T0296901

Cloud as a Service

Understanding the Service Innovation Ecosystem

Enrique Castro-Leon
Robert Harmon

Apress®

Cloud as a Service: Understanding the Service Innovation Ecosystem

Enrique Castro-Leon
Hillsboro, Oregon, USA

Robert Harmon
Portland, Oregon, USA

ISBN-13 (pbk): 978-1-4842-0104-6
DOI 10.1007/978-1-4842-0103-9

ISBN-13 (electronic): 978-1-4842-0103-9

Library of Congress Control Number: 2016961822

Copyright © 2016 by Enrique Castro-Leon and Robert Harmon

This work is subject to copyright. All rights are reserved by the Publisher, whether the whole or part of the material is concerned, specifically the rights of translation, reprinting, reuse of illustrations, recitation, broadcasting, reproduction on microfilms or in any other physical way, and transmission or information storage and retrieval, electronic adaptation, computer software, or by similar or dissimilar methodology now known or hereafter developed.

Trademarked names, logos, and images may appear in this book. Rather than use a trademark symbol with every occurrence of a trademarked name, logo, or image we use the names, logos, and images only in an editorial fashion and to the benefit of the trademark owner, with no intention of infringement of the trademark.

The use in this publication of trade names, trademarks, service marks, and similar terms, even if they are not identified as such, is not to be taken as an expression of opinion as to whether or not they are subject to proprietary rights.

While the advice and information in this book are believed to be true and accurate at the date of publication, neither the authors nor the editors nor the publisher can accept any legal responsibility for any errors or omissions that may be made. The publisher makes no warranty, express or implied, with respect to the material contained herein.

Managing Director: Welmoed Spahr
Lead Editor: Natalie Pao
Technical Reviewer: Jason Nadon
Editorial Board: Steve Anglin, Pramila Balan, Laura Berendson, Aaron Black, Louise Corrigan, Jonathan Gennick, Robert Hutchinson, Celestin Suresh John, Nikhil Karkal, James Markham, Susan McDermott, Matthew Moodie, Natalie Pao, Gwenan Spearing
Coordinating Editor: Jessica Vakili
Copy Editor: Teresa F. Horton
Compositor: SPi Global
Indexer: SPi Global
Artist: SPi Global

Distributed to the book trade worldwide by Springer Science+Business Media New York, 233 Spring Street, 6th Floor, New York, NY 10013. Phone 1-800-SPRINGER, fax (201) 348-4505, e-mail orders-ny@springer-sbm.com, or visit www.springeronline.com. Apress Media, LLC is a California LLC and the sole member (owner) is Springer Science + Business Media Finance Inc (SSBM Finance Inc). SSBM Finance Inc is a **Delaware** corporation.

For information on translations, please e-mail rights@apress.com, or visit www.apress.com.

Apress and friends of ED books may be purchased in bulk for academic, corporate, or promotional use. eBook versions and licenses are also available for most titles. For more information, reference our Special Bulk Sales–eBook Licensing web page at www.apress.com/bulk-sales.

Any source code or other supplementary materials referenced by the author in this text are available to readers at www.apress.com. For detailed information about how to locate your book's source code, go to www.apress.com/source-code/. Readers can also access source code at SpringerLink in the Supplementary Material section for each chapter.

Printed on acid-free paper

Contents at a Glance

Contents

About the Authors

Enrique Castro-Leon is a cloud technologist and strategist with the Intel Data Center Engineering Group at Intel working in cloud systems and the integration of cloud technology and platforms toward business process reengineering. He currently manages a lab piloting the use of cloud technology to increase the efficiency and agility of business, technology development and engineering processes. Users of the lab include a number of Intel business units, as well as ecosystem technology players including cloud service providers, original design manufacturers, original equipment manufacturers, system integrators and independent software and operating system vendors in the industry.

He has functioned as consultant and solution architect for data center planning with focus on energy efficiency and power and thermal modeling and analysis of data centers in large corporations. Enrique also has led technology integration projects that combine hardware, firmware and software components to deliver advanced rack-level power management capabilities applicable to cloud data centers and consistent with business requirements.

Enrique holds Ph.D. degrees in Electrical Engineering and M.S. degrees in Electrical Engineering and Computer Science from Purdue University, and a BSEE degree from the University of Costa Rica.

As a technology strategist Enrique investigates the disruptive effects of emerging technologies in the marketplace. He is the lead author of three books. The first explores the convergence of virtualization, service oriented methodologies and distributed computing titled The Business Value of Virtual Service Grids: Strategic Insights for Enterprise Decision Makers. His second book is titled Creating the Infrastructure for Cloud Computing: An Essential Handbook for IT Professionals. He co-authored a third book, titled Building the Infrastructure for Cloud Security: A Solutions View. He has published over 40 articles in conference and journal papers.

—Enrique Castro-Leon
egcastro@comcast.net

Dr. Robert R. Harmon is Professor Emeritus of Marketing and Service Innovation and Cameron Research Fellow at Portland State University. His areas of expertise are service innovation, product development, strategic marketing, and analytics. He holds a Ph.D. in Marketing and Information Systems from Arizona State University and B.S. and MBA degrees in Finance from California State University, Long Beach. Dr. Harmon is a recipient of the Oregon State Legislature's Faculty Excellence Award and the Tektronix Teaching Excellence Award. He is an American Marketing Association Doctoral Consortium Fellow. Previous faculty affiliations include the University of Oregon Executive MBA Program, Oregon Health & Science University MBA Program, and the American Graduate School of International Management (Thunderbird).

Dr. Harmon has over 30 years' experience in industries that include semiconductors, information systems, healthcare, renewable energy, displays, and software. Industry positions include financial analyst, VP of marketing, director of marketing and sales, and director of strategic planning for firms in the pharmaceutical, mobile payments, and water infrastructure industries. He is currently a consulting partner with Oregon based L.B. Day & Company, Inc., a strategic planning consultancy, in the areas of market intelligence, research and business strategy.

Dr. Harmon serves as Associate Editor in Chief for IEEE IT Professional Magazine, and serves on the editorial boards for Electronic Markets, Technological Forecasting and Social Change, and the International Journal of Innovation and Technology Management. His research has been funded by the National Science Foundation, Intel Corporation, IBM, WebMD, and Tata Consultancy Services, among others. His current research interests focus on smart systems, service innovation in the cloud, and the strategic transformation of technology firms from product to service-innovation driven business models. He is a member of the IEEE Computer Society and the International Society of Service Innovation Professionals (ISSIP).

—Robert R. Harmon, Ph.D.
harmonr@pdx.edu

Cloud-as-a-Service
Prologue

The core idea behind cloud computing is that it is much cheaper to leverage [...] resources as services, paying as you go and as you need them, than it is to buy more hardware and software for the data center.

—David S. Linthicum

The notion of service is central to cloud computing. It is so central that a capability offered through the cloud gains differentiation by appending "-as-a-service" to a legacy product offering, thus presumably increasing its perceived value. Therefore, we get the terms software-as-a-service (SaaS), platform-as-a-service (PaaS) and infrastructure-as-a-service (IaaS); and yet there is very little in the cloud literature that clarifies what service, and services, actually are. To some, the concept of service survives as a primitive notion[1]. Within a body of knowledge such as cloud computing, a primitive notion is an undefined concept that defies definition in terms of previously defined concepts. As a result, the IT practitioner informally applies meaning to a concept through experience or intuition. For instance, the Rackspace[2] and National Institute of Standards and Technology[3] publications focus on cloud-based services, but the concept itself is not clearly defined. The presentations contrast cloud services characteristics with those of customer-owned non-cloud product capabilities. The practitioner considers the features, advantages, and benefits in terms of the existing product solution.

From the traditional product perspective, services are add-on extensions of a physical product, intangible products, or services solutions that are developed and marketed as products. This services-for-a-product approach indicates a goods-dominant logic (GDL) that conceptualizes and designs services as units of output that embed and deliver value to the customer. GDL expresses as a value-in-exchange, arm's-length transaction. There is no expectation of an ongoing relationship or collaboration between the service provider and customer. This is the primitive notion that services should be defined in terms of what we know from experience, our product familiarity. Indeed, we differentiate this product view by using the plural services when a GDL perspective indicates.

---

[1]Tarski, A., Introduction to Logic: And to the Methodology of Deductive Sciences, Dover Publications, 1995.
[2]Rackspace, Inc., Understanding the Cloud Computing Stack: SaaS, PaaS, IaaS, Rackspace, https://support.rackspace.com/white-paper/understanding-the-cloud-computing-stack-saas-paas-iaas/
[3]Mell, P., and Grance, T., The NIST Definition of Cloud Computing, Special Publication 800-145, National Institute of Standards and Technology, US Department of Commerce.

The service science discipline and its service-dominant logic (SDL) provides an alternative paradigm, with service as a process that involves providers, customers and other complementary actors within a service ecosystem for the purpose of co-creating value[4]. It emphasizes a value-in-use and value-in-context to the service network approaches to value creation. Service providers and customers benefit from the collaborative exchange of knowledge, skills, technology and other resources within the service ecosystem. The co-creation process can result in superior service design, quality, pricing, customer service, and user experiences that inform compelling value propositions and realized value for all participants. Cloud computing has opened the door for the development of SDL service innovation business models. No longer constrained by GDL thinking, the cloud, especially the multi-sided platform models disrupting e-commerce, transportation, and hospitality and big data analytics, to name a few industries, have the potential to not only redefine cloud service business models, but whole industries as well. In our view, to realize the full potential of the cloud requires an integration of service science principles with cloud computing practice. The cloud is about service and increasingly service is about the cloud.

The primary goal for this book is to apply the service innovation principles to cloud computing. This book is one of the first attempts to integrate these disciplines. The motivation for this exercise is eminently practical, especially to technologists, systems and solutions architects, as well as CIOs and business strategists. As we gain insight into technology development and integration dynamics, we can reason and engage in prediction and forecasting exercises. We understand how approaches in use by product-oriented companies do not satisfactorily apply to the service-oriented cloud. We also discover that there is a path for transformation for product-oriented organizations to operate optimally in the cloud space and therefore to attain a sustained and strategic competitive advantage. This is especially applicable to technology companies with long-term product roadmaps. These companies can servitize existing product lines as an interim step in the transition toward becoming cloud-based service enterprises. The cloud-as-a-service opens up opportunities for new revenue streams and revenue modalities, converting "lumpy" revenue that depend on big bang new product launches to a more sustained service-oriented recurrent revenue.

By employing a cloud-service framework, it is now easier to understand emerging technology progressions that seemed related, but difficult to explain and operationalize. For instance, the much-heralded progression from cloud computing to the Internet of Things (IoT) domain. This understanding allows an organization to approach the cloud and IoT under a single, unified and synergistic strategy at a fraction of the cost of developing two separate strategies. In fact, the effect of two separate efforts will be less than synergistic. The overlap of the two functions will likely result in channel conflicts, with the two organizations working against each other. For this reason, we believe that traditional, product-oriented companies cannot just look at the cloud as just a new, emerging market. These companies will need to adopt a service ethic from within,

---

[4]Vargo, S. and Lusch, R., Evolving to a New Dominant Logic for Marketing, Journal of Marketing, Vol. 68, 1-17, January 2004.

meaning adopting a service ethic from within; in the methodologies used to develop technology and in the way they conduct business processes. These organizations will suffer from the drag of the dissonance between the SDL and GDL approaches. Conversely, companies adopting an SDL approach early on will enjoy an inherent and sustained competitive advantage in the cloud market.

This book comprises nine chapters in five parts:

1. The first part comprises Chapter 1, Cloud-as a Service and covers the service context for cloud computing and the convergence between historical trends toward a service economy and the information technology (IT) that enables it. The chapter introduces the goods-dominant logic (GDL) and service-dominant logic (SDL) conceptual paradigms as the primary lens by which organizations analyze, understand, and interact with their business ecosystems from a service innovation and value co-creation perspective. The chapter also covers other aspects of cloud services including the effects on employment and privacy.

2. The second part comprises two chapters that introduce the foundational principles of the emerging service science discipline with implications for service transformation as it relates to cloud computing. Chapter 2, The Service Science Foundations of Cloud Computing introduces the core principles of Service Science and SDL. Emphasis is on foundational premises and processes for value co-creation within service ecosystems. We present the product-service systems (PSS) model as a practical interim approach to service innovation as firms transition from GDL firms to service innovation enterprises. The Service Thinking section presents the five mindsets of service thinking that can inform the development of successful cloud service business plans. The chapter concludes with sections on T-shaped professionals and a view of the future in terms of the emerging frontiers of service innovation. Chapter 3, Cloud Computing: Implications for Service Transformation presents service transformation processes for GDL organizations to transition to SDL business models needed to operate in cloud space successfully.

3. In the third part, comprising chapters 4, 5 and 6, we look at a central technology component of cloud computing, namely the servers that power cloud data centers. These servers were initially developed and marketed under a GDL approach. We see that in the few years since cloud computing became a central element in the delivery of IT in the industry, the way these servers are planned, manufactured and deployed is changing fast. Chapter 4 covers the evolution of standard high volume servers, the staple for enterprise data centers and the starting point for cloud server platforms that we name application-specific cloud platforms, or ASCPs. Chapter 5 defines the ASCP concept, and Chapter 6 describes the process to build them as a variant of processes used to build enterprise servers. While the process did not change much in terms of architecture, design and manufacturing, the implementation of these processes brought new players, with cloud service providers as the platform drivers, and an original design manufacturer (ODM) carrying out a manufacture-to-order (manufacturing-as-a-service) role. This is a prime example of an emerging service-oriented technology development process to supply the needs of a service-oriented industry.

4. One of the benefits of the cloud is the potential it brings for business and technical process optimization, which in turn can bring lasting competitive advantage to its adopters and practitioners. Chapter 7 covers the concept of a hardware-as-a-service (HaaS) lab service that allows bringing together the cloud service provider driving the platform, the ODM manufacturing and other contributing technology partners all together at a single place to accelerate engineering platform debug and validation. Today these tasks are usually carried out a serial fashion, in an inefficient and time-consuming process. Collaborating partners working through a lab in the cloud can carry these tasks in parallel and complete them in a fraction of the original time. This is another example of an organization adopting service-oriented processes from within.

Chapter 8 covers additional case studies, including platform power management design, a federated database for precision medicine, and an IoT deployment. These seemingly disparate examples have in common that they are cloud-as-a-service deployments.

5.   Chapter 9 constitutes the last part, a look into the future of
     cloud-as-a-service: the next evolutionary points for cloud
     platforms are a landing with the Internet of Things, and more
     sophisticated governance through service metadata and
     meta-services. We conclude the book with a case study on
     smart cities.

The authors wish to acknowledge the contribution of Ronald
Newman as the architect, designer and implementer of the
advanced technology under the bare metal-as-a-service,
lab-in-the-cloud concepts described in Chapter 7. We would
like to thank our spouses, Kitty and Daisy for their infinite
understanding in a project that seemed to have no end.
One of the continuing challenges in compiling this book
is the ever present rapid evolution of cloud technology,
with new research results both in service science and in
cloud computing emerging at a fast pace every, and current
concepts becoming obsolete almost as fast. The conceptual
frameworks in this book are by no means definitive. The
authors hope that students in related fields use the concepts
as a departure point for their research and that industry
practitioners find the concepts useful in their quest to define
service-oriented architectures, as well as business and
engineering processes. The rapid changes in the industry
made it difficult to close the book, literally. We are grateful to
our editors at Apress, Natalie Pao and Jessica Vakili for their
patience and gentle nudging, bringing sense and practicality
to the authors to find a graceful close to the project.

PART I

CHAPTER 1

■ ■ ■

Cloud Computing as a Service

Simple can be harder than complex: You have to work hard to make it simple. But it's worth it in the end because once you get there, you can move mountains.

—Steve Jobs

Barely a decade into the cloud-computing era, most chief information officers (CIOs) and digital business managers know that the cloud is faster, cheaper, flexible, agile, and elastic. It also offers better resource utilization than legacy computing systems. Cloud computing is disrupting old markets and defining new ones and becoming the platform of choice for the development of innovative solutions that would have been unimaginable only a few short years ago. The cloud is maturing into a platform for IT services across a wide range of business functions including marketing, advertising, finance, human resources, logistics, supply chain management, and analytics. The most far-reaching impact of cloud computing is its ability to not only empower IT innovations, but to drive innovation into virtually every industry in the form of digital services. The cloud is the engine for enterprise and societal transformation.

In 2003, Nicholas Carr famously asserted that IT doesn't matter[1]. After more than 30 years of high growth that expanded the business and societal impact of IT, corporate executives at the turn of the century had embraced the strategic value of information as a primary driver of competitive advantage and the strategic transformation of the enterprise to digital business models. Carr's article certainly generated considerable debate among IT professionals, business strategists, chief financial officers (CFOs), and academics.

---

[1]N. G. Carr, "IT Doesn't Matter," *Harvard Business Review* 38: 24–38 (2003).

© Enrique Castro-Leon and Robert Harmon 2016
E. Castro-Leon and R. Harmon, *Cloud as a Service*, DOI 10.1007/978-1-4842-0103-9_1

He presented the argument that IT exhibited the characteristics of a technological infrastructure that was largely built out with commonly available commoditized components. IT investments result, at best, in strategic parity between firms, not the superior competitive advantage anticipated. Under these circumstances, developing a business strategy around IT is little different from building it around the provision of commodity services such as water and electricity. There is little expectation for improving productivity through investment in IT. IT strategy defaults to a defensive "me too" approach that emphasizes cost reduction, late technology adoption, and risk minimization.

Nobel Prize winning economist Robert Solow first identified this phenomenon in 1987 as the IT productivity paradox: "You can see the computer age everywhere but in the productivity statistics"[2]. The productivity paradox seems to come and go. During the 1990s, IT generated a productivity boom, which ended with the burst of the dot-com bubble. Since then, studies on the IT productivity paradox have proposed that it takes time to realize a payoff from IT investment. For each dollar invested in IT systems, firms had to invest additional dollars in implementation, process redesign, and training to begin to see productivity gains. In addition, during the mid-2000s, new technologies— most notably the Internet, mobile systems, and especially the digital services paradigm— were beginning to disrupt industries and their legacy IT systems. Although a case could be made in 2003 that computing power, storage, network technology, and a number of legacy applications had attained commodity status, Carr's view was not of the future. He apparently did not anticipate the rise of cloud computing, big data, and the service innovation revolution.

Cloud Computing

The introduction of service-oriented architecture (SOA) in 2003 and its subsequent manifestation as cloud computing is enabling IT to become a strategically essential factor in enterprise service transformation. The emergence of service-based business models is transforming businesses worldwide[3]. This transformation is enabled by information and communications technologies (ICT), most notably the cloud. Cloud technologies have enabled the growth of digital services, mobile computing, big data analytics, and business process innovation. The cloud provides a platform for innovation that can adapt to challenging business circumstances and drive business and market transformations. ICT-enabled services are increasingly important for the development of business, customer, and societal value.

---

[2]D. Lock, "Unravelling the IT Productivity Paradox," *CIO* 12 (2). http://www.cio.com.au/article/print/532717/unravelling_it_productivity_paradox/, November 25, 2013.
[3]P. Maglio and J. Spohrer, "A Service Science Perspective on Business Model Innovation," *Industrial Marketing Management* 42: 665–670 (2013).

The past 10 years have seen a significant increase in efficiency within IT organizations, with the most advanced operations shifting from mere cost centers to critical roles as active partners in the development and execution of corporate business strategy. Every product and service in the modern enterprise is touched by IT in some manner. Increasingly, in companies charting a path to become service enterprises, IT is at the core of the service solution or the solution itself. The adoption of cloud computing under the service innovation paradigm defines the state of the art for IT organizations. From a historical perspective, cloud-based services have moved through three IT service eras[4].

1. *Application services era (circa 1995–2003):* In the application services era, vendors such as Microsoft and the Unix community organizations offered operating systems and proprietary software frameworks to create web applications and server environments to run them. Individual vendors competed to build ecosystems around these frameworks. A typical use case was the retooling of legacy applications for e-commerce purposes. Concerns about vendor lock-in and the rise of web servers limited adoption of this approach.

2. *SOA era (circa 2003–2007):* SOA gained popularity as IT organizations rearchitected legacy applications from silo implementations to collections of service components ostensibly working together. Most of the service components are internally sourced and combined with a few noncore, third-party services. The benefits of SOA were primarily limited to large enterprises due to the high cost of the technology transformation and the demand on IT skills. Adoption by small and medium enterprises (SMEs) and individual users was limited due to costs and productivity issues.

3. *Cloud services era (2007–present):* The emergence of cloud technology and the development of resource pooling with large datacenters as drivers for IT services is the third and current era. The economic impact of cloud-service business models reduces barriers to user engagement and increases the velocity of service solutions development with the potential for redefining old markets and creating new ones. The benefits no longer accrue only to large organizations. SMEs and individual users can access the cloud from any geographical location. Cloud services are Metcalfe's Law[5] in action: The value of the network increases with the number of users actively engaged, whether they be humans, applications, devices, or intelligent machines.

---

[4]E. Castro-Leon, R. Harmon, and M. Yousif, "IT-Enabled Service Innovation: Why IT Is the Future of Competitive Advantage," *Cutter IT Journal* 26 (7): 15–21 (2013).
[5]B. Metcalfe, "Metcalfe's Law: A Network Becomes More Valuable as It Reaches More Users," *Infoworld* 17 (40): 53–54 (1995).

In 2011, the National Institute of Standards and Technology (NIST) of the U.S. Department of Commerce published guidelines for cloud computing for use by Federal agencies. Other governmental agencies, nongovernmental organizations (NGOs), and businesses could use the guidelines on a voluntary basis with attribution[6]. The key feature of the publication is a workable definition that can serve to facilitate comparisons between cloud services, deployment strategies, and use situations.

The NIST definition is as follows: "Cloud computing is a model for enabling ubiquitous, convenient, on-demand network access to a shared pool of configurable computing resources (e.g., networks, servers, storage, applications, and services) that can be rapidly provisioned and released with minimal management effort or service provider interaction. This cloud model is composed of five essential characteristics, three service models, and four deployment models." We summarize the general characteristics, service models, and deployment models in what follows and in Figures 1-1 and 1-2[7]. As we delve into the service-oriented nature of the cloud throughout the book, we discover that the NIST definition actually comprises a very small portion of a much larger service universe, summarized in Chapter 8.

Essential Characteristics of Cloud Computing

- *On-demand self-service:* Users access computing services such as server time and network storage on demand, as needed without engaging human representatives of the server provider.

- *Broad network access:* Users can access capabilities at different locations over the network through standard interfaces and devices such as workstations, laptops, tablets, and mobile phones.

- *Resource pooling:* Computing resources are pooled to serve multiple customers using a multitenant model. Both physical and virtual resources are dynamically assigned and reassigned based on user demand. From a user perspective, resources are location independent and the user has no need to know or control the exact location of the provided computing resources.

- *Rapid elasticity:* Computing resources are rapidly scaled (up or down) to meet user requirements. Users can appropriate different resources and services in any quantity, as needed at any time.

- *Measured service:* Resource use is controlled and optimized by a metering capability appropriate for each type of service, such as storage, bandwidth, processing, and active user accounts. This is usually on a pay-per-use or charge-per-use basis. Other options include subscription-based pricing models such as per hour, per day, per month, or all you can use up to a predetermined cap.

---

[6]P. Mell and T. Grance, *The NIST Definition of Cloud Computing,* Special Publication 800-145 (Washington, DC: National Institute of Standards and Technology, U.S. Department of Commerce, 2011).
[7]A. Jula, E. Sundararajan, and Z. Othman, "Cloud Computing Service Composition: A Systemic Literature Review," *Expert Systems with Applications* 41: 3809–3824 (2014).

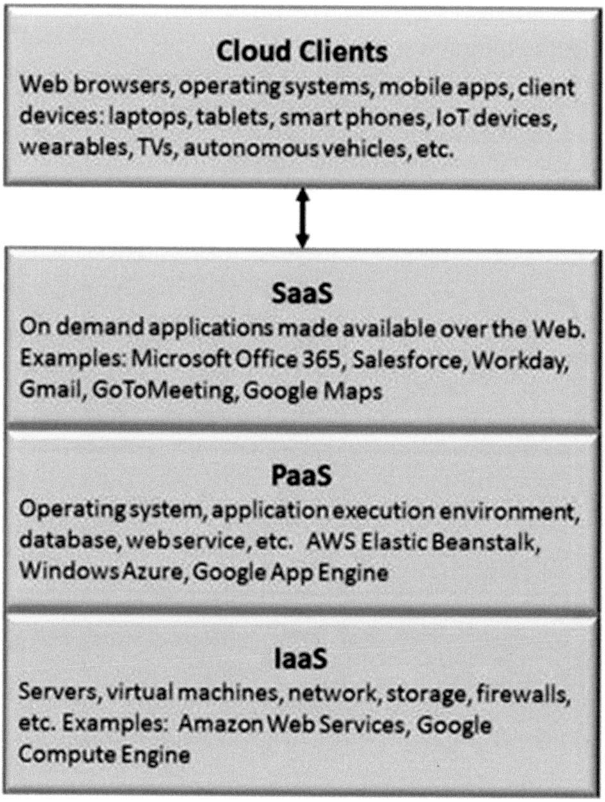

Figure 1-1. *Cloud computing service models*

Cloud Computing Service Models

- *Software as a service (SaaS):* Service consumers use the provider's applications that run on a cloud infrastructure. The applications are accessed through various client devices with a web browser, e-mail, or other program interface. The user does not control or manage the cloud infrastructure or applications beyond specific application configurations.

- *Platform as a service (PaaS):* The service provider offers systems resources such as networks, servers, storage, operating systems, middleware, databases, development tools, and other resources necessary for the user to develop, deploy, run, and manage the user's applications. The user does not manage or control the underlying platform infrastructure, but does control the deployed applications.

7

- *Infrastructure as a service (IaaS):* The consumer needs fundamental computing resources such as servers, networks, and storage that are required to deploy and run user-developed applications. The service user does not control or manage the cloud infrastructure, but does control operating systems, storage, deployed applications, and networking components such as firewalls.

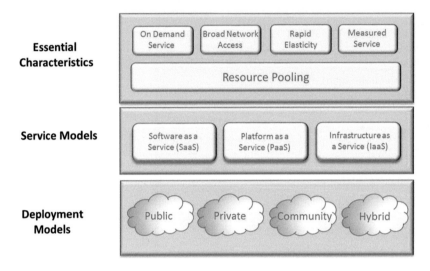

Figure 1-2. *Cloud characteristics, service and deployment models*

Cloud Computing Deployment Models

- *Public cloud:* A public cloud renders services over a network that is open for public use. It is the dominant model for cloud computing. Services can be owned, managed, and operated by a business, academic, or government organization, or some combination of them. The cloud exists on the premises of the cloud provider. Amazon Web Services (AWS), Microsoft, and Google are major public cloud service providers[8].

- *Private cloud:* Private cloud infrastructure is operated for the exclusive use of a single organization with multiple users. The cloud can be owned, managed, and operated by the enterprise, a third party, or some combination, and hosted internally or externally.

---

[8]S. Goyal, "Public vs. Private vs. Hybrid vs. Community Cloud Computing: A Critical Review," *International Journal of Network and Information Security* 3: 20–29 (2014).

- *Community cloud:* The community cloud shares infrastructure between organizations for the exclusive use of a community that shares common concerns, mission, policy, security requirements, jurisdiction, and compliance requirements. It can be owned, managed, and operated by one or more of the organizations in the community, a third party, or some combination of them, and it could exist on or off premises.

- *Hybrid cloud:* The cloud infrastructure is a composition of two or more distinct cloud infrastructures (public, private, or community) that remain unique entities, but are bound together by standardized or proprietary technology that enables data and application interoperability and portability,

As cloud computing becomes more popular and businesses shift more workloads to the cloud, the definition of what cloud computing actually is continues to be somewhat fuzzy. Larry Ellison, CEO of Oracle, captured this frustration with emerging cloud definitions in the early days of the cloud: "The interesting thing about cloud computing is that we've redefined the cloud to include everything that we already do. I can't think of anything that isn't cloud computing with all these announcements"[9]. With cloud computing entering its second decade, not much has changed since Ellison's comment. Some of the confusion comes from the computing-service providers that use the term *cloud* to characterize a wide range of applications, such as managed hosting services and other online tools that are not true cloud systems, at least by NIST standards. For instance, private cloud solutions might not be strictly cloud in nature, although public cloud solutions are more likely to be true cloud solutions[10]. *Cloud washing* is a tactic for promoting cloud-like or cloud-enabled services as true cloud services to sell services contracts. True cloud services are on demand, with shared use of software, server processing power, and computing infrastructure over the Internet on a pay-as-you go subscription. Managed hosting and other off-premises services typically do not offer the cloud's flexibility, scalability, and other benefits. Cloud-leveraged tools and systems such as the Internet of Things (IoT), which rely on the cloud, are not cloud services themselves. The lack of definitional clarity puts the onus not just on the cloud providers, but also on the cloud service users, to understand that not all off-premises computing services are cloud-based. Whether it is a true cloud or some other computing services solution, the strategic goals of the enterprise should drive service engagement decisions.

---

[9]D. Farber, "Oracle's Ellison Nails Cloud Computing," C/Net.com. https://www.cnet.com/news/oracles-ellison-nails-cloud-computing/, September 26, 2008.
[10]A. Loten, "Definition of the Cloud Remains Hazy," *CIO Journal.* http://blogs.wsj.com/cio/2016/10/18/definition-of-the-cloud-remains-hazy/, October 18, 2016.

The Services Sector

The disruptive nature of cloud computing has set the stage for IT organizations to move beyond the development and provisioning of IT systems. IT is more than infrastructure, services, and deployment models. IT has become a critical enabler of business strategy through technology integration with the business under the service paradigm. Given the commoditization of products in most advanced economies and the demonstrated ability of services as engines for value creation, organizations must rely on the development of knowledge-based services for growth. Businesses are becoming increasingly dependent on services as extensions of their product models or reimagining themselves into service companies. IT has an essential role in enabling the development and implementation of innovative service strategies.

Figure 1-3 shows that services constitute the largest global economic sector, at 63.5 percent (US$49.7 trillion) of global gross domestic product (GDP; US$78.2 trillion) in 2014[11]. Services include government activities, communications, finance, transportation and all other private activities that do not produce material goods. Practically all of these activities are supported by ICT in some manner. The United States is the largest producer of services at US$13.5 trillion and 77.6 percent of GDP. Only three developed countries—France, the United Kingdom, and Belgium—generate a higher percentage of GDP from services. China is the second largest producer of services at US$4.8 trillion but only 46.4 percent of GDP[12].

---

[11]Central Intelligence Agency, *The World Factbook 2015*. https://www.cia.gov/library/publications/the-world-factbook/.
[12]Statistics Times, List of Countries by GDP Sector Composition, 2015.
http://statisticstimes.com/economy/countries-by-gdp-sector-composition.php.

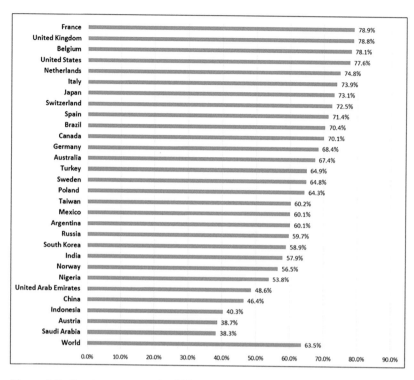

Figure 1-3. *Service sector nominal GDP percentage by country, 2014. Source: The World Factbook (2015)*

Cloud computing has applications across all major sectors of GDP growth that are characterized by process complexity and the potential for using data to improve efficiencies and effectiveness. We point out the large size and growth potential of the services sector, but we do not want to minimize the application of ICT to agriculture and manufacturing. Indeed if we adopt the perspective of service scientists that all physical products are only valuable for the services they provide, then ICT innovations have the potential to affect any GDP sectors.

During the postwar period of 1947 to 2010, the United States IT-producing industries, such as semiconductors, telecommunications equipment, telecommunications services, computers and infrastructure, the Internet, and now cloud computing, have accounted for 1.7 percent of value added for the U.S. economy. This relatively small percentage is due to the rapid price declines in hardware and software since 1973 and the decline in IT services prices since 2000. However, IT-producing industries have had an outsized impact on IT-using industries due to ICT adoption by those industries. IT-using industries accounted for approximately 49.6 percent of economic value, 8 percent of postwar economic growth, and over 32 percent of productivity growth during the postwar period[13]. The investment in new IT hardware and software can generate higher returns than

---

[13]D. Jorgenson, M. Ho, and J. Samuels, "The Impact of Information Technology on Postwar U.S. Economic Growth," *Telecommunications Policy* 40: 398–411 (2016).

11

those available from other capital and labor investments. ICT investments result in productivity growth. The impact of these investments critically affects product and service development, market creation, business models, business processes, systems, and organizational structures. During the postwar years, major innovation only accounted for about 20 percent of economic growth. As Jorgenson et al. observed, it is only a small number of economic sectors, especially the IT-producing sector where major innovations take place, that have a profound effect on society as a whole.

The 70-year ICT revolution is a product of the rapid progress of the semiconductor industry. The inventions of the transistor at Bell Labs in 1947 (see Figure 1-4), the integrated circuit at Texas Instruments in 1958 and independently at Fairchild Semiconductor in 1959, the publication of Moore's Law in 1965[14], and the invention of the microprocessor at Intel in 1971[15] set the stage for the growth of the ICT industry. Gordon Moore (see Figure 1-5), co-founder of Intel, predicted that the number of components (transistors, resistors, diodes, capacitors) in a dense integrated circuit would shrink in size and double every year, increasing exponentially for at least the next 10 years. In 1975, an updated Moore's Law predicted a doubling every 2 years, which recently increased to 2.5 years.

Figure 1-4. John Bardeen, William Shockley, and Walter Brattain at Bell Labs, 1948[16]

[14]G. E. Moore, "Cramming More Components onto Integrated Circuits," *Electronics* 38 (8) (1965).
[15]W. Aspray, "The Intel 4004 Microprocessor: What Constituted Invention," *IEEE Annals of the History of Computing* 19 (3) (1997).
[16]By AT&T; photographer: Jack St. (last part of name not stamped well enough to read), New York, New York. - eBay itemphoto frontphoto back. Public Domain: https://commons.wikimedia.org/w/index.php?curid=17898468.

Figure 1-5. *Gordon Moore and Robert Noyce, Intel co-founders, 1970*[17]

With an expectation of rapid increases in computing power and lower manufacturing costs per unit, Moore's Law became an organizing principle for the industry. The entire tech industry from capital equipment, consumer electronics, communications, and ICT-using industries had a predictably constant rate of price–performance improvement that they could depend on. As executives gained more confidence in the scalability and profit potential associated with Moore's Law, multibillion-dollar investments in semiconductor fabrication facilities became feasible. Moore's Law is about devices becoming smaller, smarter, cheaper, more powerful, and more useful over time. As a result, the services these devices provision become more capable, more encompassing, and more valuable. For instance, Apple's iPhone 6 is approximately 1 million times more powerful than an IBM mainframe computer of 1975. In 2014, the iPhone 6 cost about US$650 and fit in your hand; the IBM mainframe cost more than US$250,000 in 1975 dollars and required a large air-conditioned room[18]. The iPhone provisions services that were unimaginable in 1975. This is Moore's Law at work.

---

[17]By Intel Free Press: http://www.flickr.com/photos/intelfreepress/8429166752/sizes/o/in/photostream/, CC BY-SA 2.0, https://commons.wikimedia.org/w/index.php?curid=27922284.

[18]R. Cheng, "Moore's Law Is the Reason Your iPhone Is so Thin and Cheap," C/NET.com. https://www.cnet.com/news/moores-law-is-the-reason-why-your-iphone-is-so-thin-and-cheap/, April 16, 2015.

Moore's Law has always been about driving the next wave of innovation in semiconductors, which drives innovation for the ICT industry and for IT-using organizations and individuals. Microprocessors power the datacenters that power the cloud and the devices and software that provision cloud services. Moore summed up its impact: "Rather than become something that chronicled the progress of the industry, Moore's Law became something that drove it"[19]. It still does.

The convergence of smart devices, inexpensive bandwidth, and mobile computing combined with the increasing pace of globalization has accelerated the growth of ICT applications across industrial, agricultural, and especially service sectors internationally[20]. In 1990, the Internet had approximately 3 million users, which rapidly increased to more than 3 billion users by 2014. Mobile phone subscribers increased from 11 million to more than 6 billion over the same period[21]. What is notable about this performance is the rapid growth in the number of people connected to the Internet globally and the rapid adoption of wireless technology that in many instances leapfrogged over the both the landline plain old telephone service (POTS) and the wired Internet to mobile networks and smartphones. The infrastructure for cloud services in developed nations is largely in place. In developing nations, as Jorgenson and Vu observed, the ICT revolution and mobile phone networks have improved communications, contributed to economic growth, and increased access to essential services that have improved the lives of citizens even in the least developed countries.

Service Innovation

Innovation is the process by which ideas are generated, developed, and transformed into new products, services, and processes that generate a profit and create marketplace advantage[22]. During the industrial era, the drivers of growth and gains in productivity were largely the result of applying innovative technologies to transform natural resources in new ways to create value. Services, if thought of at all, were a low-value afterthought. This bias continues today as some manufacturers, politicians, academicians, and new college graduates view services as incidental to the real economic value and good jobs that derive from the manufacturing of products. This perception is slowly changing, as ICT innovations have transformed the very nature of services. First, ICT transformed traditional product-focused services by adopting modern manufacturing concepts such as customer centricity, division of labor and knowledge, product development processes, standardization, platformization, and coordination of production and delivery to enable new forms of value creation and consumption. This was a necessary step to begin to

[19]D. Reisinger, "Keeping up with Moore's Law Proves Difficult for Intel," C/NET.com. https://www.cnet.com/news/keeping-up-with-moores-law-proves-difficult-for-intel/, July 16, 2015.
[20]E. Brynjolfsson and A. McAfee, *The Second Machine Age: Work Progress, and Prosperity in a Time of Brilliant Technologies* (New York: Norton, 2014).
[21]D. Jorgenson and K. Vu, "The ICT Revolution, World Economic Growth, and Policy Issues," *Telecommunications Policy* 40: 383–397 (2016).
[22]M. Mogee, "Educating Innovation Managers: Strategic Issues for Business and Higher Education," *IEEE Transactions on Engineering Management* 40 (4): 410–417 (1993).

formalize services as independent sources of value. However, the service as a product conceptualization has many of the same limitations as products when it comes to commoditization and value cocreation.

Industries such as retail, hospitality, restaurants, telecommunications, health care, transportation, marketing, finance, human resources, education, and the IT industry itself are undergoing a service transformation as cloud computing increasingly enables disruptive business models. ICT has enabled the *servitization* of traditional manufacturers, as they become providers of services[23]. Apple, the world's largest technology company, illustrates a case in which a dominant product company is adding services to its product offerings, including Apple Pay, the iTunes Store, the iOS App Store, Mac App Store, Apple TV, Apple Music, and iCloud, in addition to its operating systems, browsers, and productivity applications.

ICT drives service innovation by enabling the separation of production and consumption in terms of space and time. This *separability* improves productivity, makes people and organizations more efficient, augments social and behavioral change, and provides customers[24] with more control over the consumption experience. Furthermore, ICT and other technologies are broadening the evolution of the services economy by enabling novel solutions that can create new markets. As such, the application of ICT to new service concepts has quickened service development and made services more prevalent. Service innovation has become the primary driver of economic growth and dynamism[25].

Disruptive technological innovation is recurrent in the computing industry[26]. Initially, disruptive technologies, such as cloud services, underperform established technologies in established markets. However, over time new entrants with disruptive technologies displace the established firms by redefining the established markets or creating new ones. Service innovation in particular, changes industry dynamics by reducing barriers and redefining (or ignoring) industry boundaries in term of rules, regulations, and geographic reach. Amazon disrupted the retail industry by redefining the entire retail shopping cycle and expanding geographic boundaries. It disrupted the book market by enabling customers to search and find virtually any printed book and eventually changed user behavior to prefer digital books. Apple disrupted the music industry and the phone industry and Google disrupted online search and advertising. Netflix is disrupting cable TV. Uber and Airbnb largely ignored rules and regulations to gain market footholds in their effort to disrupt taxi and hotel services, respectively[27]. In Chapter 6, we will see how Netflix and Uber also apply service transformation strategies

---

[23]J. Potts and T. Mandeville, "Toward an Evolutionary Theory of Innovation and Growth in the Service Economy," *Prometheus* 25 (2): 147–159 (2007).

[24]We recognize that the words *customers*, *buyers*, *consumers*, and *users* share a degree of commonality in meaning. We view customers as the primary beneficiary in the service provider–customer dyad. Customers could also be buyers, consumers, and users. We focus specifically on the user role with respect to the user experience.

[25]U. de Brentani, "Innovative versus Incremental New Business Services: Different Keys for Achieving Success," *Journal of Product Innovation Management* 18: 169–187 (2001).

[26]E. Danneels, "Disruptive Technology Reconsidered: A Critique and Research Agenda," *Journal of Product Innovation Management* 21: 246–258 (2004).

[27]J. Belbey, "Compliance Uncertainty and Social Media: Lessons from Uber, Airbnb, and Drones," *Forbes.* `http://www.forbes.com/sites/joannabelbey/2015/04/16/compliance-uncertainty-and-social-media-lessons-from-uber-airbnb-and-drones/#1871c85218df`, April 16, 2015.

from within in their internal ICT roadmaps. We believe that consistency between external and internal strategy is a source of strength in the marketplace by reducing dissonance and internal conflict that often exists between a product-oriented and service-oriented view of the universe. This takes us to the next section.

Service-Dominant Logic

Service-dominant logic (SDL) is a topic that we explore in detail in Chapter 2, where we discuss the service science foundations of cloud computing. We present a brief summary here to support the case that ICT services typically are developed and marketed in a manner that does not deviate significantly from the practices of product-oriented firms. ICT services have a legacy orientation of a goods-dominant logic (GDL). Of course, there are exceptions that might include the large native cloud and pure service companies such as Amazon, Alphabet (Google), Facebook, and Netflix, for example, that share some SDL characteristics. However, it is our view that even the most service-oriented cloud vendors, service providers, and cloud users view cloud services as outputs through a services as a product lens.

Within the SDL paradigm, service is defined as "the application of specialized competencies (knowledge and skills) through deeds, processes, and performances for the benefit of another entity or the entity itself"[28].The specialized competencies represent the potential value and competitive advantage. However, these competencies do not reside with only the service provider. The competencies are resources shared by actors within a service ecosystem that collaboratively engage with each other to develop customized value propositions for engaging in value cocreation. Service ecosystem actors include the service provider, customer or user, suppliers, partners, and employees that collaborate for mutual benefit.

To appreciate the differences between products and services and the concepts of value created and realized by each, it is imperative to understand the core differences between the GDL and SDL paradigms. GDL is about products, manufactured physical things and services that closely tie to products. Products and services are units of output. Within a GDL universe, all value manifests in the physical product or product-service. The customer can perceive and receive value but does not create it. Various types of value, often called *customer value drivers* include the following[29]:

1. *Economic value:* Economic value drivers relate to the customer's perceptions of the cost of acquiring, owning, installing, using, and disposing of a product or service. This value driver is associated with minimizing costs for the functional value received.

[28]S. Vargo and R. Lusch, "Evolving to a New Dominant Logic for Marketing," *Journal of Marketing* 68: 1–17 (2004).
[29]R. Harmon, H. Demirkan, B. Hefley, and N. Auseklis, "Pricing Strategies for Information Technology Services: A Value-Based Approach." In *Proceedings of the 42nd Hawaii International Conference on System Sciences* (HICSS-42), 1–10 (2009).

2. *Performance value:* Performance value is associated with the customer's perceptions of what the product or service can actually do. Does the product or service meet the customer's criteria for performing the job at hand? This value driver is associated with functional value[30].

3. *Supplier value:* The customer's perceptions about the credibility of the provider and trust in the business relationship link directly to brand image and brand acceptance. A strong brand can become a barrier to competition that is difficult to overcome. Supplier value is associated with emotional value and knowledge value.

4. *Buyer motivation:* Psychological motivations are central to the customer's decision process. Buyer motivation derives from the customer's expectations of value realized by the user experience. Can the features, advantages, and benefits associated with the solution fulfill those expectations? This value driver is a manifestation of emotional value and knowledge value.

5. *The buying situation:* Customer value perceptions occur in a situational context that can facilitate, inhibit, or have no effect on purchasing behavior. Understanding how these situational factors influence overall value perceptions is a key to gaining insight into the purchasing decision[31]. The key situational variables are as follows:

   a. *Task definition:* What tasks does the customer need to accomplish? What tasks does the product or service fulfill?

   b. *Resource capability:* What physical capacity, knowledge, and technological skills does the customer have, including proprietary infrastructure and legacy systems? The more comprehensive the customer's resources, the less is needed from the supplier.

   c. *Time horizon:* Customers with short decision time horizons tend to be less price sensitive and less selective in terms of purchase options. How far in the future is the purchase decision and how long is the solution to be in use?

---

[30]J. Sheth, B. Newman, and B. Gross, *Consumption Values and Market Choices: Theory and Applications* (Cincinnati, OH: Southwestern, 1991).
[31]R. Harmon and K. Coney, "The Persuasive Effects of Source Credibility in Buy and Lease Situations," *Journal of Marketing Research* 19 (2): 255–260 (1982).

> d. *Social influences:* How do the customer and all relevant service gatekeepers (those specifying, managing, using, and influencing the purchasing decision) affect the adoption of IT products and services?
>
> e. *Experience level:* Customers that are highly experienced with similar solutions have stronger solution-related attitudes and specific performance expectations.
>
> f. *Availability:* This situational variable refers to the availability of purchase-decision-relevant information about the solution and the actual delivery and installation dates. In some instances, availability can refer to revenue expectations in terms of time-to-revenue or time-to-profit for the solution.

When we move beyond the first two value drivers of price and performance, which are the default value drivers for GDL products and services, we need to consider the remaining value drivers that are relatively more emotional and relationship-oriented and thus more service-centric in nature. Although all value drivers can come into play for both products and services, weights vary depending on the specific situational context. These different types of value inform the differences between GDL and SDL.

A GDL orientation considers services as product-specific add-ons or intangible forms of products typically offered on a postsales basis[32]. Services are outputs that add value that the provider creates and delivers to the customer for compensation. GDL services sell on a transactional basis without an expectation of an ongoing collaborative engagement with the customer. Value is expressed as the performance benefits received from the product or product-service divided by the total cost. There is little or no acknowledgment of a service ecosystem or complementary collaboration with the customer or other actors beyond traditional supplier and partner relationships. GDL is a *value-in-exchange* transaction. The provider creates the value and delivers it embedded in the product or services. The customer receives the benefit and compensates the provider. For the provider and the customer, the price of the good and its service components defines the economic and performance value at the point where the customer exchanges money with the provider.

From an SDL perspective, the service is *product independent.* Although products often provision the service, as in the case of the iPhone or Samsung smartphone, the products are conveyances for cloud-based applications that provide myriad services. The value proposition centers on solutions to customer problems and the experiences the customer can expect. The SDL focus is on long-term relationships between service providers and customers within a service ecosystem that includes other complementary actors such as suppliers and partners. Because the customer actively engages with the service provider in the cocreation of value, the service experience should be much more customer-centric and satisfying.

---

[32]S. Vargo and R. Lusch, "Service-Dominant Logic: Continuing the Evolution," *Journal of the Academy of Marketing Science* 36 (1): 1–10 (2008).

SDL changes the game from the exchange of tangible goods and add-on service for compensation to the exchange of services between providers and customers and other engaged actors in the service ecosystem. SDL fully embraces the entire range of customer value drivers, makes them collaborative, and extends them to all members of the service ecosystem. Within this context, looking at smartphones purely from a product perspective essentially ignores the focus of the interaction between customers and their providers. Business and technology planners would have an incomplete view of the market dynamics that would make their job very difficult. It might be possible to recast service considerations into a product feature set. However, this approach would be unnecessarily complex when it is a lot simpler to explain service dynamics in terms of service concepts. There are parallels in science, for instance in the 15th century, as astronomical observations became more precise, the existing Ptolemaic system using a geocentric frame of reference became increasingly more convoluted in explaining subtle motions of the planets. Copernicus came up with a much simpler system using a heliocentric approach. Although the universe was still the same, the simpler framework made it easier to get insight into it and to make predictions.

From a legacy ICT products and services perspective, GDL is the worldview of many business executives, legacy ICT product and services providers, IT executives, technology marketers, product developers, programmers, systems architects, and business, engineering, and computer science professors. Few think in terms of service ecosystems, value cocreation, and the value potential of service business models. GDL views services (plural) as residual sources of value added to augment products. Traditional business strategies, management, marketing, and IT organizations support this product-centric paradigm. Improvements on this thinking include a more customer-centric approach, but are not sufficient to generate the power of value cocreation. The concept of service cannot be treated as an afterthought in a cloud universe where service is the focus of the discourse.

The SDL-based concept of service (singular) encompasses a service ecosystem where resources such as knowledge, skills, and technology apply in a collaborative and complementary process for the benefit of others. GDL is about creating and delivering value to the customer. SDL is about cocreating value with the customer and other supporting members of the service ecosystem. The GDL paradigm is about efficiently delivering products and services as outputs; SDL is about developing a service exchange process within an ecosystem for the purpose of value cocreation. A primary reason that the cloud concept is so powerful is that it taps into network effects that can scale the value cocreation process across large numbers of individuals, organizations, and machines. This is especially true for cloud-based service platforms such as Amazon, Facebook, Google, LinkedIn, and Alibaba, which enable service providers, customers, suppliers, and partners to network and engage with each other within a service ecosystem for mutual benefit.

Value Cocreation

A ubiquitous Internet enabled people to communicate and share information on an unprecedented global scale. This information exchange also lowers barriers for service exchange. Highly networked people are engaging with providers of goods and services in a collaborative manner that is fundamentally changing the dynamics of value creation. Customers share their experiences and opinions about products and services. Service providers encourage customer reviews, solicit satisfaction ratings, and utilize big data analytics to understand customer needs and to evaluate customers and employees. Customers desire an ongoing relationship with providers that is impactful on user experience, customer service, product and service design, quality, pricing, corporate ethics, and sustainability, to name a few issues. In essence, customers seek to engage with providers and other actors in the service ecosystem to validate their prominent role in the process of value cocreation.

Yet all of us can cite numerous personal examples where business, government, and other organizations have failed to develop high-engagement, complementary, and collaborative relationships with customers and other actors that are relevant to the value cocreation process. Such organizations lock into an internally focused GDL, thinking of how they should create and deliver value. Earlier in this chapter, we discussed the IT productivity paradox where increased adoption of technology did not produce improvements in productivity or create a competitive advantage. GDL thinking is likely a contributing factor to the paradox. ICT and other technological innovations provide companies with the operant resources (knowledge, skills, and technology) that are necessary to develop great products and services. However, without the ability to engage with customers, and what they value, opportunities are lost, brands lose relevance, products and services commoditize more quickly, and competitive advantage evaporates.

Prahalad and Ramaswamy, in their 2004 book *The Future of Competition,* defined cocreation as "the practice of developing systems, products, or services, through collaboration with customers, managers, employees, and other company stakeholders"[33]. This definition implies that companies can no longer act independently to design products and services or rely on outbound advertising and marketing communications to define customer value. Networked customers and other actors can assert their influence throughout the enterprise and the business ecosystem.

Cloud enterprises have been able to shift from linear to networked business models by developing multisided service platforms[34]. Amazon, Alphabet (Google), Microsoft, Facebook, Uber, and Alibaba have become some of the world's most valued firms through the use of multisided platforms that facilitate exchanges between individuals, online communities, organizations, and even machines. The platforms enable engagement beyond the provider–customer dyad to engage with all actors in the value network. These actors assume roles such as platform owner, suppliers, partners, developers, advertising agencies, employees, distributors, agents, competitors, and shareholders, sometimes simultaneously[35]. Value networks are synonymous with service exchange networks, service ecosystems, or platform ecosystems. Van Alstyne et al. observed that platforms facilitate service exchange and value cocreation by enabling three strategic shifts that affect the way value is created and enable service innovation[36].

---

[33]C. K. Prahalad and V. Ramaswamy, *The Future of Competition: Co-Creating Unique Value With Customers* (Cambridge, MA: Harvard Business School Press, 2004).
[34]A. Moazed and N. Johnson, *Modern Monopolies: What It Takes to Dominate in the 21st Century Economy* (New York: St. Martin's Press, 2016).
[35]P. Ekman, R. Raggio, and S. Thompson, "Service Network Value Co-creation: Defining Roles of the Generic Actor," *Industrial Marketing Management* 56: 51–62 (2016).
[36]M. Van Alstyne, G. Parker, and S. Choudary, "Pipelines, Platforms, and the New Rules of Strategy," *Harvard Business Review* 94 (4): 54–62 (2016).

1. *From control to orchestration of resources:* "Pipeline" firms, traditional GDL value-chain-centric businesses, control a linear value-added process that transforms resource inputs into value-added outputs as products and services. Alternatively, platform businesses enable the exchange of resources owned and contributed by the community of ecosystem actors. These resources typically include financial resources, knowledge, skills, critical relationships, and technologies. In other words, the service ecosystem, properly orchestrated, is the core asset of the platform.

2. *From internal optimization to external interaction:* Traditional GDL firms optimize the organization of internal resources and processes, end to end, to ensure the efficient production of products and services outputs at a profit. Platforms create value by facilitating external interactions, specifically the engagement and collaboration between service ecosystem actors.

3. *From customer value to ecosystem value:* GDL firms focus on maximizing business value by optimizing customer lifetime value (CLV), which is a measure of the future value of the firm's relationship with a customer. Platforms seek to maximize the total value of the service ecosystem.

Figure 1-6 shows the market capitalization per employee for several leading ICT companies. We use market capitalization, which depicts the market value of a firm's outstanding shares, as a relative measure of firm size, business value generated, and business model risk. Facebook Netflix, and Google, as pure-play service platform enterprises, generate exemplary market capitalization per employee. Apple, a dominant product manufacturer with small but growing cloud services, generates considerable market cap per employee as well. Ninety percent of Apple's 2015 revenues of US$233.7 billion are derived from the iPhone, Mac, and iPad products, with 63 percent of sales from the iPhone alone[37]. Still, Apple, as the world's most valuable public company, generates more than twice the revenue of Amazon, the next largest technology company. Amazon, a cloud platform company, had 2015 revenues of US$107.0 billion[38]. Amazon generates much less market cap per employee due to its extensive warehouse and logistics footprint to support e-commerce operations. Apple, although not a significant cloud services provider, benefits from its own ecosystem of product platforms and software and, most significantly, the highly profitable iPhone. It is an open question whether Apple can transform itself toward more of a service-focused company.

---

[37]Apple, Inc. Form 10-K, 2015. http://investor.apple.com/secfiling.cfm?filingID=1193125-15-356351&CIK=320193.
[38]Amazon.com, Inc. Form 10-K, 2015. https://www.sec.gov/Archives/edgar/data/1018724/000101872416000172/amzn-20151231x10k.htm.

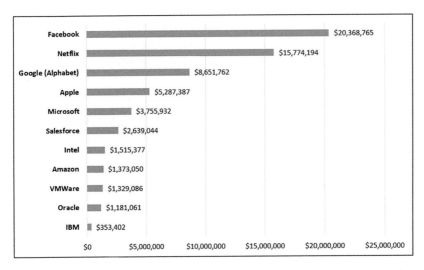

Figure 1-6. *Market capitalization per employee, December 31, 2015. Source: Yahoo Finance*

A general conclusion from Figure 1-6 is that digital platform enterprises generate more value from the efforts of their employees than other technology companies do. Notably, IBM is a company that is transitioning from a manufacturing firm to a cloud services firm with its deep learning cloud-platform-based Watson ecosystem gaining traction. Service applications and target markets include cognitive systems, analytics, finance, banking, blockchain, health care, manufacturing, smart cities, and IoT[39]. The company's relatively low market cap per employee is a measure of the current state of its service transformation as well as the value-generating potential as IBM becomes more cloud platform and service intensive.

The cloud is not all positive aspects. The financial media and other observers are becoming aware of the "winner take all" success of the digital platform companies that can generate massive value with relatively few employees[40]. Facebook, Alphabet (Google), and Netflix, all platform firms, for all the value they create, do not create many jobs (see Table 1-1). Collectively, they have 77,605 employees generating US$99.7 billion in sales. This is only 65.7 percent of the number of Microsoft employees, who generate US$93.6 billion in sales. Product-focused technology firms such as Intel and IBM have higher headcounts at much lower sales per employee.

---

[39]C. Ballavitis, "A Closer Look at IBM's Future (Part 2) – IBM Watson," *Seeking Alpha.* http://seekingalpha.com/article/4003751-closer-look-ibms-future-part-2-ibm-watson, September 2, 2016.

[40]J. Hilsenrath and B. Davis, "America's Dazzling Tech Boom Has a Downside: Not Enough Jobs," *Wall Street Journal.* http://www.wsj.com/articles/americas-dazzling-tech-boom-has-a-downside-not-enough-jobs-1476282355, October 12, 2016.

Table 1-1. Sales per Employee for ICT Companies, 2015. Source: Yahoo Finance

Company	Employees	2015 Sales $	Sales/Employee
Netflix	3,100	$6,800,000,000	$2,193,548
Apple	111,000	$233,700,000,000	$2,105,405
Facebook	12,691	$17,900,000,000	$1,410,448
Google (Alphabet)	61,814	$75,000,000,000	$1,213,317
Microsoft	118,000	$93,600,000,000	$793,220
Intel	107,300	$55,400,000,000	$516,309
Amazon	230,800	$107,000,000,000	$463,605
VMWare	18,050	$6,600,000,000	$365,651
Arm Holdings	3,975	$1,400,000,000	$352,201
Salesforce	19,742	$6,700,000,000	$339,378
Oracle	132,000	$38,200,000,000	$289,394
IBM	377,757	$81,700,000,000	$216,277

Cloud firms can be massively disruptive of industries and markets as cloud platforms redefine market boundaries by changing the rules of competition and the manner of value creation. Although employees are necessary to design, develop, implement, and manage the service platform (and act as service providers in some instances), the essential platform asset is the community of cloud ecosystem (service ecosystem) members with their knowledge, skills, technology, and other resources. Employees are members of the ecosystem as well, but in terms of numbers, the ecosystem community is much larger and more resource endowed than the platform employees. Future research will undoubtedly address the economic contributions from the platform ecosystem communities. It might be full-time jobs, new connections, new markets, and new solutions. Or, or it might be a total reconfiguration of work and the economy along the lines of the flexibility and freedom offered by a "gig economy" or a "sharing economy" that enables companies like Uber and Airbnb[41].

Service ecosystems serve critical purposes that include collaboration between actors to develop the value proposition and to cocreate value through the continuous development of innovative user experiences. Cloud platforms enable service ecosystem actors to exchange critical resources for value cocreation. New experiences can result from open innovation practices such as crowd sourcing, mass collaboration, and social networking. The *experience mindset* defines value as realized from human experiences rather than features and processes[42]. It is essential for organizations to work with customers and other actors to design the high-value experiences that will drive purchases of the solution and strengthen customer relationships and brand loyalty[43].

---

[41]L. Alton, "Is the Gig Economy a Bubble That's About to Burst?" *Forbes.* http://www.forbes.com/sites/larryalton/2016/09/26/is-the-gig-economy-a-bubble-thats-about-to-burst/#19f979b810da, September 26, 2016.
[42]V. Ramaswamy and F. Gouillart, *The Power of Co-Creation: Build It With Them to Boost Growth, Productivity, and Profits* (New York: Free Press, 2010).
[43]T. Brown and R. Martin, "Design for Action: How to Use Design Thinking to Make Great Things Actually Happen," *Harvard Business Review* 93 (9): 56–65 (September 2015).

Once designed, service experiences need to be integrated into the business processes of the enterprise[44]. This is an important notion that has become fundamental for understanding value cocreation. It informs a service-thinking mindset that is essential for service innovation.

Firms that can create a culture of value cocreation with their customers and service ecosystem partners have greater potential for business success. Engagement experiences serve to keep actors current with customers, market dynamics, innovative ideas, and other insights. ICT enables enterprises to transform the structure of value creation from physical colocated contexts to a dynamic, distributed, cloud-based service ecosystem[45]. The SDL-oriented experience mindset keeps the whole system open to real-time opportunities for service innovation. The design of the user experience strategically organizes and aligns the whole service ecosystem on its foundational responsibility, the enablement of value cocreation.

Service Mindset

When we think of reasons why IT organizations and technology firms fail to innovate, especially moving to cloud services, we usually think about inappropriate strategy or insufficient technology. A typical list of barriers to ICT innovation might include the following:

- Technical debt in legacy IT ecosystems

- Poor technology choices and lack of implementation

- Lack of or poorly designed innovation strategy

- Insufficient support from corporate leadership

- Financial barriers

- Lack of internal resources

- Lack of skilled personnel

- Organizational barriers

- Incentive system not tied to innovation

- Lack of market intelligence

- Poor marketing communications

- Organizational culture hostile to change, risk averse

---

[44]C. Christensen, T. Hall, K. Dillon, and D. Duncan, "Know Your Customers' Jobs to be Done," *Harvard Business Review* 94(9): 54–62 (September 2016).
[45]C. Breidbach and P. Maglio, "Technology-Enabled Value Co-creation: An Empirical Analysis of Actors, Resources, and Practices," *Industrial Marketing Management* 56: 73–85 (2016).

Most likely, you can add other barriers to innovation to this list from your own experience. We would like to add the *lack of service thinking*. Service thinking is an SDL mindset that holistically considers the design of service experiences, adoption of a service thinking organization culture, a flexible and adaptive organizational architecture, multisided platforms, and service analytics that are necessary to create, monitor, and support a dynamic service ecosystem. Service thinking might occur naturally to some innovators. There are ample cases where service innovation in the cloud has been phenomenally successful, such as the emergence of the cloud service platforms. The platform model, or the service ecosystem model as we might refer to it, is truly disruptive. There are obviously people and firms with a service mindset that conceived these firms. However, too many companies are not familiar with this type of thinking. Instead, they take a product thinking GDL mindset that informs their approach to innovation. Lack of service thinking will limit success in moving to the cloud and inhibit the transformation of enterprises to successful service-dominant enterprises.

So what prevents product pipeline firms from transitioning to service-oriented cloud platform enterprises, moving from product thinking to a service-thinking mindset? In our view, it is the lack of a service-thinking organization culture. Many firms do not have the right mix of service innovation skills, service resources, and team members with formal training in service innovation. Service innovation knowledge is hard to find. Whereas business schools typically offer a services marketing course, few offer service innovation courses or a degree program. The same is true for most engineering and computer science programs; product technology is the focus of the curriculum. To fill this gap, organizations such as the International Society of Service Innovation Professionals (ISSIP) work with universities to support curriculum development. The organization also offers special interest groups, community involvement, learning centers, webinars, conferences, publications, and other resources to help individuals and enterprises be successful in the global service economy[46].

Cultural change is not something to superimpose on a broken business model. Cultural transformation occurs as people buy in to new strategies and business models are developed and implemented[47]. Organizational culture generally refers to an organization's values communicated through norms, artifacts, and observed behavioral patterns[48]. From a GDL perspective, cultural change is typically associated with the development of new technologies, infrastructure, process innovations, and new applications for which the organization has to adapt. Mergers and acquisitions also can be a source of cultural change, not always beneficially.

Cultural change from an SDL perspective results from close interactions between the producer and the customer and other value-producing actors in the service ecosystem. Knowledge-based solutions constitute the primary value propositions and the service ecosystem is the source of service innovation. Technological innovation is important to the degree that it enables service innovation, but it is not the primary determining factor

---

[46]International Society of Service Innovation Professionals, www.issip.org.
[47]J. Lorsch and E. McTague, "Culture Is Not the Culprit: When Organizations Are in Crisis, It's Usually Because the Business Is Broken," *Harvard Business Review* 94 (4): 96–105 (April 2016).
[48]C. Homburg and C. Pflesser, "A Multiple-Layer Model of Market-Oriented Organizational Culture: Management Issues and Performance Outcomes," *Journal of Marketing Research* 37 (4): 449–462 (2000).

for service success. Our discussion of multisided platforms is the case at hand. Platform infrastructure technology is a readily available commodity. It is the applications and the ability to attract a critical mass of users and build a sustainable service ecosystem that matters. Innovation is a process and the result of that process, market acceptance, is critical. Innovation happens within the service ecosystem. The service culture exemplifies organizational values that support service innovation, cultural norms for innovation, artifacts of innovation[49], and innovative behaviors that will drive firm performance[50].

If service innovation is to become a cultural norm for product-focused ICT companies, then service thinking will require the training of existing leaders and employees and bringing skilled professionals in from the outside. Cloud native service companies can build a winning service culture from scratch by team building with like-minded people. For legacy companies, the creation of a separate organization to experiment with new cloud service models, "skunk works," might be useful. The skunk works isolates the innovators from the dominant culture and allows the development of success models to help transform the entire organization. Alternatively, product companies can create a hybrid business model that combines products and services with a platform business model[51]. A product-based business model develops differentiated products for specific markets. The platform model connects providers, users, and third parties. The hybrid model, such as that used by Amazon for Kindle, Fire, and Echo, and Amazon-produced films and TV series, combines the two, connecting customers and third parties and selling the platform owner's products and services as another provider in the mix. As service innovation in the cloud continues to develop, the cloud appears to be the future of digital services, and dynamic service models are the future of the cloud.

Value Creation and Service Analytics

The amount of data generated by cloud-based service ecosystems is enormous. Almost every digital interaction, whether it be a search, page view, social media post, e-mail, chat, text, Skype or FaceTime conversation, music or movie streamed, game played, photo posted, credit card purchase, or mobile phone call, generates data. Much of this data is anonymous or can be anonymized; some of it is personally identifiable. Government collects data on taxes, medical services, Social Security, homeland security, and other interactions that is personally identifiable. Businesses collect data for business intelligence, to run business operations, to develop products and services, and to market to users and potential customers. Data on markets, technologies, business operations, and customers is essential for business success.

---

[49]Innovation artifacts lead to innovative behaviors. These artifacts include attitudes, language, symbols, rituals, physical environment, and physical layout. Recall that employees are members in the service ecosystem. The team environment and its dynamics should be oriented toward engagement with other actors to develop innovation solutions.
[50]S. Hogan and L. Coote, "Organizational Culture, Innovation, and Performance: A Test of Schein's Model," *Journal of Business Research* 67: 1609–1621 (2014).
[51]F. Zhu and N. Furr, "Products to Platforms: Making the Leap," *Harvard Business Review* 94 (4): 72–78 (April 2016).

Cloud-based service innovation would not be possible without the ability to collect, analyze, and leverage information from customers and other actors in the service ecosystem. Facebook's business model depends on providing mostly free social networking services to acquire users and generate traffic and then monetizing user-generated data and analytics to target users with interactive advertising. This business model is highly successful and used by multisided cloud platforms and most online content and solution providers. Other applications of data analytics serve to transact with, engage, and monitor members of the service ecosystem to ensure effective cocreation of value.

Descriptive analytics provide insights about why specific activities happen. Social media analytics collect and analyze data from social media web sites, blogs, and online forums to measure sentiment about various issues. Predictive analytics identify patterns in historical data to predict future behavior such as using credit scores to predict payment default risks, or using past supplier performance to predict future reliability. Prescriptive analytics assess data against key performance indicators to recommend future courses of action. If the service ecosystem is the core asset of the cloud service platform, then data analytics is the service ecosystem's digital health monitor that ensures the platform is running properly, provides state-of-the-art services, develops market-leading value propositions, creates highly engaging user experiences, and generates superior value.

Privacy and Cloud Services

Annoyed by a reporter's question about online privacy, Sun Microsystems CEO Scott McNealy famously delivered this prophetic assessment: "You have zero privacy anyway. Get over it"[52]. That was 1999, before the cloud, social media, and smart mobile services era. Privacy advocates at that time were more worried about data theft and the ability of a device "phoning home" with user data than online services enterprises monetizing their personal identity. Enter Google, Facebook, Yahoo!, Twitter, LinkedIn, Netflix, Amazon, Comcast, Verizon, and a host of cloud services competitors. Do online services users have a reasonable expectation of privacy? Most people would agree that there is an expectation of privacy in terms of personal physical space, such as homes and cars, that should be free from unwanted intrusion. Nevertheless, any expectation of online privacy, as McNealy observed, is proving unrealistic given the business models of cloud services companies, Internet service providers, social media, mobile applications, and all flavors of hackers.

At the dawn of the commercial Internet in 1993, when most people had not yet heard of it, Peter Steiner published his famous cartoon "On the Internet, nobody knows you're a dog" in *The New Yorker* magazine[53]. The cartoon features two dogs, one sitting on a desk chair with a paw on a keyboard, the other sitting on the floor, an observant recipient of wisdom shared. The cartoon went viral (analog of course, via photocopies and faxes).

---

[52]P. Sprenger, "Sun on Privacy: 'Get over It'," *Wired.* http://www.wired.com/politics/law/news/1999/01/17538, January 26, 1999.

[53]M. Cavana, "Nobody Knows You're a Dog; As Iconic Internet Cartoon Turns 20, Creator Peter Steiner Knows the Idea Is as Relevant as Ever," *The Washington Post.* https://www.washingtonpost.com/blogs/comic-riffs/post/nobody-knows-youre-a-dog-as-iconic-internet-cartoon-turns-20-creator-peter-steiner-knows-the-joke-rings-as-relevant-as-ever/2013/07/31/73372600-f98d-11e2-8e84-c56731a202fb_blog.html, July 31, 2013.

It served to establish the first Internet meme: Users are anonymous on the Internet. The cartoon endures as an icon of Internet culture and the all-time most popular for *The New Yorker*. Fast forward to 2016. Can the dog remain anonymous? Absolutely not in today's world. Google and Facebook would certainly know that you are a dog, tag your photos, reference your AKC registration, fingerprint your computer, determine your location, mine your browsing and offline media habits, scan your e-mails, download your contact list, assess your credit score and purchasing behavior, create your online profile, and predict what you will likely do next. The 2016 dog soon contends with unlimited interactive ads for tasty dog snacks, high-end doggy day-care kennels, and all sorts of fashionable canine accoutrements across multiple media channels. Is this a good thing? It depends on whether the dog understands and agrees to its status as a participant in an information services market where personal data is the currency, and the benefits of that participation outweigh the costs.

The right to privacy concept is not new. An 1890 article in the *Harvard Law Review* defined privacy as the "right to be let alone"[54]. Newspapers and especially new technologies of the time such as the telegraph, photographs, and the phonograph represented threats to personal privacy. Then and now, from a service innovation perspective, it is important for service providers, users, and other actors in a service ecosystem to understand the dimensions of privacy and the factors contributing to its erosion.

Four essential dimensions of privacy affect users' trust in the provider and the service solution: confidentiality, anonymity, security, and safety[55]. Confidentiality means that information shared by customers is for the company to use for specific purposes per the user agreement. Companies have the responsibility to ensure only authorized personnel have access to customer information. Anonymity generally refers to the state of being publicly unknown. Personally identifiable information (PII) needs protection from disclosure without the owner's consent. Internet user anonymity erodes through cookies, device fingerprinting, browsing monitoring, hacking, and other approaches that allow web sites to identify users and track their locations and behaviors.

Security builds on a foundation of user confidentiality and anonymity. Security refers to the protection of personal information from theft that could cause loss of personal property or reputation. The emergence of cloud computing heightens the need for data security. The security of personal and business data is an open issue for cloud services. Almost daily, a new instance of hacking comes to our attention: the U.S. Office of Personnel Management, Yahoo!, eBay, Anthem Healthcare, JPMorgan Chase, LinkedIn, and thousands of other firms and government agencies, not to mention individuals, have been victimized. The cloud might be an undeniable megatrend, but cloud security remains a work in progress.

Finally, safety is the condition of being protected from the undesirable consequences of using an information service. Protection is needed from physical injury, emotional and psychological harm (e.g., cyberbullying), catastrophic financial loss, and life-threatening health events. Online services have opened up physical and cyber accessibility of users and reduced their ability to control online impression management and personal safety.

---

[54]S. Warren and L. Brandeis, "The Right to Privacy," *Harvard Law Review* 4 (5): 193–220 (1890).
[55]E. Chan, R. Harmon, and H. Demirkan, "Privacy, Value Co-creation, and Service Innovation: Cui Bono?" In *Proceedings of the 2012 Hawaii International Conference on Systems Sciences (HICSS-45)*, 1573–1582 (2012).

Personal locations can be determined, activities recorded and streamed, license plates scanned, homes mapped and pictured at street level, and facial recognition apps can match identities and locations to photographs and real time to individuals. All of these cloud-based services can benefit authorized users or be subject to misuse by online predators, physical stalkers, and other criminals. Indeed, our 2016 cloud-engaged dog lives in a much more complex and exciting environment.

Everything-as-a-Service

Since Nicholas Carr remarked in 2003 that IT doesn't matter, a tsunami of IT innovation has disrupted individuals, businesses, communities, nations, and indeed the entire world. A partial list includes innovations such as Internet searches, iPhones, other smartphones, wireless mobile computing, GPS for mobile phones, Google Earth, social media, online gaming, augmented reality, virtual reality, facial recognition, streaming media, electronic health records, wearable technology, mobile payments, big data analytics, cyberphysical systems, IoT, cognitive computing, artificial intelligence, robotics, autonomous vehicles, unmanned drones, cognitive assistants, software-defined networks, serverless computing, the platform economy, sharing economy, and cloud computing. IT just might matter after all.

As more and more cloud services are commercialized, it seems that Larry Ellison, CEO of Oracle, was right when he observed that he couldn't think about anything that isn't cloud computing. The cloud is the service innovation platform. To cover the incipient reality of the cloud-as-a-service business model, the term *everything-as-a-service* (XaaS), also known as anything-as-a-service, has become part of the cloud lexicon. XaaS is the shorthand for the wide variety of on-demand cloud services. XaaS is emblematic of the emerging "as-a-service" (aaS) business model that is a core component of cloud computing. The model transforms the IT cost of ownership model into a pay-as-you-go predictable expense without the need to invest up front in expensive infrastructure. Ongoing maintenance, parts, support, and periodic upgrades belong to the cloud service provider, not the user. As the cloud has matured, XaaS has grown a dizzying set of cloud-service acronyms, a sample of which are displayed in Table 1-2.

It is essential to understand the underlying dynamics of service innovation that can drive business transformation. It is also important to look at potentially cautionary tales. For instance, underlying loss of privacy is a mindset carried over from a GDL universe that assumes an *asymmetric* provider–customer relationship where the delivered product carries intrinsic value and the user consumes it. In an SDL universe, the relationship between service provider and customer should ideally be *symmetric,* as the provider also derives benefit from the customer. At the very least, this value comes from customer data and service fees, considered as rights for future services. Any entity that treats its customers as a depository for static product value is modeling an unsustainable relationship and endangering its own future.

Table 1-2. *Everything-as-a-Service Examples*

Software-as-a-Service (SaaS)	Forensics-as-a-Service (FaaS)
Platform-as-a-Service (PaaS)	Network-as-a-Service (NaaS)
Infrastructure-as-a-Service (IaaS)	Ransomware-as-a-Service (RaaS)
AI-as-a-Service (AIaaS)	Security-as-a-Service (SECaaS)
Analytics-as-a-Service (AaaS)	Sensing-as-a-Service (SaaS)
Big Data-as-a-Service (BDaaS)	Sensing and Actuation-as-a-Service
Business Process-as-a-Service (BPaaS)	(SAaaS)
Cognition-as-a-Service (CaaS)	Sensor Data-as-a-Service (SDaaS)
Data-as-a-Service (DaaS)	Storage-as-a-Service (STaaS)
Database-as-a-Service (DBaaS)	Things-as-a-Service (TaaS)
Data Integrity as-a-Service (DIaaS)	Video Surveillance-as-a-Service (VSaaS)
Data Mining-as-a-Service (DMaaS)	Virtualization-as-a-Service (VaaS)
Ethernet-as-a-Service (EaaS)	

Microsoft, not an early advocate for the aaS business model, is a legacy software firm from the PC world. It had game-changing success with operating systems and applications software. However, the firm was GDL product and services focused. The company worked to protect its dominant position in operating systems and office productivity software. It was slow to innovate. Bill Gates almost missed the Internet. Microsoft fought open source and missed the mobile revolution because it focused on the PC[56]. The company failed to see the cloud. Bing is a "me too" search engine. Windows 8 was a disaster and Windows 10 adoptions have been relatively slow, with a small installed base compared with Windows 7. Microsoft is now playing catch-up with AWS with Azure and Google with Office 365 and Outlook. Outlook is morphing from just e-mail to a platform that connects users to other Microsoft and third-party services such as Uber, Evernote, and Yelp[57]. Can Microsoft transform itself from a product GDL company to a SDL cloud-platform-based service innovation enterprise? It might take some time for success. However, the enterprise appears to be making progress. Microsoft's cloud services are gaining traction as evidenced by its market share gains on market leader AWS. Microsoft now ranks second in selling computing power and storage[58]. It appears that Microsoft has begun the transition.

We will close with a question. Consider the greatest ICT innovations of all time. Is there any innovation on the scale of the invention of the transistor, the integrated circuit, the microprocessor, or the articulation of Moore's Law that would exceed the potential of cloud-as-a-service? That is, at least until the singularity.

---

[56]J. Bort, "Kicking Bill Gates Off The Board Is the Best Thing Microsoft Can Do," *The Business Insider.* http://www.businessinsider.com/microsoft-board-bill-gates-2014-1, January 31, 2014.
[57]F. Zhu and N. Furr, "Products to Platforms: Making the Leap," *Harvard Business Review* 94 (4): 72–78 (April 2016).
[58]J. Greene, "Microsoft Soars on Cloud Gains," *Wall Street Journal.* http://www.nasdaq.com/article/microsoft-soars-on-cloud-gains--wsj-20161021-00061, October 21, 2016.

PART II

CHAPTER 2

■ ■ ■

The Service Science Foundation for Cloud Computing

Design must reflect the practical and aesthetic in business, but above all ... good design must primarily serve people.

—Thomas J. Watson

The adoption of information and communications technologies (ICT) that connect global markets and drive automation led to a migration of economies and workers from manufacturing to knowledge-intensive service industries. Under the service transformation dynamics discussed in the first chapter, by 2015 services accounted for 70 percent to 80 percent of GDP for the United States and other advanced economies and has become the primary source of economic growth[1]. The motivation for transitioning from a pure product business model to one that is more service-oriented is to increase competitive advantage by developing novel value propositions, opening new markets, and strengthening customer relationships that improve financial performance[2]. As we discuss in Chapter 3, this trend exemplifies the transition from a goods-dominant logic (GDL) to a service-dominant logic (SDL) providing the conceptual foundation for the growth of the service economy[3]. Services are less visible, harder to copy, relationship-based, relatively easy to differentiate, and enable the cocreation of value between service providers, customers, and other actors (individuals and organizations) within a

---

[1]The World Bank, *World Development Indicators: Services (% of GDP).* (Washington, DC: World Bank, 2015). http://data.worldbank.org/indicator/NV.SRV.TETC.ZS
[2]D. Kindstrom, "Towards a Service-Based Business Model: Key Aspects for Future Competitive Advantage," *European Management Journal, 28,* 479-490, 2010.
[3]S. Vargo and R. Lusch, "Evolving to a New Dominant Logic for Marketing," *Journal of Marketing, 68* (1), 1–17, 2004.

E. Castro-Leon and R. Harmon, *Cloud as a Service,* DOI 10.1007/978-1-4842-0103-9_2

service ecosystem[4]. Service solutions can make a significant contribution to growth and profitability, as product-oriented enterprises become more service dominant[5].

For ICT companies the transition to knowledge-based services is already in process. On August 1, 2011, the five largest companies worldwide by market capitalization were Exxon (US$392 billion), Apple (US$368 billion), PetroChina (US$298 billion), Industrial and Commercial Bank of China (US$240 billion) and Shell US$229 billion); three oil companies, one mobile device manufacturer, and one Chinese industrial bank. One might conclude that the most valuable firms of 2011 were symbolic of the 20th-century manufacturing ecosystem. Only five years later, by August 1, 2016, the five most valuable firms worldwide were Apple (US$571 billion), Alphabet/Google (US$540 billion), Microsoft US$441 billion), Amazon (US$364 billion), and Facebook (US$357 billion), four cloud-based services firms and one mobile device manufacturer that is migrating to cloud-based services[6]. The transformation of the world economy from products to services, as enabled by the cloud-computing megatrend, is now unrelenting. Technology firms and technology-using firms are reconsidering their business models, as cloud-based services have become a major driver of innovation.

Worldwide spending on public cloud services is projected to grow at a 19.4 percent compound annual growth rate (CAGR) from US$70 billion year-end 2015 to more than US$141 billion in 2019[7]. Cloud services can be very profitable. Amazon Web Services (AWS) reported 2015 revenues of US$7.9 billion with operating income of US$1.9 billion[8]. AWS is Amazon's most profitable business segment. As of the fourth quarter of 2015, AWS had achieved a 31 percent worldwide market share followed by Microsoft (9 percent), IBM (7 percent), Google (4 percent), and Salesforce (4 percent)[9]. The primary market segments are business-process services (BPaaS), cloud-application services (SaaS), cloud application infrastructure services (PaaS), cloud system infrastructure services (IaaS), and cloud-security services. The strong growth in cloud services will likely continue as

---

[4]P. Matthyssens and K. Vandenbempt, "Moving from Basic Offerings to Value-Added Solutions: Strategies, Barriers, and Alignment," *Industrial Marketing Management, 37* (3), 316–328, 2008.

[5]E. Fang, R. W. Palmatier, and J.-B. E. M. Steenkamp, "Effect of Service Transition Strategies on Firm Value," *Journal of Marketing, 72* (4), 1–14, 2008.

[6]S. Ovide and R. Molla, "Technology Conquers the Stock Market," https://www.bloomberg.com/gadfly/articles/2016-08-02/tech-giants-form-fab-five-to-dominate-stock-valuation-chart, August 2, 2016.

[7]L. Columbus, "Roundup of Cloud Computing Forecasts and Market Estimates, 2016," *Forbes*, http://www.forbes.com/sites/louiscolumbus/2016/03/13/roundup-of-cloud-computing-forecasts-and-market-estimates-2016/#5262975e74b0, March 13, 2016.

[8]D. Frommer, "Amazon Web Services Is Approaching a $10 Billion-a-Year Business," *Recode Magazine*, http://www.recode.net/2016/4/28/11586526/aws-cloud-revenue-growth, April 28, 2016.

[9]Synergy Research Group, "AWS Remains Dominant Despite Microsoft and Google Growth," https://www.srgresearch.com/articles/aws-remains-dominant-despite-microsoft-and-google-growth-surges, February 3, 2016.

the shift away from legacy IT services to cloud-based services drives the adoption of digital business strategies.

The International Society of Service Innovation Professionals (ISSIP) defines service as the application of knowledge for the benefit of others and service science as the study of diverse, interconnected, complex human-centered value creation systems in business and society[10]. These definitions introduce a conceptual view of the service innovation domain. Although ICT companies now appear to be rapidly adopting service-based business models, this was not always the case. For most of the industry's history, IT services were developed and marketed as products. Services were rarely at the core of corporate strategy, the development of new markets, or the creation of novel business models. Radical changes are now taking place in the industry. The purpose of this chapter is to present an overview of the foundations of service innovation as they might apply to cloud computing. Topics to be covered are service science, service-dominant logic, product-service systems, service thinking, T-shaped people, and the emerging frontiers of service innovation.

Service Science

A brief history of IBM Corporation as the pioneering thought leader for the transition to service and the continuing development of the new field of service science is in order. The continuing transformation of IBM to a service-dominant enterprise was born of necessity more than two decades ago. The megatrend revolutions of personal computers, followed by networked client/servers, broadsided IBM and wrecked its proprietary enterprise integrated-solutions mainframe business. Both IT revolutions transformed how customers perceived value and how they purchased and used IT. IT became cheaper, more pervasive, individualized, and decentralized. Individual users and business units were able to assert control over IT strategy and purchase decisions. By 1993, IBM faced a net loss of US$9 billion on sales of US$64.5 billion. IBM's board considered breaking the firm into independent businesses[11]. Instead, they looked for leadership from outside.

On April Fool's Day 1993, Louis Gerstner became CEO and Chairman of IBM. It was the first time that IBM had hired an outsider for its top position. Previously, Gerstner held positions as Chairman and CEO of RJR Nabisco, Chairman and CEO of American Express Travel Related Services Company, and a director for McKinsey & Company. Gerstner immediately set out to change the company's strategy and culture to become more customer centric and service oriented. He kept IBM together, rebuilt the product line, downsized the workforce, and redefined its core competence with integrated business solutions to emphasize IBM's world-class technology expertise aligned with industry-leading IT services. At COMDEX 1995, Gerstner announced the new strategy. Network computing services would drive the company going forward. Services soon became the

---

[10]R. Badinelli, "What Do We Mean by Service?," International Society of Service Innovation Professionals, www.issip.org/what-do-we-mean-by-service/, 2015.
[11]IBM Archives, *History of IBM: 1990s, IBM Corporation*. http://www-03.ibm.com/ibm/history/history/decade_1990.html, 2016.

fastest growing business segment. By 2000, IBM had reestablished itself as a leading IT service innovator[12]. IBM's success revolutionized the industry. Microsoft, HP, Oracle, Salesforce.com, SAP, Siemens, Cisco, and other technology companies soon adopted business models that were more service oriented as well[13].

THE INVENTION OF SERVICE SCIENCE

In 2004, Dr. Jim Spohrer, the new Director of Almaden Service Research at IBM, complained to Dr. Henry Chesbrough, Director of the Center for Open Innovation at University of California, Berkeley, that graduates with the right mix of computer science, engineering, management, and social science were hard to find. Chesbrough noted that IBM in the 1940s and 1950s had seeded the development of computer science by donating computers and curriculum assistance to universities: "IBM started computer science. You should start service science." Paul Horn, Director of IBM Research, supported the idea and the development of the service science discipline was underway.

Service-oriented ICT firms that developed business models to exploit technology could gain advantage over firms that merely implemented technology. Formal service research should complement technology and business research. This conversation proved to be the genesis for the discipline of service science.

Source: IBM Corporation, "The Invention of Service Science," *IBM at 100,* 2011. http://www-03.ibm.com/ibm/history/ibm100/us/en/icons/servicescience/.

The strategic shift to service for IBM was only the beginning of the story. In a product-dominated world, corporate strategy, organization structure, culture, technology, processes, and approaches to markets and customers are the result of product thinking. Indeed, most business executives, employees, university professors, government regulators, and politicians still think this way. Even today, as more firms have recognized the strategic potential of service innovation, product thinking dominates, especially in technology firms. The formative issue for service science is the need to develop a better understanding of how service innovation can transform industries and markets. Surely if services can potentially provide more value and innovation opportunities, then service thinking must be different from, and superior to, product thinking. That thought became the genesis for the development of the scientific discipline that became service science.

IBM coined the term *service science management and engineering* (SSME) as an integrative label for the discipline of service science, which embraces both academic theory and business practice. Service science merges technology with an understanding of business management, processes, organizational design, and culture to develop

---

[12]L. V. Gerstner, *Who Says Elephants Can't Dance?* (New York: Harper Business, 2002).
[13]L. Young, *From Products to Services: Insights and Experience from Companies Which Have Embraced the Service Economy* (Hoboken, NJ: Wiley, 2008).

and apply tools to address business problems and create market opportunities. It is an interdisciplinary field that "combines organization and human understanding with business and technological understanding to categorize and explain the many types of service systems that exist as well as how service systems interact and evolve to co-create value"[14]. Managers seeking to develop innovative service solutions will need to understand how to apply their organization's unique resources and capabilities in an effective, efficient, and value-creating manner.

Over the past decade the growth in global services, and especially the incidence of digital services based on ICT, most notably the cloud, has elevated service innovation to a high priority for companies, governments, and individual citizens. Accordingly, there is an increasing awareness of the need for an interdisciplinary science of service that can develop a systematic approach for innovation that is reliable and more sustainable[15]. A core tenet of service science derives from the ubiquitous nature of service and the notion that all businesses are service businesses. Actors cocreate value within a service ecosystem that consists of service providers and customers along with other collaborative economic and social actors that possess the knowledge, skills, technology, and other resource-based capabilities necessary for arriving at mutually beneficial outcomes.

Service science is about rethinking the where and how of value creation. Historically, managers and scholars adhered to a manufacturing-oriented logic where value creation is the purview of the firm. The firm delivers value to the customer (as buyer or user) in product form. A service-oriented logic recognizes that value creation occurs within service systems that can involve service providers and customers in addition to a whole network of actors collaborating to cocreate value. Maglio et al. asserted the notion that the service system is the fundamental abstraction (defining concept) of service science[16]. The service system is an ecosystem of organizations, people, technologies, shared information, and other resources that engage with other service systems for mutual benefit. The service system abstraction provides the foundation for developing a systematic approach for understanding value cocreation toward the goal of advancing an integrated science of service.

The core research propositions that are foundational to the continuing development of the service science discipline follow here[17]:

- Close engagement between service providers, buyers, suppliers, and other economic and social actors in the service ecosystem is necessary to enable value cocreation. This interaction can be separable from the actual physical proximity of the actors due to cloud-based service platforms.

- Value cocreation involves the integration of knowledge into useful systems.

---

[14]P. Maglio and J. Spohrer, "Fundamentals of Service Science," *Journal of the Academy of Marketing Science, 36,* 18–20, 2008.

[15]P. Maglio and J. Spohrer, "A Service Science Perspective on Business Model Innovation," *Industrial Marketing Management, 42,* 665–670, 2013.

[16]P. Maglio, S. Vargo, N. Caswell, and J. Spohrer, "The Service System Is the Basic Abstraction of Service Science," *Information Systems and E-Business Management, 7,* 395–406, 2009.

[17]H. Chesbrough, and J. Spohrer, "A Research Manifesto for Services Science," *Communications of the ACM, 49* (7), 35–40, 2006.

- The cocreation of value among actors in service exchange is simultaneous.

- All parties to the value cocreation process need to understand the nature of the knowledge exchanged. The core assumption is each actor can assess the complementarity of the other actors' knowledge to negotiate the exchange. Actionable knowledge is the principal means for value creation and the fundamental source of competitive advantage. Knowledge networks drive value creation. For example, knowledge of customers through direct engagement and data analytics has become a major source of value for cloud-based service providers.

- Gaining an understanding of the service exchange process and its relationship with relevant experience points is a key factor in customer relationship management that extends to the combined roles of all actors in creating the customer experience.

- Recognizing the role of service science as a discipline for developing and exploiting ICT-based service innovations. The digital transformation that virtually all organizations are addressing creates opportunities for service innovation.

Service-Dominant Logic

In 2004, Stephen Vargo and Robert Lusch, in their seminal works on SDL, defined service as "the application of specialized competencies (knowledge and skills) through deeds, processes, and performances for the benefit of another entity or the entity itself"[18][19]. SDL presents a service-oriented alternative to the traditional goods-oriented model offered by GDL for understanding economic exchange and value creation. The authors advocated for a service-centered view of business with the following requirements[20]:

- Develop service-oriented core competencies, knowledge, and skills that represent potential competitive advantage.

- Identify potential customers (or other stakeholders) that can benefit from the competencies.

---

[18]S. Vargo and R. Lusch, "Evolving to a New Dominant Logic for Marketing," *Journal of Marketing*, *68*, 1–17, January 2004.
[19]S. Vargo and R. Lusch, "The Four Service Marketing Myths: Remnants of a Goods-Based, Manufacturing Model," *Journal of Service Research*, *6*, 324–335, 2004.
[20]S. Vargo and M. Akaka, "Service-Dominant Logic as a Foundation for Service Science: Clarifications," *Service Science*, *1* (1), 32–41. 2009.

- Engage in collaborative relationships that involve customers (and stakeholders) in developing customized, competitively compelling value propositions to meet specific needs.

- Monitor service outcomes to improve customer collaboration and firm performance.

To implement a service-centered approach it is important for managers to understand the conceptual differences between products and services, the types of value created by each, and its realization. It involves understanding the distinction between the GDL and SDL paradigms. GDL views services from a product perspective as add-ons or intangible products offered on an after-sale basis[21]. In this view, services are designed and conceptualized by a service provider as outputs that "add value" that is created and then delivered to the consumer in exchange for financial or other compensation. It is an "arm's-length" transaction. There is no assumption of an ongoing relationship or collaboration with the customer or other complementary actors to cocreate value. Therefore, GDL is a *value-in-exchange* or, in some instances, a value-in-use conceptualization. Value-in-exchange represents the amount of money actually paid for a product or service. For the enterprise, the price of a good (including its service components) defines its economic value. Value manifests at the point where the customer exchanges money for the good. The consumer is the recipient of the embedded value in the good created and delivered by the enterprise. Alternatively, value-in-use recognizes the role of the customer, or user, in generating value. Products are distribution mechanisms for services. Value results from the customer's value-creating process, as the service value of the product is determined during its use. Both value-in-exchange and value-in-use emerged out of the GDL-based provider–customer dyad that assumes value is the provenance of the provider or the customer, or both. As we will soon discover, these concepts inform the migration to an SDL perspective of value creation.

SDL envisions *service* to be product independent, although goods can play a role in service provisioning. The value proposition is service centered. SDL focuses on the development of continuing relationships between service providers and customers within a service network that includes other complementary actors. Service value is always cocreated within the service network. This is a key distinction between SDL, which is based on the service system, and GDL, which is dyadic (provider–customer) in nature. Cocreation involves the process of proposing value (the value proposition), the acceptance of the proposal, and the realization of the proposal by (at least) two service systems, the provider's service system and user's service system, at a minimum[22]. It should be clear that value propositions are not stand-alone statements from the provider's perspective only. The provider, customer, and other actors jointly and iteratively design them, as the case may be. The service system, which might be individual providers and customers or a larger group of collaborative actors, engage each other to apply and integrate resources to cocreate value and realize the service experience. Active

---

[21]S. Vargo and R. Lusch, "Service-Dominant Logic: Continuing the Evolution," *Journal of the Academy of Marketing Science*, *36* (1), 1–10, 2008.
[22]P. Maglio, S. Vargo, N. Caswell, and J. Spohrer, "The Service System Is the Basic Abstraction of Service Science," *Information Systems and E-Business Management*, *7*, 395–406, 2009.

engagement by the customer with the provider's service system in the value cocreation process should ensure that the outcome of the service experience is more customer-oriented and satisfying. An SDL perspective transitions the dominant logic from the exchange of tangible goods for compensation toward the exchange of services for the benefit of the engaged actors in the service ecosystem.

To summarize, GDL is the legacy worldview of traditional economists, marketers, technology executives, product developers, manufacturers, and industries that extract and transform natural resources into products. GDL centers on the product that consists of tangible goods and intangible services as units of output. GDL views *services* as a residual type of good or noncore add-ons that enhance the value of the goods. The GDL perspective assumes that the same principles and management strategies that are applicable for goods production, marketing, and delivery are applicable to services, with some modification based on the relative share and intensity of services in the product mix. Alternatively, service within an SDL perspective is a value-creating process where competencies, such as knowledge and skills, create benefits for another party.

The use of the word *service* as a value-creating process versus *services* as an intangible unit of output recognizes the present understanding of the nature of value in terms of *operand* and *operant* resources[23]. Operand resources are typically tangible and static in nature, such as raw materials. Some type of operation by operant resources is required to make operand resources valuable. Operant resources act on operand resources (and other operant resources) to produce effects that can multiply the value of operand resources. Operant resources are often invisible and intangible (e.g., knowledge, skills, core competencies, organizational processes, and technology). Operant resources are scalable, as they are dynamic and infinite in nature. Operant resources can create additional operant resources (e.g., microprocessors, cognitive computing, artificial intelligence [AI], and robotics). In the case of the microprocessor, human inventiveness embedded silicon (operand) with knowledge (operant) to enable the creation of other operant resources such as computers, software, networks, and the cloud[24].

From a GDL perspective, operand resources are primary. Manufacturers take operand resources as factors of production and apply operant resources to produce outputs to deliver to customers. Similarly, in GDL thinking, customers and markets take on operand characteristics, as they are researched, shaped, segmented, positioned, penetrated, and marketed to. In SDL thinking, operant resources are primary because they produce beneficial effects. Operant resources are important for the services they produce and the value they can create in collaboration with other actors in the value cocreation process, not as inputs to a production process.

Service Ecosystems

Over the last decade, SDL evolved from its initial focus on value cocreation between providers and customers to encompass a broader network-centric view of value cocreation between relevant actors within a *service ecosystem*. The term service

---

[23]Maglio, Vargo, Caswell, and Spohrer, *Ibid.*, 2009.
[24]S. Vargo and R. Lusch, "Evolving to a New Dominant Logic for Marketing," *Journal of Marketing*, *68*, 1–17, January 2004.

ecosystem provides a networked view of value creation and service innovation. Vargo and Lusch defined a service ecosystem as "a relatively self-contained, self-adjusting system of resource-integrating actors connected by shared institutional arrangements and mutual value creation through service exchange"[25]. The service ecosystem focus entails a more comprehensive consideration of the structural details that include the service network actors, technology, institutions, and institutional arrangements that serve to facilitate value cocreation.

Chandler and Vargo introduced the concept of *value-in-context*, which derives from a "set of unique actors with unique reciprocal links between them"[26]. *Context* refers to the dynamics of the service ecosystem and its key players (actors). Service ecosystems emerge through continuous and simultaneous processes where context is the essential value cocreation dimension. Value-in-context emanates through collaborative relationships among actors, providers, users, and others, in dyad, triad, and complex networks. Each instance, consisting of a set of actors with reciprocal relationships within a service ecosystem, constitutes a specific context that affects how value is cocreated. Each actor brings its own unique characteristics, resources, and situational differences to the relationships within the ecosystem, which embodies the context. It encompasses the quantity and quality of business resources, the rules that govern interactions, the size and sophistication of service demand, and the availability, capabilities, relationships, and characteristics of key stakeholders. Actors within the service ecosystem need to understand how context affects value cocreation.

As we mentioned previously, the value-in-exchange and value-in-use concepts can extend beyond their GDL roots to play roles in the SDL domain as contributors to value-in-context. For example, service provider–customer dyads often exist between two actors in a complex network of multiple actors. Value propositions proposed by the service provider might include specific mentions of product-service attributes such as features, pricing, performance, and quality, which have direct value-in-exchange implications for the customer and potential indirect influences on other actors in the service ecosystem as they might have to react to requirements that are more stringent in terms of quality. For value-in-use implications, knowledge of the customers' brand preferences, experience with similar products, online product reviews, search history, purchase intentions, financial situation, and user experience expectations can directly affect the service provider's and customer's behavior and indirectly influence other actors in the service ecosystem. In both instances, information shared from the service provider–customer dyad within a complex network can affect value cocreation by directly or indirectly influencing the behavior of other actors, which in turn affects value-in-context.

For our purposes in focusing on the service science, and hence SDL, foundations of cloud computing, we primarily consider the business-to-business (B2B) and business-to-consumer (B2C) orientations of SDL to consider a broadened actor-to-actor (A2A) focus. A2A considerations also apply to consumer-to-consumer (C2C) and business-to-business-to-consumer (B2B2C) relationships, which also characterize segments of the cloud domain. An A2A orientation enables the consideration of the resource integration,

[25]S. Vargo and R. Lusch, "Institutions and Axioms: An Extension and Update of Service Dominant Logic," *Journal of the Academy of Marketing Science, 44*, 5–23, 2016.
[26]J. Chandler and S. Vargo, "Contextualization and Value-in Context: How Context Frames Exchange," *Marketing Theory, 11* (1), 35–49, 2011.

service-for-service exchange and value cocreation roles of a set of actors within the service ecosystem (see Figure 2-1). The purpose of service exchange is to provide access to complementary resources that can provide benefits (value) for actors within their own individual context. The service ecosystem provides a platform for bilateral or multilateral actor engagement that ultimately joins networks together when individual actors connect with each other[27]. Cloud-based platforms can function as multisided intermediaries for communications and other connections that enable actors to engage other actors in resource integration for value cocreation. Actors include service providers; customers, consumers, or users; suppliers; partners and allies; and all enterprises from individual humans to large organizations involved in service-for-service exchange in a specific service ecosystem. Actors could also include machines, smart technologies, and machine-to-machine and technology-to-technology interactions. Sensor-based smart systems, the Internet of things (IoT), robotics, AI, cloud-based big data analytics, cognitive computing, and autonomous vehicles are examples of technology-based actors that can have important service-development and value cocreation roles in A2A service ecosystems.

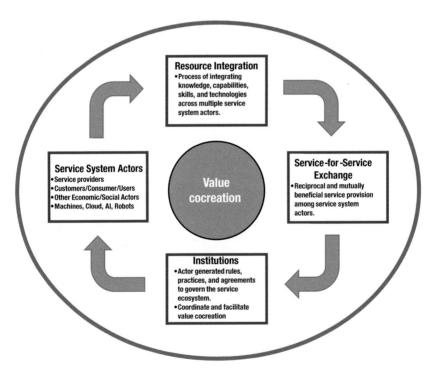

Figure 2-1. Core SDL processes within the service ecosystem. Adapted from Vargo and Lusch[28].

[27]K. Storbacka, R. Brodie, T. Bohmann, P. Maglio, and S. Nenonen, "Actor Engagement as a Microfoundation for value cocreation," *Journal of Business Research, 69,* 3008–3017, 2016.

The A2A orientation has several implications. First, it recognizes that value creation occurs in networks because other actors collaborate to provide and integrate resources for service-to-service exchange. Second, each service exchange changes the network in some manner, which suggests a systems orientation is necessary to understand the working of the service ecosystem. Third, instruments for coordination of actors to facilitate resource integration and service exchange are necessary[28]. In SDL, these instruments, or institutions, are often referred to as "rules of the game" that are typically normative and procedural in nature.

Although institutional rules could be formal laws, norms, regulations, statutes, conventions, doctrinal principles, and constitutions, they also include informal agreements, rules of conduct, accepted practices, protocols, and culturally defined expectations that actors share. Their role is to facilitate communication, judgment, and trust with the service ecosystem. Established institutions can enable a value-creation network effect that results from greater coordination of efforts by all actors. It follows that actor-generated institutions can form interdependent associations with each other. These institutional arrangements, or sets of interrelated institutions, extend the coordination and facilitation of value cocreation within service ecosystems comprised of a network of networks.

Foundational Premises

There are 11 foundational premises (FPs) that underpin SDL as expressed by Vargo and Lusch[29]. FPs are concepts, propositions, and theories that are essential for the development of a field or discipline. They define the discipline and inform the development of a conceptual framework for service-dominant thinking that can drive research and industry practice. This set of principles will very likely continue to evolve as the service discipline innovates and reflects shifts in service thinking. The 11 FPs are as follows:

- *FP1:* Service is the fundamental basis of exchange (Axiom 1).

- *FP2:* Indirect exchange masks the fundamental basis of exchange.

- *FP3:* Goods are distribution mechanisms for service provision.

- *FP4:* Operant resources are the fundamental source of strategic benefit.

- *FP5:* All economies are service economies.

- *FP6:* Value is cocreated by multiple actors, always including the beneficiary (Axiom 2).

- *FP7:* Actors cannot deliver value but can participate in the creation and offering of value propositions.

---

[28]S. Vargo and R. Lusch, "Institutions and Axioms: An Extension and Update of Service Dominant Logic," *Journal of the Academy of Marketing Science, 44,* 5–23, 2016.
[29]Vargo and Lusch, *Ibid.,* 2016.

- *FP8:* A service-centered view is inherently beneficiary oriented and relational.

- *FP9:* All social and economic actors are resource integrators (Axiom 3).

- *FP10:* Value is always uniquely and phenomenologically determined by the beneficiary (Axiom 4).

- *FP11:* Value cocreation is coordinated through actor-generated institutions and institutional arrangements (Axiom 5).

Five FPs have been elevated to axiom status by virtue of their summative interrelationships with the other premises and their bedrock importance to SDL. Axioms are widely accepted statements based on intrinsic merit or established principles. For emphasis, we repeat the five axioms of SDL here:

- *Axiom 1:* Service is the fundamental basis of exchange (FP1). Service is a process for the application of operant resources (knowledge, skills, and technology) for the mutual benefit of actors engaged in value creation. The exchange of service for service by ecosystem actors is essential for value cocreation.

- *Axiom 2:* Value is cocreated by multiple actors, always including the beneficiary (FP6). Value is always cocreated. Value cocreation results from the actions of multiple actors that contribute to each other's well-being.

- *Axiom 3:* All social and economic actors are resource integrators (FP9). Social and economic actors within a service ecosystem are resource integrators in service-for-service exchange networks and networks of networks.

- *Axiom 4:* Value is always uniquely and phenomenologically determined by the beneficiary (FP10). All value is perceived by the beneficiary of that value. Value propositions (value intended) might differ from value perceived. Service exchange initiates if, and only if, beneficiaries accept the value proposition.

- *Axiom 5:* Value cocreation is coordinated through actor-generated institutions and institutional arrangements (FP11). Institutions are actor-generated rules, norms, and practices that are aids to collaboration. Institutional arrangements are interdependent associations between institutions. Together they form the basis for governance of the service ecosystem and facilitate actor collaboration for value cocreation.

The axioms focus on four core constructs that define SDL: service exchange, value creation, resource integration, and actor roles and institutions within the service ecosystem. Table 2-1 depicts the focus of the axioms across the SDL construct spectrum. Beyond their primary focus as stated earlier, each axiom affects the entire service construct spectrum. Axiom 1 highlights service as the basis for exchange and encompasses the processes, actors, and systems necessary for value cocreation. Axiom 2 indicates value is cocreated by multiple actors, which are both beneficiaries and resource integrators within the service ecosystem. Axiom 3 states that all actors within the service ecosystem are resource integrators. Axiom 4 states that value is always determined by the beneficiary. Perceived value enables service exchange and connects to resource integration and collaboration by actors within the service ecosystem. Axiom 5 emphasizes the importance of actor-generated institutions and institutional arrangements that ensure collaboration between actors and provide for governance of the service ecosystem.

Table 2-1. SDL Axioms by Service Construct

Axiom	Service Exchange	Value Creation	Resource Integration	Actors/ Ecosystems
Axiom 1	**Service is the fundamental basis of exchange**	Service exchange is a key element in the value cocreation process	Service exchange is a function of resource integration	Collaborating actors in service ecosystems engage in service exchange
Axiom 2	The beneficiary role is critical for the service exchange process	**Value is cocreated by multiple actors, always including the beneficiary**	Actors are resource integrators	Service ecosystem actors are both beneficiaries and resource integrators
Axiom 3	Resource integration is critical for service exchange	Resource integration enables value cocreation	**All social and economic actors are resource integrators**	Actors integrate resources within the service ecosystem
Axiom 4	Service exchange depends on the value perceived by the beneficiary	**Value is always uniquely and phenomenologically determined by the beneficiary**	Implies actors' dual roles of beneficiary and resource integrator	Beneficiary is a key role for all actors in the service ecosystem
Axiom 5	Institutions set the rules for service exchange	Value cocreation is coordinated by actor institutions	Institutions facilitate resource integration	**Value cocreation is coordinated through actor-generated institutions and institutional arrangements**

From GDL to SDL

SDL is a revolutionary concept that transcends the output-based orientation of GDL to recognize that service is a process of applying resources for the benefit of other actors. SDL is foundational for understanding the value creation process. As firms shift from analog to digital technologies, the opportunity for disruptive service innovation is apparent. SDL encompasses this shift from manufacturing-dominant to service-provider business models where operant resources, especially ICT innovations, are driving the rapid growth of high-value service applications. Table 2-2 depicts the generic characteristics of firms as they transition from GDL to SDL, categorized by the four service constructs: service exchange, value, resource integration, and actors and service ecosystems. The 14 characteristics for each instance of the migration from GDL to SDL are not mutually exclusive, as there is necessary overlap conceptually.

Table 2-2. *Characteristics of Firms from GDL to SDL (adapted from Vargo, Lusch, and Mele[30])*

Service Construct	#	Goods-Dominant Logic Concepts	Transitional Concepts	Service-Dominant Logic Concepts
Service Exchange	1	Goods	Services	Service
	2	Products	Offerings	Experiences
	3	Features/attributes	Benefits	Solutions
	4	Transactions	Touchpoints	Relationships
Value Creation	5	Value-added	Coproduction of value	Cocreation of value
	6	Embedded value/utility	Value delivery	Value proposition
	7	Value-in-exchange	Value-in-use	Value-in-context
	8	Economies of scale: products	Economies of scale: products and services	Economies of scope
	9	Business value	Customer value	Ecosystem/societal value

(continued)

---

[30]This section draws from S. Vargo, R. Lusch, and C. Mele, "Service for Service Exchange and Value cocreation: The Service-Dominant Logic Perspective." In R. Fisk, R. Russell-Bennet, and L. Harris (Eds.), *Serving Customers: Global Services Marketing Perspectives* (Prahran, Australia: Tilde University Press, 2013), 208–228.

Table 2-2. (*continued*)

Service Construct	#	Goods-Dominant Logic Concepts	Transitional Concepts	Service-Dominant Logic Concepts
Resource Integration	10	Operand resources	Operand/operant resources	Operant resources
	11	Producing	Resource acquisition	Resourcing
Actors/ Ecosystems	12	Value delivery sequence	Supply chain, electronic data interchange (EDI), customer relationship management (CRM)	Actor-to-actor value network
	13	Equilibrium systems	Dynamic systems	Complex adaptive systems
	14	Internal IT systems, Client/server	Datacenters, service-oriented architecture (SOA), SaaS	Cloud, smart systems, multisided platforms

Table 2-2 serves as a summary of the differences between GDL and SDL characteristics and the conceptual steps from one orientation to another. The migration from GDL to SDL involves the following changes in perspective:

- The shift of focus from manufacturing products and services as units of output to service as a system for cocreating value.

- The creation of actors' experiences rather than units of output.

- A firm's offerings are contributions to solutions rather than product features and attributes.

- A shift from arm's-length transactions to relationships.

- The migration from value-added to cocreation of value.

- Service firms do not deliver value, they offer value propositions.

- Value cocreation is context specific.

- Service enterprises enjoy economies of scope; anything that can be digitized can be customized.

- Service enterprises exist in a service ecosystem that is affected by society and the natural environment.

- The creation and application operant resources that are dynamic and reusable (knowledge, skills, and technology) contrasts with consumption of static operand resources.

- Resourcing refers to the conversion of resources into benefits as opposed to producing specific products or services.

- Actor-to-actor value networks are based on a system of reciprocal service provisioning among actors.

- Service ecosystems are complex adaptive systems that are dynamic networks of interactions that can self-organize according to a change-initiating microevent or collection of events.

- Cloud computing, multisided platforms, and smart systems are emblematic of the ICT technologies that are driving service innovation and hastening the adoption of SDL principles.

Cloud industry professionals and other ICT practitioners who are considering or currently pursuing the adoption of service-oriented business models should become conversant with the fundamentals of SDL and its axioms. The axioms define a service-oriented domain and inform a service-dominant mindset enabling the exchange of ideas that can reduce the cognitive gap that often exists between theory-based research and operations-based practice. Each axiom and premise contributes to a better understanding of the service ecosystem its participants, formative principles, value cocreation processes, and strategic benefits. Each is essential for SDL-based business strategy. As enterprises move beyond their legacy product-market orientations to embrace an active role in creating new markets and redefining old markets, they will create service ecosystems where innovative value propositions result from the novel integration of resources with collaborative actors for the purpose of cocreating outstanding value.

Product-Service Systems

In highly competitive markets, companies have recognized the need for the dynamic alignment of production with complex, continually changing customer requirements and market conditions. The ongoing transition from the primary emphasis on goods has led to the development of a synergistic system of products and services combined into comprehensive value propositions. Researchers in product development, product management, design, engineering, services marketing, and management disciplines refer to such solutions as product-service systems (PSS). PSS business models are associated with service innovation[31].

---

[31]F. Beuren, M. Ferreira, and P. Miguel, "Product-Service Systems: A Literature Review on Integrated Products and Services," *Journal of Cleaner Production, 47,* 222–231, 2013.

The PSS concept originated in northern Europe, primarily Scandinavia and the Netherlands, in the late 1990s as international competition increasingly threatened the manufacturing base of those nations[32]. The general idea underlying PSS is companies create products and can customize them with services. As markets become more competitive, product manufacturers adopt differentiation strategies to become more customer-oriented and innovative by adding more services to the product mix. Some researchers have found that companies with a higher reliance on services can improve the value of their firm[33]. Accordingly, as manufacturers are intensifying efforts toward innovation and customer engagement, they are also redirecting their focus from products to services. Instead of services being viewed as add-ons, value-added, residual intangible forms of products, or otherwise supporting product sales, they are assuming a shared role at the core of the value proposition[34].

From a product management point of view, PSS refers to product-service combinations where the service component is positioned as an extension of the product or as a new service component that is marketed as a product[35]. However, a problem arises when a company can identify the need for PSS solutions, especially a more service-intensive solution, but the implementation of the design, production, and marketing executes from a product perspective. In other words, value embeds in the product and its associated services delivered as units of output to customers. The process is dyadic (firm-to-customer) in nature and typically (at first view) does not embrace the dynamic SDL multiple-actor service ecosystem value cocreation concept.

From an SDL perspective, PSS solutions are milestones in the journey from GDL to SDL business models. PSS are product-oriented business models with a heavier emphasis on the integration of services into the value proposition. We include the discussion of PSS here in recognition that although the disciplines have evolved on parallel conceptual paths, SDL and PSS commonalities are compelling and a case can be made for their convergence within an SDL framework.

Definitions

In the general case, a PSS is a product and a service (or products and services) combined in a system to deliver superior value that is not available from either individually. The goal of the PSS is to increase competitive advantage by offering superior value through adding services to the value proposition. Services serve to help differentiate product-service solutions and to improve market positions.

---

[32]Beuren, Ferreira, and Miguel, *Ibid.*, 2013.
[33]E. Fang, R. Palmatier, and J.-B. Steenkamp, "Effect of Service Transition Strategies on Firm Value," *Journal of Marketing, 72,* 1–14, September 2008.
[34]H. Gebauer, A. Gustafsson, and L. Witell, "Competitive Advantage Through Service Differentiation by Manufacturing Companies," *Journal of Business Research, 64,* 1270–1280, 2011.
[35]N. Morelli, "Designing Product/Service Systems: A Methodological Exploration," *Design Issues, 18* (3), 3–17, 2002.

Table 2-3 presents commonly accepted definitions for PSS that appear to be stable from the inception of the PSS to present. Summarizing the key points, we have the following general characteristics of PSS:

- *Strategy:* PSS is an innovation strategy that shifts the business focus from physical products only to a system of products and services to improve competitiveness.

- *Products and services:* PSS is an integrated system of tangible products and intangible services. The product service ratio is variable and can be set in terms of function fulfillment or economic value.

- *User needs and value delivery:* PSS are designed to be jointly (products and services) capable of satisfying specific customer needs. PSS deliver value-in-use.

- *System:* PSS is a system of products, services, and supporting networks in infrastructure.

- *Sustainability:* PSS aims to achieve sustainable development goals by employing the dematerialization properties of services.

PSS focused on sustainability since concept inception. However, the most notable addition to framing the PSS domain is the centrality of the value-in-use concept. From a PSS perspective, value-in-use is defined as "all customer-perceived consequences arising from a solution that facilitate or hinder achievement of the customer's goals"[36]. The value-in-use concept specifies that value will emerge as the customer or user experiences the use of the product-service. The user, not the solution provider, determines value. This loosely maps to SDL Axiom 4 but it lacks the service ecosystem multiple actor perspective for cocreating value. Value-in-use is an interim step into the transition from GDL to SDL, as indicated in Table 2-3. The sustainability dimension argues that PSS offerings deliver value-in-use by reducing material consumption through the dematerialization properties of services[37]. The emphasis on the service component reduces the total solution's environmental costs by using less product-based materials. Value emerges at the point where the user (and society) experience it through use of the more environmentally friendly PSS-based solution.

---

[36]E. Macdonald, V. Martinez, and H. Wilson, "Towards the Assessment of the Value-in-Use of Product-Service Systems: A Review," *Performance Management Association Conference*, New Zealand. 2009.

[37]See R. Tercek, R. *Vaporized: Solid Strategies for Success in a Dematerialized World* (LifeTree Media, 2015).

Table 2-3. Product-Service Systems Definitions

Authors	Product-Service Systems Definitions
Goedkoop et al. 1999[38]	"A marketable set of products and services capable of jointly fulfilling a user's need. The product/service ratio in this set can vary, either in terms of function fulfilment or economic value."
Mont 2002[39]	"A system of products, services, supporting networks and infrastructure that is designed to be: competitive, satisfy customer needs and have a lower environmental impact than traditional business models."
Brandsotter et al. 2003[40]	"A PSS consists of tangible products and intangible services, designed and combined so that they are jointly capable of fulfilling specific customer needs. Additionally, PSS tries to reach the goals of sustainable development."
Manzini and Vezzoli 2003[41]	"An innovation strategy, shifting the business focus from designing (and selling) physical products only, to designing (and selling) a system of products and services which are jointly capable of fulfilling specific client demands."
Baines et al. 2007[42]	"A PSS is an integrated product and service system that delivers value in use. A PSS offers the opportunity to decouple economic success from material consumption and hence reduce the impact of economic activity."
Boehm et al. 2013[43]	"A PSS is an integrated bundle of products and services which aims at creating customer utility and generating value."

[38]M. Goedkoop, C. van Halen. H. te Riele, and P. Rommens, "Product-Service Systems, Ecological and Economic Basis," *Report for Dutch Ministries of Environment (VROM) and Economic Affairs (EZ)*, 1999.
[39]O. Mont, "Clarifying the Concept of Product-Service System," *Journal of Cleaner Production, 10* (3), 237–245, 2002.
[40]M. Brandstotter, M. Haberl, R. Knoth, B. Kopacek, and P. Kopacek, "IT on Demand – Towards an Environmental Conscious Service System for Vienna," *Third International Symposium on Environmentally Conscious Design and Inverse Manufacturing (EcoDesign'03)*, 799–802, 2003.
[41]E. Manzini and C. Vezolli, "A Strategic Design Approach to Develop Sustainable Product Service Systems: Examples Taken from the 'Environmentally Friendly Innovation' Italian Prize," *Journal of Cleaner Production, 11* (8), 851–857, 2003.
[42]T. S. Baines, H. W. Lightfoot, S. Evans, A. Neely, R. Greenough, J. Peppard, R. Roy, E. Shehab, A. Braganza, A. Tiwari, J. R. Alcock, J. P. Angus, M. Bastl, A. Cousens, P. Irving, M. Johnson, J. Kingston, H. Lockett, V. Martinez, P. Michele, D. Tranfield, I. M. Walton, and H. Wilson, "State-of-the-Art in Product-Service Systems," *Proceedings of the Institution of Mechanical Engineers, Part B. Journal of Engineering Manufacture, 221* (10), 1543–1552, 2007.
[43]M. Boehm and O. Thomas, "Looking Beyond the Rim of One's Teacup: A Multidisciplinary Literature Review of Product-Service Systems, Business Management, and Engineering Design," *Journal of Cleaner Production, 51*, 245–260, 2013.

PSS can be viewed as a special instance of *servitization* or *service infusion,* where manufacturers offer a fuller bundle of customer-focused combinations of products, services, and knowledge with the goal of adding value to the core product offering[44]. At its service-oriented limit, PSS is a sale of use instead of a sale of product. When the service component of PSS is transcendent, customers pay for using the asset, rather than its outright purchase. In the case where the product actually provisions the service, the benefits of PSS can multiply. Cloud services, mobile communications, and social media services are examples of this type of solution. Benefits from the user perspective include reduced up-front and operating costs, increased scope and scalability, shift of ownership responsibilities to the provider, increased asset efficiency, reduced environmental impacts, fewer risks, and improved competitiveness. The service provider retains direct access to the asset that enables collection of data on performance and use. This data enables product and service improvements, control over maintenance schedules, improved performance, improved asset utilization, and lower environment costs[45].

Hybrid Offerings

Hybrid offerings are a form of PSS that combine industrial goods and services in business markets. Conceptually, hybrid offerings can provide a strategic roadmap for transitioning from GDL solutions, where services support the product, to SDL-like solutions that support the customer's business processes or perform them on behalf of the customer. This aligns with the SDL notion of the shift in value creation from products to services and from the firm to the customer. It is helpful to envision a product-service continuum with the product-dominant endpoint (with add-on services) and the service-dominant endpoint as hybrid services (services provisioned by products). At some point along the continuum, as firms increase the service component, services revenues, and profits will reach sufficient intensity to support a more service-dominant, customer-centric PSS business model.

Hybrid solutions provide a pathway for firms to move toward high-value services. Three questions have motivated research on hybrid solutions[46]:

1. What *distinctive capabilities* (operant resources) do product firms need to have or acquire to develop and implement a hybrid solution-based business model?

2. What *existing resources can companies shape and integrate* with distinctive capabilities to develop and deploy hybrid solutions?

3. How can these service-oriented *capabilities and resources* be combined and leveraged strategically into innovative hybrid solutions that can achieve positional advantage in existing markets and create new markets?

---

[44]S. Vandermerweand J. Rada, "Servitization of Business: Adding Value by Adding Services," *European Management Journal*, *6* (4), 314–324, 1988.

[45]Baines et al., 2007.

[46]W. Ulaga and W. Reinartz, "Hybrid Offerings: How Manufacturing Firms Combine Goods and Services Successfully," *Journal of Marketing, 75,* 5–23, 2011.

Distinctive capabilities are operant resources that refer to a firm's leadership, skills, knowledge base, organizational processes, and technologies that enable the firm to effectively shape and integrate with other resources to deploy innovative solutions. They are not ordinary day-to-day proficiencies; they are dynamic in nature. Firms with strong dynamic capabilities have the ability to learn and adjust by modifying their resources to execute strategic transformations that are necessary for business success[47]. A capability is dynamic if it enables the development of innovative solutions to address opportunities in rapidly changing markets[48].

Goods-dominant firms will need to acquire service-oriented distinctive capabilities (or adapt existing capabilities for service applications) for the development of hybrid offerings. These capabilities include service-oriented leadership, cloud-based ICT capabilities, service-related data processing and customer analytics, design-to-service capability, service marketing and sales capabilities, and product-service platform development and deployment capabilities. These distinctive capabilities will shape and integrate with the firm's existing product-based resources to form the foundation for hybrid solutions development. Existing product-based resources typically include installed-base customer databases, product-focused organizational processes, product development and manufacturing assets, product platforms, brand assets, product sales force and distribution networks, supply chains, and industry partnerships and alliances. Most of these operand resources will need to be adapted to support hybrid solutions.

Product-oriented firms transitioning to hybrid offerings will need to add human resources with strong SDL-based backgrounds and train existing employees to drive the development of service strategy, development, operations, and organizational culture. From a risk management perspective, firms might need to consider creating a new hybrid solutions organization or skunk works to enable and support the new service focus in a product-oriented company.

---

[47]D. J. Teece, *Dynamic Capabilities and Strategic Management: Organizing for Innovation and Growth* (Oxford, UK: Oxford University Press, 2011).

[48]S. Madhavaram and S. D. Hunt, "The Service-Dominant Logic and a Hierarchy of Operant Resources: Developing Masterful Operant Resources and Implication for Marketing Strategy," *Journal of the Academy of Marketing Science, 36,* 67–82, 2008.

Service Orientation and PSS

To provide clarity for the PSS concept, it is useful to classify PSS forms into a typology of three categories according to the degree of service orientation of each. The typology distinguishes among the three forms of PSS with respect to who owns the product, the provider or the customer, the provider's role in value creation, and the importance of service to the PSS solution. Researchers identify three forms of PSS[49]:

1. *Product-oriented PSS:* Traditional product firms primarily focus on manufactured goods, including add-on services that can be bundled with the product, sold separately, or made optional. These companies offer services at the time of sale or after sale in the form of warranties and service contracts for training, maintenance, and repair. The seller typically specifies the terms of the service that might include conditions for the repurchase, reuse, or recycling of the customer-owned product. This form of PSS relies on the execution of transactions and value-in-exchange-based GDL thinking. The service component is relatively minimal and residual in nature. Embedded value and product ownership transfers to the customer. The goal is to increase transaction value and minimize costs by ensuring the customer has well-maintained, reliable, efficient, long-lasting products over the product's life cycle.

2. *Use-oriented PSS:* Customers are more interested in the service the product provides rather than its ownership. Customers purchase the use of physical products that they do not own, and the provider retains ownership. However, the customer has a greater role in interacting with the provider during a specified use period. The customer experiences the value-in-use offered by the service provisioned by the product. Numerous users share individual products. Examples include leasing, renting, or sharing of physical products such as auto and equipment leasing and rental, Uber ride sharing, Airbnb home rental service, and so on. The PSS provider's goal is to maximize use of the product and extend the life of the product and materials used to produce it. Use-oriented PSS are primarily GDL in nature but share some SDL qualities in terms of a focus on the user experience.

---

[49]Baines et al., 2007.

3. *Result-oriented PSS:* The provider and user agree on a specific result or a capability without predetermining a product-service configuration. Result-oriented PSS provide value-in-use services that include activity management, outsourcing, and pay-per-service options. Activity management and outsourcing involve assuming a client's function or process such as manufacturing, maintenance, accounting, finance, marketing, logistics, and IT services. The service provider owns the resources that constitute the service and the client pays for agreed-on customized results. The pay-per-service unit category typically has a physical product or system at its core. However, the user only buys the output of the product according to the level or time of use. Examples include data services, cloud computing services, storage services, and printing services. Users change their purchasing behavior from buying physical products or infrastructure to purchasing the use of a product or system when it is required. This form of PSS has dramatic financial implications for both providers and customers in terms of the timing of revenue recognition and costs (up-front investment vs. pay as you go). Result-oriented PSS typically involve significant engagement between providers and users. The service experience is most apparent to the user, although significant product resources such as datacenters, software, and network infrastructure are required to enable the services. This category is value-in-use based and the most service-oriented PSS.

Figure 2-2 depicts the evolution of the PSS concept in terms of its transition from the product-oriented PSS to the result-oriented PSS. The PSS evolution transitions from product-dominant to service-dominant business models. Both use-oriented and result-oriented PSS rely on value-in-use as a core concept. This is a concept shared by SDL. However, are PSS business models based solidly on service science/SDL principles? At this point, that is not the case. The A2A service ecosystem that is the foundation for value cocreation within service systems is the bedrock concept for SDL. Although some PSS literature alludes to SDL, it has not been foundational to the development of the PSS domain. It is interesting that the parallel universes of PSS and SDL might be converging. SDL has evolved into a paradigm characterized by complex service systems, actor engagement, collaborative institutions and institutional arrangements, and a cross-disciplinary approach to theory development. It is the theory behind the practice. PSS, on the other hand, has a practical goal to add value to products by including the service component with the intent to differentiate manufacturers' solutions and improve the market positions for product-based solutions. The derivative goal is to use the dematerialization characteristic of services to lessen the environmental impacts of product-based solutions.

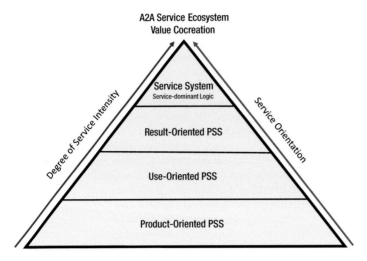

Figure 2-2. *Service orientation and product-service systems*

To be within the service science/SDL domain, PSS will need to incorporate service innovation thinking into its conceptual framework and business practices. At present, PSS is more of a subset of service science/SDL where manufacturers are in the service transition process as they move to embrace service innovation concepts more fully. Service transformation might be the end state, but PSS is not as rich in theory. Looking forward, we believe that PSS will eventually integrate into the SDL domain. Some retrofitting of SDL concepts will be necessary, but PSS and SDL are playing in the same conceptual ballpark.

Benefits of PSS

The PSS approach offers a wide range of benefits. PSS is important from both micro- and macroeconomic perspectives. Strategically, PSS benefits product firms because manufacturing directly strengthens the science and engineering research base, drives exports, and enables the service-based economy. Firms can move up the value chain and deliver knowledge-based PSS solutions, which drives overall economic growth[50]. PSS-based competitive strategy uses technical knowledge of products and services, process, and customer expectations to enhance value by lowering costs and increasing benefits. Companies can also move beyond transactions to customer relationships. Relationships are much more difficult to copy. This is the very reason the northern European countries have developed the PSS approach.

---

[50]H. Lightfoot, T. Baines, and P. Smart, "The Servitization of Manufacturing: A Systematic Literature Review of Interdependent Trends," *International Journal of Operations & Production Management, 33*, 1408–1434, November 2013.

PSS can provide benefits to the consumer, provider, environment, and society. For the manufacturer it means a more easily differentiated offering of higher value. For the customer it is a release from the responsibilities of asset ownership, and to society a more sustainable approach to business[51]. PSS provides customers with superior value through customization and higher quality. The service component is flexible and can deliver new functionality to meet consumer needs. Service shifts monitoring and administrative tasks away from the customer and to the provider. Due to flexibility, the customer receives value that aligns better with current needs. PSS does provide a foundation for service innovation by emphasizing the role of the product in service provision. PSS increases total value to the customer through increased service and encourages experimentation through quick introduction of new service options. PSS enhances competitive advantage because services are hard to copy and serve to engage the customer to provide feedback about the product-service package. PSS enables the continuous improvement of the business, innovation, quality, and customer satisfaction. For sustainability, PSS enables providers to minimize material requirements and enables take-back, recycling, refurbishment, and reuse to minimize environmental impacts.

Barriers to PSS Adoption

The primary barriers to PSS adoption emanate from both manufacturing firms and their customers. The cultural shift required for product-oriented companies to become service- oriented businesses is perhaps the most significant barrier to adoption of PSS. PSS adoption affects revenues, costs, markets, customers, competitors, employees, and other stakeholders and requires rethinking the approach to risk management. Companies must carefully plan for PSS adoption because they will likely sell less products and more services. First, services affect how companies generate profits. Value-in-use services often rely on pay-as-you-go or time-based subscription pricing models. This can produce significant shifts in revenues and expenses during the service transition period. Second, the product mindset in manufacturing firms might not easily translate into strategies for designing, producing, and marketing successful new services. This can create cultural tension as organizations and processes are reengineered, new service-skilled employees hired, and existing employees redeployed, retrained, or replaced.

Cloud-based software companies are more likely to transition to PSS models as a competitive necessity as new pure service entrants to the market can leverage the value creation of the cloud and might not have legacy products to protect. A cultural change might be necessary for customers as well. In some markets, customers are used to purchasing products and might be reluctant to accept a pay-for-use or subscription-only service approach. This might be less of problem for younger consumers who have readily adopted digital-platform sharing-economy services. However, cultural effects are situational and market segment specific. A customer who regularly uses Uber's car-sharing service during the work week in the city might also own a luxury car for weekend travels. Market research and customer analytics are requirements for sorting this out.

[51]F. Beuren, M. Ferreira, and P. Miguel, "Product-Service Systems: A Literature Review on Integrated Products and Services," *Journal of Cleaner Production, 47,* 222–231, 2013.

Service-Dominant Logic Thinking

You might not be willing to admit that service thinking is the type of thinking you are *not* doing today. Perhaps you work for a product company and just do not think about service innovation. Alternatively, you work in a successful services firm and want to consider how to become more successful by adopting a service-dominant thinking approach to service innovation. Understanding service science/SDL concepts is essential for advancing your service thinking. First, we should look backward a bit. Product thinking has evolved from its roots in the Industrial Revolution. Firms make things they can sell profitably to customers. That mindset influences strategy, product innovation, market development, consumer behavior, and economic growth, to name a few obvious effects. Until recently, product thinking had exclusive reign over both business and academia. Over the past half-century, primarily due to competitive pressures and other market dynamics, firms started to add services as a value-added component to their product mixes. This marketing tactic generated considerable interest among academics and practitioners as they sought to understand its impact in a product-oriented business world. Until recently, the research and practice focused on services. Now we recognize services as a subset of the larger SDL domain. This section provides a framework for the evolution of service thinking from its services thinking roots.

Services Thinking

The dawn of services thinking more than 50 years ago initiated efforts to define services by identifying differences between products and services. How are they different, what characteristics are unique to services, and are these differences important in defining the role of services in a product-focused economy? To address the questions, marketing scholars began to develop what eventually became *services* marketing, a subset of the marketing discipline.

The acronym IHIP (intangibility, heterogeneity, inseparability, and perishability) refers to the most common characteristics used to define and describe the uniqueness of services.[52] Intangibility refers to the immateriality of services. Goods are material objects; services are deeds or performances. Heterogeneity refers to the inability to standardize services in the same manner as goods. This is due to human involvement in face-to-face service provision that introduces variability into the process. Inseparability denotes that the producer and consumer of the service must interact simultaneously. Finally, perishability refers to the notion that services cannot be stored for later consumption. Because services are intangible, production and consumption are simultaneous. As you might have observed these services' characteristics emanate from the perspective of the product provider, not the customer or user.

---

[52]V. Zeithaml, A. Parasuraman, and L. Berry, "Problems and Strategies in Services Marketing," *Journal of Marketing, 49*, 33–46, Spring 1985.

By identifying services in terms of what they lack when compared to goods (i.e., tangibility, standardization, separability, and the ability to be inventoried), service characteristics imply qualities that could actually require remediation. However, because goods marketers approach both products and services in product terms as units of output, the four characteristics are arguably inadequate and perhaps unimportant for differentiating between products and services. Fundamentally, all economic exchange is about service provision; services provided directly to the consumer or indirectly provisioned by tangible goods. Therefore, all economic exchange is about service provision and tangible products are only valuable for the services they provide. From this broader view, everything is a service[53]. Revisiting the IHIP characteristics from a customer-oriented service perspective, the implied differences between products and services become less apparent:

1. *Intangibility.* Services can have very tangible results in terms of customer experiences and knowledge-based features such as car insurance provisions that affect the customer. Products also have intangible qualities associated with brand image and emotions associated with ownership and use.

2. *Heterogeneity.* Services can be standardized and customized. For cloud-based services, the modularity of the standardized service systems components can enable the configuration of highly customized solutions. Alternatively, products are often differentiated, made more heterogeneous, to appeal to various markets.

3. *Inseparability.* ICT services *are* separable from a customer-oriented perspective. The consumer does not have to interact with a physically present service provider. Cloud service providers are some distance away from the customer's physical location where they access the network. Alternatively, from an SDL perspective, service providers, customers, and other actors are inseparable, engaged in the act of value cocreation within the service ecosystem.

4. *Perishability.* Cloud and other ICT services are storable as various software and infrastructure modules (SaaS, IaaS, PaaS, etc.) reside in datacenters that customers can access on demand. Similarly, video and audio services have large inventories of streaming-ready content. In a larger sense, because SDL views both products and services as service, both tangible and intangible capabilities and resources can be inventoried.

---

[53]S. Vargo and R. Lusch, "The Four Service Marketing Myths: Remnants of a Goods-Based, Manufacturing Model," *Journal of Service Research, 6* (4), 324–335, May 2004.

Service Thinking

It is appropriate to think of SDL thinking, or *service* thinking, as a transformational and transcendent service mindset[54]. This mindset enables a holistic view of the service ecosystem in terms of opportunities, value propositions, value cocreation, dynamic resources and capabilities, customers, suppliers, partnerships, alliances and other engaged actors, service networks, markets, positioning, revenue mechanisms, and strategies for opportunity maximization. In short, service thinking is about developing and executing innovative business plans by mobilizing resources and actors for the cocreation of value that can redefine markets, create new markets, and lead to strategic success. Service thinking depends on developing a service culture within organizations that can drive and support service transformation. Service innovation adopts a view of strategy that requires business organizations to reinvent themselves continuously within dynamic complex service systems.

Service innovators are change agents. ICT innovations such as cloud computing are especially disruptive to existing industries, markets, and customer relationships. The move from face-to-face services to cloud-based customer support, e-commerce, hospitality, transportation, government, search, video and music streaming, social media, business services, and military operations has disrupted the traditional user experience. This affects the customer relationship, satisfaction, and brand choice, among other factors. Successful innovators have advantageously driven or responded to changes in customer and other ecosystem relationships by incorporating service thinking into their business models. Figure 2-3 depicts five key mindsets for service-thinking innovators: service design thinking, service thinking culture, service-ready business architecture, multisided platforms, and service analytics, which are necessary for the development of a service thinking enterprise.

---

[54]Recall that *services* is a goods-dominant logic concept. *Service* refers to the service-dominant logic concept.

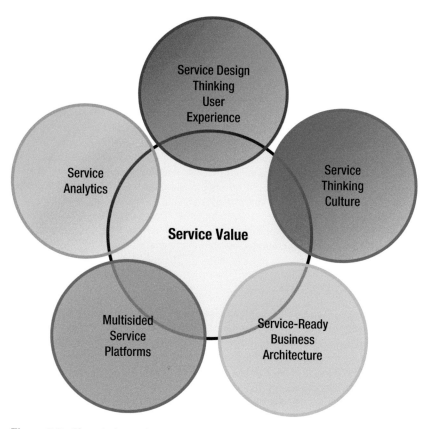

Figure 2-3. *The mindsets of service thinking*

Service-Design Thinking

Design has historically been the goods-dominant domain of objects, things, and commercial products. Transformation to a service-dominant approach began when design community leaders such as Tim Brown of IDEO introduced the notion that the design process is a collaborative effort among diverse participating stakeholders, competencies, and resources, where ideas are envisioned, prototyped, and explored in a hands-on manner. Innovative designs need to be human centered, aspirational, and infused with empathy and optimism[55]. Designers for high-technology firms initially engaged in the design of hardware such as computers, mobile phones, electronic devices, and appliances. Over time, these responsibilities morphed to include designing graphical

---

[55]E. Bjogvinsson, E. Pelle, and P.-A. Hillgren, "Design Things and Design Thinking," *Design/ Issues, 28* (3), 101–116, Summer 2012.

user interface (GUI) software and eventually the user experience itself[56]. Design thinking is a discipline that integrates the sensibilities and methods of the designer with the understanding of the users' expectations, the feasibility of technology, and the strategy for the business to convert market opportunity into customer value.

Design thinking helps multiple actors work collaboratively together as a system to create value. It drives the creation of the user experience. It is only a short conceptual journey to arrive at the design of the service itself and the framework, infrastructure, and processes needed to create the collaborative interfaces for the user and other actors within the service ecosystem. Thinking like a designer helps develop better business strategy. Design thinking is applying the principles of design to strategy development and how people working together can integrate knowledge, technology, and other resources into innovative user experiences that build strong brands and transform markets. Indeed, Elizabeth van Kralingen, Senior Vice President of IBM Global Business Services, argued, "There's no longer any real distinction between business strategy and the design of the user experience. The last best experience that anyone has anywhere, becomes the minimum expectation for the experience they want everywhere"[57].

Service-Thinking Culture

Building a strong organizational culture for service innovation is a key consideration for any enterprise transitioning to service-based business models. Visionary leadership is required to develop a service-ready organization with the right mix of service innovation skills, individuals and team members with a service thinking mindset, service-specific resources, and technologies to ensure service innovation is the priority for the enterprise. Service-relevant processes ensure collaboration among employees, customers, and service network stakeholders. Service innovation champions within product companies are rare but necessary for driving cultural change. Engagement with suppliers and customers to educate them on your strategy and to encourage their service thinking is essential.

For cloud-based enterprises, service innovation is global in scope and high-volume in scale. Increasingly, cloud services are mobile, social, and on-demand. Service thinking leaders need to expand employees' thought horizons accordingly. Situation awareness by individuals, teams, and entire organizations is necessary. Service transformations require cultural change, achieving a service-ready organizational structure, and developing a ubiquitous service mindset.

---

[56]T. Brown and R. Martin, "Design for Action: How to Use Design Thinking to Make Great Things Actually Happen," *Harvard Business Review,* 56–65, September 2015.

[57]A. Vanrenen, "IBM Commits $100M to Globally Expand Unique Consulting Model That Fuses Strategy, Data and Design," IBM News Release, https://www-03.ibm.com/press/us/en/pressrelease/43523.wss, March 27, 2014.

Service-Ready Business Architectures

The experience economy embraces rapidly changing consumer expectations and continuous reconfigurations of cocreated value within dynamic service ecosystems. As a result, service enterprises experience continuing pressure to respond by redesigning or repositioning business functions, assets, and resources such as engineering, production, marketing, finance, human resources, and IT from slow-growing businesses to those with greater potential. For instance, enterprises transforming from client/server-based IT to cloud business models such as SaaS, PaaS, or IaaS can choose among private, public, or hybrid cloud resources. Other options include firm-to-firm collaboration, mergers, or acquisitions of firms that have already transformed themselves into service-dominant enterprises.

Componentized business architectures are an approach for enterprises to react to complexity and rapid change in service systems[58]. The basic question is what components and systems are essential for the enterprise to retain and develop in-house versus what can be outsourced to other actors in the service ecosystem? Outsourcing can free up resources, promote specialization, and benefit from comparative advantage within the service ecosystem. The other consideration is identifying what organizational functions, systems, and procedures need to be in place to develop and deliver the service solution. Service thinking informs resource integration and relationship development among a variety of actors for the purpose of value cocreation. Think in terms of large systems integrators such as Boeing and Airbus. Do they make every part and system for their airplanes? On the other hand, do they manage, coordinate, and integrate internal and external components, capabilities, and requirements from a large number of suppliers and demand-side actors to create their solutions for enabling an experience that will transport their customers' customers anywhere in the world in a day?

Multisided Service Platforms

Multisided platforms (MSPs) have enabled enterprises to shift from linear to networked business models[59]. This shifts value creation from the firm to a network of users, partners, and other actors within a service ecosystem. It is not necessary for platform owners to own the product or service content because the platform enables service providers and users to engage directly, such as merchants and credit card users. MSPs facilitate value creation by enabling direct and indirect interactions between two or more distinct actors, each of which affiliates with the platform. Direct interactions occur when no intermediary is involved in the interaction between actors. Direct interactions might involve commercial transactions, relationships, or communications between various actors. Indirect connections are typically suppliers or other service providers for direct participants.

---

[58]H. Hastings and J. Saperstein, *Service Thinking: The Seven Principles to Discover Innovative Opportunities* (New York, NY: Business Expert Press, 2014).

[59]G. Parker, M. Van Alstyne, and S. Choudary, *Platform Revolution: How Networked Markets Are Transforming the Economy and How to Make Them Work for You* (New York, NY: W. W. Norton, 2016).

Platform affiliation requires a collaborative relationship with other actors for integrating resources for the purpose of value cocreation. A two-sided platform directly connects buyers with third-party sellers. Cloud service MSPs such as those used by Google, Facebook, Netflix, Microsoft, Amazon, and Alibaba are the result of service business models where the platform supports and facilitates an external ecosystem that connects platform managers, service providers, users, customers, payment systems, suppliers, partners, alliances, products, services, and complementary resources, and facilitates feedback between the ecosystems' actors. MSPs are digital platforms for value cocreation, which places them at the core of service thinking. The potential for value creation and rapid growth is much greater than that of a single product or service.

MSPs include search engines, social networks, auctions, cloud-based software, and mobile operating systems that connect two or more distinct types of customers (actors) in a matchmaking relationship[60]. For example, mobile operating systems such as iOS and Android are MSPs that integrate various types of customers that demand services from the platform, including users, handset makers, component manufacturers, network operators, app developers, and advertisers[61]. Platforms engender a network effect where the more users (and other ecosystem actors) that use the platform, the more valuable the platform becomes to each user, and the more attractive the platform becomes for new users. For cloud enterprises the MSP and its associated service innovation ecosystem is SDL in action.

MSPs capture mountains of data from the service ecosystem. Associated analytics provide near real-time insights for shaping, managing, and controlling the ecosystem and its individual actors. The platform manager does not have to control all the resources in its ecosystem, just those whose value creation potential is greatest. Multisided cloud platforms can act as institutions that regulate service ecosystems. The emerging platform economy is rapidly reshaping markets, businesses, and global societies. Cloud service platforms are in position to dominate economic growth.

Service Analytics

Service thinking drives becoming a smarter enterprise: smarter about markets, customers, solutions, processes, systems, operations, and value creation. A smarter enterprise connects people, integrates processes, and makes intelligent use of big data analytics to make better decisions[62]. *Analytics* has replaced the term *business intelligence* (BI) to refer to computerized decision support applications. Analytics involve the extensive use of data, quantitative analysis, and explanatory and predictive models

---

[60]D. Evans and R. Schmalensee, *Matchmakers: The New Economics of Multisided Platforms* (Boston, MA: Harvard Business Review Press, 2016).
[61]M. Campbell-Kelly, D. Garcia-Swartz, R. Lam, and Y. Yang, "Economic and Business Perspectives on Smartphones as Multi-Sided Platforms," *Telecommunications Policy, 39*, 717–734, 2015.
[62]B. Dietrich, E. Plachy, and M. Norton, *Analytics Across the Enterprise: How IBM Realizes Business Value from Big Data Analytics* (Indianapolis, IN: IBM Press, 2014).

to drive decisions and create value. Application areas extend throughout the service ecosystem including marketing, business operations, IT, finance, human resources, supply chain, production, solution development and delivery, and service optimization. Analytics are particularly useful for the optimization of systems and network performance.

When thinking about big data, the five Vs come to mind: volume, variety, velocity, veracity, and value. Internal and external data from traditional sources and increasingly from new sources such as cloud-based services and social applications contribute to the ever-growing tidal wave of data. For service thinkers, value is of primary concern. Big data analytics can extract the hidden value in data to uncover market opportunities and drive growth. Companies that can acquire accurate situation awareness by leveraging a wide variety of high-volume, rapidly growing data types are likely to grow faster than competitors that do not have this capability[63]. We provide an overview here of the three fundamental classes of analytics—descriptive or diagnostic, predictive, and prescriptive—that are useful for service thinking considerations.

Descriptive Analytics

Descriptive analytics is the simplest and most used class of business analytics. It condenses big data to report past and current performance with the goal to determine why things happened. Descriptive analytics offer a visualization format for analyses that uncover patterns in the data that offer insights about underlying causes and trends relevant to changes in business performance[64]. *Social media analytics* is a special type of descriptive analytics. It analyzes data from blogs, social media web sites, and forums to mine community sentiment. Its most common use is to support marketing and customer service activities such as obtaining product feedback and customer satisfaction. Sentiment volume and trends on specific topics typically display visually on a dashboard.

Predictive Analytics

The next level of big data reduction, *predictive analytics* use statistical data mining, modeling and machine-learning techniques to forecast events that might happen in the future. A typical approach is to identify patterns and trends in historical data to make predictions about what is likely to happen. For instance, predictive credit scoring models use past payment history to predict the risk profiles for customer loans. CRM and other data can predict*predictive* customer retention and churn (brand switching), future purchases, and responses to marketing campaigns[65].

---

[63]M. Lock, "Managing Rapid Data Growth: A Trial by Firehose," Research Report, Aberdeen Group, http://aberdeen.com/research/10279/10279-rr-fast-data-growth/content.aspx, March 2015.

[64]F. Provost and T. Fawcett, *Data Science for Business: What You Need to Know About Data Mining and Data-Analytic Thinking* (Sebastapol, CA: O'Reilly Media, 2013).

[65]E. Siegal, *Predictive Analytics: The Power to Predict Who Will Click, Buy, Lie, or Die* (Hoboken, NJ: Wiley, 2013).

Entity analytics focus on resolving multiple references to the same entity across several data sources[66]. The goal is to improve data quality that will increase the accuracy of analytic models. For instance, it is important to determine if three transactions belong to three people or one person. In addition, several records might have incomplete data on one person. Aggregated data from those incomplete records creates a more complete profile of that person. *Context computing* uses an incremental process for context accumulation for relating new data to existing data gain understanding of entity-relevant relationships, such as those that occur in service ecosystems. A more accurate picture of an entity results as more context identifiers accumulate. Achieving a more accurate picture of the entity provides for better model development and better outcomes such as determining which customers are better risks for bank loans, or which suppliers have superior performance.

Prescriptive Analytics

Prescriptive analytics aid decision making by providing recommendations for one or more courses of action associated with likely outcomes on key performance indicators. The goal is to achieve the best possible performance outcomes to solve specific problems or to address specific opportunities. As a type of predictive analytics, it predicts multiple futures based on the actions of the decision maker[67]. Prescriptive analytics uses existing data and data on actions taken to feedback decision outcomes iteratively to guide decision makers to a desired outcome. It can recommend the best course of action for any prespecified outcome. What is missing is execution, so actual outcomes might vary from desired outcomes. Prescriptive analytics have been used in marketing, finance, insurance, mobile communications, e-commerce, and supply chain optimization, among others.

Service Value

At its core, service thinking is about value. From a traditional GDL marketing perspective, value is what firms create and deliver through products and services. Value is expressed in terms of the trade-off between benefits and costs within an exchange transaction. In the traditional provider–customer/user relationship that characterizes many IT organizations, the creation of *business value* and *customer value* are primary concerns. A third type of value, *societal value,* derives from business and customer value concepts broadened to encompass the long-term well-being of the social and environmental ecosystems. Finally, we discuss the asymmetric characteristics of value that cloud-based technologies can amplify within service ecosystems.

---

[66]L. Sokol and J. Jonas, *Using Entity Analytics to Greatly Increase the Accuracy of Your Models Quickly and Easily,* IBM Redguides for Business Leaders, http://www.redbooks.ibm.com/redpapers/pdfs/redp4913.pdf, 2012.

[67]M. Wu, "Big Data Reduction 3: From Descriptive to Prescriptive," *Science of Social Blog,* https://community.lithium.com/t5/Science-of-Social-blog/Big-Data-Reduction-3-From-Descriptive-to-Prescriptive/ba-p/81556, April 10, 2013.

Business Value

Business value is the total value received by the enterprise resulting from sales of its products and services[68]. However, business value is a complex concept not easily defined. Business value is difficult to measure solely in monetary terms, and is it not easily allocated between operating units in large enterprises. At a high level, business value is the aggregation of all forms of value that determine the long-term value of the firm such as economic value added, employee value, supplier value, alliance partner value, managerial value, and societal value. Intangible assets such as intellectual capital and business model value might also be considered. However, such value is difficult to measure and rarely accounted for. Therefore, evidence of business value creation typically includes revenue growth or decreases in costs that can lead to increased profits, return on investment (ROI), and shareholder value. Although this definition of business value implicitly recognizes the necessity for creating customer value, the primary focus of business value is generating returns for the enterprise.

Business value initiatives tend focus on internal, short-term, pricing and cost-based solutions that are easily quantifiable. Common metrics include product cost and operating cost reductions, supply chain efficiency, productivity increases, headcount reductions, asset utilization rates, risk avoidance, and price increases that can overlook the best interests of customers and the enterprise itself[69]. Business value conceptually aligns with GDL. Business value typically relies on customer input, but it is not cocreated. As cloud-based enterprises migrate to service thinking and value cocreation with collaborative actors within a service ecosystem, business value will look beyond the enterprise to align more closely with SDL principles.

Customer Value

Customer value is the "overall benefit derived from the product or service, as perceived by the customer, at the price the customer is willing to pay"[70]. A focus on customer value requirements defined around desired customer experiences enables cloud enterprises to look beyond their organization to engage the customer both individually and collectively as a market. Engagement with the customer and other ecosystem actors for the purpose of value cocreation should be the focus of business activity. The type and degree of engagement is critical. From a GDL view, engagement could mean merely asking user groups about their preferences for new products and services, delivering the output, and later assessing their satisfaction with the experience. This situation would describe coproduction, value-in-exchange, and most software services. Alternatively, from a value-in-use or SDL value-in-context perspective, a cloud-based service relationship would entail the continuous engagement with customers and other ecosystem actors. That actor engagement occurs within a collaborative service ecosystem for integrating their

---

[68]D. Sward, *Measuring the Business Value of Information Technology* (Intel Press, 2006).

[69]R. Harmon, H. Demirkan, and D. Raffo, "Roadmapping the Next Wave of Sustainable IT," *Foresight, 14* (2), 121–138, 2012.

[70]J. Sheth, B. Newman, and B. Gross, *Consumption Values and Market Choice: Theory and Applications* (Cincinnati, OH: Southwestern, 1991).

complementary resources in the process of service exchange. Currently, an SDL approach would likely be a departure for many enterprises from their existing cloud services business models where GDL short-term business value priorities prevail.

Societal Value

Societal value holds that companies should meet their business goals in such a way that enhances the long-term well-being of customers and society. This approach maximizes both customer value and business value. Societal value calls on organizations to include ethical, social responsibility, and environmental considerations into their business practices. Therefore, companies must balance profits, customer requirements, and social responsibility in their business models. Both customer value and societal value are amenable to an SDL conceptualization based on the creation of value-in-use and value-in-context, where higher ratios of service in the solution can minimize societal impact. Societal value is ecosystem based, which raises awareness of the need for aligning the economic and social health of the service ecosystem with the physical health of the natural ecosystem.

Asymmetric Value

Asymmetric value is realized when some actors in an exchange-based relationship achieve differential outcomes that result from one-sided advantages over other actors that can increase their relative benefits and lower costs. In SDL, the potential for asymmetric outcomes is associated with the underlying principle of value-in-context. Each actor's context affects its ability to directly access and leverage resources and indirectly do the same beyond its immediate context. These contextual advantages could be derived from superior information and other resources such as brand power, installed base of users, IT and other infrastructure, processes, solution scope, financial capability, logistics systems, long-standing relationships and partnerships, and the ability to preferentially leverage institutional complexity within a given service ecosystem[71]. Asymmetric value can be situational in nature due to felicitous timing of business decisions, favorable economic conditions, new laws and regulations, social changes, and technology disruption. Asymmetry considers the relationship between proprietary resource inputs relative to performance-based outcomes for each actor. If one considers intangible value dimensions such as strength of brand affiliation, customer satisfaction, and the emotional signature associated with the service experience, the asymmetry of the value could be defined differently for each actor. The primacy of the service provider–customer relationship contributes to value asymmetry.

---

[71]J. Siltaloppi, K. Koskela-Huotari, and S. Vargo, "Institutional Complexity as a Driver for Innovation in Ecosystems," *Service Science, 8* (3), 333–343, September 2016.

Cloud service providers and platform managers, as keystone actors in a cloud service ecosystem, have tremendous relational advantages over other actors due to the quality, scope, and scale of their knowledge, infrastructure, and technology resources. Of particular importance is their ability to leverage multisided cloud platforms that can exchange resources that are practically unlimited in scope, scale, geography, and availability. Cloud service providers pursue value cocreation through service-to-service exchanges that can engage dyads (provider–customer), triads (exchange among dyads), complex networks (exchange among triads), and service ecosystems (exchange among complex networks). Each actor rationalizes its position in the service ecosystem.

Asymmetric Relationships

SDL essentially relies on collaborative business relationships among actors within a service ecosystem for the value cocreation process to succeed. Nevertheless, enterprise managers might conclude that close interfirm relationships do not always provide positive results. The effectiveness of the relationship is affected by the nature of the service exchange partner and the associated business context. From an SDL perspective, actors engage in the exchange process to create value for themselves and other actors whether they assume the roles of suppliers, service providers, customers or other actors. For example, in a B2B context, supplier relationship management (SRM) is an approach for the systematic assessment of suppliers' resources, capabilities, and ability to perform that are essential for a successful business relationship. The goal of SRM is the development of two-way relationships with strategic suppliers that can lead to greater levels of innovation and competitive advantage than one-off transactions. Strategic supplier status can create value for the seller by lowering ordering, acquisition, and operating costs and increasing sales and profits. Such relationships can generate value for both actors that they could not achieve alone.

Relationship value is especially challenging to achieve in international markets due to the potential for asymmetric outcomes. Given the high degree of outsourcing of manufacturing and the migration of ICT services to Asia over the last decade, international interfirm (interactor) relationships have become increasingly important. Accordingly, it is more difficult to create relationship value in an international context. This is due to buy-local initiatives; language, cultural, social, economic, geopolitical, legal, and business practice differences; and in some cases, mercantilist governmental interventions that can affect cross-border relationships. Looking at relationship value from the importer's (customer) perspective provides a practical evaluation of the business relationship. To increase the likelihood of positive relationship value and to reduce asymmetric outcomes, actors should consider knowledge-sharing practices, relationship-specific investments, complementarity of resources and capabilities, and adhering to established norms (institutions and institutional arrangements) that can increase openness, quality, and perceived relational value in cross-border A2A relationships.

Information Asymmetry

Information asymmetry occurs when some participants in an exchange relationship have superior information that is not available to all participants. This creates an imbalanced state where superior information can cause inequitable sharing of resources and superior outcomes for the actor or actors that can exploit their superior knowledge to the detriment of other network participants. Asymmetric information can result in market failure if the disadvantaged actors become aware of the imbalance and choose to exit the exchange network or take other action.

We assume that actors in a service exchange relationship work collaboratively for the benefit of all. This is not always the case. It is up to the service system to police network performance. On a two-sided platform, the primary actors are the service provider and the customer in a direct relationship. Depending on who owns the platform, there might be a third-party platform owner or manager as well. All other actors in the network might have direct relationships with the service provider as suppliers and integrators of resources. Their relationship with the final customer is indirect. On an MSP there could be direct relationships between each actor and indirect relationships between actors on the platform and those that are not (typically component or software suppliers). It is important to understand and monitor the roles, capabilities, resources, past performance, and goals of each actor. Some actors will assume short-term transient roles, whereas others will have well-established and trusted roles in the network. Information asymmetry is less of a problem when each actor in the network has an open and collaborative relationship where all critical information is available to all relevant actors. Continuous monitoring, big data analytics of actor performance, and openly available crowdsourced ratings of actors can reduce information asymmetry. Actors that exploit information asymmetry to the detriment of other network actors, especially on an MSP, can contribute to relationship or network failure.

Cloud computing enables new opportunities for IT service providers in terms of new business models, greater scope, economies of scale, and innovative solutions that are deployed "as-a-service." Cloud users benefit from low up-front capex, up-to-date IT resources, lower operating costs, and increased business flexibility. However, not all potential cloud adopters are rushing to adopt. In particular, small and medium-sized enterprise (SME) IT service providers and service users have been slower to embrace the cloud. A major reason for this is information asymmetry within the overall cloud ecosystem[72]. Large companies have the capability to acquire information to assess the benefits, costs, and risks associated with changing to cloud-service business models. Smaller companies have similar requirements. However, they have been more cautious and less trustful of cloud service provider promises. SMEs need approaches and metrics to compare cloud service quality, reliability, privacy, and security requirements with their current approach to IT services. They need to understand security, privacy, and other legal compliance requirements concerning the adoption of cloud services in specific industries. Cloud service certification systems need to address this information asymmetry[73]. Certification seeks to validate the adherence of cloud services to a set of requirements. Metrics for security assurance and transparency are key requirements for increasing trust for cloud service customers[74]. Continuous monitoring of the cloud

---

[72]A. Sunyaev and S. Schneider, "Cloud Services Certification," *Communications of the ACM, 56* (2), 33–36, February 2013.

[73]P. Stephanow, C. Banse, and J. Sch, "Generating Threat Profiles for Cloud Service Certification Systems," *2016 IEEE 17th International Symposium on High Assurance Systems Engineering (HASE)*, 260–267, January 2016.

[74]R. Trapero, J. Luna, and N. Suri, "Quantifiably Trusting the Cloud: Putting Metrics to Work," *IEEE Security & Privacy, 14* (3), 73–77, 2016.

service provider's performance is key to the assessment of their ability to meet their agreements. Certification is a starting point for creating information transparency for actors in the cloud computing service ecosystem.

T-Shaped Professionals

Cloud computing is rapidly becoming the foundation for enterprise IT infrastructure and a primary driver for service innovation. However, companies are having considerable difficulty finding qualified candidates to plan, develop, and implement cloud solutions. A recent study of 250 business managers and 250 IT managers found 54 percent of the IT managers stating their teams struggled to form a cloud strategy and 52 percent had no formalized cloud strategy at all[75]. Although 75 percent of business managers believe working with IT is critical for implementing new cloud services, 48 percent said they could do it faster in their business units. This opens the door for unsanctioned "shadow IT" cloud solutions, which highlight the IT organization's weaknesses and failures to innovate[76]. Alternatively, shadow IT could assume the role of service innovation incubators developed and implemented by boundary-spanning, strategic-thinking visionaries.

One IT director affirmed the skilled resource problem: "There's incredible opportunity for businesses if they move to the cloud, but with a lack of skilled resources they are not able to realize those benefits as quickly. At best, this affects revenues and profit potential in isolation. At worst, competitiveness and market relevance suffer"[77]. Enterprises have difficulty finding well-rounded cloud engineers. IT organizations look for the skills of experienced systems engineers; knowledge of the full range of the public cloud's native services, tooling, and solution potential; and a DevOps approach to managing configurations, infrastructure, software deployment, and integration. Notice that this list does not include deep knowledge of business strategy, markets, industries, or the ability to work cross-functionally across teams and business units. The transition from product-oriented to service-oriented cloud business models opens new opportunities for the development of novel service solutions, the creation of new markets, and the redefinition of existing markets. Unfortunately, most organizations lack the requisite resources in terms of people skills and cultural DNA to make this transformation. They will need a new type of service-thinking talent known as *T-shaped professionals* to drive the development of service-innovation-oriented organizations and solutions.

---

[75]Softchoice, "The State of Cloud Readiness: Transformation and Strategic Adoption Measured," *Softchoice.com*, http://campaigns.softchoice.com/state-of-cloud-readiness-study/, April, 2016.
[76]D. Linthicum, "CIOs: Shadow IT Is Actually Great for Your Cloud Strategy," *CIO*, http://www.cio.com/article/3099106/cloud-computing/cios-shadow-it-is-actually-great-for-your-cloud-strategy.html, July 22, 2016.
[77]S. White, "Businesses Struggle to Hire Workers with Cloud Skills," *CIO*, http://www.cio.com/article/3093453/cloud-computing/businesses-struggle-to-hire-workers-with-cloud-skills.html, July 8, 2016.

Historical examples of T-shaped professionals from the product era include Thomas Edison, Nikola Tesla, Henry Ford, Thomas Watson, and Steve Jobs. T-shaped professionals have two types of competencies symbolized by the T. For IT (cloud) professionals, the vertical stanchion of the T represents the depth of knowledge in at least one system and discipline with contextual knowledge relevant to a vertical industry and business function (see Figure 2-4). This is an indication of the skills background that can enable them to contribute to the creative process. These skills can be from a number of different fields, such as computer science, engineering, mathematics, physics, business, or social science, for example. The horizontal crossbar is emblematic of the individual's boundary-spanning abilities to lead, collaborate, and apply knowledge across groups, teams, disciplines, cultures, locations, and business situations. Ernst and Chrobot-Mason defined horizontal boundaries as "the walls that separate groups by areas of experience and expertise"[78]. These walls can prove difficult to overcome. In our opinion, these horizontal boundaries constitute significant cultural and operational barriers to cloud adoption and the transformation from product to service-innovation-oriented business models. T-shaped professionals' ability to collaborate, communicate, and work across various disciplines and levels of expertise is critical for team alignment for organizational success.

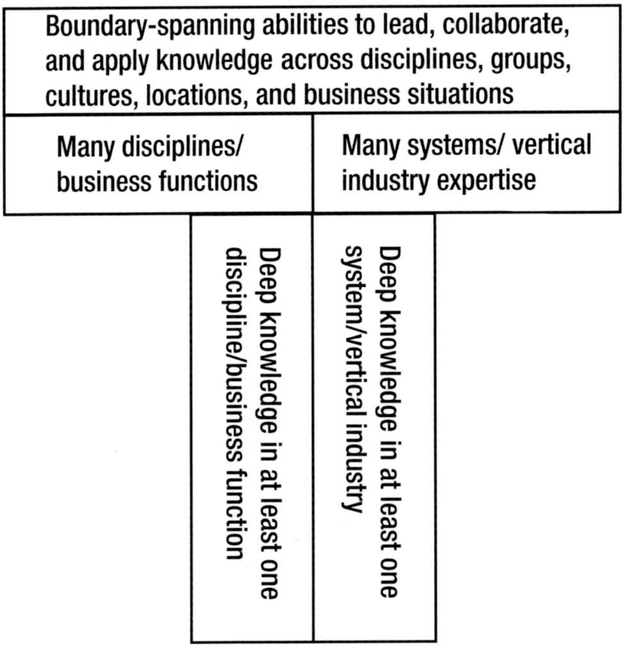

Figure 2-4. *Attributes of the T-shaped professional*

---

[78]C. Ernst and D. Chrobot-Mason, *Boundary Spanning Leadership: Six Practices for Solving Problems, Driving Innovation, and Transforming Organizations* (New York, NY: McGraw-Hill, 2011).

T-shaped professionals exhibit both depth and breadth in their skill sets. As T-shaped individuals gain additional experience and knowledge, they can develop additional vertical skills and horizontal capabilities. The underpinnings of the T-shaped concept relate to design thinking and systems thinking in that such highly skilled T-shaped individuals are able to appreciate how their actions affect an entire system. T-shaped professionals are essential for enabling diverse connections and for breaking down silos in organizations. They are good at empathy, strategic thinking, leveraging technology, operational excellence, and aligning the organization on market opportunities for value creation[79].

For technology firms, it is useful to consider a second type of employee, the *I-shaped professional*. I-shaped professionals are deep specialists in a specific area of expertise and work to improve their skills by going deeper into that area. Firms need both I- and T-shaped professionals. T-shaped professionals are better at identifying and building consensus and executing on exceptional ideas. I-shaped people are better at specific technologies, but are not necessarily collaborative. They might not be willing to contribute their insights or see the market opportunity or the "big picture." Each discipline represents its own point of view and priorities. Tim Brown of IDEO commented that competing points of view could lead to "gray compromises" where the lowest common denominator prevails[80]. One head of R&D for a major technology company complained about the dominance of I-shaped professionals in his organization: "We have a lot of Is. What we need are more Ts"[81].

Some authors, especially in the software development domain, refer to T-shaped professionals with oxymoronic subtlety as *generalizing specialists*[82]. These specialists are also known as T-skilled people, multidisciplinary developers, cross-functional developers, deep generalists, polymaths, and Renaissance developers. A generalizing specialist is a person who:

- Has one or more technical specialties (e.g., cloud computing, smart systems, AI, Java programming, database administration, big data analytics, etc.).

- Has a general knowledge of software development.

---

[79]H. Demirkan and J. Spohrer, "T-Shaped Innovators: Identifying the Right Talent to Support Service Innovation," *Research-Technology Management*, 12–15, September–October, 2015.
[80]M. Hanson, "IDEO CEO Tim Brown: T-Shaped Stars: The Backbone of IDEO's Collaborative Culture," *Chief Executive Magazine*, http://chiefexecutive.net/ideo-ceo-tim-brown-t-shaped-stars-the-backbone-of-ideoae%E2%84%A2s-collaborative-culture/, January 21, 2010.
[81]A. Boynton, "Are you an 'I' or a 'T'? *Forbes*, http://www.forbes.com/sites/andyboynton/2011/10/18/are-you-an-i-or-a-t/#4daec562351b, October 18, 2011.
[82]S. Ambler, "Generalizing Specialists: Improving your IT Career Skills," *Agile Modeling*. www.agilemodeling.com/essays/generalizingspecialists.htm, 2014.

- Has a general knowledge of the business domain in which he or she works.

- Actively seeks to gain new skills in his or her existing specialties and other technical domain areas.

For example, the advantages for building software development teams with generalizing specialists include improved communication and collaboration, less documentation, improved flexibility, less risks, fewer bottlenecks, and faster times to implementation. A good articulation of T-shaped advantages is apparent in a DevOps context.

At the corporate level, Gartner coined the word *versatilist* to describe those (essentially T-shaped) people with a depth of skills and experiences that can be applied across a broad range of situations. They are able to build new alliances, consider multiple perspectives, apply multiple competencies, and assume varied roles for the creation of business value[83]. As organizations transition toward being process and service innovators, versatilists can fulfill multiple roles and assignments in various projects with greater insight than specialists can. Gartner claimed that businesses can stretch their expertise budgets further than is possible with specialists. The experience and competencies of versatilists enable them to integrate knowledge contextually into viable solutions. These IT and business professionals with deep process and industry competencies will help companies incorporate innovation into IT-based processes, products, services, and technologies.

Cloud-based service innovation is not just about IT, although every business unit's budget now includes IT. Enterprises will need T-shaped professionals from all disciplines that can shape their service innovation future. A key success factor is the need is to infuse service thinking throughout the organization. First, the enterprise needs to acquire T-shaped service expertise. This is already beginning to happen. The chief digital officer (CDO) role has arisen over the last five years as companies begin to change their business models to respond to nimbler, more innovative competitors that entered the market with web and cloud-based service solutions. The CDO is primarily responsible for driving an organization's transformation from traditional to digital innovation business models[84]. The job description includes creating the digital vision for cloud services, social media, mobile computing, big data analytics, and e-marketing, among other disciplines. Most CDOs have backgrounds in technology, marketing, or both. These C-suite members are a bridge between IT, data, marketing, and business operations. From fewer than 100 in 2011, more than 2,000 CDOs were in place globally by the end of 2015[85]. Many global

---

[83]D. Morello, "The IT Professional Outlook: Where Will We Go From Here?" *Gartner Report*, https://www.ee.iitb.ac.in/~hpc/.old_studs/hrishi_page/outlook/report.pdf, September 14, 2005.

[84]F. Desai, "Transformation and Innovation Agendas Point to Need for Chief Digital Officers," *Forbes*, http://www.forbes.com/sites/falgunidesai/2016/01/14/the-need-for-more-chief-digital-officers/#258d83392e07, January 1, 2016.

[85]T. Bourgeois, "One-in-Three Chief Digital Officers Bring General Management Skills to Job," *Chief Digital Officer*, https://www.chiefdigitalofficer.net/one-in-three-cdos-bring-general-management-skills-to-job/, December 23, 2015.

brands including GE, Cisco, IBM, Michelin, Under Armour, Nike, Samsung, Starbucks, and Louis Vuitton have created CDO positions.

Closer yet to the core element of service innovation is the chief experience officer (CXO), also called the chief customer experience officer. Customer, or user experience (UX), involves customers' perceptions of their relationship with a brand. It is concerned with value expectations and value realization over the entire life cycle of the service relationship. The CXO is responsible for developing the overarching experience design for the company and making it the essential element of business culture, strategy, and execution. In the last decade, the C-level CXO position has become prominent due to the need for a consistent customer experience across all of the customers' service engagement touchpoints, internally and externally. More companies are recognizing that the customers' experience needs to be at the center of business strategy. For many companies, the customer experience implementation uses two major channels: online customer service and personal interactions for sales and customer service at physical locations or by phone. Social media comments, reviews, and other sentiment indicators are also part of the experience. To ensure satisfactory experiences online commentary needs monitoring, shaping, managing, and proactive responses. The CXO spans boundaries across marketing, sales, IT, operations, product management, and customer service. Successful CXOs integrate employees, vendors, suppliers, wholesalers, distributors, and other actors into the mix, as all members of the service ecosystem contribute to the quality of the service experience. It is the CXO's job to build a consistent experience throughout the service network. Lack of engagement anywhere in the system can lead to bad service experiences everywhere. The CXO is the single point of contact for quality of service experience for all actors, whether internal or external[86].

We end this section with a parting thought; Will the T-shaped professionals of the future be humans, or T-shaped Watsons? Cloud-based service industries are heavily dependent on data collection and processing that are readily susceptible to automation. Could a 21st-century HAL 9000 design and manage real-time customer experiences by leveraging streaming data analytics for AI-driven engagements at the point of service? Can cognitive assistants such as Siri, Cortana, and Alexa become more T-shaped and capable than they already are? We have already seen AI augment and replace humans in functional areas such as advertising, finance, human resources, IT, and big data analytics. It is not difficult to imagine that higher level service innovation capabilities such as monitoring and managing the entire service ecosystem for the creation of optimally individualized user experiences will automate as well. AI technology likely will apply, at least in part, to every business model that is dependent on data. If all businesses are service businesses, then cloud-based service innovation will continue the transformation by AI technologies. The transition toward the service-oriented enterprise involves changes in business resources, processes, and practices. Developing enterprise-wide support for this transition will involve reshaping mindsets, behaviors, and organizational culture to be focused on service innovation. T-shaped professionals have the ability to create the direction, alignment, and commitment across organizational boundaries that are critical to the success of service innovation transformation.

---

[86]S. Olenski, "Does Your Brand Need a Chief Experience Officer?," *Forbes*, http://www.forbes.com/sites/steveolenski/2015/10/24/does-your-brand-need-a-chief-experience-officer/#1023bb6d22a8, October 24, 2015.

Emerging Frontiers for Service Innovation

Up to this point, we have covered underlying conceptual foundations of the service innovation domain. Service innovation creates new opportunities through the integration of knowledge and technology into useful systems for the cocreation of value. The service ecosystem is the fundamental construct for service innovation, and value cocreation is the fundamental innovation process. As we have seen, service innovation is a dynamic and disruptive domain. We now look into the emerging technologies that will affect the future of service innovation.

Emerging Challenges

The mission for the International Society of Service Innovation Professionals (ISSIP) is to "promote service innovations for our connected world"[87]. To that end, ISSIP sponsored a service innovation research and applications workshop, "Emerging Digital Frontiers for Service Innovation," held at the 48th Annual Hawaii International Conference on System Sciences[88]. The following section summarizes some of the key results from the workshop with regard to the emerging technologies and challenges for service systems and the dynamics of value cocreation.

Challenge 1: Developing Cognitive Assistant Services

The goal of cognition-as-a-service (CaaS) is to augment and scale human performance with cognitive assistants. CaaS can enable service providers to augment the capabilities of employees, customers, and other service ecosystem actors. Cognitive assistants have the opportunity to improve how various business functions work and how complex service systems operate. These are the key challenges:

- How to make the development of cognitive assistants for all occupations in smart service systems more scientific, rigorous, and cost effective.

- Defining effective ways to organize human–agent teamwork.

- Using cognitive computing systems to identify and specify decision models for context-dependent service.

- How to stimulate investment and use of cognitive assistants while ensuring robust demand for workers across a spectrum of skills that have committed to working in human–agent relationships.)

---

[87]International Society of Service Innovation Professionals, "About ISSIP," www.issip.org/about-issip/, 2015.

[88]C. Peters, P. Maglio, R. Badinelli, R. Harmon, R. Maull, J. Spohrer, T. Tuunanen, S. Vargo, J. Welser, H. Demirkan, T. Griffith, and Y. Moghaddam, "Emerging Digital Frontiers for Service Innovation," *Communications of the Association for Information Systems, 39* (1), 136–149, 2016.

Challenge 2: Creating Smart Service Systems and Smart Services

Making services and service systems smarter should create more engaging customer experiences and improve overall value creation. However, there are unresolved issues:

- Understanding and realizing the value of big data that is necessary to support smart service systems.

- The lack of decision models for understanding the impact of smart systems and smart services on user behavior and value creation.

Challenge 3: Development of Cyberphysical Systems and Services

Cyberphysical systems and services (CPSSs) are physical and engineered systems that are monitored, coordinated, controlled, and integrated by ICT. These systems can enable value cocreation through the development and implementation of ICT-enabled processes that integrate system-developed value propositions with customer value drivers. The integration of ICT into products and services creates opportunities for SDL thinking about entirely new ICT-enabled services. Examples of CPSSs include smart medical devices, intelligent highways, robotic systems, autonomous vehicles, defense systems, process control systems, factory automation systems, building and environmental controls, smart spaces, and associated real-time analytics. Unresolved issues include the following:

- The application of SDL principles to CPSSs and how value might be cocreated with these systems and services.

- Assessing the impact of infusing ICT into services and SDL thinking with CPSS development.

- Understanding CPSS applications in B2C, B2B, C2C, machine-to-machine (M2M), machine-to-business (M2B), and machine-to-consumer (M2C) environments.

Challenge 4: Understanding Human-Centered Service Systems

Human-centered service systems (HCSSs) depend on sharing resources and capabilities within formal and informal social networks to create value. At this point, these complex service systems are not well understood. HCSSs might include cities, social media platforms, family households, nongovernmental organizations (NGOs), nonprofit social enterprises, aid organizations, churches, shopping malls, office complexes, universities, schools, airports, and hotels, among others. These networks can exhibit similar complex behaviors due to relationships between people and shared information, skills, resources, infrastructure, organizations, and institutions. The challenge is to understand these sociotechnical service systems through interdisciplinary research to develop theory, models, measurement, and the design, engineering, and management of HCSS applications.

Challenge 5: Leveraging the Potential of Personal Data

Two new issues remain unresolved concerning the use of personal data:

1. The first involves the *ethical use of data* in the decision-making process. By analyzing and combining data, especially within service ecosystems, new sociotechnical systems are developed. This raises concerns about data privacy, security, and ownership. In what contexts can data be used, and what value does it have? The key use of data is to better understand and improve service systems; however, these attendant issues need attention.

2. The second issue about personal data concerns the *human side of service*. How can data ethically be used in fields such as health care, education, government, and social services to ensure the human side of service is paramount? Challenges include establishing rights for responsible use of personal data, privacy guarantees, connecting open and crowdsourced data with personal data, the use of personal data from MSPs, how to incentivize users to provide personal data, and who uses personal data for what purposes and who benefits from its use.

Challenge 6: Designing Service System Institutions

How can enterprises design service institutions (and institutional arrangements) to support the various kinds of service systems? Key challenges include the following:

- Understanding the institutional language needed to discuss sociotechnical structures.

- Learning about the levels, how each level works, or how levels interact in institutions as coordination functions.

- Understanding and defining institutional boundaries.

- Understanding the role of technology in institutions.

- Understanding the linkages of institutions to the service system.

- Determining if service systems can automate to cocreate value without humans being involved in direct interactions and how this affects people.

Challenge 7: Service Transformation

We know a great deal about the service transformation process. However, there are gaps in that knowledge that offer opportunities for improved clarity and further topic development. Challenges include the following:

- Understanding the difference between the service transition process and service transformation.

- Developing further insight into service platform strategy, especially for product companies transitioning to service innovation business models.

- Hybrid services that combine products and services represent a logical evolution on the service transformation continuum from product dominance to service dominance. What dimensions or factors characterize the threshold where product dominance gives way to service dominance? Can we define, predict, and effectively map this point of service transformation?

- What impact will new technologies that can drive asymmetric service innovation such as 3D printing, robotics, autonomous capabilities, cognitive computing, energy harvesting devices, smart systems, smart sensors, and the IoT have on product manufacturing companies?

Conclusion

This chapter has presented an introduction to the service science discipline and the SDL concept. Presently, it is reasonable to conclude that all SDL implementations are works in process. However, many companies, especially in ICT industries, are embracing the SDL concept to good effect. Native cloud service companies such as Facebook, Amazon, Netflix, Facebook, and Uber have experienced spectacular growth. Other ICT firms such as Salesforce, IBM, and Microsoft are integrating their service business models with the cloud. It would be fair to say that none is a pure SDL enterprise at this point, but all have adopted some aspects and are certainly improving their service thinking.

Managers in business enterprise, government, and social organizations that are considering the transition from a GDL to an SDL logic approach to innovation might consider the following important steps:

- Develop an appreciation for service principles defined by service science and SDL. You might already offer services or product-service systems. However, do you have sufficient knowledge and experience with the service transformation process to lead the change necessary to become a service innovation leader?

- Define and map your market-specific service ecosystem. Who are the actors? What roles do they play? What unique resources do they have? Do they share your vision of the service value proposition? Do they understand their roles in the creation of the desired user experience? How will you manage the value-creation process?

- Adopt a service thinking mindset. There are six service mindset dimensions: service design, service culture, service architecture, service platforms, service analytics, and service value.

- If you are not already, become a T-shaped person and identify those in your organization who align with T-shaped capabilities. T-shaped requirements will affect recruiting, training, and retention decisions.

- Create a service innovation agenda. Work with service ecosystem members, both internal and external, to identify the best strategic service innovation opportunities and approaches.

- View the future through a service innovation lens. What will your enterprise look like in three to five years? What does it need to look like to remain or become a market leader in service innovation? What technologies will drive the market and how will you leverage them?

Service enterprises are disruptive innovation organizations. They need to innovate or rapidly lose market relevancy. We close with a checklist of recommendations for implementing service innovation initiatives. Once considered radical, but more commonplace now, these recommendations from IDEO, the T-shaped global service design firm, will energize your service transformation[89].

1. *Develop insights about the market:* Monitor your industry, markets, customers, technology, competitors, and business operations concurrently. Look for patterns of unmet or underserved needs. Develop strategic frameworks that describe the opportunity space and customer pain points that can lead to meaningful ideation.

2. *Create radical value propositions:* The goal of radical innovation is to acquire and retain new customers. In a crowded marketplace, people need a good reason to try your new service. Go beyond what they experience from their current service. Help them appreciate the value of your new service. Consider new services that fill a market gap, steer markets in new directions, or create a new class of service. Prototype, simulate, or act out new service experience scenarios. A good prototype will engage designers to consider consumer desirability, business viability, and technical feasibility.

---

[89]M. Jones and F. Samalionis, "Radical Service Innovation: Strategies on the Frontiers of Service Design Demand a Blend of Creativity and Discipline," *Bloomberg Business Week*, http://www.bloomberg.com/news/articles/2008-10-20/radical-service-innovationbusinessweek-business-news-stock-market-and-financial-advice, October 20, 2008.

3. *Explore creative service models:* Innovations that redefine markets usually result from fundamental changes in the industry, technology, and customer requirements. Creative solutions are necessary to make new service offerings viable. Google's service model enables the monetization of service offerings through ad revenues without compromising the service experience. Championing the desirability of an innovation forces the organization to build new constructs to nurture radical innovations. Facebook is a marketing platform that captures user information on interests, behaviors, and personal networks to target advertising and other services. Creative new service models will further drive the monetization of that information.

4. *Bend the rules of delivery:* Part of the innovation process is learning from failure. Service design teams need reassurance that it is acceptable to try new service concepts that have many unresolved questions. Fear of failure makes radical service innovation impossible. Get buy-in to experiment and learn from the results. The often ambiguous nature of early-stage radical service concepts might not have an immediate business case that will meet existing corporate financial or Six Sigma guidelines. This is a major barrier to innovation. Design new metrics for success that focus on customer value, emotional design, and customer experience. As the new service concept matures, measures that are more traditional can come into play.

5. *Iteratively pilot and refine the new service:* Radical innovation is new-to-the world services. It redefines and creates new markets. Conducting a pilot test of the new service is a recommended way to assess and manage risk before the service scales. However, test marketing a new service exposes the company's intent to competitors. Understandably, companies are reticent to pilot if they are to protect first-mover advantage. One approach is to go with the results from beta testing. Radical innovation depends more on the evolution of customer behavior, market trends, and technology rather than quick breakthroughs. Success of a new service can depend on a small nuance that is hard to pinpoint in a market test. Monitoring reactions to your service and making quick iterative refinements is critical to risk management. In the rapidly evolving marketing landscape for new services, customers expect nimbleness as a key element of innovation.

CHAPTER 3

Cloud Computing: Implications for Service Transformation

The day science begins to study non-physical phenomena, it will make more progress in one decade than all the previous centuries of its existence.

—Nikola Tesla

The cloud computing business model is evolving into a compelling platform for service innovation that is transforming the behavior of users and organizations to disrupt existing markets and create new ones. Cloud computing offers a convenient, inexpensive way to lower IT costs, broaden distribution, and improve the quality of IT services. The essential advantage of cloud computing derives from the ability to leverage IT to engage users and other actors in the creation of innovative value propositions and to reengineer existing ones.

A number of emerging cloud-based business models have been highly successful. Cloud technology is being adopted by product and service firms, government, health care, education, and the military. E-commerce, mobile computing, social networking, media, finance and banking, transportation, travel, digital advertising, and big data analytics are examples of industries that were either born in the cloud or were transformed by adopters of cloud-based business models. Examples include Amazon, eBay, Google, Facebook, and Netflix. IBM, Microsoft, Salesforce, and Intel are companies that are transitioning from a product orientation to a service orientation in their businesses.

© Enrique Castro-Leon and Robert Harmon 2016
E. Castro-Leon and R. Harmon, *Cloud as a Service*, DOI 10.1007/978-1-4842-0103-9_3

Cloud adopters can be classified into three primary categories:

1. Native cloud firms such as Amazon, Facebook, Uber, Lyft, Google, and Airbnb.

2. IT-focused firms such as ISVs, cloud services and infrastructure providers including Amazon Web Services (AWS), Microsoft, Salesforce, and IBM.

3. Product-oriented firms that either have not adopted the cloud, are in the process of doing so, or have some business units that are cloud based such as Apple, Intel, GE, and Rolls Royce.

Of importance here is whether the cloud services are actually products or extensions of products in terms of how they are conceived, developed, and implemented in the marketplace or the result of a true service-innovation-focused business model. Developers of product-oriented software and services support a *goods-dominant logic* (GDL) business model, whereas the service innovation orientation is based on a *service-dominant logic* (SDL). GDL-oriented services are developed and marketed like products. GDL is focused on transactions and based on an exchange of value with customers. SDL-oriented services are conceived, developed, commercialized, and supported to cocreate value with customers and other actors in the service ecosystem. SDL is based on collaboration among various actors, including the service provider and user, to cocreate value within a service ecosystem. This chapter presents an overview of the fundamental principles and strategies for the transformation of GDL-oriented firms and their IT organizations to service-innovation-centric SDL enterprises that leverage cloud computing as a key factor in their service-oriented business models.

Incumbent firms in mature markets (characteristic of most businesses) are being challenged by slow-growth, increasing competition from emerging market competitors, rapid technological change, high labor costs, rising energy and materials costs, long and slow supply chains, and uncertain economic conditions. These issues are particularly pressing for manufacturing firms and their IT organizations, but they also apply to service firms. As a result, there is an increasing emphasis on IT-enabled service innovation as firms look for sales growth and profits.

A similar dynamic applies to legacy *services* companies that are managed under a GDL approach where services are treated not in terms of value creation, but as a cost to be minimized. The quintessential examples are airlines, health care, cable and satellite content providers, and providers of cellular services, where SDL notions of value are ignored in the operating business model. Services offered by these companies become *service products*. Examples are class of service and a la carte pricing for passenger ticketing, baggage fees, leg room, and on-board food. This approach applies to programming packages with specific "features" driven by short-term goals to maximize revenue versus delivering long-term customer value leading to a sustainable competitive advantage. The dissonance from shoehorning GDL solutions onto what otherwise could be a cocreated service offering leads to inscrutable fee structures that create significant customer discontent[1]. In most cases the status quo prevails because these business run under near-monopoly conditions or as regulated monopolies in low-growth environments. In the long term, these industries are vulnerable to disruptive innovation such as we are seeing with video streaming, online retailing, and ride-hailing services. Later in this chapter we cover processes for service transition and transformation under the rubric of *servitization*. The process of productizing a service offering is the opposite, namely a process of deservitization with the goal of maximizing short-term revenue at the expense of long-term risk.

From a marketing perspective, innovation refers to the process that enables breakthrough ideas to be generated, developed, and transformed into new processes and solutions that create marketplace advantage. For manufacturing companies as well as traditional IT companies, innovation that results in increased productivity and growth is typically the result of applying new technologies that can transform resources in new ways to create value. Traditionally, services have been viewed as add-on "intangible" products that are typically associated with the core business and used to increase the value of the overall solution[2]. Examples include warranties, training, and consulting services. IT firms and organizations have approached service innovation in much the same way.

In most advanced economies, services account for the more than 70 percent of economic activity and represent the primary driver of growth[3]. Organizations seeking to grow must rely on service innovation for continued business success. It is convenient to think of disruptive service companies such as Amazon, Google, Facebook, and Uber, but most service innovation is incremental in nature. In a GDL-oriented world, it has been relatively rare and difficult for a company to develop a service that redefines and disrupts an existing market and rarer still to develop a service that creates an entirely new market space.

This historical reality is changing as new information technologies have changed the very nature of services. First, IT-enabled innovation has transformed traditional services by adopting manufacturing concepts such as division of labor, knowledge sharing, standardization, and coordination of production and delivery to enable new forms of value creation and consumption. Industries such as retail, hospitality, restaurants, telecommunications, health care, transportation, finance, and education are presently undergoing this type of transformation. They are making progress, but with varying degrees of success. Second, ICT has enabled traditional product manufacturers to become providers of services[4]. IBM and Apple are good examples of manufacturing firms

---

[1]K. Holloway, "10 Ways Monopoly Airlines Use 'Calculated Misery' to Make Flying an Increasingly Overpriced Nightmare," *Alternet.org*, http://www.alternet.org/news-amp-politics/10-ways-monopoly-airlines-use-calculated-misery-make-flying-increasingly, 2015.
[2]I. Gremyr, N. Loftberg, and L. Witell, "Service Innovations in Manufacturing Firms," *Managing Service Quality, 20* (2), 161–175, 2010.
[3]The World Bank, *World Development Indicators: Services,* http://data.worldbank.org/indicator/NV.SRV.TETC.ZS, 2015.
[4]J. Potts and T. Mandeville, "Toward an Evolutionary Theory of Innovation and Growth in the Service Economy," *Prometheus, 25* (2), June 2007.

that are in the process of transitioning their business models to be more service-centric. Indeed, IBM is in the process of transforming itself away from a product orientation into a service-innovation-focused company.

ICT drives service innovation by enabling the separation of production and consumption in terms of space and time. This separability improves productivity, makes organizations more efficient, augments social and behavior change, and provides customers with more control over the consumption experience. ICT can set the stage for value cocreation. For example, wireless cloud platforms in conjunction with Global Positioning System (GPS)-enabled mobile devices are broadening, deepening, and quickening the evolution of the service economy by empowering service providers and customers to cocreate high-value solutions that can redefine old markets and create new ones. Examples abound, such as the rapid development of the "sharing economy" with companies such as Airbnb, Uber, and Lyft that were developed, tested, deployed, and run in the wireless cloud. ICT, and especially the cloud, is rapidly becoming a primary driver of economic growth and commercial dynamism.

There is a long-running, and often spirited, discussion among IT professionals and business leaders about what the true role of the IT department should be or whether there should be an IT department at all. Criticisms include the lack of alignment with business strategy, the internal focus of IT departments, and the lack of user orientation that affects both internal users and external customers. Indeed one frustrated business unit leader disclosed, "I am really disappointed with our IT organization. They ask us for requirements that never seem to get into the final system roll out. There is little collaboration. They always export their inefficiencies to us." The IT organization's failure to engage in value cocreation had serious implications. The business unit developed its own "shadow IT" stealth solution that subsequently spread to other business units.

This example is emblematic of IT organizations embracing a business orientation that is similar to product-focused companies. IT often designs and deploys systems that address the IT organization's internal issues, but not the user's problems. Too many IT managers approach services as if they were products and manage accordingly, leaving considerable value on the table. Others might be well on their way toward delivering services to customers but are still more product oriented than service oriented. The transformation is not complete and might not be based on strong service innovation principles.

Market Creating Service Innovation

The transition to service-oriented business models increases customer engagement and offers new opportunities for cocreation of value. Services can be instrumental for creating new markets by redefining industry boundaries and changing the competitive rules. Companies that redefine markets can make the competition irrelevant as the value that services create pulls in new customers. Markets can be metaphorically conceptualized in terms of two distinct spaces—red and blue oceans[5]. Red oceans represent existing

---

[5]W. C. Kim and R. Mauborgne, "Blue Ocean Strategy," *Harvard Business Review, 82,* 76–84, October 2004.

markets, the known highly competitive market space. Red oceans are characterized by well-defined market segments with understood industry boundaries and competitive rules. Over time, existing markets become crowded with competitors and products and services become commoditized. The lack of differentiation and emphasis on taking share from competitors leads to intense price competition where profits and growth are limited.

Alternatively, blue oceans represent new markets that are not yet well defined. They are untapped market spaces that lack significant competitors. Blue oceans might arise from the creation of entirely new-to-the-world innovations such Facebook's social media services or Google's online search. Blue oceans can result from new entrants that totally redefine old red oceans, such as Apple's entry into the music business with iTunes or the introduction of the iPhone. Most blue oceans are created from within red oceans by existing players such as Netflix using cloud-based streaming to revolutionize the video business and Uber using the cloud to disrupt the taxi business.

Creating new markets or redefining existing markets to create uncontested market spaces is not necessarily dependent on disruptive technology. Technology is not disruptive unless it disrupts customer value. New applications of existing technology can increase value by solving new problems that redefine old markets. Breakthrough technologies, such as cloud computing, by redefining industry value metrics, can create entirely new markets. Disruptive technology can lead to new capabilities and lower costs that change the basis of competition. Disruptive value can derive from any element of the company's resources that affects the value proposition as perceived by the customer. It redefines industry boundaries and market spaces to create new opportunities. The focus on new conceptualizations of customer value enables redefinition of an existing problem or articulation of an unfilled need. Companies that create disruptive value focus on differentiation strategies with superior benefits and lower costs, which can increase customer value.

Discontinuous Innovation and Service-Dominant Logic

If firms are to remain successful, they have to address the value requirements of both today's and tomorrow's customers. To satisfy today's customers, firms need to have strong exploitation capabilities. Exploitation refines and extends existing resources, competencies, and business models to maintain predictable returns. Addressing tomorrow's customers involves exploring for new opportunities to create value through innovative new products and services. Exploration activities involve risk taking, experimentation, and innovation. To satisfy both today's and tomorrow's customers, firms must master both exploitation and exploration activities[6].

One method for limiting exploration risk is to adopt a continuous innovation strategy. Continuous innovation is managed by a predictable and steady innovation process that derives increased performance from improvements in the technology

---

[6]M. Corso and L. Pellegrini, "Continuous and Discontinuous Innovation: Overcoming the Innovator's Dilemma," *Creativity and Innovation Management, 16* (4), 333–347, 2007.

that is embedded in the product or service. By innovating incrementally, firms improve on existing knowledge and capabilities. This approach fits very well with the service transformation process, which benefits from experimentation with new value propositions and explorations of new service models.

Firms that seek to develop new markets by quickly creating disruptive value must innovate beyond their normal incremental approach. Discontinuous innovation often requires different processes, resources, management attention, and organizational culture. The notion of discontinuous innovation is at the core of market creation and destruction. The traditional GDL approach alone is insufficient for arriving at an understanding of the patterns of discontinuous innovation that can reshape markets. Therefore, discontinuous innovation might be better understood if both a GDL and an SDL approach are considered.

SDL defines services as the use of one's resources for the benefit of another entity. SDL argues that service is the basis for all economic activity. SDL focuses on the process of service, whereas GDL focuses on the production and provision of outputs. SDL views goods and tangible resources as appliances that provision the customer's service. Goods are a distribution mechanism for services. The product enters into a value-creating process to be integrated with other resources to provide a flow of service. The essential transition of IT organizations to service-oriented business models is the transition from a GDL organization that is focused on the provisioning of outputs to an SDL organization that focuses on customers for the purpose of relationship building for value cocreation.

GDL is tied to economic exchange. It is transactional in nature and defines value as value-in-exchange. Alternatively, SDL recognizes value-in-exchange, but focuses on value-in-use. It is the value that users receive from the experience of using an offering and integrating it with other resources. For this reason customers are always cocreators of value and only the user can determine value[7]. Therefore, value-in-exchange exists only if (and when) value-in-use occurs for the customer. As a result, an innovation can be defined as discontinuous if, and only if, it significantly alters how customers cocreate value and affects market size, definition, price, margins, or market share. Chapter 2 introduced the SDL concept of value-in-context that derives from the unique reciprocal relationships among the service ecosystem actors as it affects value cocreation. For this chapter we primarily focus on the service provider–customer/user dyad. Therefore, we focus primarily on value-in-use while recognizing the importance of the larger service ecosystem in value cocreation.

SDL defines goods as operand resources to be acted on to create value. Operand resources, such as traditional IT systems, are typically tangible, static, and serve to provision the customer's value-creating process. Operant resources such as knowledge skills, competencies, dynamic capabilities, and technology are largely intangible and dynamic and act on operand and other operant resources to create compelling experiences that enable value cocreation. Operant resources define the basic unit of exchange and are the primary source of competitive advantage. GDL emphasizes operand resources that embed value during the development and production processes. SDL emphasizes the cocreation of value outside the traditional production process as the

---

[7]S. L. Vargo and M. A. Akaka, "Service-Dominant Logic as a Foundation for Service Science: Clarifications," *Service Science, 1* (1), 32–41, 2009.

solution engages the customer. GDL is value added to operand resources, whereas SDL is value cocreated with customers and other service ecosystem actors.

Discontinuous innovation is caused by changes in the value integration roles of the firm, its customers, and other actors in the service ecosystem where the integration of operant resources affects the cocreation of value. IT changes value-creation capability by improving the embedded operand resources (IT infrastructure) and enabling operant resources (cloud solutions) that can dynamically change the configuration of the market's value ecosystem. Innovation is often triggered at this level by members of the value ecosystem, the cooperative networks of value cocreating providers and customers.

Finally, discontinuous innovation changes the role of the customer. Customers are members of the service ecosystem and have specific roles to play as users, buyers, and payers that impact value creation. The roles apply to both businesses and individual consumers and conform to SDL notions of value: payers with value-in-exchange, users with value-in-use, and buyers with either or both, depending on the situation.

Service Transition and Transformation

The term *service transition strategies* describes the processes firms go through in adopting service-oriented business strategies[8]. Service transition implies a step-by-step process that organizations can follow as they migrate from an internal focus or a product orientation to business models dominated by services. Alternatively, the term *service transformation strategies* is often used to describe the same processes. In some instances, the terms service transformation and transition strategies are used interchangeably[9]. Is there a real difference or are these terms describing the same phenomenon?

A *transition* can be defined as a movement, development, or evolution from one form, stage, or style to another[10]. More dynamically, a *transformation* is a complete or major change in an entity's appearance or form. As such, service transitions and service transformations can be perceived in terms of the designated business purpose and the magnitude of change with respect to business goals, transition periods, processes, strategies, end states, and investment requirements. Transitions are a series of smaller changes necessary for improved solution development and deployment and transformations involve a complete redesign of the value proposition, solution development, infrastructure, organization, organizational culture, and successful customer engagement.

For IT organizations and enterprises, a *transition* to cloud-oriented services occurs when an application migrates to the cloud with minimal changes to its design and delivery continues to support current performance and security requirements[11]. For a cloud-based service *transformation,* much more is required. IT objectives drive larger,

---

[8]E. Fang, R. W. Palmatier, and J.-B. Steenkamp, "Effect of Service Transition Strategies on Firm Value," *Journal of Marketing, 72* (4), 1–14, 2008.
[9]A. Salonen, "Service Transition Strategies of Industrial Manufacturers," *Industrial Marketing Management, 40,* 683–690, 2011.
[10]*The Merriam-Webster Dictionary*, Revised Edition (Springfield, MA: Merriam-Webster, 2004).
[11]S. Garforth, "Transitions vs. Transformation," *Cloud Services World,* https://samjgarforth.wordpress.com/2013/08/08/the-roadmap-to-cloud-by-sam-garforth/, July 30, 2013.

comprehensive application changes. Transforming the IT organization to embrace cloud-based service innovation involves rethinking and redesigning the organization's approach to its customers. Often this involves the adoption of a more open computing model and service-oriented architecture (SOA) considerations enabling integration across custom and prepackaged applications, storage, and business support services. Service transformation requires the development of new business models and a redesign and development of new methods, architecture, infrastructure, applications, organization, information requirements, security, operations management, and the creation of a customer-focused, service-oriented culture. The bedrock of the transformation is the successful transition from a value-in-exchange transactions model to a value-in-use relationship model that fosters value cocreation.

Both transition and transformation involve varying degrees of service and process innovation. Transition steps are quicker and might be less expensive, whereas transformations are long-term changes that might be much more expensive. Service transition is the process organizations go through as they move from pure product providers to service providers. Service transformation refers to the achievement of the service-dominant end state. It is helpful to consider transitions from product to service to be more continuous in nature and initially focused on adding value to core products or existing IT solutions. Service transitions are typically not initially intended to result in a service-dominant business model. There might be no expectation to morph a product company from its product-dominant business model. Therefore, service transitions are smaller steps and more tactical in nature. The goal is to support the product by incrementally adding and deploying service functions to match competitors or for differential purposes.

Service transformations, on the other hand, are larger and more comprehensive, with the intent to fully change the organization's business model to focus on service innovation. Transformations are meant to be disruptive. Transformations involve redesigning the enterprise to be service driven. Service transition models might eventually end up transforming the enterprise to service dominance, but service transformation models have shorter time horizons and a sense of strategic urgency. In both instances, the issues to consider are the nature of the market opportunity, customer expectations and readiness, the role of products and services in the value proposition, the service focus of the business model, organizational culture, service-related resources and capabilities, desired end state, time horizon, risk management, investment requirements, and potential returns[12]. The differences and similarities between the definitions of service transition and service transformation are not entirely clear in the academic literature and warrant further explication. However, in the professional world of cloud, mobile, gaming, and social media services, the distinction is very clear: Transitions are too slow.

---

[12]IBM Corporation, "Transition and Transformation: Transitioning to Services with Minimal Risk," IBM Global Technology Services White Paper, http://www-935.ibm.com/services/au/igs/pdf/tt_booklet_final_web.pdf, 2007.

Service Infusion and Servitization

The term *service infusion* typically refers to the transition process used by organizations to create value by adding service offerings to their product portfolios. In IT organizations that are moving to the cloud, it has been referred to as *lift and shift*. Service infusion is conceptualized as the unidirectional transition from the old product orientation to one of service provision. Services have typically been viewed as add-ons to the core product to stay competitive. Initially, the add-on services typically increase overall product costs but are necessary to maintain market share. The emphasis here is on services that support the product (SSP) or, for IT organizations, services that support the product-like software solutions. SSP typically include warranty, repair, and maintenance, but service infusion is more than that. As depicted in Figure 3-1, at its limit, the shift from SSP to services that support the customer (SSC) can involve the transformation from a product-oriented company that adds on services to its core solutions or to a service-dominant enterprise where products provision the services (e.g., cloud-based real-time jet engine monitoring), or very disruptively to a pure service company (web services provider, digital advertising, or data analytics service provider). Service infusion can be disruptively implemented in large chunks or, more likely, in smaller incremental steps[13]. This process has been described as *agile incrementalism,* which refers to an exploratory process that continually builds step by step from an initial state in relatively small degrees. This enables the service developer to experiment with various services to gauge customer interest, test service performance, and limit execution and other risks[14].

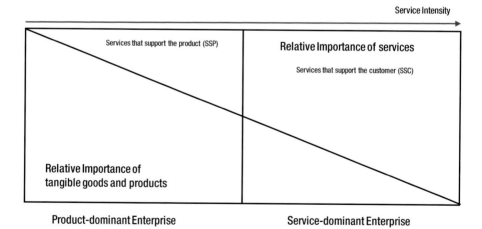

Figure 3-1. *Transition from products to services (Source: Adapted from Gebauer et al., 2008[15])*

---

[13]P. Matthyssens and K. Vandenbempt, "Moving from Basic Offerings to Value-Added Solutions: Strategies, Barriers, and Alignment," *Industrial Marketing Management, 37* (3), 316–328, 2008.
[14]C. Kowalkowski, D. Kindstrom, T. B. Alejandro, S. Brege, and S. Biggemann, "Service Infusion as Agile Incrementalism in Action," *Journal of Business Research, 65,* 765–772, 2012.
[15]H. Gebauer, C. Bravo-Sanchez, and E. Fleisch, "Service Strategies in Product Manufacturing Companies," *Business Strategy Series, 9* (1), 12–20, 2008.

Service infusion is perhaps a clearer and more modern descriptor of the *servitization* process. Servitization refers to the offering of bundles of customer-focused combinations of goods and services to add value to core product offerings[16]. The dominant perspective in the servitization literature is companies should be focused on developing integrated product-service solutions that have been referred to as *product-service systems* (PSS). Similar to the service infusion concept, servitization typically refers to lower cost service add-ons such as warranty and self-service support to high-value core products. Moving past these initial steps, firms are implementing strategies where services are the primary differentiator in an integrated products and services solution. For many IT organizations and firms, services are becoming the essential value-creating element in the value proposition with products diminished to a secondary role in the solution.

Service Platforms

Platform strategy is the foundation for product and service strategy especially in companies that have multiple products or services that share a common technology. Platforms define capabilities, development parameters, cost structure, and the differentiation potential of the family of product or service versions. A well-developed literature base exists for product platform strategy. However, the academic literature on service platform strategy, service innovation platforms, service development platforms, and indeed how to integrate service elements into the product platform is virtually nonexistent. The few studies available tend to define service development in product development terms, yet services differ significantly from products[17][18][19].

Undoubtedly, the lack of focus on service platform development and strategy emanates from the dominance of product thinking at the university level. Most MBA and engineering schools have courses on new product development, but few have courses or programs on service innovation, service development, or service science, and certainly not on service development platforms. In practice, it is relatively straightforward to conceptualize and design the common and unique elements of a product platform because each element is a tangible product feature or attribute. It is much more difficult to design and model intangible service attributes such as embedded knowledge, emotional signatures, and user experience. The primary exceptions to this situation are the pure play ICT services, such as web retailing, digital advertising services, mobile services, social media, and big data analytics, which are all part of an evolving cloud services ecosystem. The designers of these business models are service innovation pioneers.

---

[16]S. Vandermerwe and J. Rada, "Servitization of Business: Adding Value by Adding Services," *European Management Journal, 6* (4), 314–324, 1988.

[17]M. H. Meyer and A. DeTore, "Creating a Platform-Based Approach for Developing New Services," *Journal of Product Innovation Management, 19,* 188–204, 2001.

[18]M. P. Papazoglou and W. J. van den Heuvel, "Service-Oriented Design and Development Methodology," *International Journal of Web Engineering and Technology, 2* (4), 412–442, 2006.

[19]S. Pekkarinen and P. Ulkuniemi, "Modularity in Developing Business Services by Platform Approach," *International Journal of Logistics Management, 19* (1), 84–103, 2008.

Service Transformation Strategies

Service innovation initiatives involve the development and integration of new service "products" and processes. The innovation could derive from a new core benefit or a new service delivery system. Often product-oriented firms envision new services in terms of their old core businesses and use them to increase the value of the overall product. As we discussed earlier, services such as warranty, maintenance, financing, and support services are characterized as SSP or *product services*[20]. These services are often simply characterized as the intangible dimensions of the product. They might be delivered before, during, or after the sale. They typically do not enable significant customization or increase the intensity of the customer relationship. They are GDL value-in-exchange transactions.

Alternatively, SSC, by enabling the cocreation of value, are characterized as *services as a product,* which can be experienced independently from the product or be provisioned by the product. SSC involves the development of high-value services such as taking over the customer's maintenance function, offering IT services such as cloud computing, and outsourced design, manufacturing, inventory, and fulfillment services, to name a few examples. These services integrate the provider's solution with the customer's systems and organization in a collaborative way. SSC aligns with SDL in that it moves the provider away from reliance on one-off value-in-exchange transactions to value-in-use customer relationships, and eventually to SDL-based value cocreation within the service ecosystem. SSC can provide significant differentiation, are difficult to match by competitors, and can enable opportunities for the long-term cocreation of value with customers beyond the initial service collaborations. Because SSC is based on relationships, it offers a high degree of customization through the integration of the supplier's value proposition with the customer's systems and organization. IT organizations and manufacturing firms are finding that SSP is not sufficient for differentiation and sustained competitive advantage because the service intensity is low. SSC, on the other hand, provides a primary avenue for responding to increasing customer expectations by creating differentiated solutions that deliver superior value that is more difficult for competitors to emulate. SSC is therefore characteristic of a high degree of continuous innovation, with the potential for the creation of disruptive service innovation through cocreation of disruptive value within the service ecosystem.

SDL conceptualizes a compelling approach to service innovation through the application of competencies and dynamic capabilities such as knowledge and skills. It provides a perspective for understanding the transition from a product to a service orientation[21]. The transformation process gives rise to solution selling as a viable service strategy. Solution selling, which integrates products and services, leverages the synergy between the core product and the service. Solution selling is typically SSP in nature,

---

[20]V. Mathieu, "Product Services: From a Service Supporting the Product to Services Supporting the Client," *Journal of Business and Industrial Marketing, 73* (1), 39–58, 2001.

[21]A. Ordanini and A. Parasuraman, "Service Innovation Viewed Through a Service-Dominant Logic Lens: A Conceptual Framework and Empirical Analysis," *Journal of Service Research, 14* (1), 3–23, 2011.

but it is not inherently so. It is an important transition step that enables the growth of service intensity, or the proportion of total sales that derive from services. At the limit of service intensity where service value dominates, solution selling strategy is a service innovation strategy. An important class of solution provider is the systems integrator that designs and integrates both internally and externally supplied product and service components into a custom solution. Systems integrators, by their very nature, are more SSC oriented. This business model has the advantages of specialization of solution, modularity of components, standardization of interfaces, and multivendor sources of technology, products, services, and other resources[22]. Top solution-selling systems integrators include Lockheed Martin, Boeing, IBM, HP, Computer Sciences Corp., L-3 Communications, Booz Allen Hamilton, and Verizon Communications.

Service Transformation Business Models

The service innovation discipline is not yet robust or prescriptive concerning strategic and operational approaches for the transition from products to services. Recognizing this deficit, researchers have adapted Chesbrough's Business Model Framework (BMF) to develop a service-based business model approach that identifies and categorizes key factors in the service transformation process and the connections between new service development and service innovation[23]. The elements of the service-oriented business model are as follows:

1. Value proposition.

2. Target market.

3. Value chain.

4. Revenue mechanisms.

5. Relative position in the value network.

6. Competitive strategy.

One observation is that most new service development is focused at a granular level on introducing new service offerings, developing the underlying processes, and developing infrastructure without directing sufficient attention to the strategic changes that are necessary at the firm level. Firms should adopt a holistic business model approach that can foster customer relationships, enable the visualization of the service value, and enable the creation of a service portfolio that is dynamically adaptable to customer needs[24].

---

[22]A. Salonen, "Service Transition Strategies of Industrial Manufacturers," *Industrial Marketing Management, 40,* 683–690, 2011.

[23]H. Chesbrough, "Business Model Innovation: Opportunities and Barriers," *Long Range Planning, 43,* 354–363, 2010.

[24]D. Kindstrom, "Towards a Service-Based Business Model: Key Aspects for Competitive Advantage," *European Management Journal, 28,* 479–490, 2010.

The antecedents for successful innovation in product-related services are becoming clear. The success of both integrated product-services and independent service innovations are influenced by the involvement of frontline employees, information sharing, multifunctional teams, funnel tools (mapping of delivery processes), ICT infrastructure and applications, internal organization structure, training, and education. The presence of a service champion, the independence of service employees, market testing, and market research had a beneficial impact on separate service innovations. However, these factors could negatively affect integrated product-service innovations if a dominant product-oriented culture minimizes the importance of the service component of the value proposition. Management support, availability of resources, and the development of strong service-based relationships with partners and customers are characteristics of companies that understand the importance of service innovation. These factors are favorably associated with both integrated product-service business models and pure service business models, but more so for pure service models.

For the development of service-oriented business models consider three factors:

1. *The service transition strategy:* Strategy development is initiated by consolidating product-related services, entering the installed base market with new product-based services, expanding relationship-based or process-centered services, and taking over end users' operations, such as maintenance. Internal service champions often drive strategy development.

2. *Conceptualizing the service offering:* This a departure from services as an add-on to an existing product. The business model is moving from transactions to relationships, developing a service-dominant mentality, conceiving IT-enabled services, and increasing the degree of service complexity.

3. *The development project:* Developing and implementing the new service. These could be improvements to current offerings or new-to-the-world solutions. Attention is focused on markets and building strong customer relationships based on value cocreation. The typical project is a goods-to-services transition that features a migration from SSP to SSC.

Hybrid Solutions

The end of World War II marked the beginning of the consumer economy. In 1950, employment in the growing service economy surpassed 50 percent of the U.S. population. Fast growing B2C firms were first to recognize this trend and to develop complex service-oriented business models. Retailers and firms that manufactured consumer goods found that competitive advantage could be achieved by shifting the strategic focus from what could be produced to what customers wanted; from a sales orientation to a customer-focused marketing orientation. GE, in its 1952 annual report, introduced the marketing concept that placed marketing planning at the beginning of the production cycle rather than at the end and integrated marketing into each phase of the business. The marketing concept recognizes that a firm can achieve long-term business success by understanding and meeting the needs of its customers[25]. This shift in strategic philosophy was supported by increased emphasis on market research, customer relationships, and value cocreation opportunities that underlie modern service innovation business models.

Traditional internally focused IT organizations share a lot in common with B2B product-oriented manufacturers. They have been slower to engage in value cocreation with customers and to develop service-oriented business models. Market-driven services, to the extent they exist, support the internal workings of the IT department and the employees and processes of the firm. These services are typically not aligned on business strategy or customer value creation, or based on service innovation principles. However, a logical starting point for the service innovation transformation is to embrace the development of hybrid offerings. A hybrid solution that features a combination of IT infrastructure, applications, and customer-oriented services is a logical evolution on the service innovation continuum that can enable strategic alignment with the business, stronger market positions for the firm, and strategic legitimacy for the IT organization.

Hybrid solutions are a combination of one or more goods with one or more services that have the potential for creating more customer value than if the good or service were commercialized separately[26]. Hybrid solutions are a form of PSS that is common in industrial and other B2B markets (refer to Chapter 2 on hybrid solutions). Hybrid-solution value propositions can be categorized as either a service oriented toward the supplier's good (SSP-like) or a service oriented toward the customer's process (SSC-like), each of which can be subcategorized as a supplier's promise to perform a specific act (input) or supplier's promise to achieve a specified level of performance (output)[27].

Figure 3-2 presents a classification scheme of four types of hybrid solution offerings. In Quadrant 1, *product life-cycle services* (PLS) are SSP-like and input-based. PLS facilitate and enable the customer's access to the supplier's product and ensure its performance over the use life cycle. Examples are deployment, setup, inspection, testing, warranty, product-specific support, and life-cycle management of the product. In Quadrant 2, *asset efficiency services* (AES) are SSP-like and output-based. The services are designed to improve the productivity potential of the product and associated customer assets. Examples include services for risk assessment, cost reduction, scalability, remote monitoring, and cloud-based services, if they are primarily efficiency based. In Quadrant 3 *process support services* (PSS) are SSC-like and input-based. These services move beyond improving the efficiency of the product to focus on improving the business processes of the customer. Examples include business process improvements, training, logistics, energy use, and data analytics. Cloud-based applications can be dominant in this space. Finally, in Quadrant 4, *process delegation services* (PDS) are SSC-like and output-based. They are services to perform processes on behalf of customers. The goal is to make the supplier's solution indispensable for the successful execution of the customer's business strategy. These services could be embedded or colocated at the

---

[25]W. Ocasio and J. Joseph, "Rise and Fall – or Transformation? The Evolution of Strategic Planning at the General Electric Company, 1940–2006," *Long Range Planning, 41,* 248–272, 2008.
[26]V. Shankar, L. Berry, and T. Dotzel, "Creating and Managing Hybrid Innovations," *Proceedings of the American Marketing Association Winter Educators' Conference*, February 2007.
[27]W. Ulaga and W. Reinartz, "Hybrid Offerings: How Manufacturing Firms Combine Goods and Services Successfully," *Journal of Marketing, 75,* 5–23, November 2011.

customer's site or hosted by the provider or a third party. From a customer's perspective, PDS are outsourced solutions. They include maintenance management, inventory management, and remote monitoring and maintaining of jet engines, for example.

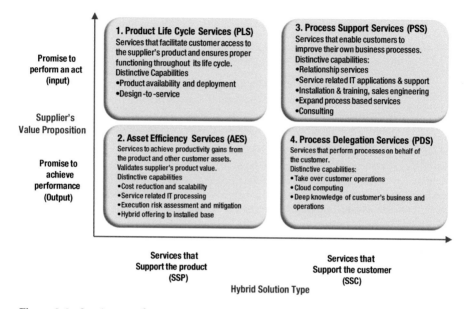

Figure 3-2. *Service transformation strategies for hybrid solutions (Source: Ulaga and Reinartz, 2011[27])*

A typical service migration path is thought to be from PLS to AES to PSS to PDS as the manufacturer, or product-oriented IT organization, gradually adds service capability to the product and subsequently focuses more on services that support or take over customers' processes. Hybrid solutions can increase positional advantage through two avenues: differentiation that can favorably impact pricing and the creation of cost advantages.

Superior capabilities and resources are essential for the development and execution of low-cost or differentiated hybrid offerings. The following are these capabilities and resources:

1. Corporate leadership and an organizational culture that supports the transition to a service innovation business model.

2. Human resources that have service training and skills.

3. Marketing intelligence including competitor analysis, product research, and customer usage and process data from the firm's installed product base.

4. Service-related data processing for monitoring and management of hybrid solutions.

5. Execution risk assessment and mitigation capability that includes the ability to a priori assess the fit and potential efficacy of the hybrid solution.

6. Design-to-service capability that includes the product-service design, platform strategy, and development skills and abilities.

7. The ability to produce and integrate products and services into solutions.

8. Commercialization and deployment capability for hybrid solutions including highly capable marketing and sales functions, distribution network, applications infrastructure, engineers, support functions, and field service organization.

A firm's commitment to service innovation can affect its business value. Service innovation capabilities and resources, or lack thereof, can affect service transition strategies. On the positive side, leveraging service knowledge to engage the customers in value cocreation can result in better relationships and increased customer loyalty. On the negative side there is the potential for conflict between product and service priorities and the loss of strategic focus from ill-conceived and implemented service initiatives that can lead to strategy failure. The good news is that once the critical mass for service capability is reached the potential for success improves. The *service intensity ratio* of actual sales from services to the total sales of the organization is a performance metric that indicates the progress of a firm's service strategy migration. The notion of a service ratio of actual service sales to total sales is useful. As service intensity reaches 20 to 30 percent of sales, the business effects of transitioning to services become apparent in terms of increased profitability. Higher returns result from service innovation that can develop new markets and redefine old markets with the potential to achieve higher margins. Successful companies that have become sufficiently service oriented have transitioned beyond the product-focused, transaction-based customer relationship to service-focused collaborative relationship with customers based on the cocreation of value.

Table 3-1 summarizes and provides an overview of the service transformation process. Of particular interest are the linkages between service transformation strategies, the hybrid services model, the type of value created, degree of service intensity, the type of customer relationship, and the type of services offered. The transition between Stages 2 and 3 of the service strategy migration from SSP to SSC is where the value proposition changes from being predominantly product oriented to being predominantly service oriented. This might indicate the existence of a service intensity threshold that, when reached, triggers a change in enterprise approaches to customer engagement and value cocreation activities. This threshold effect could be the result of a deliberate service transformation strategy on the part of the enterprise, or perhaps an organic change in the nature of customers' value requirements and service innovation expectations. In any event, navigating through the threshold would involve a change in customer expectations and value migration that enables both the customer and the provider to engage in service readiness activities for more innovative and relationship-oriented service solutions. The progression through the various stages of the hybrid services model needs to be better understood: Is the migration step by step and orderly, or is the process less deterministic and more random and potentially more disruptive and risky?

Table 3-1. Stages of the Service Transformation Process

Transition Stage	Offering Type	Service Migration	Service Strategy	Primary Value Orientation	Customer/Actors Relationship	Services
0	Pure Product	Product manufacturer	None or minimal SSP	Goods-Dominant Logic Value-in-exchange	Transaction focus Product dominant	No services or industry standard customer service
1	Product Lifecycle Services (PLS)	Hybrid services that ensure product availability and performance over its useful life	SSP	Goods-Dominant Logic Value-in-exchange Input-based: supplier promises to perform specified activities	Low service ratio Transaction focus Product dominant with services required to support product	Product integration services (design-in), Field engineering support, Transportation, Installation, Quality assurance, Documentation, Inspection & testing, Refurbishing & Recycl, 24/7 hotline-help desk
2	Asset Efficiency Services (AES)	Hybrid services to increase output and/or reduce customer costs associated with supplier's product	SSP	Goods Dominant Logic Value-in-Exchange Output based: Supplier promises to achieve a specified result	Low to moderate service ratio, Mostly transaction focus, Service enables product efficiencies, rudimentary service systems	Productivity improvement Upgrades/updates Product customization Consulting-product/technology Training-product/technology Cloud-based customer service
Service Intensity Threshold						
3	Process Support Services (PSS)	Hybrid services to enable improvement of the customer's operations	SSC	Service-Dominant Logic Value-in-use Input based.	Moderate to high service ratio, Developing actor-to-actor service ecosystem, Service leads-product provisions	Co-development, Process consulting, Process training Process R&D, Proprietary cloud software services
4	Process Delegation Services (PDS)	Hybrid services that perform processes for the customer	SSC	Service Dominant Logic Value-in-use Output based	High service ratio, Actor-to-actor service ecosystem, Service, provisioned by product, takes over end-user processes	Inventory & maintenance mgmt, Process mgmt, Engr. services, Mktg, sales, & analytics services, Smart systems services, Cloud-based service platforms
5	Pure Service No product required from same supplier	Integrated cloud services that are product agnostic	SSC	Service Dominant Logic Value-in-use Value-in-context	Highest service ratio, scope, scale, and engagement with service ecosystem, Service system institutions and arrangements	Multisided cloud platforms, Social media, sharing economy, Streaming media, Mobile services, Digital media, Cognitive services, Autonomous services, Open systems, Cloud-centric service innovation

Service Transformation Process

Market Creating Cloud Services Innovators

This section provides overviews of five cloud-based service innovators to assess their service transformation strategies and stage of the process. Four of these companies, Intel, Rolls-Royce, Cisco, and IBM, are attempting to migrate from product-oriented GDL models. Google has a more mature service strategy and is developing the characteristics of pure service innovators.

Google

Google's mobile service transition strategy has been to drive its open wired Internet-based business model to the fast-growing wireless space. Google's vision is to organize the world's information and make it available to all. In 2005 Google purchased the Android OS and subsequently adopted an open-innovation platform-based model for the development and deployment of application services (Android Market) for smart phones, netbooks, and tablet computers. This was a blue ocean service innovation opportunity for Android.

The Android platform provides everything a device manufacturer needs for rapid introduction of new smart phones and tablets. Android's open-innovation strategy is to gain OS dominance to implement its cloud-based search, advertising, and data analytics model across multiple device manufacturers and mobile network providers. In 2010 Android market share surpassed the iPhone's iOS and by May 2015 was 70 percent worldwide versus 14 percent for iOS[28]. Android is based on SDL principles and occupies several stages of the transformation model depending on the market. For original design manufacturers (ODM) and original equipment manufacturers (OEM) of mobile devices Android is solidly in Quadrant 2 because the OS enabled these companies to lower costs, enter the market, and scale more rapidly.

For business users, Google occupies Stage 3 of the service transformation process because the advent of bring your own device (BYOD) has enabled businesses to leverage and improve IT operations to address mobile business requirements. Google also occupies Stage 4 of the model as educational and other organizations have outsourced their IT organizations to the Google cloud, featuring Google Chrome, Gmail, Calendar, Google Docs, Google Drive (cloud storage), and Google+ as Google becomes more SDL in nature. If Google continues to populate the service ecosystem with smarter applications it could challenge the pure service companies such as Netflix, Uber, and Airbnb in Stage 5. It is already challenging Facebook with Google+. Google's cloud services market share is about 5 percent[29]. When compared to Amazon Web Services at 28 percent and

---

[28]D. Olenick, "Apple iOS and Google Android Smartphone Market Share Flattening: IDC," *Forbes.com,* http://www.forbes.com/sites/dougolenick/2015/05/27/apple-ios-and-google-android-smartphone-market-share-flattening-idc/#12c486c2d4e6, May 27, 2015.
[29]*The Economist,* "The Cheap, Convenient Cloud," 59–61, http://www.economist.com/news/business/21648685-cloud-computing-prices-keep-falling-whole-it-business-will-change-cheap-convenient, April 18, 2015.

Microsoft at 10 percent, this is relatively small. However, Google appears to be executing its service transformation strategy across a wide range of markets and applications. It dominates wireless OS and online search, and has the cloud infrastructure (datacenters and applications) that can enable the value cocreation with customers that drives service innovation.

Intel's Collaborative Cancer Cloud

Intel is leveraging its hardware expertise to position itself in health care services. Intel is motivated to explore service innovation initiatives as the microprocessor market matures and changes focus to less expensive mobile processors. In 2011 Intel and GE Healthcare's Home Health Division formed Intel-GE Care Innovations, a telehealth joint venture. The new company's goal is to develop new telemedicine models of care to enable the elderly to live more independently, assist people living with chronic conditions, and to lower health care costs by allowing earlier intervention. Areas of focus include remote patient management that features patient engagements with caregivers, in-home wireless, sensor-based, near-real-time patient wellness monitoring, and fall prevention. Intel looks to save its insurance companies and health-care provider-customers money by shifting some of the burden of monitoring patients to the home and out of the hospital. As the Care Innovations business model has matured, it has shifted from device engineering to cloud and data analytics services for managing patient care[30].

In 2015 Intel announced its Collaborative Cancer Cloud software initiative for sharing medical images, clinical information, and genome research results among researchers and medical professionals[31]. The software is being developed in partnership with Oregon Health and Science University. The project involves a software platform for a system to allow collaboration across disciplines and institutions. Intel will distribute the Cancer Cloud software under an open source license that is free to share and modify. Because Intel chips dominate the market for large-scale data processing and personalized medicine requires massive computing power, the Collaborative Cancer Cloud platform could become an important player in the health care cloud ecosystem.

The Care Innovations business model is approaching Stage 4 of the service transformation process. It is enabling and has started to assume some the functions of outpatient care with its telemedicine-based patient monitoring capabilities. It is also setting the stage for a higher degree of value cocreation between patients and health care providers, which in turn creates opportunities for value cocreation between Intel-GE Care Innovations and its business customers, the health care providers and insurance companies. Intel's Collaborative Cancer Cloud is a Stage 3 initiative that makes improvements in the customers' operations. It is a customer-focused cloud model.

---

[30]K. Robertson, "Intel-GE Care Innovations Shifts Business Model," *Sacramento Business Journal*, http://www.bizjournals.com/sacramento/news/2014/02/25/intel-ge-care-innovations-business-chang.html, February 25, 2014.
[31]E. Dwoskin, "Intel Joins Race to Build Platform for Medical Data," *The Wall Street Journal*. http://blogs.wsj.com/digits/2015/08/21/intel-joins-race-to-build-platform-for-medical-data/, August 21, 2015.

Rolls-Royce Civil Aerospace Services

Rolls-Royce is the number one manufacturer of large turbofan aircraft engines. More than 500 airlines rely on Rolls-Royce power, with more than 11,000 engines in service. Since 2004, approximately 60 percent of sales have come from services. For its airline customers, Rolls-Royce offers TotalCare maintenance service, which provides a single-source solution for the overall lifetime support of the engine. The core elements are service integration of real-time, cloud-based engine health monitoring, comprehensive engine overhaul, engine reliability improvements, and Rolls-Royce initiated specialized maintenance. Rolls-Royce analytics monitor engine status to determine whether and when an engine needs maintenance or repair at a central facility[32].

Customers benefit from predictable costs, improved reliability, and less downtime. This enables customers to transfer the technical and financial risks associated with engine care to Rolls-Royce, concentrate on their core business, increase control of financial planning, and increase efficiency. Customers are not just buying engines; they are buying cost-predictable, long-term, reliable thrust. Rolls-Royce benefits because maintenance revenues over the 20 to 25 years of a jet engine's service life can run more than seven times the original cost of the engine. A Trent 1000 engine for the Boeing 787 can cost more than $40 million. Rolls-Royce stresses "peace of mind" to their customers. Virtually all of the Rolls-Royce engines in service are covered by the plan. Rolls-Royce TotalCare maintenance service is a Stage 4 process delegation service. Both customers and Rolls-Royce benefit from the high degree of value cocreation in this service innovation business model.

Cisco Systems, Smart+Connected Communities

Cisco has launched the Smart+Connected Communities cloud-based smart-systems service initiative for the purpose of achieving economic, social, and environmental sustainability goals[33]. Cisco envisions the network as the platform for the development and delivery of services that transform physical communities to smart-connected communities. The network and its cloud-based software platform facilitate the development and delivery of building management, transportation, utilities, security, entertainment, education, health care, and other services. A major goal is to enable high levels of collaboration to increase economic growth, improve resource efficiency, lower costs, and reduce or eliminate environmental impacts. Cisco envisions a family of smart service "experiences" to enhance work and lifestyle activities. The experiences cover home, office, wellness, learning, shopping, travel, entertainment, sports, and government interactions that can be accessed around the clock from any location.

---

[32]A. Derber, "No Afterthought: Rolls-Royce and the Aftermarket," *MRO Network*, http://mro-network.com/analysis/2013/07/no-afterthought-rolls-royce-and-aftermarket/1345, July 19, 2013.
[33]Cisco, "Smart+Connected Communities: Changing a City, a Country, the World," Cisco Systems, Inc. http://www.cisco.com/c/en_in/solutions/industries/smart-connected-communities.html, 2010.

Songdo City, near Incheon, Korea, is the first Smart+Connected Community. The project is a showcase for green and clean technology, in addition to serving as a laboratory for the development of the smart experiences service platform. This is a blue ocean opportunity, a new-to-the-world market for new-to-the-world services, for Cisco's smart systems services that are based on its networking infrastructure, databases, and software applications. Although other companies are attempting similar projects, Cisco is becoming an SDL service innovator that is defining what smart systems can do in the sustainable IT services arena. From a city manager's perspective, Cisco's Smart+Connected Communities is a Stage 3 SSC initiative. As Cisco continues to build smart service infrastructure and applications, it might become engaged in Stage 4 process delegation services as the company takes over city services. Application experiences that directly engage in cocreation with the citizen customer would strengthen Cisco's market position in smart cities.

IBM Watson Health Cloud

The Watson Health Cloud provides a secure and open platform for physicians, researchers, insurance companies, and firms and governmental organizations that are focused on health and wellness solutions[34]. IBM has been developing applications for its Watson cognitive computing system to improve the quality and efficacy of personal health care. The Watson Health Cloud is compliant with the Health Insurance Portability and Accountability Act (HIPAA). The service enables secure access to individual health data and a comprehensive view of the factors that affect personal health.

The foundation of the service is Watson's advanced cognitive computing capabilities to connect the Health Cloud's ecosystem of researchers, practitioners, and partners into a community on an open, secure, and scalable platform. IBM recently acquired Explorys and Phytex to enhance Watson's medical analytics services. The IBM Watson Health business unit will manage the initiative. IBM is partnering with Medtronic, Johnson & Johnson, Apple, and other organizations to engage in data collection, analysis, and solution development. For example, IBM and Apple will integrate mobile cloud services and analytics with HealthKit and ResearchKit as key applications for iOS and Apple iWatch. The Watson Health Cloud platform will collect and analyze data from users who opt in to contribute personal data for medical research. Medtronic will use the platform to collaborate on the development and delivery of highly personalized care management solutions for diabetes patients. Johnson & Johnson will focus on pre- and postoperative patient care and the management of chronic health conditions that account for more than 80 percent of global health care costs.

---

[34]D. K. Taft, "IBM Launches Watson Health Cloud, New Health Unit," *eWeek.com*, http://www.eweek.com/cloud/ibm-launches-watson-health-cloud-new-health-unit-2.html, April 4, 2015.

The IBM Watson Health Cloud could be viewed as a Stage 3 SSC initiative that improves the customer's operations. This is similar to the Intel Collaborative Cancer Cloud. However, it promises more than that. Fully implemented, the IBM service innovation platform could assume many of the Stage 4 SSC functions such as diagnostics and health management applications now performed by individuals in health care organizations that lack Watson's cognitive computing capabilities.

Service Innovation Transformation

All of these firms are engaged in a service transition process that might or might not result in full transformation to a world-class provider of innovative service solutions. All are utilizing the cloud as a platform for service development and delivery. Google and Rolls-Royce have demonstrated that service models based on the cloud can be very disruptive in terms of defining new markets and delivering superior customer value. Intel might well succeed in moving beyond its manufacturing base. However, Intel's initial intent with its partnership with GE was to find a new market for its core semiconductor capabilities. Intel's DNA is GDL and the medical device and telemedicine markets already have plenty of entrenched competitors. Without the GE Healthcare joint venture, Intel was risking being just another "me too" competitor, but even that has moved beyond hardware to cloud services. The Collaborative Cancer Cloud might not be disruptive enough when compared with Watson's cloud power.

Similarly, Google was late to enter the mobile services market. It made early attempts to bring its wired search-based advertising model to the mobile Internet without much success. It had to contend with the walled gardens of the network carriers that resisted the open-innovation model. Apple disrupted the market with its iPhone, which provided Google a strategic opening with the non-AT&T carriers. Android, although it was a late mover, is a superior open solution and is likely to continue to gain strength in the mobile space at Apple's and the network operators' expense. Google's initial migration path was through a market development strategy that didn't work well, followed by an Android-based information services development strategy that did. Its move to the cloud for its entire suite of applications is enabling it to confront Microsoft even in business settings.

Rolls-Royce has taken a core capability in manufacturing and repairing engines and turned it into a successful service by taking over its customers' maintenance responsibilities, an SSC approach. Its path to the blue ocean was through new service development. Cisco followed a path similar to Intel through market development. It was looking for new markets for its core technologies. As it developed expertise in smart systems it chose sustainable IT services as its strategy, which is being driven by the sustainability megatrend. It reached for a market space with little competition and high potential for future growth and might find itself navigating a blue ocean.

IBM is taking a big risk by selling its hardware divisions and fully committing to cloud-based service innovation as its future. Watson and its cognitive computing combined with the cloud is just starting to gain traction. Big risks can mean big rewards. IBM initiated the service science discipline, and it is now becoming its greatest test case.

Conclusion

To improve business outcomes in challenging market conditions, goods-oriented organizations are transitioning to business models that are more service oriented. Service innovation can provide competitive advantage for such organizations as means for repositioning away from commodity markets and price-oriented competitors that are not yet capable of developing sophisticated service offerings, much less marketing and deploying them. Organizations that adopt a service innovation strategy can extend their value proposition and market scope to gain advantage over slower moving competitors.

Although much is known about the service transformation process for manufacturers, when it was applied to the initial development of product-oriented cloud-based business models it had a somewhat static or even retro old-line ambience. However, new technologies such as cognitive computing, robotics, autonomous capabilities, cloud-based analytics services, energy harvesting devices, smart systems, smart sensors, and the Internet of things (IoT) will drive more asymmetric and disruptive service innovation. The new service business models now being developed are resetting the competitive arena with the advantage going to high-technology innovators that can design, produce, and deploy smart solutions that can provision even smarter services. For many of the old-line companies and IT organizations this oncoming wave of new technologies will likely present huge challenges to their existing business models. The next generation of service transformation research will indeed be very dynamic and interesting.

For IT managers the lessons derived from a deeper understanding of the service transformation process are important and provide essential insight into how to become more competitive, at least in the short run. The real challenge will be how to integrate the next generation of truly disruptive technologies into the process. The transformation of old-line organizations to service innovation powerhouses is one of the most important trends of our time. In the future, only enterprises that fully embrace service innovation are likely to be the leaders of the next transformation.

PART III

CHAPTER 4

Evolution of Cloud Server Platforms

"Make sure your business is creating a service experience so good that it demands loyalty."

—Steve Maraboli

Cloud Server Platforms and Their Ecosystems

The largest *cloud service providers* (CSPs) worldwide today—Amazon, Google, Microsoft, and Facebook in the United States, and Baidu, Alibaba, and Tencent in the People's Republic of China—operate very large datacenters housing hundreds of thousands of servers. The replacement rate for these machines also runs in the hundreds of thousands per year. The cost of a server can run anywhere from a couple of thousand U.S. dollars to five or even six figures, depending on the configuration: number of processors, amount of memory, composition of peripherals, and level of fault tolerance built in[1]. Given the large capital outlay that these acquisitions represent, it is understandable that these companies make every effort possible to minimize per-unit cost. These CSPs also seek to reduce operational costs through unusual measures such as locating datacenters in sparsely populated but low-energy-cost areas.

Cloud operators realized early on that servers originally designed for enterprise datacenters were not optimal for their application. These servers are well-known, branded machines from manufacturers such as Dell, Hewlett-Packard Enterprise, or SuperMicro, known as *original equipment manufacturers* (OEMs). Instead, they deploy in-house designs with machines built by contract manufacturers. This strategy allows strict control over the technology ingredients going into the servers, the platform architecture, and the manufacturing supply chain, as we discuss later in this chapter. The names of these contract manufacturers, such as Quanta, Inventec, Wiwynn, Foxconn, and Jabil, are not exactly household names with the public. The appellation in the industry for these contract manufacturers is *original design manufacturers* (ODMs), meaning that the machines ODMs manufacture are third-party designs, not those of the ODMs, as would have been the case with OEMs. OEMs themselves have evolved and adjusted their product strategies to satisfy requirements for cloud markets.

---

[1]This capability is also known in the industry as reliability, availability, and serviceability (RAS).

© Enrique Castro-Leon and Robert Harmon 2016
E. Castro-Leon and R. Harmon, *Cloud as a Service*, DOI 10.1007/978-1-4842-0103-9_4

All the cloud server designs are instances of *standard high volume server* (SHV) platforms. If picked apart, the technology ingredients in these servers are not much different from equivalent OEM platform offerings. These platforms use the same processors, memory, networking, and storage technology found in any OEM offering. However, the layout of components on a circuit board, the layout and geometry of the board itself, or number of memory slots and I/O ports might be unique to the design and purposely designed to the CSPs' applications.

Initially the cloud providers kept their in-house designs proprietary and secret, and that is still the case today. However, some realized there were certain strategic advantages in sharing designs with the industry along the same notion of open source software, which had revolutionized the industry a quarter-century earlier. In other words, sharing these designs involved the concept of *open hardware*. The earliest initiative toward in-house, user-driven, open hardware server designs came within the context of the Open Compute Project (OCP). Facebook launched the initiative in April 2011 with the charter to share designs for datacenter products.

OCP was unique not in that it was the first in-house design by a large CSP. It was general knowledge at that time that other large players were building their own in-house designs. What made Facebook unique is that the company took the bold step of sharing its design details with the industry and invited other partners to join in and do the same. We cover later in this chapter some of the reasons why Facebook was motivated to "open source" their hardware designs. Significant partners have joined the initiative since then, including Apple, Microsoft, Rackspace, Cisco, Juniper Networks, Goldman Sachs, Fidelity, and Bank of America. Some of these participants might see themselves as competitors to Facebook. However, common interests trump competitive concerns: Microsoft created another specification, Windows Cloud Server, and submitted this spec as an OCP contribution under the name of *Open Compute Server*. The Scorpio cloud chassis specification in use by Baidu, Alibaba, and Tencent in the People's Republic of China went through a similar process.

Evolution of Cloud Platforms

An analysis along the following two dimensions will make it easier to understand the dynamics playing out in the design and manufacturing of cloud platforms:

- The process of platform *development* involving the *design, test and validation,* and *integration* of the machines with respect to the technologies and components inside each machine. Design involves the development of *computer-aided design* (CAD) diagrams for the circuit boards and the mechanicals of the machine. Testing involves the initial power-on of the machine, affectionately known as the *smoke test,* testing the integrity of the individual subsystems in the machine, including CPUs and chipsets, memory subsystem, and I/O subsystem, and ensuring that the firmware in the various controllers implements the server management and housekeeping functions as specified. Validation processes verify functionality across subsystems and that the server meets the equipment specifications. Integration includes configuring and provisioning nodes into turnkey chassis for the intended application. We cover this process in more detail later in this chapter.

- The *business* processes within which this development takes place. These processes involve multiple partners or participants. We call these processes *platform execution*. Crucial considerations for platform execution are cost, time to market, and a low defect rate. The CSP goals are a low-cost platform that meets the design specifications, with a low defect rate, and specifications that match the application with manufacturability in the scale needed for the application.

As suggested, cloud platforms represent the latest instantiation of the notion of SHV. From a design perspective, the rise of cloud platforms represents the latest iteration of evolving technology integration processes with origins that date to the dawn of the computer era. Beyond that, we can go even earlier in history and notice similar patterns in other industries. For instance, the railroad industry during the 19th century experienced significant acceleration once the industry adopted common standards and specifications for the design and operation of steam engines and locomotives that allowed for interoperable railway networks, including the use of the adoption of the Stephenson gauge set at a width of 4 feet, 8 1/2 inches. These norms reduced the likelihood of steam engine accidents and allowed use of the railway network by rolling stock regardless of origin within the network. We need to note that this progress was not continuous: A number of companies and even some countries sought a tactical advantage in *preventing* their grid from being interoperable with adjacent networks to preserve tariff advantages, or to minimize the risk of military invasions. These flight-or-fight dynamics are still very much at play for companies trying to decide whether to stay out or join in or take on new roles. Furthermore, participants make these decisions relative to the network instead of independent technology instances.

Commoditization of Computer Platforms: A Historical Perspective

Until the early 1960s, building a computer system meant a complete redesign from the ground up. Manufacturing was done in house, and therefore bringing up the new system meant a complete retooling with very little reuse from the old to the new system. The seven-figure selling prices for this machinery, in dollars at the time, not in today's dollars, reflected the steep development costs.

For end users deploying the equipment, the transition to a new generation was also painful. If an enterprise customer outgrew the capabilities of the present installation, the limitations of a fixed model design constrained the range of attainable upgrades. The soup-to-nuts approach to design did not allow much variation without introducing undue risk, as opposed to the continuous refinement process prevalent today. End users received little more than the basic operating system and some software tools such as compilers and runtime libraries. Because the breadth of the toolset was limited, users wrote their own compilers on occasion. Applications written in house were the norm. Therefore bringing in a more capable machine of the new generation meant a complete infrastructure remake that included literally a forklift replacement of the hardware and a rewriting of the application software. It was some consolation that, given the enormous capital outlay associated with these machines, the labor costs involved in the transition were still a fraction of the total investment. Furthermore, there were few options for efficient capacity planning. Installing a machine with room to grow also required a large investment up front, and unused capacity at the beginning of the deployment cycle went to waste.

In this environment, when IBM announced the System/360 (S/360) in 1964, it was a revolutionary concept, decoupling architecture from implementation. The initial announcement in 1964 included a broad range of models: 20, 30, 40, 50, 60, 62, and 70, enabling customers to achieve a finer grained degree of application scaling when it came to capacity planning. True to this concept, the following generation, System/370 (S/370) introduced in 1970, incorporated a number of advances in the hardware technology and the programming environment, such as support for virtual memory, yet it was capable of running the S/360 software unchanged. For IBM this allowed a somewhat shortened development cycle at the tail end of development due to software reuse.

Although the development of System/360 represented a multiyear effort by IBM, IBM could bring in new architecture machines at a minimal level of disruption to existing customers. Under the old rule, customers expected that an application retooling was the price to pay to move to the next generation. The S/360 architecture changed that. For IBM, of course, this new value proposition vector made the newer machines easier to sell, generating revenue earlier in the platform life cycle. This was possible because customers were able to run legacy applications immediately without the time and labor investment of porting applications to the new environment.

IBM carried out this concept to the successor S/370. These machines could run the prior generation OS and applications unmodified, albeit in emulation mode with some overhead. Users chose this path for economic reasons: The extra hardware to compensate for this overhead cost less than the labor to retool as well as the opportunity cost for faster time to market. For IBM as well, this approach to building computers shortened development cycles and gave the company a time-to-market capability and advantage and a position of technology leadership that lasted for decades. In other words, the broad range of models within the S/360 series allowed IBM to fine-tune offerings in a modular fashion without the need to redevelop a whole system from the ground up.

In spite of the modular architecture in the IBM S/360, until the mid-1970s the process of building computers was still single-sourced: A single company managed the bulk of the supply chain, from the fabrication of critical semiconductor devices to the delivery of finished computers and the handling of postsales service and maintenance contracts. IBM directly manufactured CPUs, made out of discrete components at the time, peripheral devices including keyboards, the operating system, and even some applications. Although competitors such as Amdahl Corporation provided an alternative for plug-compatible S/370 mainframes in 1975, customers had few alternatives for technology sourcing.

Digital Equipment Corporation (DEC) used a similar approach of distinguishing architecture from implementation that made IBM so successful. This time, the company applied the approach to a landmark line of minicomputers, the PDP-11[2].

---

[2]C. Gordon Bell, C. Mudge, and J. E. McNamara, *Computer Engineering: A DEC View of Hardware Systems Design* (Bedford, MA: Digital Press, 1978).

The range of models within the PDP-11 line offered by DEC was even broader than that of the IBM S/360, spanning two decades and a number of manufacturing technologies in the implementation.

Still, PDP-11 installations in the mid-1970s were vertically integrated. An installation might have consisted of a PDP-11/45 computer, a VT100 combined keyboard and CRT display, a DECtape tape drive, an RX11 floppy disk drive, and a DECwriter II LA36 printer terminal, all manufactured by DEC. Inside the computer, the processor bus, Unibus was a DEC design. There was a choice of operating systems: RT-11, RSTS/E, and RSX-11, all made by DEC. Only certain applications were left out to other companies or to hungry graduate students, including the author at that time.

Due to advances in technology management, PDP-11 systems evolved at a much faster rate than the IBM S/360, with these changes occurring at multiple levels of abstraction. For instance, the IBM S/360 and derivatives never left the mainframe market. In contrast, PDP-11 systems found a first home as minicomputers for processing lab data in the 1970s, and transitioned to departmental computers in the 1980s, eventually to become a significant player in a growing OEM industry. The machines found a home in Eastern European countries and the Soviet Union, where they were reverse-engineered, reimplemented, and cloned. Most of these designs were unlicensed and not under the oversight of DEC. DEC sold significant portions of PDP-11 machines to an emerging OEM market. These sales channels were different from today's OEMs, who manufacture computers from widely available commodity technologies and market their offerings under their own brand. Instead, PDP-11 computers were embedded into larger applications, usually in industrial process control, signal processing, and data path switching[3], as well as end user applications such as word processing marketed as a vertical capability. Nonetheless, these changes foreshadowed the emerging era of commodity computers.

From an implementation technology perspective, initial implementations of the processor used *small-scale integration* (SSI) circuits and discrete logic that required multiple boards to implement the CPU. Subsequent implementations used medium-scale integration (MSI) to reduce the number of parts until large-scale integration made single-chip implementations practical, enabling space and cost reductions of several orders of magnitude. Likewise, DEC replaced its initial core-based memory with CMOS, semiconductor-based memory.

As radical as these changes might seem, they were actually very evolutionary, each one happening on top of a preexisting technology base. Each change brought benefits without the need to throw away prior technology investments.

The single-supplier pipeline model for computer manufacturing did not last forever. IBM, perhaps unwittingly, started the next revolution. An IBM design team in Boca Raton, Florida, working on the upcoming model 5150 decided to make heavy use of outsourced technologies, including operating system software from a then obscure company called Microsoft.

---

[3]C. Gordon Bell, "United Engineering Foundation and IEEE STARS Program and Engineering and Technology History Wiki," http://ethw.org/Rise_and_Fall_of_Minicomputers, February 2016.

IBM introduced the PC in 1981. The primary driver for working through outsourcing was time to market. The development team wanted to complete the project in an unprecedented time frame of less than a year. In order to expedite expedite time to market, the 5150 architects made the specifications for some of the components public. In what eventually proved a transformative decision, the team made extensive use of commoditized components, including the operating system, outsourcing it to a fledgling startup at the time, Microsoft. IBM also took on a new role that surged in prominence at the beginning of the third millennium: a systems integrator.

We now realize that this role represents a common pattern in many industries old and new: Companies like Boeing and General Motors represent only the tip of an iceberg. If we look at the size of the Boeing 787 project, the dollar amount associated with supplier economic activity is many times over the economic activity by Boeing. It is not that Boeing is intentionally trying to downsize. This process is disruptive for Boeing and places enormous cost pressure on the members of the supply chain to deliver parts that fit, under predefined time constraints and at the targeted cost. The transformation is taking place because the third-party development paradigm minimizes the cost per aircraft delivered.

The decision or ability to take advantage of a third-party supply chain is not casual or arbitrary. It is actually a function of technology development. If made too early, the necessary support system might not exist, resulting in no economic advantage. On the other hand, if made too late, the first mover advantage is lost to competitors. For computer manufacturers, this supply chain began to form after multiple generations of IBM and DEC computers. The 5150 development team was one of the first organizations to take advantage of third-party suppliers to accelerate computer development and manufacturing. The relative openness of the PC provided opportunities for emerging, fast-moving companies to step in and become suppliers, first to IBM, and later within the industry segments that arose.

What IBM did not realize at that time were the emerging supply dynamics characterizing the behaviors of the different elements in the supply chain. The most consequential change probably went unnoticed at the time: A turning point was taking place in the economics driving the supply chain. The single-supplier development pipeline made sense when the computer industry was nascent and there was little in the way of collective knowledge. Even while the company was outsourcing portions of the technology, it was not clear that the development team was aware of its groundbreaking role, the changes it was driving, and the forces it was unleashing. Perhaps even IBM did not internalize the strategic significance of this development until other companies started building "IBM-compatible" PCs and IBM realized it was losing control over the platform architecture.

The company made belated attempts to regain control. In spite of these efforts, the development of the PC had its own momentum beyond IBM's, or as a matter of fact, beyond any single company or organization's ability to control.

One effort to put the genie back in the bottle was the introduction of the IBM Personal System/2 (PS/2) system in 1987, featuring the successor of the first system bus, the Industry Standard Architecture (ISA) bus. IBM designed the successor of the ISA bus, the Micro Channel Architecture (MCA) bus, and promptly proceeded to control its specification and licensing. It did not work. Other manufacturers found the licensing terms to develop compatible machines too onerous and supported industry consortia to develop alternatives, first the extended ISA (EISA) bus, followed by the PCI bus a few years later. The MCA bus was never widely adopted, and the industry, for practical purposes, bypassed this technology.

When IBM published the specifications for expansion cards for the PC, it fueled a market for third-party add-on cards. The initial, basic machine had very limited capability, initially configured with 16 kilobytes (KB) of memory up to a maximum of 64 KB.

The initial machine had rudimentary features with line graphics in the display, and the I/O capability went little beyond the keyboard, display, and a cassette tape. However, the expandability of the machine captured the imagination of the technical community, and the availability of third-party expansion cards quickly took the machine's capabilities well beyond the intent of the original designers and correspondingly increased the machine's value to users. In addition, the variety and functionality of third-party cards went beyond what IBM could have built singlehandedly, bringing value to PC consumers.

PCs have a firmware program built into the machine that runs first when the machine is powered on that allows the machine to recognize certain hardware devices such as hard drives and the video card in preparation for the installation of the OS. This program is known as the *Basic Input/Output System* (BIOS)[4]. IBM required a license for the manufacturers to use the BIOS. In the early 1980s, companies such as Computer Data Products and Compaq reverse-engineered the BIOS, opening the path to the manufacture of PC-compatible machines built without the intervention of IBM. The BIOS has since been replaced by the Unified Extensible Firmware Interface (UEFI), an industry standard.

The decisions IBM made worked as intended in terms of accelerating development schedules, but also had unintended effects: They created new supply chains to provide peripheral cards and storage and memory devices, and eventually the whole machine in the form of IBM-compatible or "IBM clone" machines. The events may not have resulted in the best business outcomes for IBM. However, they fueled new industries in entirely new ecosystems, including platforms for cloud computing today.

The First Wave for Servers: Standard High Volume Servers

By the early 1990s, interoperable and commoditized computer components such as CPUs, memory modules, hard drives, BIOS, and BMC[5] firmware and shrink-wrapped operating systems and firmware became openly and widely available. A new class of companies, the computer OEMs, came onto the scene to participate in this market. The largest participants in this market were IBM, Dell, Hewlett-Packard, and Compaq. At that time, one opportunity ripe for picking, following the pattern of extending the capability of the PC with commoditized components and a scalable supply chain, was to use a PC as a small server. These circumstances led to the concept of standard high-volume server (SHV), horizontally integrated servers built using processes learned from the PC industry.

---

[4]BIOS stands for basic input/output system, a preboot environment that runs immediately after a platform is powered on implementing low-level I/O and configuration functions. For most platforms, a third-party independent software vendor develops the BIOS.

[5]BMC stands for baseboard management controller, a microcontroller installed in a baseboard to implement platform management functions such as power and thermal management, chassis intrusion, and orchestration of the functions of various sensors and actuators installed in the baseboard. In more advanced servers the BIOS implements complex runtime functions such as adding processors to the mix and reconfiguring the system after a memory failure. Most OEMs and ODMs outsource the BMC firmware to third-party firmware independent software vendors (ISVs).

The opportunity ripe for picking was to use components, processes, and supply chains from the PC industry to deliver servers at a fraction of the cost of the existing, vertically manufactured purpose-built servers.

The standard high volume server started taking root when Intel developed derivative CPUs and chipsets for enterprise servers under a model that had worked well for PCs before. This was to become the case for the next 25 years, with OEMs as the largest channel for delivering SHVs.

OEMs function as technology integration powerhouses, with a diversified supply chain to source all the components going into a server, including CPUs, chipsets, memory, storage components, and baseboard or motherboard firmware. In sum, OEMs carry development tasks, including design, test, and validation as defined at the beginning of this section, as well as the platform execution of bringing the platform to market and taking care of customer support. Most OEMs also provide consulting services that go beyond platform-specific services.

Today, specialization and division of labor in the SHV ecosystem has quickened the rate of innovation. For SHVs using Intel processors there is a new generation introduced every year, which brings in a new processor microarchitecture every two years with a process "refresh" in the second year with an improved fabrication process under the well-publicized Intel *tick-tock* model, where the tick brings manufacturing process improvement and the tock brings a new microarchitecture. Introducing innovation at this rate requires significant investment. Completing each cycle is a three- to five-year endeavor from planning to sustaining, and therefore at any given time there is a pipeline with each generation in different stages of completion. This level of investment is possible only because of the demand coming from the large SHV ecosystem. In terms of ecosystem impact, the number of servers OEMs ship collectively every year in this ecosystem is two or three orders of magnitude larger than the numbers in the vertically integrated servers from the prior era.

OEMs have been playing a significant role in terms of their research and development and technology integration perspective. The fact that they use components built to common standards reflects more potential than reality, especially when integration occurs across multiple parties. In practice, standards are subject to interpretation. Beyond that, there might be variances in implementation that could make components behave in unexpected ways or not work at all. Customers expect a working platform when they purchase it, and even when something does not work as expected, from purchasing the product, the OEM provides a support line and an entitlement to get the issue fixed.

To summarize, and as shown in Figure 4-1, OEMs strive to become the single source for server needs to a variety of customers. Customers range from a small business deploying a back-room server to a large enterprise deploying a mission-critical machine in a highly redundant Tier 4 datacenter that requires dual-powered mechanical equipment, fault-tolerant site infrastructure, and local power generation and storage.

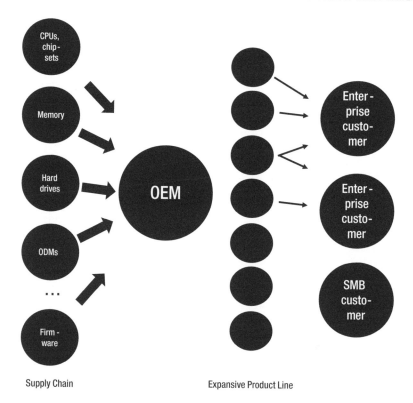

Supply Chain   Expansive Product Line

Figure 4-1. *First-wave server platform ecosystem: the OEM server ecosystem 1990 to 2007, before the cloud, with OEMs as technology integration powerhouses*

In order to satisfy such a broad customer base, the OEM builds and offers an extensive range of server product line. This line could range from small, inexpensive single-CPU PC-derivative servers that can sit under a desk or closet to highly complex, state-of-the-art, 8- to 32-CPU mission-critical, fault-tolerant servers for large enterprise customers deploying servers in their datacenters. The fact that servers at the low end are PC derivatives is a testament to the PC roots of present-day SHV servers.

On the left side of Figure 4-1, we see the technology ingredients and supply chain that feeds the production at any given OEM. The number of alternatives that an OEM can take in the pursuit of a successful business strategy is practically infinite. The strategy could involve deciding which technologies to throw into the mix as well as build versus make decisions. An OEM could manufacture the server or components, such as baseboards, or outsource to third-party contract manufacturers (ODMs), or sidestep the whole issue by purchasing a third-party prefab board. Each decision has an impact on cost, functionality, and product differentiation. OEM offerings also include unique features developed in house. OEMs also need to decide how valuable these features will be to their customers and to assess customer acceptance. A highly valuable feature might only get lukewarm acceptance if customers have trouble integrating the feature with their current infrastructure.

117

The Second Wave: Hyperscale Cloud Servers

When large cloud service providers (CSPs) tried to integrate OEM offerings into their datacenters, they discovered that the established turnkey SHV acquisition model was less than optimal in terms of access to the latest technology, platform cost, manageability, and fitness to business processes. These CSPs had such large orders that working across multiple OEMs became the norm, not the exception, and managing equipment from different OEMs was logistically challenging. In some cases, a large OEM might be able to fulfill such an order from a CSP. However, doing so posed risks on both sides of the transaction. On the OEM side, such large orders imposed considerable pressure on logistics planning for supply chain and manufacturing capacity allocations. The OEM would need follow-through guarantees to ensure that all these elaborate planning efforts would not be wasted in the eventuality of an order cancellation. On the other side, the CSP might feel it was conceding too much authority to the supplying OEMs, with little control over delivery schedules. Because of the heavy investment in the relationship on both sides, qualifying and switching to a new supplier was expensive. A new supplier would bring equipment that, even when mostly built from the same technology components, had different personalities, especially when it came to hardware management and management tools. All these considerations detracted from the objective of cloud for agile, on-demand service delivery.

Advanced server features in which OEMs had a large investment as their value added and to differentiate their products in many cases went unused, either because the features did not work across OEM offerings because of the complexity imposed by large deployments, or because they plainly did not fit the target environment. For instance, CSPs favored scale out, software-based redundancy with fail-in-place policies, and therefore scale-up reliability-availability-serviceability (RAS) hardware-based features became less useful. These RAS features, perhaps useful in an enterprise setting, became overkill and a nonoptional cost drag built into the platform.

The numbers of servers involved in CSP orders were so large that per-unit extra items insignificant in enterprise settings could become deal breakers: a $10 per-board item becomes a $1 million additional cost in an order of 100,000 servers. An example is a strong consideration for boards without BMCs. A powerful BMC with an embedded web server might cost between US$10 and US$25. Some cloud servers use a less capable BMC that might cost only US$2.50, or dispense with the BMC completely by using embedded microcontrollers already present in the processor control hub (PCH) chip such as the Innovation Engine (IE) or the Management Engine (ME). These servers might have a BMC without graphics capability or dispense of a web server supporting a Redfish[6] engine for server management.

Conversely, if a CSP needed a feature not available from an OEM, an engineering change request (ECR) or a product feature request was obligatory, both involving onerous and time-consuming processes. In some cases, the CSP had to wait until the next product cycle to have a necessary feature implemented, a situation they found unacceptable.

---

[6]Redfish is a DMTF standard specification and schema using a RESTful interface using JSON to describe the data object and allows rapid integration of server management. See `https://www.dmtf.org/standards/redfish`.

The resolution of the dissonance between the cloud providers' new requirements and the traditional SHV model brings us to the current situation today, at least with the largest cloud providers (see Figure 4-2). Under the current state of the art, a company with a demand of 100,000 servers or more per year can afford not just to have an OEM build a special model or stock-keeping unit (SKU). At these demand levels, customers can justify the development of a server architecture to suit their application needs. This dynamic led to the notion of an application-specific cloud platform (ASCP), which we cover in the next few chapters. Under this dynamic, every instance of this architecture is essentially a custom architecture. Leading CSPs like Google, Facebook, and Amazon started building their own specifications and in some cases skipped OEMs altogether, using the manufacturing services of ODMs.

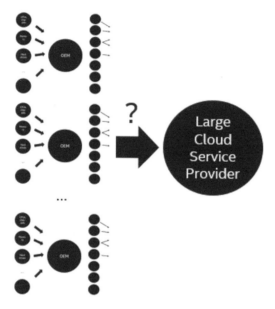

Figure 4-2. *The traditional SHV model breaks with hyperscale dynamics and procurements over 100,000 servers*

Initially the CSPs kept the details of their in-house architecture under wraps. However, in 2011 Facebook realized that the same open source dynamic that played out with software development 15 years before, especially with OS software, could also apply to cloud server designs and specifications, and therefore took a bold step to make their server specifications public under the *Open Compute Project* (OCP).

Since then OCP has become an independent, nonprofit entity. Facebook stood to gain from this move on two fronts: By open sourcing their design, and by virtue of the momentum of their initial demand, Facebook made it worthwhile for engineers, architects, and contributors industry-wide to join the effort. These contributions to architecture and product development reduce Facebook's cost per unit, even with customizations. OCP participants get a ready-made technology base requiring only incremental development to get the customized capabilities they want. All participants get the benefit of amortizing development costs over a much larger production base than if they had gone alone. The result of this effort is a considerable enrichment of the initial design through the participation of the new players, with a very small incremental research and development expenditure for the platform owners.

In other words, a virtuous circle takes place whereby external participants working with other CSPs adopt and deploy OCP designs, and have the designs manufactured to order by ODMs. Because OCP is an industry specification, there is minimal retooling cost for ODMs with experience manufacturing OCP-specification platforms. The additional platform demand increases the OCP demand base, lowering the cost per unit. OCP platform procurement transactions are no longer private transactions between Facebook and an ODM contract manufacturer. By the end of 2014 and early 2015, an ecosystem of OCP solution providers began to form. A cloud provider, or as a matter of fact, any organization that can make use of OCP hardware, can go to any of these solution providers and purchase OCP spec platforms. These players include Quanta Computer, Hyve Solutions, and Hewlett-Packard Enterprise. The participation of Quanta Computer, one of the ODMs that built OCP platforms for Facebook initially, is notable, trying to capitalize their OCP manufacturing experience.

For Quanta Computer this trajectory has been nothing short of transformative. The analyst firm Moor Insights & Strategy estimates that Quanta's direct sales to datacenter customers constituted about 85 percent of their server business by the end of 2014[7]. Likewise, Hewlett-Packard Enterprise represents a traditional OEM transforming itself to play in the cloud platform market, through the HPE Cloudline products, manufactured in partnership with Foxconn, another prominent ODM player worldwide[8].

Figure 4-3 illustrates the new dynamic for cloud servers, where manufacturers not only use standardized parts, but also build to a common specification, driving economies of scale and lowering cost per unit. This scheme becomes economically feasible because of the large, concentrated demand coming from the community of cloud service providers. These servers are customized or purpose-built to the needs of the end user CSPs. We refer to servers designed and built under this dynamic as instances of application-specific cloud servers (ASCS).

[7]Moor Insights & Strategy, "Quanta's Server Business: Can They Scale Beyond Hyperscale?," http://www.moorinsightsstrategy.com/research-paper-quanta%E2%80%99s-server-business-can-they-scale-beyond-hyperscale/ 2014.

[8]P. Moorhead, "OCP Summit: HP and Foxconn Blur Server Industry Lines with Cloudline," Forbes, http://www.forbes.com/sites/patrickmoorhead/2015/03/10/ocp-summit-hewlett-packard-and-foxconn-blur-server-industry-lines-with-cloudline/#41f22b733e94, March 10, 2015.

Manufacturing and integrating ASCPs places traditional players into new roles. As mentioned earlier, bringing a new platform to market requires a number of steps, regardless of who performs them. The names for each step and the boundaries between them can vary slightly depending on particular cases. For the purposes of this discussion, we identify three:

- *Platform design:* Design involves taking the standardized components and producing a blueprint for the target platform. One of the most complex parts for a new platform is the baseboard schematics, including the printed circuit CAD diagrams. For baseboards using Intel processors, a design is a pipeline delivering a new product roughly every year. Because a design cycle can last two to three years, a new generation design needs to start even when the prior generation design is still in midflight.

- *Platform test and validation:* Platform testing refers to performing functional testing of the various subsystems individually in a new platform with less emphasis on how the different subsystems interact. Platform validation is an engineering process to ensure that the newly designed platform meets the specified functional and performance behaviors. For example, the platform might have a memory RAS capability to map out a whole chip in a DIMM memory module. However, being able to do so depends on a complex procedure that operates two DIMM ranks in lockstep, executed by an interrupt handler and the BIOS. A validation exercise will actually run a platform through this sequence to verify that all the steps execute correctly, and most important, that no data is lost when a fault of this type (i.e., a chip malfunction) actually occurs.

- *Systems integration:* Systems integration repeats the design and validation pattern, but at the application level. For cloud servers it usually means provisioning the manufactured servers with memory and peripherals, populating the expansion slots, and placing the servers into racks. One of the focus areas for systems integration is rack-level power management; for instance, ensuring that the rack power draw is within specs at various loading levels and that group power management policies for servers in the rack work as expected.

The process in Figure 4-3 brings certain ambiguity that puts actors in new, unfamiliar roles. The platform specification might be in a relatively high-level form that defines functional behavior, perhaps at the register transfer level (RTL). ODMs will be familiar with instantiating an actual design from an RTL description, figuring out the actual board layout and the values for circuit components. However, validation is a more traditional OEM function, and the absence of an ODM in its traditional role brings challenges and can create conflict with an unspoken expectation from the CSP to take on validation tasks, based on prior experience with OEMs. On the other side, the ODM might resist taking on this new role on the assumption that this requirement is beyond the traditional scope of contract manufacturing. The downside to this dynamic is an impact on quality control and development delays while participants solve role issues. Delays due to process ambiguity tend to be more serious than regular implementation delays.

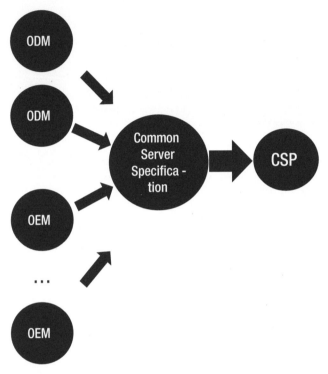

Figure 4-3. Second wave cloud server ecosystem: resolves the multi-OEM quandary for CSPS, with a diversity of manufacturing entities building up to a common specification

The Third Wave: Platforms for Vertical Cloud Operators

One interesting consideration in this analysis is figuring out how to amortize the cost for *nonrecurring engineering* (NRE). This cost covers the development of the platform specification and producing the first design instance. Facebook defrayed the cost for the original OCP platform. Microsoft did the same with the Windows Cloud Server that eventually became an OCP contribution and became the Open Cloud Server (OCS) specification. There is a minimum manufacturing run of server units (nodes) needed to justify the investment. Our estimate is that at the current state of the art, this break-even point lies at around 100,000 servers.

Newer entrants beyond the largest seven worldwide operators (Amazon, Google, Microsoft, Facebook, Baidu, Alibaba, and Tencent) are smaller and do not have the critical mass to create a cloud subecosystem by themselves or to build an ASCS architecture by themselves as the largest seven do. Participants in the third wave tend to be vertical players. Examples are JD.com in China and FlipKart in India with a play in e-commerce; and eBay, PayPal, and Rackspace in the United States, leaders in electronic auctions, payment systems, and bare metal services, respectively. In addition, even for the largest seven CSP operators, the Scorpio specification was not the work of a single company, but the fruit of an industry collaboration of Baidu, Alibaba, Tencent, and Intel in the People's Republic of China. For newer entrants in the third wave, there are opportunities that were not available at the ramp of the second wave. The cost of entry or price to play will be much lower, probably by at least an order of magnitude, for several reasons.

- First, the heavy lifting of creating a cloud platform spec is already in place. OCP provides a public, ready-made, existing platform usable as a launching pad for additional development by third-wave entrants.

- Second, there is the learning curve factor: On the supply side, ODMs like Quanta, Inventec, or Wiwynn already have experience building platforms to OCP spec from manufacturing platforms for the large service providers and can potentially deliver valuable customizations with much lower NRE given that they have already made the investment in manufacturing processes to build their OCP offerings. These customizations are valuable to match the OCP platform to the third-wave players' needs in their vertical niches.

- Third, a supply chain for OCP spec platforms began forming in late 2014 and early 2015; therefore new entrants can order product from a competitive diversity of ODMs offering OCP products as a regular line-of-business product offering instead of building them under a special, one-of-a-kind project. The original platform sponsors benefit from the economies of scale of a much larger installed base.

Given these considerations, Figure 4-4 shows a likely evolution of the second-wave environment into a third wave, with multiple adopters of a common cloud platform specification. These platforms are public, making them effectively an open hardware specification. In practice, there will be more than one common specification: The original OCP spec and OCS represent two different form factors. OCP machines come in third width, two OpenU tall modules plugged into to respective direct current bus bars in the back. The original OCP from Facebook specifies a *power shelf* with seven power supply units (PSUs) in the middle of the rack, whereas OCS platforms feature six power supplies located behind the blades. OCS platforms come packaged in 12U-tall chassis with a variety of blades. The OCP OpenU pitch is 48 mm, slightly larger than the standard EIA 1.75-inch rack unit pitch.

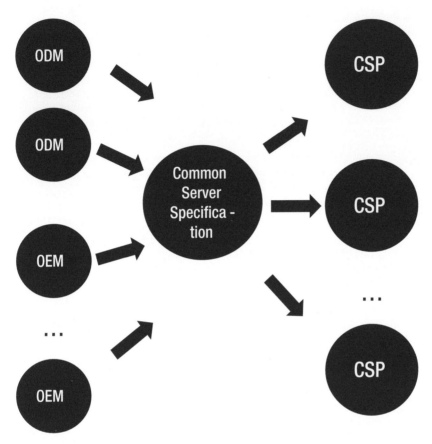

Figure 4-4. *Third wave: Evolved common server ecosystem serving multiple CSPs in a more diversified cloud service ecosystem*

The published specifications are not necessarily complete; the spec creators left certain components unspecified, or with proprietary, undisclosed implementations. In particular, Scorpio, for instance, is mainly a rack specification. It specifies the size of the PSU bay in the power shelf but not the number of PSUs or the size of the PSUs to install. These gaps allow for innovation and for additional industry players to provide alternatives to fill in these gaps as additional OCP contributions. Proprietary implementations are an option to use as implementation plug-ins or modules to fill in functionality gaps. However, doing so could increase the platform average selling price and generate some customer resistance. This path requires some investment in OCP, as it still requires negotiating and publishing the appropriate interfaces. Whether or not this path makes sense depends on the particular business strategy in place.

The NRE to bring up customized cloud platforms under a third-wave platform will be much lower than in the prior wave given that only the NRE cost to build a platform instance will accrue, not the cost to architect a new platform from the ground up. Our estimate is that the break-even point for NRE will go down by about one order of magnitude, to the order of 10,000 delivered nodes. We might start seeing the beginnings of vertical specialization. Even in cases where a single organization does not have the resources to cover the NRE, similar organizations could work together and form consortia to develop OCP variants addressing the needs of a specific vertical segment; for instance, e-commerce or analytics platforms, or platforms for small financial institutions such as credit unions and savings and loans banks.

Fourth Wave: Emergence of Service Networks

For the fourth wave and beyond, with the industry having gone through successive learning curves, we can anticipate even lower barriers to server customization. We expect the cost for customization to go lower by another order of magnitude, to about 1,000 servers. Crossing this threshold will allow new, even smaller entrants, namely value added resellers (VARs) and systems integrators (SIs). A VAR is a company that operates within a specific area of expertise or vertical segment and takes a baseboard design, configures and customizes it, integrating in applications to deliver a turnkey solution.

Today, companies that cater to VARs, such as SuperMicro, carry dozens of SKU variants to address every single need. These variants include the board form factor, number of CPUs supported, number and type of expansion slots, the type of chipset, the way the available PCIe lines are allocated, number and type of memory slots, presence of ECC and RAS features, and so on. Under current manufacturing processes, these manufacturers carry a SKU for each variant primarily because verifying correct functionality for each variant requires allocation of validation engineering resources. As previously described, validation is labor-intensive and usually represents the main gating factor for the delivery of a design variant. With increased manufacturing process and technology integration maturity, we can expect more predictable product outcomes, where it becomes possible to build most of these variants on a build-to-order (BTO) basis. ODMs might need to perform validation anyway, but ideally executed in days, not months. This enhanced design for a manufacturing capability would allow a VAR, perhaps building a solution for a smaller ISP or datacenter operator, to go to a manufacturer portal, place an order for a customized product, and have it delivered a few weeks later.

Depending on business need, cloud assets might be deployed externally through the public cloud, or internally in private clouds. The same dynamics driving the need for customization will be present for private cloud deployments. However, these single-enterprise deployments, by definition encompassing one business, will each be smaller than those at CSPs subject to demand aggregation. Therefore the private cloud market will likely be better served by value-added resellers or VARs.

Business dynamics will also be different; the transactions will not be just about server procurement, but will be also about VARs integrating cloud services into their offerings as well as other kinds of devices, not just servers. At this point we can see a convergence between cloud computing and the Internet of things (IoT).

With the continued learning curve, we can expect that the break-even point for customizations getting smaller and smaller, thereby bringing up opportunities for VARs and SIs as previously noted. The focus of the supply chain will shift to smaller and smaller CSPs. There are two distinguishing transitions in this new environment:

- *Transition from monolithic services to infrastructure services:* Second-wave CSPs have a large footprint with a deployed server base of hundreds of thousands, if not millions, of servers. Their business model depends on offering a broad portfolio of services to businesses large and small as well as to individual consumers, where they strive to become the one-stop provider of cloud services to their customers. These large operators can be self-sufficient in their infrastructure, and yet offer a broad portfolio of externally visible services.

- For instance, Microsoft lists more than 50 services under Azure, including PaaS to publish and manage web sites, Active Directory, business analytics, and development environments, to cite a few. Services to the consumer include Windows Live Hotmail, Skype video and voice calling, Xbox gaming, and Onedrive storage. Likewise, Amazon Web Services (AWS) lists more than 50 services in 12 primary areas in computing, storage and content delivery, and enterprise applications, to cite a few[9]. Figure 4-5 shows this pattern. Interestingly, this pattern bears a certain resemblance to the OEM ecosystem shown in Figure 4-2, where the offerings are not from an extensive line of server products, but in terms of various service offerings.

- *Transition to infrastructure services and service networks:* The transition to the third wave, with smaller players, saw some degree of vertical specialization across the portfolio of services represented in Figure 4-5; for instance, with eBay providing auction services to individual consumers and former subsidiary PayPal providing online payment services. However, the actual business dynamics are richer than that: eBay customers continue using PayPal services, even though PayPal is now a different company. Conversely, PayPal established partnerships with MasterCard to enable PayPal customers to generate a single-use MasterCard number at checkout time for vendors that do not accept PayPal directly. PayPal has similar arrangements with Discover card.

---

[9]See https://aws.amazon.com/products/ for a current listing.

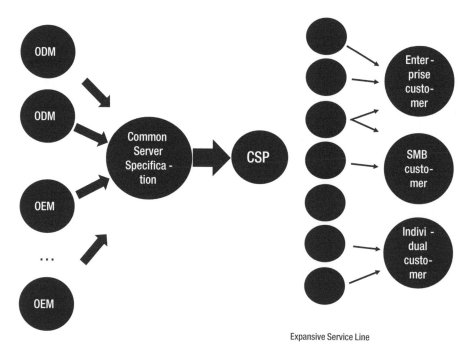

Expansive Service Line

Figure 4-5. *Third-wave one-stop shop service model.*

What we are seeing here is a transition from a flat, single-level service ecosystem where every customer is the direct consumer of a cloud service from a CSP to an ecosystem of *infrastructure cloud services*. The consumer of an infrastructure service might not be an end customer, but uses third-party service offerings as components to build higher level service offerings to be marketed separately. The new composite service in turn becomes a component for other services, effectively defining a new supply chain. In other words, instead of flat universe consisting of end customers purchasing services from a CSP for a direct user, now we have a *service network*. Figure 4-6 captures the conceptual notion of a service network. There are two types of nodes in this network: nonterminal nodes, or CSPs, and terminal nodes, the service consumers. A service consumer can be an individual node or a business, a direct service consumer in the sense that there is no intent to ue service resources to provide services to other entities.

We expect that as the industry matures, the offerings in this new service supply chain will eventually become normalized, subject to specifications in a way not much different from the OCP specifications today. We would like to think that technology components, whether physical as a JEDEC-spec memory DIMM, or virtualized or a service, are conceptually the same and part of the same service supply chain. Under the current state of the art, we are not there yet. Although the breadth of service offerings might be useful and immediately convenient to some users, in the long term it makes it difficult for these users to switch service providers, or even combine offerings from other providers into an existing application portfolio. This is one of the ironies of the cloud service ecosystem today: Although clouds use interoperable hardware technology components at the bottom of their implementation stacks, the service offerings coming from service providers tend to be unique. As we see in the Amazon–Netflix case study, this situation makes it very difficult to switch providers, or even to seek additional providers to complement Amazon's offerings. A healthy cloud ecosystem will require interoperable service offerings available to customers from multiple providers, large and small, in a diversified and level competitive field. We expect that this transition will occur in the fourth wave, in the transition to infrastructure services and service networks.

A service provider has a choice between building and deploying in-house assets, such as a datacenter to build composite services, or outsourcing the acquisition of services from third-party providers to augment a service portfolio. Even a large CSP operating hyperscale datacenters worldwide might decide to deploy servers hosted by third-party providers to deliver services from certain localities, whether required by regulation or for performance reasons.

In a similar pattern to what took place in enterprise space, the supply chains established to supply the needs of the large CSPs in the second wave will continue. The growth of this segment will likely taper off gradually, to be picked up by the demand from the smaller CSPs, much in the same way large CSPs caught some of the demand that would have gone to the enterprise segment during the first wave.

Extrapolating this pattern, demand from third-wave service providers will also taper off, giving way to fourth-wave entrants in an emerging IoT ecosystem. We can expect some cloud customers, especially large enterprise customers, to shun the one-stop shop service model and gravitate toward a diversified portfolio of service providers, as shown in Figure 4-6.

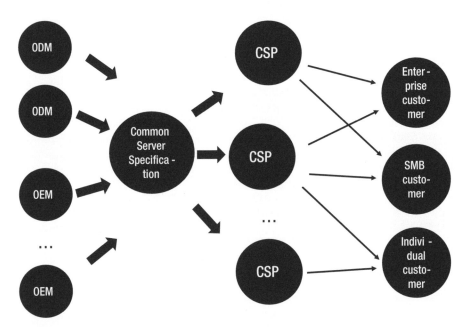

Figure 4-6. *The beginning of the fourth wave: Customers opting for a diversified service portfolio*

The CSP world will not stay flat for long as Figure 4-6 depicts, with each CSP maintaining a physical infrastructure looking left, and serving end customers on the right. It is reasonable to expect that some SaaS players will not be bothered with maintaining an in-house physical infrastructure and would rather use PaaS offerings from other CSPs. We can also expect a degree of specialization whereby some CSPs will cater to end customers as most of them do today, whereas others will focus on offering servicelets for use by other service providers. We can distinguish the former as *edge* CSPs, and we can call the latter *infrastructure* CSPs, whether or not they deploy physical infrastructure. Figure 4-7 represents this evolved fourth-wave infrastructure, where the initial flat service environment becomes a service network.

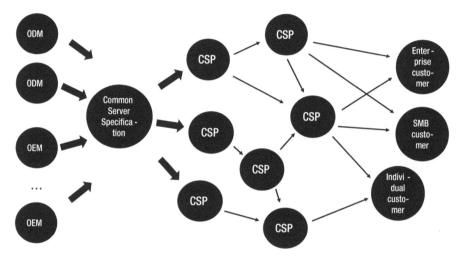

Figure 4-7. *Evolved fourth wave: Customers opting for a diversified service ecosystem*

A very powerful force drives this transition toward service networks: It is the same dynamic in Coase's principle, the desire for each player individually and collectively to lower transaction costs. The CSP nodes in this emergent service network will likely exhibit some degree of functional specialization: Some CSPs provide a storage service, others offer media rendering services, and yet other CSPs are part of a content delivery network. In turn, this functional specialization suggests that these CSPs might benefit from deploying platforms especially tailored to the CSP's mission, assuming that these platforms can be configured to the CSP's requirements.

In other words, we begin to see that the dynamics that applied to large CSPs in the second wave also applied to smaller CSPs, possibly with small, but not fundamental differences. For instance, some aggregation might be necessary, perhaps across CSPs operating in a similar field to amortize platform development NRE across the larger base of like-minded CSPs. In other words, the ASCP concept also applies to smaller

CSPs. These customizations, being cost driven, will likely be small variations over a base platform, for instance:

- Adding an FPGA processor when called for a content rendering application.

- The use of nonvolatile memory for applications needing lower latency than can be attained with solid state drives.

- The implementation of a specific power management behavior through a baseboard logic modification.

- By "de-contenting" components expected to remain unused during the machine's life cycle.

- By precisely provisioning and configuring the hardware platform according to a published specification. The published platform specification allows configuration to the needs of the target application. One example is the memory footprint. Overprovisioned memory might be wasted, and underprovisioning could result in an underperforming platform.

Figure 4-8 captures a more detailed snapshot of the service network, where we see CSPs making a business from the servicelets they implement. These servicelets are not self-standing; they use servicelets from other CSPs. Conceptually the CSPs in this evolved environment can be large, effectively as large as AWS, or as small as a single-person business. Actually, it can be even smaller, at which point the CSP need not be a business entity; it can be a machine communicating with another machine and providing services for other machines to consume. We can even extend this line of thought to a virtualized environment, where the nodes are virtual machines or even processes in the traditional sense of OS service processes or daemons.

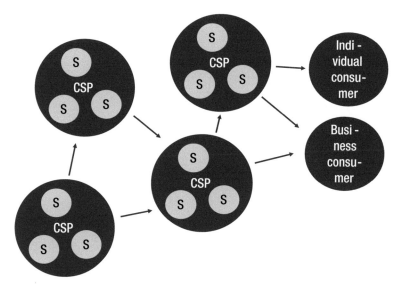

Figure 4-8. *The fourth wave: Transition to a cloud infrastructure ecosystem and convergence with IoT*

Innovative new cloud services might come less from established cloud players and more from highly innovative and nimble smaller players. These players will not be saddled by the task of developing basic services from the ground up; they can build new services by composing lower level services. If called for by their business needs, they can avail themselves of the composition of finer grained, composable hardware components, manufacturable on demand, effectively bringing the convergence between today's customized cloud platforms and the IoT.

Internal Intel studies suggest that in the middle of the decade of the 2010s, two thirds of the server demand goes to fulfill the needs of cloud operators delivering services directly to consumers and only one third of the demand goes to serve infrastructure and private cloud services. Out of that two-thirds ratio, 40 percent belongs to demand from the largest one-stop-shop cloud providers. We can expect this ratio to reverse by the early 2020s, when the majority of servers will be for servers in organizations delivering infrastructure services. This dynamic suggests new business models not yet implemented, at least on a large scale; for instance, a directory service for services. Google started as a directory service for humans accessing Web sites. This hypothetical service directory would need to provide automated machine access through an application programming interface (API), instead of a web site for humans. Existing protocols such as UDDI and WSDL are useful to get started, but likely insufficient; users of the service also need to get information about quality of service, including historical information and forecasts, information about security, and bindings to established management protocols. Also important will be the business aspects: licensing, legal, technology import and export restrictions, pricing, billing, and account settlement. These concepts relate to data about services and auxiliary services, covered in Chapter 9.

Cloud Platforms Evolution Summary

We have covered 60 years of computer history and the dynamics that led to the concept of SHV. Figure 4-9 provides a synthesis of the concept we have covered so far regarding the evolution of cloud platforms starting with their SHV incarnation. The graphic tracks four overlapping waves in this evolution; this is the reason we call them *waves* and not *generations,* because earlier waves persist as a new one comes in. We can expect traditional SHVs to continue having a significant segment of market play in the marketplace in the near future. Likewise, second-wave platforms continue growing at a fast pace.

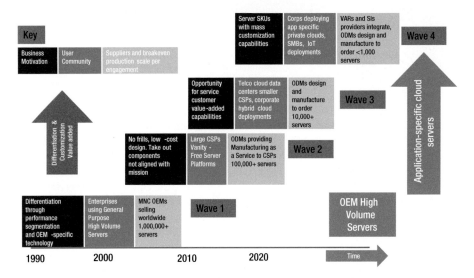

Figure 4-9. *Evolution of cloud platforms*

We track three parameters for each wave: the business motivation behind the server platform, the user community, and break-even points to make production viable. The dynamics of the first platform are well known, starting in the early 1990s with large OEMs delivering highly differentiated platforms and the main consumers being enterprises large and small. The production scale needed to deliver this degree of differentiation is on the order of 1 million servers per year. Smaller OEMs start from reference designs, and their collective demand is still in the millions.

The era of ASCS starts with the second wave, where the main drivers are large CSPs seeking optimized, low-cost, no-frills designs. The second wave started around 2009 or 2010. ODMs, functioning as contract manufacturers, delivered these platforms. From patterns of market participation, the NRE break-even threshold is on the order of 100,000 servers per year.

The third wave, with lower barriers to entry, opens opportunities for new, smaller entrants to deploy customized cloud platforms. This wave started around 2015, when a supply chain for OCP platforms emerged, enabling businesses to order and customize these platforms. The third wave effectively rides on the learning curve from the second wave. Our estimation is that a customized cloud platform is now viable for an ODM delivering on the order of 10,000 to 100,000 servers per year. The ODM can make a business by delivering variants to more than one end customers to achieve the necessary production scale, as shown in Figure 4-4. There are new entrants beyond the very large edge CSPs such as Amazon or Microsoft. We will see increasing participation from infrastructure CSPs and smaller edge CSPs with minimal physical infrastructure, implementing their services mostly on top of third-party services. There is also participation from niche cloud providers, for instance telcos such as NTT Communications providing very high-quality, near-mission-critical cloud services and serving large corporations. This strategy avoids direct competition with large CSPs providing utility-like services to millions of individual consumers.

We anticipate that the fourth wave will ramp up in full force around 2020, although we are beginning to see inklings of it as suggested in the discussion of Figure 4-8. A fundamental requisite to make the fourth wave viable is a capability to perform manufacturing to order in small batches, preferably in quantities less than 1,000. One challenge under the current state of the art is that changes in the board layout from a customization imply significant cost in time and labor from revalidation. A higher level of manufacturing automation than what is available today is needed, from the ordering process to compiling the customization requests into a design variant and having it built at a factory with the expectation that the board will work without further intervention.

Because of the IoT component, we can expect increasing participation of smaller players in the fourth wave, in other words. These nodes or players in the graph might not be strictly CSPs; they might be implemented as VAR solution instances or by SIs. In the end, the majority of nodes will be simply machines talking to other machines in an automated fashion; these nodes consume data, but also generate data to be consumed by other entities in the service network.

Traditional OEMs are also evolving with changes in the industry, with the largest two OEMs establishing divisions to deliver customized servers into cloud space, with Dell DCS having a capability to design and build customized boards, and Hewlett-Packard Enterprise joining forces with ODM Foxconn to manufacture their Cloudline servers, built under an OCP specification.

Enterprise systems will coevolve with the cloud in the next few years. Moving forward, studying the underlying processes driving cloud platform demand can give us some insight about how the demand for enterprise servers will evolve in the near future. The graph in Figure 4-10 depicts an estimate of the growth of the total addressable market (TAM) for enterprise and cloud servers. It suggests that after 2007, when the cloud started, we can expect the demand for enterprise servers to remain flat for the near future. This suggests that as IT functions migrate to the cloud, cloud platforms take out all the expected growth that would have taken place in the enterprise segment. We can expect second-wave demand to continue growing at least through 2020. Third-wave demand will start picking up in 2016, and eventually might surpass second-wave demand. Fourth-wave demand will start picking up around 2020. This demand includes servers deployed in cloud datacenters and does not include embedded IoT nodes or edge devices, which technically are not servers. Business planners will be interested in breaking out the ODM server component in the graph by second-, third-, and fourth-wave participants. Unfortunately, we are not aware of any forecasting model that would allow estimating these numbers.

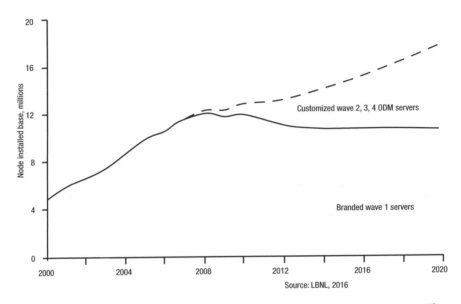

Source: LBNL, 2016

Figure 4-10. *Installed base, enterprise OEM branded servers versus application-specific ODM cloud servers*[10]

Looking at Figure 4-11, and as previously mentioned, growth in the enterprise segment tapers off during the second wave as applications or application components migrate to the cloud. We can expect this segment to retain significant presence in the market through 2020. Deployments in corporate datacenters will continue growing overall, except that most of this growth is for private clouds and counted in the ODM segment. This migration is a gradual process; enterprises need to tread cautiously to avoid affecting their internal SLAs. In addition, migration of individual applications proceeds in small quanta; large, complex applications are not monolithic; software and service-oriented architecture (SOA) engineers will redesign applications into service collaborating service components (*servicelets*) with servicelets moving to the cloud selectively depending on SLA. For instance, storage for some noncritical back-end databases might end up outsourced to storage providers, whereas the enterprise crown jewels stay in house.

<hr>

[10]*Data Center Energy Usage Report* (Lawrence Berkeley National Laboratory: U.S. Department of Energy, 2016).

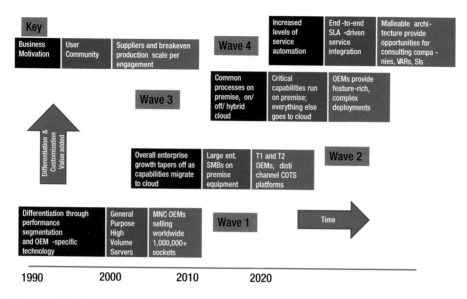

Figure 4-11. *Co-evolution of enterprise platforms with the cloud*

The proliferation of application-specific platforms during the third wave does not necessarily imply balkanization or the formation of technology islands. To the contrary, for end users it will be highly valuable to be able to deploy common business and manageability processes regardless of whether a resource is local or remote, implemented in hardware, or in a private or a public cloud, even across customized platforms. The valuable lesson learned from CSPs is the leveraging of common abstract platforms regardless of manufacturer, building up to compatible hardware and software APIs. For instance, customers will value a common experience regardless of brand or level of customization. We can expect increased deployments of bare metal facilities because it will facilitate uniform manageability schema for hybrid deployments and because bare metal deployments can deliver higher levels of security and privacy and a mitigated noisy neighbor problem. Innovation takes place through integration at multiple levels, whenever there are opportunities to deliver improvements in functionality, performance, and reliability to customers.

For the fourth wave, we can expect to see increased levels of automation in the form of automated service discovery, negotiation, billing, and cost settlement, all based on standardized technical and business processes. Highly specialized application-specific platforms will become valuable in this context. Examples are a scale-out service scheme using similar services from multiple providers to improve throughput and reliability. A highly secure scheme might include partitioning or striping a data set through multiple providers. Applications could be domain specific where a consulting house, a VAR, or an SI add significant value to the solution stack.

Long term, we expect in-house, hybrid cloud and pure cloud deployments to coexist. The expectation is that all resources will follow a common management framework, and the actual location of resources will be driven by SLA objectives and not technical limitations.

Uber Service Transformation Example

Let us look at a couple of service transformation examples. Uber and Netflix reflect two different architectural approaches, yet both companies have realized that the traditional approach with a focus on the physical infrastructure does not provide the agility required to meet their fast growth. They cannot move atoms fast enough to track the turns and twists of business, and they have both internalized that a set of loosely coupled, collaborating services will get them as close to meeting business demands as technology today allows. In the following sections we analyze the two case studies presented in[11] and[12].

Uber works like a utility, providing rides on demand in hundreds of cities across the world. The number of cities served is growing at a fast pace. The company has been scaling the engineering and IT organization to match this growth, where the size of the staff has gone from 40 to 1,200 in less than two years.

Having control over the complete technology portfolio is an important consideration for Uber, and the company has elected to deploy most resources in house, including practically all components down to procuring servers, except the datacenter physical infrastructure. Uber hosts its servers from several infrastructure providers to remove dependencies on any single provider, and does not use technology components from a large provider such as Amazon to eliminate the possibility of lock-in. This is contrary to what many startups do, using prepackaged and proprietary cloud servicelets in the interest of time to market.

There are two critical mobile applications for Uber operations across the globe: The first application interacts with drivers and customers to dispatch a car and track progress toward a passenger pickup and toward the destination. The second application handles customer enrollment and fare calculations. The dispatching application runs on the *Node.js* JavaScript runtime, whereas the billing application uses the Python interpreted programming language.

For historical reasons two separate development teams were in charge of the two applications, with minimal coordination between them. During the current period of rapid growth, the two teams could implement new capabilities faster by working as independent teams. There were simmering conflicts across teams due to the two different subcultures and development philosophies, however. Eventually the two functions grew up into two silos in the classical sense. The only common resource in this environment was the shared, leased datacenter buildings. The limited communication led to resource duplication for some of the stack components above the physical infrastructure. Figure 4-12 shows this structure.

---

[11]A. Efrati, "Inside Uber's Engineering Struggles," *The Information,* https://www.theinformation.com/inside-ubers-engineering-struggles, September 21, 2015; R. Miller, "Uber Scales up Its Data Centers to Support Growth, Data Center Frontier," http://datacenterfrontier.com/uber-data-center-expansion/, January 12, 2016.

[12]Y. Izrailevsky, S. Vlaovic, and R. Meshenberg, "Completing the Netflix Cloud Migration," https://media.netflix.com/en/company-blog/completing-the-netflix-cloud-migration, February 11, 2016; J. Brodkin, "Netflix Finishes Its Massive Migration to the Amazon Cloud," *Ars Technica,* http://arstechnica.com/information-technology/2016/02/netflix-finishes-its-massive-migration-to-the-amazon-cloud/, February 11, 2016.

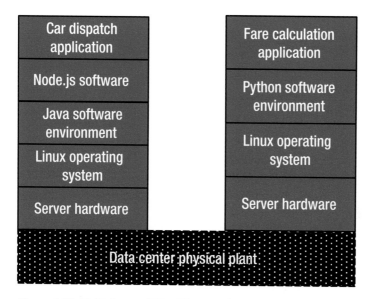

Figure 4-12. *Initial state of IT at Uber: Application silos*

There were a number of subsystem outages under the silo environment traced to dissonances in implementation processes, quality control, and coordination of operational procedures. Fortunately, most of the outages did not affect actual service delivery, but served as warning calls for a much needed system architecture retooling.

The solution that Uber came up with is a classic SOA transformation, breaking apart the siloed layers and reorganizing the layers into loosely coupled servicelets, about 450 in total. This architecture allows consolidating servicelets with like functionality, thereby reducing duplication of resources. This environment reduces operational expenses compared to the previous multiple-stack, tightly coupled architecture. Loose coupling allows services to be replaced, optimized, or modified to improve security and as part of capacity planning, minimizing side effects with neighboring services. Loose coupling also implies late binding. With tight coupling in a stack, changes in components in the stack might require rebuilding and revalidating the whole stack, a time-consuming and risky task that could lead to scheduled and even unscheduled outages. Figure 4-13 captures the new architecture, essentially Uber's instantiation of the infrastructure services ecosystem depicted in Figure 4-7. Instead of the traditional chimney stacks below the two applications, the transformed application infrastructure now runs on top of a service network undergirding. Each circle with an *S* represents a supporting servicelet. The servicelets run on Uber computers installed at third-party hosting providers, represented by circles with a *C*. Uber uses a multiplicity of physical infrastructure providers. The service network running on top of the hosted server is entirely Uber's.

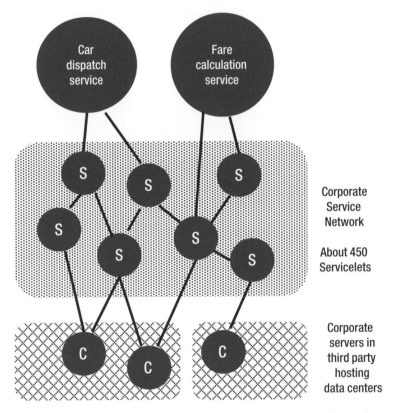

Figure 4-13. *Uber application architecture after a service-oriented transformation*

This architecture is not intrinsically cloud-oriented, except for the trivial case of the third-party hosted infrastructure. However, this modular structure allows functional components to be moved to the cloud, horizontally, for instance, by rehosting the components on top of a third-party *Node.js* IaaS offering, or vertically by replacing selected components with cloud SaaS offerings. Uber can carry out this second phase replacement based on specific architectural or business criteria instead of a forklift replacement to the cloud, which would carry its own risks.

The two example applications from Uber are not necessarily only endpoints, in the sense of having these applications consumed exclusively by paying customers or car drivers. Uber could define APIs for third-party developers to adopt and implement additional capabilities, for example:

- Scheduling the delivery of a car at a certain time.

- Scheduling large groups requiring multiple cars.

- Integrating the Uber service with other applications, such as arranging transportation for tours.

- Scheduling multimodal trips or tours, such as airport pickups.

Netflix Service Transformation Example

Netflix represents the case of a company that internalized early on the use of the cloud for scalability. In our initial snapshot, Netflix has already deployed one of its main applications in the cloud, streaming video content on top of Amazon IaaS and PaaS. Unfortunately, their business applications, such as billing and customer and employee data management were still running on a traditional in-house stack. Netflix realized that due to its demand growth, it also needed to migrate the business applications to the cloud.

Figure 4-14 depicts the initial state, where Netflix runs its streaming services on top of an application service network, represented by the solid *S* circles. The service network in turn runs on top of Amazon-provided PaaS servicelets or on top of Amazon Elastic Compute Cloud (ECC) virtual machine IaaS servicelets. The virtual machines in turn run on top of servers housed in Amazon datacenters.

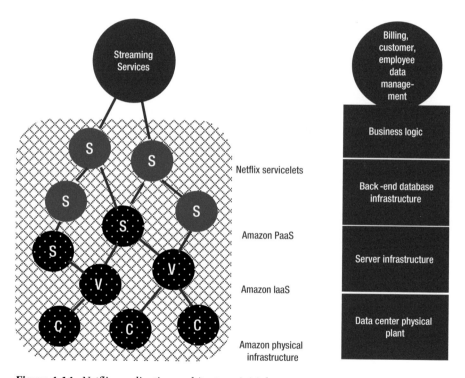

Figure 4-14. *Netflix application architecture, initial state*

Figure 4-15 depicts the evolved system, showing some of the actual servicelets. Some synergies become immediately evident: Some of the databases could be deployed using Amazon NoSQL database servicelets, and it is now possible to start sharing servicelets across applications, such as databases and the analytics and recommendations engines, regardless of whether it is a Netflix or an Amazon-provided servicelet. This obviates potential data synchronization and resource duplication issues. Netflix can carry out tactical optimization for some of the servicelets and switch between Netflix and Amazon offerings, depending on performance or security considerations, such as the transcoding modules. In addition, although Figure 4-15 does not show it, under the evolved architecture, Netflix still has the option of hosting critical databases on premises, although the claim is that Netflix does not contemplate this alternative anymore given that it has decommissioned all its datacenters and instead the company relies on Amazon-provided services. We can look at Figure 4-15 as an instantiation of a third-wave environment where Amazon is the one-stop shop unique provider and Netflix is a corporate customer.

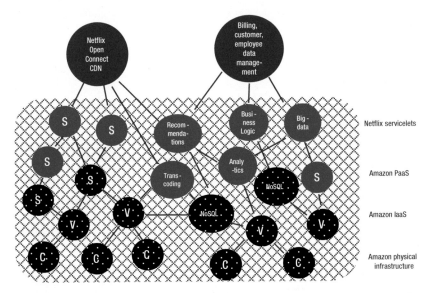

Figure 4-15. *Netflix application architecture after the integration of business applications*

The resulting architecture is highly reliable, allowing service replication for redundancy as well as for capacity planning. This type of redundancy is scale-out redundancy at the service level rather than with hardware RAS technology. Netflix can enforce redundancy along specific service metadata attributes, such as the zonal or geographic location of the services. One type of redundancy not possible under this architecture is provider redundancy; Netflix has a 100 percent dependency on AWS. It does not have the option of switching service providers because many of the service PaaS service offerings from AWS are not available anywhere else. There is also potential risk from the fact that Amazon and Netflix are both in the business of content delivery, although it can be argued that content delivery is only one of the many services that Amazon provides.

CHAPTER 5

■ ■ ■

Application-Specific Cloud Platforms

A business absolutely devoted to service will have only one worry about profits. They will be embarrassingly large.

—Henry Ford

A number of events in IT practices paved the way to the adoption of the cloud we see today. One of these events took place primarily in large organizations: the service-oriented architecture (SOA) transformation between the turn of the century and 2007, in which application silos were broken up into loosely coupled reusable service components (servicelets) linked by web services or RESTful application programming interfaces (APIs). This is the transformation described in the Uber and Netflix case studies in Chapter 4. IT became modular, with the servicelet as a unit of composition. The employee roster is an example of a servicelet that most any organization must implement. In an evolved system, a number of human resources applications access a single instance of this servicelet, such as payroll, travel planning, and expense reporting, as well as the company employee directory.

Change did not stop there. Although the first generation of servicelets might have been sourced internally, including the travel scheduling and reservation system, eventually it became more efficient to outsource these capabilities to specialized companies: travel to American Express, Concur.com for expense reporting, Salesforce.com for customer management, and so on. Cloud technology gives these companies a choice of running certain servicelets either in house or outsourced to external IaaS or PaaS providers based on technical and business criteria. Before the cloud, the only choice was to run the applications in house regardless of readiness.

Cloud services run on pooled infrastructure over a network. A service offering might encompass other supporting services and might run on infrastructure from providers delivering infrastructure services. In the end, applications still run in physical datacenters. However, by the time this chain of delegated functionality gets resolved into the actual physical infrastructure, it represents the aggregate demand of thousands of companies and perhaps hundreds of millions of individual users. This is the dynamic driving the build-up of hyperscale datacenters. In fact, large service providers were the first to experience and capitalize from this dynamic during the second wave of the cloud

© Enrique Castro-Leon and Robert Harmon 2016
E. Castro-Leon and R. Harmon, *Cloud as a Service*, DOI 10.1007/978-1-4842-0103-9_5

platform evolution. The design, development, and deployment of these platforms called for the specialized, customized designs described in Chapter 4, the first instance of application-specific cloud platforms (ASCPs), the main topic for this chapter.

The need for customized platforms will persist in the third wave of the evolution of cloud platforms with additional demand coming from providers delivering specialized infrastructure services. An additional challenge for platform providers will come in the form of delivering customized platforms economically, yet in smaller numbers. The trend will continue through the fourth wave to support application and security demands from the Internet of things (IoT).

Service-Oriented Platforms

Under a goods-dominant logic worldview (GDL), computer hardware represents an invariant asset. Product planners assess future needs the best they can to develop a product roadmap and an architecture to suit customer needs using available market research and sales data. System architects and engineers build the platform to forecasted needs. Unfortunately, requirements information is always forward looking, and therefore incomplete, and the resulting product needs to address a broad audience. However, each user is different with specific needs. Every need not met can potentially erode market segment participation and puts a product's success in the marketplace at risk. Also given the long lead time to execute a technology development pipeline, from the initial conceptual architecture to product launch, new business requirements will certainly arise beyond those in the initial planning. Engineering organizations do not take new requirements in the middle of the development very kindly because development in process can easily lead to rework and cost overruns. Processes for change requests do exist but are expensive and slow, commensurate with the potential disruption they cause. With the cloud, business conditions drive change and not necessarily with a schedule. Cloud processes assume change is an essential part. Development methodologies, such as DevOps incorporate this assumption, and the ability to track change, otherwise known as nimbleness is an important figure of merit for any methodology.

Continuing with platform development under a GDL approach, when the product launches, it comes with a set of features primarily defined at its planning inception years before. Furthermore, it falls to the system integrator (SI) or the user to map features in a product's spec sheet to business needs. The vendor participates indirectly in this process through sales, marketing, and training efforts, or in the case of large procurements, by participating in long procurement processes or by bidding in public tenders. The seller hopes the product specifications as developed will satisfy the user enough to close a sale. The execution of a technology pipeline has always been an exercise in guessing where the market will be at launch time. Reasonably good guesses can be made through extensive market research and focus group exercises, but they are still educated guesses.

In spite of its limited capability to incorporate midcourse changes, this form of planned technology development worked well for first-wave platforms targeted to the enterprise. Most companies had a centralized IT function and every IT organization hosted a predictable mix of applications: enterprise resource planning, business intelligence and analytics, productivity and collaboration, sales support, finance, and human resources. A relatively balanced portfolio of applications favored the deployment of general-purpose servers with requirements that did not change much year over year.

The cloud involves pooling and specialization not just for the physical infrastructure, but just about every entity in IT all the way up to application components to applications to service providers. Requirements for e-commerce providers will be different from search providers and these in turn are different from social media providers or for providers of human resources applications. Today, within their area of specialty, business conditions for each service provider change at a furious pace, and with it, the associated technology requirements. Given the high barriers for customization during the first wave and the fact that all platform providers had similar limitations, platform customers had to live within a level of inconvenience, which, although present, did not make or break the business.

Prompted by their enormous product demand, large cloud service providers (CSPs) were the first to revolt against the status quo. They were unhappy about the fit of product feature sets to application and the variation across platform providers. These CSPs could afford and started deploying in-house technology assessment teams to develop customized technology planning and deployment roadmaps. For developers of general-purpose platform providers, the cloud market moves so fast that by the time of launch, creeping obsolescence is already nibbling at the heels of these platform providers. Although the actions by these cloud providers accelerate the path to obsolescence for traditionally developed cloud platforms, they also create competitive opportunities for those willing to embrace customizability.

There is risk for the status quo as well. A platform strives to provide an extensive range of technology features. Every feature, whether or not it is used, represents an investment by platform providers. Unused features, whether by the end customer or indirectly by supporting other capabilities, represents an unrecovered sunk cost that affects profitability. If enough features do not make it, the development project as a whole might not break even. In other words, the most expensive feature to implement is the one that does not get used. Every user gets a basket of technology capabilities with a platform purchase, and every capability not used represents an avoidable cost to the technology provider and a hidden cost to the customer in the form of additional complexity.

Traditionally, with computer hardware assumed invariant, there is an unvoiced expectation about the goal of application optimization, which is to modify the application to fit the requirements of the new technology. An implicit assumption is that an emergent platform technology is inherently valuable, and that the mission of the application developer or SI is to "unlock" the value of the technology.

The cloud operates under a service-dominant logic (SDL), which turns these assumptions upside down. Under an SDL, a product offering holds no intrinsic value. Value does not exist until it expressed by the user, under a concept known as *value-in-use*. This is the other side of avoidable technology cost under the product-service duality. A technology or feature might have cost a couple hundred million dollars in labor and equipment to develop and manufacture. Unfortunately, if it does not find a paying customer, what it cost to develop is irrelevant; for this case the value this technology delivers is exactly zero.

This situation underscores a sobering dissonance between product-oriented suppliers and their service-oriented customers. Suppliers, using processes that worked well in the past, build a technology roadmap to an extrapolated set of requirements possibly years into the future. Yet cloud players, whether public service providers or private cloud organizations, must deal with changing requirements where a minute matters, let alone years. A successful technology execution strategy requires reconciling these two opposites.

How do we reconcile these opposites? The development of a fundamental technology, such as achieving the next rung in logic density according to Moore's Law still might take years and billions of dollars in capital investment. Although the hard work and the capital investment are nonnegotiable, a change in approach might be helpful. Much in the same way that business planning starts making more sense in a service-oriented ecosystem when the analysis assumes that the customer determines the exchange value, it might make more sense to start defining roadmaps not as abstract roadmaps, but with the goal to address customer needs as a continuous feedback loop. In practice, there are multiple, concurrent feedback loops of varying time scales to incorporate a number of different planning time horizons.

Determining requirements just at the inception of a technology development project does not cut it. Technology providers need more end-to-end involvement in the product delivery cycle. Success in a service-oriented ecosystem requires integrating change into the development cycle, not viewing change reactively and a problem to be managed and minimized. This is a cultural dissonance between GDL and SDL. Rather than change being a problem, incorporating change into product development provides a vital feedback loop and directional input to the project that increases its likelihood of success.

Platform providers internalizing this transition will start seeing themselves as equipment *service* providers. They will find it easier to bridge the product-service gap from selling products into a service market. With no product-service chasm to bridge, business planning actually becomes easier, with more predictable and increased likelihood of positive outcomes. In retrospective, the pressure for this kind of change goes back to the beginnings of the first wave in the early 1990s. As noted earlier, prevailing application methodologies such as the waterfall method, made it obligatory to lock in project requirements during the planning phase. Change was so expensive that in many cases a change in business requirements meant abandoning the project during development. It also meant having to accept misaligned capability right off the launch due to evolving business conditions[1]. Agile programming was born out of this need in the early 2000s, with emphasis on project front-loading, with no "magic happens" at the end or other expressions of wishful thinking, and in delivering working code early on, with iterative development built right into the methodology. For service providers, the goal is creating value to customers as early as possible, following an end-to-end approach instead of blindly following a stepwise approach. The latter is akin to dead reckoning in navigation where a ship is set to sail to a destination with a trajectory calculated only from the current position and data from currents and wind en route with no possibility of calculating intervening positions.

Service providers are highly motivated to deliver value to their customers as early as possible on the assumption that revenue follows value. In cloud computing, the concept of *DevOps* followed a few short years thereafter. DevOps is a methodology to carry out application development and operations as concurrent steps, and bringing the corresponding teams together, with the goal of reducing the time to execute on an application as quickly as possible to get revenue started[2]. Following this line of thinking, in the not-too-distant future it will make sense to integrate cloud platform development into an *extended and generalized DevOps process*. It must be noted that Agile and DevOps are still two separate methodologies, and there is no established methodology to optimize the entire flow, let alone integrating ASCP development for a cloud application. Given current needs in the industry, this is an excellent area for process development.

---

[1]TechBeacon, "To Agility and Beyond: The History and Legacy of Agile Development," `http://techbeacon.com/agility-beyond-history%E2%80%94legacy%E2%80%94agile-development`, August 26, 2015.

[2]M. Marschall, "How Are Lean, Agile, and Devops Related to Each Other?," `http://www.agileweboperations.com/lean-agile-devops-related`, July 12, 2012.

Under an SDL approach, the platform vendor becomes an integral part of technology development for CSPs in a tight feedback loop that radically shortens the time to deployment for emerging technologies and increases the economic efficiency of whole ecosystems. Sales and marketing functions shift from traditional push selling to facilitating and expediting SLAs and partner management as well as building trust relationships with these partners. Performance benchmarking and engineering tasks become tasks directed toward specific landings and tied to revenue, less on a speculative basis to win business, as understood in a product-oriented environment. These considerations reduce business uncertainty and shorten time to revenue.

In the emerging service-oriented environment for platform development, exchanges between a CSP and an equipment provider cease to be *transactional* and become *relational*. The optimal outcomes do not take place when the producer sells a bill of goods at a "good" price in a one-time *transaction*. Carrying out this transaction implicitly assumes a mercantilist approach with a "winner," usually the seller intent on making a profit and a loser locked in a zero-sum game, usually the buyer, intent on acquiring a capability. The platform asset is not the goal, but the means to achieve a goal. Unfortunately, the buyer bears the burden of converting the newly acquired asset into something useful. In actuality, this GDL-SDL clash in a cloud environment produces no winners, only lost opportunity. The product-service chasm introduces friction that slows down the ability of participants to close business and realize value.

A vendor embracing a service-oriented approach with a CSP commits to deliver a platform *service*, not a platform *product*. The interactions between vendor and service provider become relational in that the vendor commits to develop a capability, perhaps over an extended, possibly indefinite period and participates in the mapping of product features to customer service capabilities, and that the vendor, now a *platform service provider*, commits to integrate the platform capabilities to enhance a CSP's portfolio. The dynamic playing out here is that of a service network as depicted in Figure 4-7, with platform vendors, now platform service providers, fully integrated into a service network.

The business goal becomes not to maximize profit margins as a tactical exercise but to maximize value delivered to customers over time. Maximizing value delivered opens the possibility of higher revenue in a win–win situation. Under these circumstances, a "customer" cloud platform roadmap in our case becomes as important, if not more, as the vendor roadmap.

Vendor roadmaps are still useful for planning purposes, but the goal is not to organize vendor features; the goal instead is to provide a technology basis and a framework to support customer-specific roadmaps. A single roadmap for a whole industry might not be granular enough to satisfy individual customer requirements. The vendor roadmap would function more like a proto-roadmap or roadmap generator or launching pad for instantiating, adding value and customizing to user needs.

Flexibility to satisfy customer needs becomes more important than designing a feature portfolio with 100 percent coverage. Although this scorched earth approach might help in preventing competitors from entering a given space, it represents an expensive and wasteful approach because it ensures at least a few zero-value technology dead ends as defined earlier. Methodologies that align vendor roadmaps with end user roadmaps bring in efficiency, reduce wasted effort, and ensure that every engineering effort has a purpose rooted in customer demand.

Under a relational business exchange model, customer feedback processes become an integral part of technology development where every technical task is part of a *directed engineering* strategy driven by customer need. By definition, there are no technology dead ends because every activity carries a purpose expressed by a customer in a customer interaction from delivering a service. Customer feedback is no longer strictly a product planning activity carried out as market research at the front end and blindly followed through product launch. It becomes a continuous process throughout technology development. The term we use for this mode of technology development is *platform codevelopment,* under the assumption that no technology is context free; this development takes place in the context of customer requirements on a continuous basis.

ASCPs customized cloud platforms are instances of *product-service systems* (PSS) covered in Chapter 2, designed by collaborating consortia technology providers in a supply chain using a codevelopment approach with the goal of maximizing value cocreation. A supply chain or ecosystem, operated in this mode, effectively defines another service network, namely a design and manufacturing service network operating on behalf of CSPs deploying the platform. CSPs in turn use ASCP assets and services to deliver their own services. This process is inherently more efficient than traditional design and manufacturing processes. By definition, participants in these processes allocate every hour of labor and every physical component in response to demand directly from a consumer, or indirectly through the service network. There is improved asset utilization and process efficiency compared to a system with products built to forecast. A forecast carries a speculative component that requires push marketing, with the possibility of unsold stock if the forecast is too optimistic, or missed revenue opportunities if the forecast is too pessimistic.

The largest cloud operators worldwide, namely, Amazon, Microsoft, Google, and Facebook in the United States, and Baidu, Tencent, and Alibaba in the People's Republic of China, were instrumental in transforming platform development from the product-oriented approach prevalent during the first wave toward a service-oriented approach through cloud platform codevelopment. This is the defining characteristic for second-wave cloud platforms. These CSPs involved were small in number but at the same time constitute the largest operators of datacenters worldwide, each deploying well in excess of 100,000 servers, up to possibly several million.

Without exception, all these operators deploy servers built to in-house specifications. In other words, the CSP end user determines the specifications for these cloud spec standard high-value server (SHV) machines. As described in Chapter 4, the CSP customers bypass traditional original equipment manufacturer (OEM) procurement channels and hand their designs to contract manufacturers, the original design manufacturers (ODMs) for direct sourcing. Because these platforms are purpose-built, we call these machines, along with peripheral attachments, customized firmware and configured operating environment applications *application-specific cloud platforms* or *application-specific customized platforms* (ASCPs).

An event that catalyzed the adoption of ASCPs beyond first-wave players is the Open Compute Project (OCP), launched in April 2011 by Facebook along with Rackspace, Intel, Goldman Sachs, and Andy Bechtolsheim[3]. By that time, Facebook had been working on

---

[3]Open Compute Project, "About OCP," http://www.opencompute.org/about/, 2016.

their own ASCP, not just a custom server design, but also an efficient, integrated cloud platform that incorporated rack and datacenter architecture as well as the operating environment and applications. Facebook realized that the same dynamics that played out with open software 20 years before would apply to cloud platforms, and in a gutsy move, decided to make their designs public, inviting contributions from other industry players.

Facebook and the launch partners were hoping OCP would become a platform that industry partners joining the effort could use to build additional capabilities, and in the process, enrich the technology base for OCP ASCPs, thereby closing a turn of a virtuous circle. Facebook's server designs contain customizations synergistic with deployment in Facebook's highly efficient datacenters such as the Prineville, Oregon, datacenter.

The impact of Facebook's OCP designs in the industry goes well beyond this initial deployment. As a developing process at the time of writing, there is not yet a benefit of hindsight, but our prediction is that OCP is serving as the main catalyst for the third wave, for the following reasons:

- OCP as a proof point of the paradigm of ASCP, showing how platform customizations can fulfill the unmet needs of CSPs in spite of fast-changing requirements.

- Smaller CSP players in the third wave also benefit from customized platforms. However, without the critical mass of Facebook's large volume demand, most CSPs would have encountered insurmountable technical barriers building their own ASCP, mainly footing the bill for the associated nonrecurring engineering (NRE). Facebook and OCP contributors, in the process of pursuing the benefits and scale of an open hardware platform, did the heavy lifting in creating the OCP ASCP and lowered the barriers to new entrants to build additional ASCPs. Facebook benefits from the economies of scale and from the technical contributions of the new entrants.

- A supply chain of OCP solution providers is developing[4]. These providers are in a good position to become *cloud platform service providers* as explained earlier, further fueling the OCP technology dynamic and its economic relevance for the entire ecosystem.

OCP has been successful, with significant contribution from other large CSPs such as Google and Microsoft. Microsoft, in particular, published the specifications of its own in-house cloud server, Windows Cloud Server, as the Open Cloud Server (OCS) specification as a contribution to OCP. Other notable participants are Apple, Cisco, Juniper Networks, Fidelity, Bank of America, AT&T, SK Telecom, and platform providers such as Hyve Solutions, Penguin Computing, Stack Velocity, HP Enterprise, Quanta, and Wiwynn.

A succinct analogy culled from Physics provides insight into the GDL and SDL approaches to cloud platform development: The GDL approach is absolutist, whereas the SDL approach is relativistic. Under the GDL worldview, the ideal platform is immutable. The goal for developers is to discover requirements to design the appropriate platform

---

[4]Open Computer Project, "Become a Solution Provider," http://www.opencompute.org/about/open-compute-project-solution-providers/, 2016.

that satisfies the requirements. The design requires iteration due to imperfect knowledge of requirements. The SDL worldview assumes a process of co-creation, and therefore the shape of the platform depends on this process, which takes place in the context of a relationship between the service provider and the consumer.

ASICs and ASCPs: Dynamics of Customization

Customization is powerful. It allows a practitioner to develop a platform that meets the needs at hand exactly. However, there is a trade-off between the benefit gained and the cost to build such a platform. To understand the dynamics of ASCPs, it is useful to review a lower level earlier development closer to silicon, the notion of the *application-specific integrated circuit* (ASIC).

An integrated circuit (IC) or "chip" consists of a number of electronic devices such as AND or OR logic gates or a transistor imprinted on a substrate material. Chips usually come affixed to a package with connectors, ready to be soldered to a circuit board. Current technology allows packing these devices very densely; a microprocessor IC can carry several billion transistors on a chip only a few millimeters square.

A board made up of discrete logic, with single device components, offers the utmost flexibility; a designer can lay out a board one gate at a time as needed. However, for most applications this method is expensive in terms of labor, the bulk of the resulting design, and the cost of packaging. As an example, it is not practical anymore to construct a memory cell in terms of its constituent transistors or even packaging a single cell. A single memory chip can carry hundreds of millions of memory cells. Discrete components are a good fit in some applications, for instance as a quick way for interconnecting other chips in a baseboard or for power circuitry where high currents are involved.

Memory chips are examples of general-purpose, stock, or *commercial off-the-shelf* (COTS) products. They might be part of a family of products, built and designed with a certain set of specifications purchased in the open market and selected from a manufacturer catalog.

Stock chips are not an optimal alternative for certain applications. Examples include the following:

- Compact mobile devices with extremely low power consumption.

- Instrumentation devices where available alternatives can't be easily integrated and would result in unnecessary complexity.

- Incorporating logic and radio frequency functions into a single device helps in reducing a device's footprint as well as integrated digital and analog hybrid designs. The reduced footprint yields an efficient and competitive product that consumers will likely find more attractive and convenient to use.

If a stock chip is not available for one of these applications and the cost of using discrete logic would make the product unaffordable, an alternative is to build a custom chip. An example of an ASIC is a *complex programmable logic device* (CPLD) that manages power management in a server baseboard. The practical effect of an ASIC is to squeeze the components that otherwise would have been in a large and bulky baseboard design into the substrate of a single chip.

A primary consideration for incorporating an ASIC in a design over a general-purpose chip is cost. Every design carries a fixed cost, the NRE cost, and variable cost, the incremental cost of fabricating each chip. The NRE cost includes the cost of requirements analysis, the logic design, simulation and verification, logic synthesis, creating masks, setting up fabrication processes, manufacturing test samples, the cost of marketing and sales, and the labor involved in these tasks. Most of these costs are present in both general-purpose and ASIC designs[5]. The difference is that in an ASIC design one customer, the requester, must bear the NRE costs, whereas a general-purpose design allows amortizing this cost over a much larger customer base to the point that for purchasers, this cost is already included in the unit price. Customers might see the fixed cost indirectly when they get price breaks when ordering in large quantities.

A number of methods are available to carry out ASIC implementations:

- Using silicon layers and predefined gate arrays where the design process consists of defining the interconnections between the gates through a custom metallization layer. This method is relatively inexpensive but least flexible, with limited density, and wasteful in the sense that not all the gates provided end up used. This method is appropriate for projects of relatively low complexity where the expected production run is small.

- Using standardized cell libraries, building a device using component libraries. These components could be as complex fully formed microcontrollers, Ethernet, Universal Serial Bus (USB) or Bluetooth I/O, A/D or D/A converters, serializers/deserializers (SerDes) or embedded, in-chip memory. Some components might even be third-party intellectual property protected components used as functional blocks. This method allows fast time to market through the reuse of standardized components from a component library. Additional licensing costs might be involved in the use of the third-party components.

- Full-custom designs provide even higher flexibility than the previous two methods, essentially through the same methodologies used for COTS products where the designer can define detail down to the single gate level. This method is also the highest cost method appropriate to projects requiring fabrication of a large number of parts.

The space spanned by customization is very large (see Figure 5-1). We can divide this space into three main categories for our analysis:

- Custom architectures.

- Custom models or stock-keeping units (SKUs).

- Customized configurations.

---

[5]D. Chakravarty, "Marketing ASICs," in *Application Specific Integrated Circuit (ASIC) Technology*, ed. N. Einspruch, pp. 27–57 (New York, NY: Academic, 2012); Ian Poole, "ASIC Design, Development and Layout," http://www.radio-electronics.com/info/data/semi-cond/asic/designs-development-layout.php, 2016.

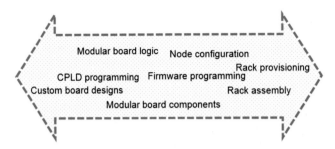

Figure 5-1. Customization range for server system designs

The lightest form of server customization is through a product's *configuration*. Modifying a configuration involves the selection or the arrangement of the product's components using stock parts, without involving the manufacture of special-purpose components. The customized configuration might involve special assembly and test procedures, or even modified management software or the selection of specific components for performance or cost reasons.

When an OEM builds a server model offering, say a Dell PowerEdge R520, bringing this model to market involves a significant investment in engineering, marketing, and sales resources. A model carries a baseboard and sheet metal of unique specifications. The dynamics fixed and variable costs are similar to those of COTS chips. One characteristic to note is that present-day computer manufacturers (OEMs) are actually so efficient that they can usually offer a product at a lower price than a similarly capable single unit assembled from COTS parts.

Still, there are circumstances where it makes economic sense to build a custom SKU. A first consideration is economy of scale, namely demand for enough units to amortize NRE costs. A second issues is a need for features beyond the range of configurability of COTS models. This could be an I/O rich board, used as a storage controller. Such a board would carry just one CPU but four Ethernet ports embedded on the baseboard itself. This setup makes sense if the required features go beyond the range available with stock models. A custom SKU is not necessarily a complete makeover. For instance, Intel creates reference board designs for each generation of CPU and chipsets. An OEM could take one of these designs and use it as a baseline to build their COTS offerings.

An example of a custom SKU is eBay's concept of servers with a "gas pedal"[6]. eBay is deploying water-cooled servers with water heat exchangers directly attached to CPUs[7]. At 4.186 joules/gram–°C, water has a specific heat higher than almost any

---

[6]R. Miller, "EDI Wins eBay Modular Design Contest," http://www.datacenterknowledge.com/archives/2010/12/15/edi-wins-ebay-modular-design-contest/, December 15, 2010.
[7]R. Miller, "eBay Shifts to Water-Cooled Doors to Tame High-Density Loads," http://www.datacenterknowledge.com/archives/2014/05/20/ebay-shifts-water-cooled-doors-tame-high-density-loads/, May 20, 2014.

common substance, meaning that it can absorb a lot of heat without a commensurate temperature rise. It is also 24 times more heat conductive than the air used to cool most servers. These servers carry a special CPU SKU capable of handling more than 200 watts, or twice the power of most stock CPUs used in servers. It would be very difficult to extract heat at this rate from a CPU drawing 200 watts with standard air cooling. Running a CPU at this power level allows higher frequencies and an extra kick in performance when needed to ride out peaks in application demand. This also allows the operator to reduce the number of servers allocated to a certain workload just to handle momentary peaks. The extra performance extracted is linear with frequency. The trade-off is power consumption increasing at a faster than linear rate when a CPU is overclocked. This is an acceptable trade-off when a server operates in this mode for short periods.

An example of a server architecture is the Dell PowerEdge R-series, with a range of models or SKUs of different capabilities through the R200, R300, R400, R500, R600, R700, R800, and R900 models. The architecture is multigenerational where it carries over multiple generations of underlying CPU, chipsets, I/O, and networking technologies. The large investment in developing such a series is amortized over a large and diversified enterprise and cloud customer base. For a large CSP deploying hundreds of thousands of servers, it makes economic sense to develop a custom architecture to optimize the deployment of such a scale when the fixed costs of developing the architecture are smaller than the variable cost premium from using COTS equivalents.

The original Facebook OCP specification captures an example of a custom cloud architecture, carried over for at least three generations[8]. Within the architecture, there are model and configuration instances to support different application profiles such as compute intensive for analytics applications and I/O intensive for data-intensive applications.

To summarize, a custom architecture is a customer-driven platform architecture with unique capabilities planned for deployment across a number of technology generations. Customer-driven does not mean a vendor trying to guess customer requirements, but a roadmap developed under the customer direction on top of some base or reference technology. As in customized SKUs, a customized architecture can be incremental over a reference board design. In the customization example that follows, we describe a board with circuitry that allows it to survive the failure of one or more power supply units (PSUs). This is a modification on top of a stock board design.

The roadmap depicted in Table 5-1 is an example of an end-user-driven roadmap built on top of a technology provider's processor roadmap as covered earlier in the chapter, with processors from Intel Corporation in this particular example. This process benefited Facebook by providing a technology roadmap precisely tailored to Facebook's needs. However, the open hardware dynamic of OCP amplifies the impact of the OCP in the industry: OCP in turn becomes a technology base enabling new participants small and large.

---

[8]Open Compute Project, "Server Specs and Designs," http://www.opencompute.org/wiki/Server/SpecsAndDesigns, July 13, 2015.

Table 5-1. *Facebook Open Compute Project Architecture Pedigree*

Baseboard Model	CPU Generation	Processor Model
Windmill	Thurley	Nehalem, Westmere
Winterfell	Romley	Sandy Bridge, Ivy Bridge
Leopard	Grantley	Haswell, Broadwell

Attributed technology contributors in the compilation of server specifications and designs for OCP include Facebook, Microsoft, Netronome Systems, Rackspace, AMD, Intel, Quanta, Wiwynn, and Gigabyte, taking Facebook beyond its initial seed contribution and fulfilling Facebook's strategic objectives. The technical contributions from these players expands the OCP technology base beyond what Facebook could have achieved on its own, perhaps presenting Facebook and OCP participants with competitive benefits beyond those that could be achieved through secrecy and by going alone. Furthermore, the aggregate demand from these new entrants augments the customer base for OCP platforms, reducing costs per unit to all participants.

The augmented technology base for OCP in turn becomes the launching point for even more innovations with new players thereby completing one turn of the virtuous spiral coming out of the open hardware approach. The dynamic driving the adoption of open hardware for OCP is the same that fired up the open software revolution of the mid-1990s.

The large number of units involved in OCP has delivered benefits, not just to Facebook, but has made OCP a market mover by itself. On the deployment side, CSPs can now order OCP form factor machines from suppliers such as Hyve and Stack Velocity. Companies beyond Facebook, such as founding members Goldman Sachs, Fidelity Bank, and Bank of America, have been deploying OCP form factor machines in their datacenters since 2014[9]. On the technology development side, Microsoft has presented OCS as another architecture available under OCP, and Baidu and Quanta have taken a similar action with the Scorpio chassis specification, and an effort to converge Scorpio with OCP started in 2013[10]. Any CSP can now place orders to these OCP suppliers and have a platform fabricated to order. Given that the OCP specifications are public, and the solution providers are already experienced in fabricating OCP platforms, the participants in a design project can focus their attention on the variants from the base design needed

---

[9]T. Prickett, "Goldman Sachs and Fidelity Bank on Open Compute," http://www.enterprisetech.com/2014/01/29/goldman-sachs-fidelity-bank-open-compute/, January 29, 2014; Y. Sverdlink, "Wall Street Rethinking Data Center Hardware," http://www.datacenterknowledge.com/archives/2015/03/11/open-compute-wall-street-rethinking-data-center-hardware/, March 11, 2015.

[10]F. Frankovsky, "OCP Summit IV: Breaking Up the Monolith," http://www.opencompute.org/blog/ocp-summit-iv-breaking-up-the-monolith/, January 16, 2013; G. Huang, "Optimizing Your Datacenter with Open Compute," http://cloudadvisorycouncil.com/workshops/2014/china/pdfs/Grant%20Huang_Quanta.pdf, March 10, 2014; L. Luo, "China's Open Source Initiative Starts with Server Standards," http://www.datacenterdynamics.com/content-tracks/servers-storage/chinas-open-source-initiative-starts-with-server-standards/93902.fullarticle, May 6, 2015.

to satisfy the CSP buyer requirements. The NRE involved in the incremental design is a fraction of the cost to do a baseboard design from the ground up. This is the dynamic enabling third-wave players to break even on customization projects at production numbers far smaller than those required for hyperscale players.

Platform Customization Examples

As mentioned earlier, and shown in Figure 5-1, a number of customization techniques are available to server providers today, ordered from left to right by difficulty, technical challenge, and the amount of labor involved. A customized platform could carry one or more of these techniques. Probably the most sophisticated form of customized platform is a custom board design. The baseboard described in the OCS blade specification exemplifies one such instance[11]. A less complex customization might include custom CPLDs to consolidate certain logic functions, modular board logic reused across boards of the same family, and the selection of specific modular board components, such as storage controllers and custom firmware including BIOS and Intel Innovation Engine firmware.

Lighter forms of customization include specific node (baseboard) configurations in the form of specifically provisioned accessory cards or firmware parameters and customized processes for rack assembly and provisioning. Special capabilities might include more dynamic behaviors than those supported by COTS models. For instance, a bare metal cloud provider might find it useful to reconfigure BIOS parameters for specific customers or even load custom firmware at customer provisioning time, tasks currently carried out only at manufacturing time. The notion of customization is relative: A rack manager deployed with custom algorithms implemented in the top of rack manager is by definition a customized rack, yet the nodes themselves might be stock nodes.

The example that follows shows the implementation of a default power cap (DPC) as a baseboard customization. When the DPC is triggered, the baseboard readjusts its power demand to a predefined level. This readjustment happens very quickly, typically in less than 0.1 seconds. In other words, if the current power draw of a board or *node* is 275 watts and the DPC is 175 watts, the baseboard will readjust its power demand from 275 watts to 175 watts in less than 0.1 seconds. On a chassis with 48 nodes a power swing of 100 watts per node means a 4.8 KW fast readjustment is possible. An application of this capability is as an alternative to physical redundancy and overprovisioning to handle power supply failures. Dense cloud platform designs usually feed the nodes in a chassis or rack out of a pool of six to eight power supplies on a tray or chassis backplane. Having one or two power supplies in reserve is expensive. The cost comes from having an asset in standby, doing no useful work except for being there in case of emergency. There are passive losses from having them online all the time. In addition, overprovisioning reduces the load factor where power supplies are less efficient.

An alternative to overprovisioning is to add intelligence to the system to reconfigure its power consumption profile in response to a contingency, namely the loss of one, two, or even three power supplies. There is no extra equipment needed. The trade-off is that

---

[11]Open CloudServer (OCS) Blade Specification, V2.0, http://files.opencompute.org/oc/public.php?service=files&t=1c2ed966035b8b83aaeadc80b4a5b356, 2016.

when the contingency occurs, the system shifts to a power-reduced mode, which will affect application performance. Beyond that, applications continue to run normally and perhaps most important, there is no impact during normal operation.

In a server baseboard, power management is a complex function implemented through the collaborative participation of multiple subsystems from different technology providers. One such function is the implementation of processor throttling.

The principle of operation for throttling is simple: There are certain emergency situations where quickly rolling back power demand in a server is helpful, where "quickly" means anything less than 1 second, and preferably less than 0.1 second. PROCHOT# and MEMHOT# are digital signals (general-purpose I/Os, or GPIOs) attached to the CPUs for this purpose. The hash mark symbol (#) indicates the signal is "active low," meaning that when set to logical zero, PROCHOT commands the CPUs to reduce frequency from its normal operating frequency to a low baseline known as low frequency mode (LFM). For the current generation CPUs, this frequency is about 800 MHz, down to about one third to one fourth of the normal operating frequency. This transition happens very quickly, in 1 to 4 milliseconds. When this transition happens, server power demand is reduced anywhere from one half to one third of its normal level. Likewise, MEMHOT# commands the memory controller in the CPU to reduce the number of lanes used in memory requests, an action that also reduces power demand.

Being able to reduce power demand this fast is useful to ensure the survival of a system under certain contingencies. In a cloud server, power into server baseboards typically comes from tightly provisioned PSUs. If one or more PSUs fail or go offline, there might not be enough power left to go around. In this case inducing LFM for all nodes in a rack or chassis essentially puts the system in a safe mode to enable other elements in the system to assess the situation and reconfigure the system to continue operating with the remaining resources without crashing.

Figure 5-2 represents an example of customization at two levels: a customized power management subsystem in an ASCP, and second, the logic of this design is a good fit for an ASIC implementation, in this case precisely a CPLD. At a first blush the logic design is very simple, consisting of just four gates: a NOT gate, two AND gates, and a NOR gate. This is not as it appears to be. General-purpose I/O (GPIO) pinouts in a chip are usually overloaded. GPIOs might have functions depending on the state of the machine, perhaps one immediately after power-on, another when the firmware is running the power-on self-test, another while the OS is booting, and yet another when the system is up and running. In this case, the CPLD implements the different configurations and topologies depending on system state.

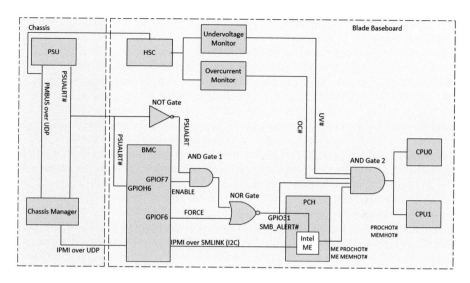

Figure 5-2. *Implementation of processor throttling with undervoltage and overcurrent protection*

In particular, asserting PROCHOT# too soon, within a few milliseconds of power-on, the CPU assumes there is an anomaly and this triggers a safe boot where the OS boots with only one core. To avoid triggering this sequence by accident, the throttling logic also implements an inhibit feature that prevents this circuitry from acting too soon and inadvertently deconfiguring the system.

The logic represented in Figure 5-2 is distributed. A server system might consist of a chassis and a number of blades, anywhere from 12 to 96. The chassis houses a chassis manager computer and about a half-dozen PSUs shared across all nodes. Individual designs differ as part of the customized design. Assume for the purposes of this example that there are three types of microcontrollers: one in the chassis managing the PSU complex, the baseboard management controller (BMC) overseeing the baseboard functions, and the ME or the Intel Management Engine embedded in the Processor Control Hub (PCH), informally known as the chipset. There are many more management microcontrollers not relevant to this example and therefore not represented for simplicity, for instance the Intel Innovation Engine microcontroller in the PCH, the main CPU running the BIOS, and the power control unit, a microcontroller inside the CPU that actually catches the PROCHOT# signal and executes it. The CPU itself can also initiate a PROCHOT# action whenever the PCU reads the internal temperature sensors and determines that the CPU is overheating. This is the origin of the PROCHOT monitor in the first place. All power going into a server eventually becomes heat. The PCU can reduce thermal gradients in a server by reducing CPU power demand. All energized components in a server produce heat. However, CPUs are usually the most energetic and therefore represent the richest target for power control.

155

At the highest level, the chassis manager coordinates management actions across PSUs and baseboards in a chassis (nodes). Communication takes place through standard protocols, Power Management Bus (PMBUS) a standard from the Server Management Industry Forum (SMIF) and Intelligent Platform Management Interface (IPMI). The physical transport convey these protocols depends on the application. User Datagram Protocol (UDP) over Ethernet is probably the best alternative for communication with the chassis manager. Serial communication (RS-232) is possible but suffers from high latency because of the limited number of available ports and the time it takes to set up a connection. For the intraboard communication between the BMC and the ME, the *inter-integrated circuit* protocol (I2C) is the most common physical transport. In the node shown in Figure 5-2, this link has been renamed SMlink, following industry practice.

In Figure 5-2, any of the power supplies can set PSUALRT# low to send a distress signal. The signal is routed to the chassis manager and each of the nodes. This transition is merely an indication of an incident. It is up to the entities involved to evaluate the situation and take the appropriate action. Assuming the appropriate logic is present, the chassis manager interrogates the controller in the PSU complex to determine the extent of the fault and reallocates the remaining power to the nodes following a predetermined policy. However, carrying this process over the all nodes in a chassis might take a minute or more. Meanwhile each node needs to take autonomous action to stay alive while the chassis manager figures out the global policy. The BMCs in each node execute a local action, the DPC. Because all nodes received PSUALRT# simultaneously, the BMCs in each board should be able to establish the DPC in less than 0.2 seconds.

Unfortunately, 0.2 seconds to establish the DPC might not be fast enough to prevent a collapse of the DC bus in the remaining power supplies and subsequent cascading failure and therefore this design uses LFM activated through PROCHOT to hold power down while the DPC sets. Operating a system in LFM affects the OS and application performance severely, and therefore it is critical to keep this time to a minimum, just long enough to allow the DPC to take hold.

Operators who do not want to use this mechanism can disable it through GPIO GPIOF7 in the BMC. An IPMI command to the chassis manager will accomplish this. The chassis manager in turn relays the command to all nodes. Conversely, there is a provision to intentionally trigger the LFM sequence by pulling the FORCE signal out of GPIOF6 and into the NOR gate high.

At the top left of the baseboard diagram in Figure 5-2 is the hot swap controller (HSC). Among other functions, the HSC works as a local proxy for the power supply complex in each node. The ME uses sensors in the HSC to determine the instantaneous power consumption for that particular node. The HSC also monitors the DC voltage level and current consumption for the node, and if the voltage goes under a preset level or current consumption exceeds a predetermined limit, it also initiates the LFM sequence. This action prepares the system for handling power failure such as putting the node in asynchronous DRAM self-refresh or ADR where memory buffers in the CPU are flushed to memory and memory is placed in self-refresh mode.

All system inputs are eventually consolidated through the AND gate 2. If any of the signals coming into the AND gate 2 is pulled low, the node enters LFM.

156

Identifying Opportunities for Cloud Platform Innovation

ASCP instances can define their own platforms in the sense that functionality is not fixed. Once an ASCP design becomes publicly available in a venue such as OCP, other industry players, be it a CSP with a pain point to address, or a technology provider intent on bringing a new capability to the industry can take the base design and augment it.

There are at least two possible paths to bring up new functionality: by improving on the original design through enhanced firmware algorithms or through a more sophisticated baseboard logic design, or perhaps more interestingly because it mimics the pattern seen in service networks, by composition. We revisit this example from an application design perspective. For now, let us focus on the original example of inoculating a rack with pooled power supplies against PSU failures without overprovisioning PSUs. Because of the large number of nodes relative to the available space for PSUs, overprovisioning is not a feasible alternative in practice.

Contemporary server baseboards exhibit a highly dynamic power consumption behavior, with very low idle power draw in the 50- to 60-watt range for a dual-CPU baseboard. This power consumption figure can rise as much as 350 to 400 watts when an application drives the CPUs to full utilization. Figure 5-3 shows a measurement of a lightly configured cloud platform baseboard with only two DIMMs running the Intel Power and Thermal Utility (PTU) stress test showing a power draw of 351 watts. These boards have fulfilled the aspirational requirements called for by Barroso and Hölzle in their classic 2007 paper[12].

Figure 5-3. *Power draw of a cloud platform baseboard running the Intel PTU stress test*

The base chassis configuration for OCP can fit 15 nodes. Therefore, the potential peak draw for a fully loaded chassis is 15 × 400 watts = 6 KW. The chassis can be provisioned with up to seven PSUs of two possible capacities: 700 watts and 450 watts. Even with 700-watt PSUs, the maximum capacity in a chassis is thus 7 × 700 watts = 4.9 KW. This is clearly not enough to meet potential peak demand. We cover application and power provisioning considerations with more detail in the case study in Chapter 8. We focus on the recovery measures from PSU failures for now.

In the base OCP design, any PSU can send a distress signal by asserting the SMBAlert wire. All SMBAlert wires are strung together in a scheme known as *wired OR*, and the combined signal is routed to each of the nodes. Any PSU that runs into trouble can assert the SMBAlert signal. With the topology as shown, this signal eventually maps out to a PROCHOT assertion into all the CPUs in the chassis. The effect can be rather dramatic where the consumption drops to the 30- to 40-watt range or about half a kilowatt for the whole chassis down from about 5 KW. Unfortunately, this action has a severe effect on application performance. The power demand drop is achieved by severely lowering processor frequency by about two thirds from the normal operating frequency. This design has severe drawbacks:

- It relies exclusively on PROCHOT throttling and it cannot be modulated. Under the emergency operation, the OS and applications could become unresponsive to the extent that the only recourse is shutting down the whole chassis anyway.

- Because the SMBAlert signals out of the PSUs are wire ORd, there is no means to determine which power supply failed, except perhaps by visually inspecting the machine looking for a fault LED signal. This defeats the purpose of lights out operation.

- There is no agent, such as a chassis manager to carry out fault recovery actions. The operator would need to identify the offending PSU and physically remove it to clear the fault. This sequence is tricky and can result in secondary faults: Even if a hot PSU swap is possible, removing the bad PSU clears the fault. Unfortunately, if the chassis is now operating at a power deficit because of the missing PSU, the voltage in the DC bus will sag, resulting in a chassis crash. Ideally it would be desirable to establish a limp-home profile with nodes operating at slightly reduced power to have nodes still operable, albeit at a somewhat impaired performance, but not as severe as if they were throttled. This would allow the system operator to carry out graceful recovery procedures that would avert a chassis crash.

Enhanced Chassis-Level Power Management for OCP

Let us elaborate the DPC-enabled baseboard design covered in the previous section and orchestrate this capability to implement chassis-level power regulated throttling. Developers can take the DPC capability just described and use it as the basis for subsequent development; in essence, this concept becomes a *platform* for further development, either through further hardware evolution or through algorithmic development using this hardware architecture basis.

Figure 5-4 depicts a chassis view of the processor throttling capability in Figure 5-2. PMBUS 1.2 compliant PSUs or more recent ones carry two control physical transports, an I2C bus to implement relatively complex interactions between the PSU and managing controllers and the SMBALERT# wire, a GPIO signal to trigger an interrupt and raise an immediate alarm when a PSU is in distress.

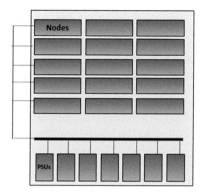

Figure 5-4. *Power throttling scheme for base OCP design*

The PSUs are pooled for the chassis and can serve anywhere from 15 to several dozen nodes. It is not practical to connect every PSU to the BMC in every node in the system from many aspects, wire management and electrical noise not being the least. Assume the existence of an integrated chassis and PSU controller as shown in Figure 5-5.

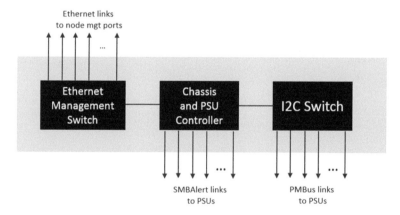

Figure 5-5. *Integrated chassis and PSU controller*

It is possible to implement this controller board with off-the-shelf IC components in a small footprint and have it embedded inside the OCP power shelf. No modifications would be required in the OCP chassis proper.

The chassis manager captures the PMBus links from each PSU through an I2C switch and features GPIOs to capture the SMAlert signals from each PSU. The chassis in turn communicates with the BMCs for each of the nodes in the chassis through an Ethernet management switch. This scheme simplifies wire management enormously. It enables the chassis and PSU controller to manage the SMBAlert signals from each PSU as an interrupt, as well as to carry out power management policies across the power supplies using the PMBus I2C links. The chassis manager is connected to each of the BMCs in the blades through Ethernet, either in a separate management network or a network shared with the data network depending on application requirements. In either case, only a single wire from the chassis manager to each node is required. The chassis manager uses UDP to signal the target BMCs. UDP carries relatively low overhead. It is useful as a transport for IPMI or Redfish and is fast enough as a transport for GPIOs for alerting purposes.

The PSU controller can now keep track of the number of PSUs installed, their health, and how much power is available collectively. It provides this information to the chassis manager on request, communicating with each PSU through its PMBus I2C link. If a PSU fails, it signals distress by pulling down SMBALERT#. Upon receiving SMBALERT#, the BMC in each node executes the DPC autonomously to put its node in a safe mode. Meanwhile the chassis manager starts a discovery and triage process. It can find out which PSU failed from the PSU SMBALERT# line activated. The specific triage algorithm to be used depends on application and customer requirements on the chassis nodes.

We revisit this architecture in Chapter 8 as a component of a comprehensive power management macroarchitecture for cloud computing.

CHAPTER 6

Building Application-Specific Platforms

> *The purpose of a business is to create a mutually beneficial relationship*
> *between itself and those it serves.*
> *When it does that well, it will be around tomorrow to do it some more.*

—John Wood

We covered the evolution of cloud server platforms in Chapter 4 and technical characteristics of these platforms in Chapter 5. Now let us look at processes and methodologies for building application-specific cloud platforms (ASCPs) as well as the companies and organizations that manufacture ASCPs.

Defining Cloud Platforms

Up to this point, we have managed to talk about platform ecosystems and the underlying technologies behind platforms based on the intuitive and commonly accepted meanings of the term. Similarly, it is possible to carry out deep discussions about object-oriented programming or service-oriented architecture (SOA). However, before we embark on the subject of building cloud platforms, it will help to define what we are building.

For this purpose, we use the concepts from Gawer, Cusumano and Evans[1]. The authors started by defining an *internal* or *product* platform as "a set of assets organized in a common structure from which a company can efficiently develop and produce a stream of derivative products." The authors proceeded to build a notion of an *external* platform as an extension of an internal platform "as products, services or technologies that are similar to the former but provide the foundation upon which outside firms (organized as a business ecosystem) can develop their own complementary products, technologies,

[1]P. C. Evans and A. Gawer, *The Rise of the Platform Enterprise: A Global Survey*. The Emerging Platform Economy Series (New York, NY: The Center for Global Enterprise, January 2016); A. Gawer and M. A. Cusumano, "Industry Platforms and Ecosystem Innovation," *The Journal of Product Innovation Management, 31* (3), 417–433, 2013.

© Enrique Castro-Leon and Robert Harmon 2016
E. Castro-Leon and R. Harmon, *Cloud as a Service*, DOI 10.1007/978-1-4842-0103-9_6

or services." It is interesting to note here that the notion of *product* in this definition is product as an operant resource as described in Chapter 2, and not in the more traditional sense of a consumable asset. Because cloud platforms involve cross-company ecosystems, they are instances of external platforms.

Internal platforms enable a company to increase economic efficiency through reuse of technology, processes, and capital assets. External platforms amplify this benefit through network effects where additional companies join the effort, effectively forming a platform ecosystem. The presence of an ecosystem increases the level of reuse of the original technology, systems, and processes, but what's more important from the standpoint of economic impact, more often than not, external platforms open up opportunities for ecosystem participants to bring in complementary innovations.

The better known platforms are well-known digital platforms such as Amazon Marketplace, eBay e-commerce, Apple iCloud, and Alibaba e-commerce. The business objective of these platforms is to capture and monetize business and personal data by processing, analyzing, and sharing it over networks. A platform relies on network effects to achieve scale and amplify revenue, where the presence of an ecosystem brings economic opportunity to new participants bringing products and services. The new products and services bring value and attract new users. The concentration of new users in turn brings new participants in a self-reinforcing cycle.

For the platform owner, ecosystem scale for external platforms increases demand for products and services. It can reduce operating costs through a more reliable and mature supply chain. However, direct investment for growth is not a practical choice for achieving scale. The growth dynamics for a cloud platform are different from traditional companies or even consortia. Executive mandates do not apply to complementary contributors given that they are separate companies and can run afoul of antitrust regulation. Platform owners can influence, but not directly control the ecosystem. Most strategies tend to be indirect, geared toward reducing barriers for participating complementary actors, such as establishing and subsidizing developer communities and investing in tool and market development.

Cusumano and Grawer defined four types of platforms:

- *Transaction platforms* connect users, buyers and suppliers for the facilitation of the exchange of goods or services. Examples are eBay and Amazon Marketplace for goods and Monster.com for resumes. Spotify.com matches artists, music studios, and recording companies with consumers.

- An *innovation platform* provides a set of base technologies for other companies in the ecosystem to build complementary technologies or derivative platforms. An example is the Intel family of processors, 3D XPoint Technology for storage and Field Programmable Gate Arrays from Altera. Successful innovation platforms are multidimensional, generating cascading, derivative ecosystems. Figure 6-1 is a partial snapshot of such a system, the Intel technology ecosystem of ecosystems.

- An *integrated platform* combines elements of both an innovation platform and a transaction platform. An example is the Sabre reservation system. As a transaction platform, Sabre allows customers to search, price, and book airline tickets, hotel reservations, and car rentals. As an innovation platform, it allows third-party developers to access a RESTful application programming interface (API) to build other applications on top of the Sabre capability.

- *Investment platforms* allow investors to purchase or sell securities online. Investment firms providing financial services build portfolios of services, some in house, some from third-party providers through the cloud. These portfolios, replicated across instances in different geographic locations, or in franchises, are also instances of investment platforms.

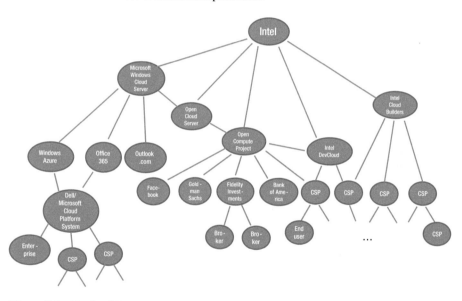

Figure 6-1. *The Intel Xeon processor technology cloud platform ecosystem*

One important characteristic of cloud platforms is that they do not exhibit a flat structure. Instead, they are richly complex and multilayered. It is easier to visualize cloud platforms as sets of connected platforms, each defining a local environment. A platform is more likely to succeed if it is flexible, rapidly adaptable, expressive, and responsive to its environment. This is where platform customization plays a role. Intel, as a platform provider and the sponsor of an innovation platform, has a stake to see the technologies in its portfolio adopted by the largest and most diverse cloud end users. In particular, the placement of servers can occur in a corporate datacenter, or indirectly through enterprises and individual users consuming services at a hosting or cloud service provider (CSP) datacenters.

Figure 6-1 shows a conceptual view of a small portion of the cloud ecosystem behind the Intel Xeon processor technology. Each oval represents a platform, and behind each platform, there is an ecosystem of platform builders and users. Each connector represents a "uses technology from" relationship. On the left side, the Microsoft Windows Cloud Server platform designed by Microsoft Server Engineering, uses Intel Xeon processors. A number of Microsoft business units in turn deploy this platform, such as Windows Azure, Office 365, and Outlook.com. The OEM Dell, in turn, manufactures the Microsoft Cloud Platform System (CPS) Powered by Dell for Azure[2] supporting hybrid cloud deployments outside Microsoft datacenters. Note that the graph represents a conceptual view with a few examples of what amounts to a vast platform ecosystem to describe platform dynamics without attempting to be comprehensive; platform instances with a different processor, or in fact, any other technology, would show as another graph with the appropriate topology. These are deployed in enterprises building private clouds, or by CSPs offering a Windows Azure service in a hybrid cloud setting. CSPs can define subsidiary platforms to their customers based on CPS, represented by the open links underneath. The fact that the shape of the graph depends the player, that is, on who is looking at it, reflects the relativistic nature of cloud services.

Continuing with Figure 6-1, Open Cloud Server (OCS) is a publicly available derivative of Windows Cloud Server that Microsoft contributed to the Open Compute Project (OCP). There are notable OCP deployments, manufactured by original design manufacturers (ODMs) or original equipment manufacturers (OEMs). These include deployments by OCP founders Facebook, Goldman Sachs, Fidelity Investments, and Bank of America fulfilling their strategic goals in harnessing platform scaling benefits for their own companies. These companies can generate subsidiary platforms in their particular ecosystems; for instance, Fidelity Investments supports investment platforms, providing services for security brokers to carry out their business. It is perfectly logical to see integrated or investment platforms sprout out of innovation platforms.

ASCP Demand-Side Historical Background

The demand for IT services drives the profile, character, and demand for ASCPs. In other words, the evolution of IT services and capabilities, and the hardware and the application and software technology ecosystems that support them have been co-evolving through recent history starting in the 1990s. It will be useful at this point to look at the evolution of IT in parallel with the evolution of cloud server platforms. In this co-evolution, first-wave enterprise servers cover the golden era of enterprise platforms. When cloud computing started ramping up in 2007, large CSPs drove the creation and demand for cloud platforms. The third wave, driven by customized CSP platforms, started in 2016. We expect a fourth wave of ASCPs providing the datacenter foundation for the Internet of things (IoT) ramping up around 2018. Chapter 4 covers the four waves of the evolution of cloud platforms, summarized in Figure 4-11.

---

[2]See https://blogs.technet.microsoft.com/windowsserver/2014/10/20/unveiling-the-microsoft-cloud-platform-system-powered-by-dell/.

Figure 6-2 captures the corresponding evolution of IT across the four waves. The rectangles on left side show an approximate timeline for hardware components, platforms, and providers, whereas the rectangles on the right side track application and software solution providers. The ovals in capture the main technological milestones for IT. We cover the various aspects illustrated in Figure 6-2 in the next few sections, starting with the appearance of the Web as a universal application front end. Designed initially as a human–machine interface, the universal interoperability of the Web was so useful and appealing that it morphed into a machine-to-machine application communication interface starting in 2000, with the introduction of web services technology. We will see that web services led to SOA, Web-based APIs, and the emergence of the cloud in 2007. For IT, one of the drivers for the cloud was the ability for CSPs, especially large CSPs such as Amazon Web Services (AWS) to deliver foundation capabilities such as IaaS in a way that was more convenient and economical. In the next stage, smaller CSPs are entering the market, effectively defining a cloud service network. For the next stage, IoT, we can expect increased economies of scale and increasing levels of automation. The promise of SDI is the ability to instantiate not just individual servers, but an entire infrastructure with computation capability, networking and storage, based on a set of service-level agreements (SLAs), templates, and operational policies.

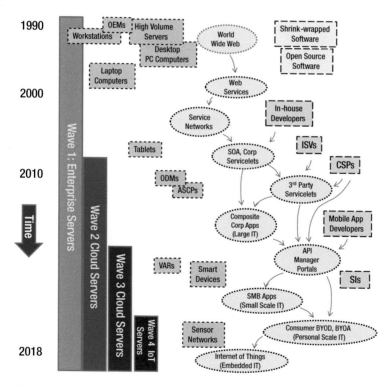

Figure 6-2. *The evolution toward fine-grained IT*

There are a couple of patterns present throughout this evolution: increasing automation and technology evolution enabling ever fine-grained services. An example of the first is the transition from the first Web, to web services, and from SOA, which was essentially breaking monolithic applications into in house, handmade services, to the use of public APIs such as the AWS APIs. Case in point are web servers. As evidenced by their name, web servers were originally applications set up to dispense HTTP content configured by humans. Today embedded web servers vastly outnumber "manual" server-based deployments. There are embedded web servers in most every piece of network equipment, such as network interface devices (modems), routers, and switches, including consumer network equipment. Also practically all standard high-value servers (SHV) today carry one or more embedded web servers, usually implemented by the baseboard management controller (BMC). This server provides an interface to set up firmware parameters (BIOS, UEFI, CPU, chipset, I/O controllers and other devices within). It also provides the RESTful API needed for automated management protocols such as Redfish. Let us review each of the evolutionary stages in detail in the next few sections. We use Figure 6-2 as a reference throughout this discussion.

The First Web and the Rise of Wave 1 Servers for the Enterprise

By the late 1980s, distributed computing and networking was well entrenched in the industry. However, there was no easy way to exchange documents and files, especially across machines from different manufacturers and architectures. Tim Berners-Lee experienced this problem while working as a contractor for CERN in Geneva. Lower level protocols such as TCP/IP were already in widespread use, but higher application layers were still missing; scientists were stymied when they tried to share papers and technical reports electronically. Berners-Lee developed the basic capabilities of the Web, including a method to access other people's documents, setting up a server for this purpose in a proof of concept using a NeXT workstation in his lab. He achieved this goal by creating and integrating three fundamental technology components:

- The Hypertext Markup Language (HTML) defining a data model for the Web.

- The Hypertext Transfer Protocol (HTTP), the protocol for carrying out document exchanges.

- The notion of uniform resource identifiers (URIs) or uniform resource locators (URLs) functioning as universal, platform-independent pointers to access a document. A URL allowed a user to locate the server containing the document and its location within the server in a transparent manner.

When standard high-volume (SHVs) servers running Microsoft Windows became available in the early 1990s, these machines significantly reduced the cost of computing compared to the cost of servers running on RISC processors with the Unix operating system. Most software became available as shrink-wrapped software. Economies of scale allowed shrink-wrapped software to be purchased at a fraction of the cost over software developed in house, with instant gratification. Requests for in-house development could languish for years before development would start. In-house development and integration required high levels of expertise, always in short supply. With lower anticipated costs for hardware and software, IT organizations began purchasing these servers, provisioned with shrink-wrapped software, in large numbers. Another development in the mid-1990s was the broad adoption of Linux and open source software.

The combined availability of shrink-wrapped and open source software enabled SHV servers to provide a predictable and inexpensive computing environment to run the Web, in the process giving it considerable adoption momentum. CERN released Berners-Lee's source code to the public domain in 1991. Even today, much of the Web runs on generic LAMP software bundles or their successors. A LAMP stack was the initial moniker for a stack consisting of the Linux OS, the Apache web server, a MySQL relational database, and the PHP server-side scripting language. Today the term applies to any Web installation made up of open source components.

The diffusion of web technology happened fast. Less than five years later, by 1995, there were thousands of web sites deployed across the world, 23,500 according to an estimate by Internet Live Stats[3]. This growth continues exponentially to date. The statistic for 2016 is slightly above 1 billion. The value of the Web resides mainly in providing a universal, compatible human–machine interface allowing access to data and applications across the Internet regardless of differences in machine architecture.

The beginning of this period saw a shift from running in-house software to widely available, prepackaged, shrink-wrapped applications. Prime examples were productivity applications, such as the Microsoft Office suite and the Windows 3.1 operating system on which it ran. This software ran on PC computers from a diverse array of manufacturers. This development was highly disruptive to IT organizations, which, up to that time, had an iron grip on the development and delivery of corporate applications. We see the first inklings of the move toward a *self-service* view of technology that would become a distinguishing characteristic of the cloud. Another pattern that started becoming apparent is that of *shadow IT*, applied to teams or individuals adopting a self-service approach for a technology capability formerly provided by their IT organization. Even today, business units keep driving this shift, prompted by the need for economic efficiency and by the business need and time-sensitive nature of these capabilities, and the perception or inability of IT organizations to deliver on these requirements. The adoption of shrink-wrapped software was prompted by mainframe application backlogs of three years or more in the 1980s[4]. An ad from Phaser, Inc. in 1984[5] cited a survey that reported a 3.5-year delay between an application request and the development to begin in mainframe environments and touted the use of a development environment running on an IBM PC to shorten editing and compilation cycles. The irony here is that PC computers did not only get used as development tools, but eventually became vehicles to run applications by themselves.

---

[3]World Wide Web Consortium (W3C) and World Wide Web Foundation, "Total Number of Websites," http://www.internetlivestats.com/total-number-of-websites/, July 2016.
[4]"Application Backlogs," *Computerworld*, December 14, 1987.
[5]"m3278/SPF Puts Micros On-line to Mainframes and Cuts Application Software Backlog," *Computerworld*, January 16, 1987.

At the beginning of this period, there was little functional differentiation between PCs, workstations, and what would become SHV servers. Berners-Lee's first web server was a repurposed NeXT workstation, and workstations were just PCs, but with a more powerful RISC processor. However, by the mid-1990s well-differentiated SHV servers had significant market presence. These servers featured multiple processors, and higher bandwidth extended Industry Standard Architecture (EISA) slots for peripheral cards instead of the Industry Standard Architecture (ISA) slots found in PCs, and the use of the Small Computer System Interface (SCSI) standard for I/O instead of the lower performing Integrated Drive Electronics (IDE) standard in PCs[6].

Web Services: Platforms for Corporate Service Networks

The next step in technology evolution occurred with the realization in the technical community that the World Wide Web was good not only for human-machine communication, but also for interoperable machine-to-machine communication, meaning a computer communication not directly initiated by humans. This realization led to the development of web services technology in the early 2000s. Two flavors of web services were developed: Simple Object Access Protocol (SOAP) and Representational State Transfer (REST). Web services technology is firmly established today. Web services add a few more foundational technologies: XML, WSDL, and UDDI. Extensible Markup Language (XML) is a way for encoding documents using human-readable characters, yet it is machine-readable. Web Services Description Language (WSDL) is an XML-encoded interface definition language describing the functionality of a web service. Universal Description, Discovery and Integration (UDDI), a discoverable registry, is also XML-encoded, listing web services to allow machines to determine which web services are available.

Web services protocols allow accessing resources with just a URI. All negotiation and handshaking between entities takes place at the time of access under a modality called *late binding*. Systems supporting late binding are known as *loosely coupled* systems. In contrast, *strongly coupled* legacy systems require significant software context and configuration before the any exchange could happen. Thus, although functionally similar from a programming perspective, distributed object model protocols such as Distributed Component Object Model (DCOM) from Microsoft or Common Object Request Broker Architecture (CORBA) or Remote Procedure Call (RPC) for Unix systems and the Java Remote Method Invocation (RMI) imposed considerable deployment overhead and restrictions[7]. These included requirements to compile the code together, or supporting communication only through a relatively narrow range of peer software versions, possibly from the same vendors. Protocols available did not support communication across objects from different OSs. This state of affairs was obviously unrealistic for applications running on the Internet.

---

[6]"Server Upgrades: Vendors Hop Aboard Extended Express," *InfoWorld*, p. 25, August 21, 1995.
[7]J. Levitt, "From EDI to XML and UDDI: A Brief History of Web Services," http://www.informationweek.com/from-edi-to-xml-and-uddi-a-brief-history-of-web-services/d/d-id/1012008?, September 27, 2001.

There were deployment restrictions for some application implementations in the sense that one component could only support one instance of the application, and therefore must be replicated for each application instance. This approach led to unnecessary replication, bloat, and complexity as the different instances evolved over time, diverged, and compatibilities showed up. Multiple instances also led to increased licensing costs. The availability of loosely coupled web services allowed factoring out functions to a single, common service. These common functions then would run as self-standing services. An application needing the capability simply invokes that particular service through a RESTful interface.

As an example, applications as diverse as human resources, the internal phone directory, and expense reporting all need to access information about the employee roster in an organization. Having separate copies of these resources means allocating infrastructure to run the multiple copies. Running multiple copies also increased database software licensing fees. Having several copies of the same data also brought the problem of propagating updates and keeping data synchronized across the different copies.

Before the cloud, applications circa 2000 ran in stovepipes with strongly coupled architectures as the norm. As an illustrative example, Figure 6-3 depicts three applications, A1, A2, and A3, each running a separate copy of the application on dedicated hardware. The common practice was to run each instance on a separate machine, even if they were nearly identical deployments. If the three applications ran from common data, such as an employee roster database, it was also necessary to replicate the database using a batch process. Real-time updates were not practical. If the stacks were from different vendors, it was worse; the data from one database had to be dumped offline to some common format such as text and reloaded to the target database using complex and cumbersome extract-transform-load (ETL) processes. With web services late binding, it became possible for any application to access a shared database through a RESTful interface.

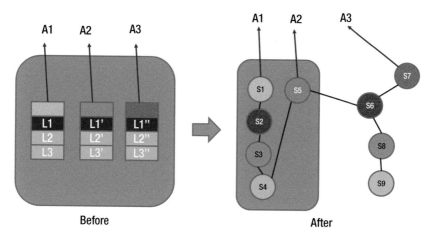

Figure 6-3. *Transition from application stovepipes to services and a service ecosystem*

In sum, loosely coupled web services enable abstracting out common capabilities across multiple stack instances, such as the employee roster just mentioned, to a single or small number of instances. All applications needing access to the employee database now plug in to the employee database service. The original, tightly coupled, duplicated stacks in the stovepipes morph into a graph, with each node representing a coalesced capability delivered as a service. In other words, the stovepipe "forest" morphs into a service network, depicted on the right side of Figure 6-3.

Each node in the network defines a *service component* or *servicelet*. Servicelets are self-standing application components, accessible through a URI and discoverable through a registry (UDDI) using WSDL. Of course, there is a bit of oversimplification for clarity; the single instance requires redesigning to support concurrency and performance for the new environment. This redesign is usually not viable unless it is part of a multiyear conversion to SOA.

Redesign issues notwithstanding, Figure 6-3 shows the original stack on the right redesigned and replaced by services S2, S3, and S4. The servicelets being self-standing allows external hosting as servicelets S6, S8, and S9. The decision to use S2, S3, or S4 and not S6, S8, and S9 might come down to quality of service (QoS) or business issues. Assume that application A1 has stringent security requirements and therefore deployed with servicelets running in an internal cloud. Application A3 carries more relaxed requirements and therefore uses servicelets deployed as a SaaS application hosted by a third party. Application A2 is somewhere in between, using external components, but plugging in to the internal database.

An example of a type A1 application is an employee directory and organizational chart. An example of type A2 application is an expense reporting human resources application. All the logic comes from a third-party provider, which reaches to the employee roster servicelet. Type A3 applications could be applications posted on the company's web site.

Servicelets might not be fully formed applications given their intended use as components; they might be accessible only through a web service API. In their present-day incarnation, servicelets usually run in a virtualized environment hosted in a pool of servers. Workloads can be rebalanced across this pool by managing how they are launched or even moving virtual machines around following specific performance policies.

Applications built out of service components are called *composite* applications, and the architectural style for building this type of applications is known as an SOA. The primary goal of the SOA as defined in the mid-2000s was to achieve radical cost reductions in the delivery of IT to the enterprise through the elimination of duplicate or redundant functions. An IT organization can now deploy a specific function, such as the employee information database, just once as a service, instead of deploying a copy for each application with the added resources and cost of data synchronization.

During this period, in-house developers in IT organizations played a significant role in rearchitecting corporate applications toward an SOA. Independent software vendors such as TIBCO brought in tools such as the implementation of the notion of enterprise service buses as a transport for servicelets to interact, first inside the enterprise and then outside.

Wave 2 Server Platforms for the Large Clouds

SOA adoption took place primarily inside large organizations through the middle of the decade of the 2000s. Because URIs are truly universal handles, practitioners noted that it mattered little whether the resource lived inside or outside the corporate walls. IT organizations realized that it was not always desirable or cost efficient to host generic services in house, especially those unrelated to the organization's line of business, such as e-mail and messaging or even storage. Therefore, when a specific capability became available as a third-party servicelet, it became a target for outsourcing, especially for those capabilities not related to line of business.

Kin Lane[8] noted significant milestones in web APIs: Two pioneers for web APIs are Salesforce.com and eBay, who published their first APIs in 2000, the same year as the introduction of web services. Facebook and Twitter launched theirs in 2006. The year 2006 also saw the launch of Mashery, one of the first, if not the first, API service provider, and AWS. The availability of servicelets from large providers such as Amazon or smaller providers through API portals facilitated the externalization of internal servicelets such as S1 through S5 in Figure 6-3 to servicelets hosted by third parties, such as S6 through S9 in Figure 6-3. An early servicelet was Amazon S3 (Simple Storage Service); it was offered only as an API, specifically a RESTful API supporting HTTP PUT and GET requests on objects and files.

The emergence of the cloud around 2007 came up with perfect synchronicity, representing a development synergistic with the SOA transformation. A little documented, unintended effect of the transition to composite applications is that although service components might have started as in-sourced service components within the confines of the enterprise boundaries, in reality there were no fundamental reasons why they had to. Castro-Leon and Chang[9] postulated the externalization service components in 2007, especially generic components such as compute or storage, services currently associated with cloud infrastructure as a service (IaaS). The drivers were pure economics, whereby third parties offered servicelets at a lower cost than using in-sourced equivalents. This was due to two factors: Providers specializing in a specific type of service develop skills and knowledge and therefore build and deliver these services more efficiently than corporate IT can; and second, a virtualized cloud infrastructure enabled amortizing physical assets over a larger customer base, allowing economies of scale well beyond what the few internal clients in a corporation could allow. Most of these providers were also motivated to charge as little as possible to prime the network effect as quickly as possible and gain scale and market presence.

Large servicelet providers such as Amazon, Google, and Microsoft created demand for second-wave servers, the first ASCPs where ODMs started taking a prominent role.

---

[8]K. Lane, "History of APIs," http://history.apievangelist.com/.
[9]E. Castro-Leon, J. He, and M. Chang, "Scaling Down SOA to Small Businesses," *IEEE International Conference on Service-Oriented Computing and Applications,* June 2007.

Wave 3 Server Platforms for the Small Clouds

Externalized services were useful not only to large corporations outsourcing functional components for their applications. Because these servicelets were available for just a few dollars per month, small and medium business could also afford them, acquiring the same capabilities as their large corporate brethren without spending hundreds of millions of dollars building a datacenter. This phenomenon marked the transition from the era of *large IT* to *small-scale IT,* as shown in Figure 6-2. A small business struggling to maintain two or three servers in a room to run a few applications could afford to have these applications served as a cloud service at a lower cost.

Beyond servicelets with APIs, third parties began offering fully formed applications accessible through a web browser, the universal interface. Early, pioneering examples are web-based mail applications such as Google Mail and Yahoo! Mail and the customer relationship management (CRM) application from Salesforce.com. These applications required little more than a simple registration process to set up, to the point that individual consumers could use them just as easily. At this point, the small-scale IT with SMBs became *personal IT* for individual consumers. This event marked the *democratization* of IT[10] where capabilities that used to require IT staff to implement were now available to individuals on a self-service basis. The cloud truly had transformed the industry.

The Wave 3 universe evolved into the rich, multipolar universe illustrated in Figure 4-7. Demand for Wave 2 platforms from large CSPs is still there, growing fast. Likewise, demand for first-wave enterprise servers is also still present, although not growing as fast. Smaller CSPs providing specialized servicelets or hosting APIs have an option to outsource some of their servicelet needs to second-wave providers, especially commodity services unrelated to their line of business. Doing so allows these companies to focus on their core strengths and provide services in areas where they are competitive. This specialization makes the notion of developing customized platforms for sustained and strategic competitive advantage the same dynamic that motivated large cloud players to design theirs. We will cover some possible approaches to address this type of demand later in this chapter.

Please note that smaller CSPs does not necessarily mean small companies. Some of these companies are members of giant telecom conglomerates such as T-Systems or NTT Communications. These companies have a strong tradition of service delivery, and are poised to deliver, for instance, very high-quality cloud services to corporations in segments not well served by one-size-fits-all service offerings. This addresses some of the initial objections some consumers of cloud corporate services had at the beginning about take it or leave it, nonnegotiable QoS promises. There is no inherent lower QoS in cloud offerings when compared to equivalent corporate services. The initial complaints were likely due to service expectation mismatches between service providers and service consumers, and due to operators going through a learning curve. By definition, if there are metrics to track QoS and the service provider carries and implements internal and external processes to track service quality, this will allow the provider to build up meet any target QoS objectives the customer desires.

---

[10]E. Castro-Leon, J. He, and M. Chang, *The Business Value of Virtual Service Grids* (Intel Press, 2008).

Wave 4 Server Platforms for IoT

Figure 6-2 at the bottom points to one more evolutionary step toward finer-grained IT where there are no people involved, just machine-to-machine communication. We use the moniker *embedded IT* for this particular case. This is a defining characteristic of the IoT. IoT devices can be small, but also large, or very large. An example of a large object is a networked vehicle, such as the Chevrolet Volt or the Tesla electric cars. In particular, the Chevrolet Volt is an example of an edge device connected to the General Motors OnStar servicelet. This servicelet allows the exchange of diagnostics as well as the implementation of certain functions, such as operating the windows or locking or unlocking the vehicle from another edge device. An example of a potentially very large node is the out-of-band management infrastructure for a datacenter. This will allow a company to leverage a large number of servers as bare metal resources using an IPMI infrastructure in a uniform manner regardless of whether the resources are inside or outside the corporate walls.

We anticipate that demand from this segment will initially come from smaller value-added resellers (VARs) or system integrators (SIs). Our assessment is that the technology frameworks to satisfy this kind of demand are still in their infancy. A typical scenario would be for a VAR to place an order of fewer than 1,000 platforms at a provider web site for a customized server, have it manufactured to order, and retrieve the order a few weeks later.

The barrier today is that even minor feature or functionality changes in a platform require revalidation, currently a long and arduous process. With increased automation, it might be possible to deliver baseboard variants without compromising board quality.

IoT will also drive demand for third-wave devices. The edge devices mentioned thus far are the most visible exponents. However, enabling edge devices requires a strong and robust service network powered by third-wave platform services to facilitate device communication and to carry out core computations.

Developing Hardware for the Cloud

Within the Intel technology ecosystem that underlies many cloud platforms, manufacturers can be one of three types:

- *Original equipment manufacturers, or OEMs* design servers using CPUs, chipsets, network and I/O controllers, and other semiconductor components from various suppliers, adding significant technology content and supply chain expertise on top of the embedded technology capabilities. Some of the system features, for instance the CPU instruction set, are determined by the underlying CPU architecture. Different platform designs can be endowed with unique capabilities where these capabilities use common technologies embedded in silicon. Bringing these unique capabilities requires vast resources. Smaller manufacturers tend to rely and stay closer to reference designs provided by the semiconductor manufacturers. OEMs derive significant revenue from support contracts.

- *Original design manufacturers, or ODMs* have traditionally taken logic designs from OEMs to manufacture them into finished servers on contract. Their expertise resides in efficiently manufacturing boards at the lowest possible cost. Some ODMs have a global presence in their manufacturing facilities but have less name recognition than their OEM counterparts because the manufactured products carry the OEM brand name.

- *Value-added resellers, or VARs* bring expertise in a particular knowledge domain, developing and customizing applications in that domain to resell to end users as turnkey solutions. The customization work includes hardware, which might come from an OEM or an ODM as unbranded "white box" systems. VARs derive revenue from the sales of the solution and associated activities: consulting, integration, training, and support. A company that emphasizes the integration of existing components is known as an SI.

Hardware Development for Second-Wave Platforms

During the first wave, most enterprise end users purchased their platforms from OEMs. If there was a need for a turnkey platform optimized for a certain application, a customer could go to a VAR or a system integrator (SI) specializing in that particular application. These VARs would build their application on top of a turnkey OEM server, or at most, use a bare bones or unbranded white box server. In any case, whether OEM or white box, there were few opportunities to customize baseboards or anything finer grained. Manufacturers like Supermicro have a large selection of chassis in their portfolio where customers selected one of the offerings. There was no provision to change a form factor to fit an application, beyond cosmetic changes such as nameplates.

Figure 6-4 summarizes the relationships for players in the high-volume server market during the first wave and before second-wave or hyperscale cloud platforms became pervasive. SHVs share silicon technology from technology providers in the form of CPUs and chipsets, I/O, network and management controllers, and other basic components. OEMs source components from different technology providers. The OEM selected components might have different implementations, for instance an OEM could source SCSI controllers from different manufacturers, including Adaptec, Western Digital, or Symbios Logic, but in spite of different hardware implementations, these controllers were built up to meet the SCSI interface standards. Technology providers make available reference designs for OEMs to adapt into their platforms with a few modifications. OEMs made sure that the offerings from different technology providers worked together in spite of the unavoidable differences and small variances in the implementation of the standard interfaces.

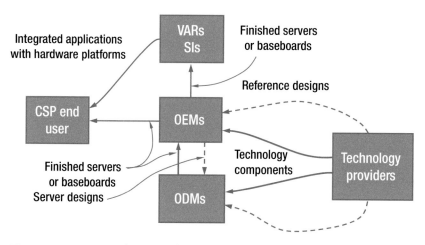

Figure 6-4. *First-wave [enterprise] server supply chain*

The investments OEMs made to carry this integration required a large technical development and manufacturing capability. OEM designs could be manufactured at an in-house facility, or under contract at an ODM factory, and hence the *original design* moniker, where an ODM would carry out manufacturing using someone else's blueprints, OEM blueprints in this case. The OEM then proceeded to ship the finished product to end users or to VARs and SIs. Because of the large investment needed in their design and manufacturing, these servers usually address broad market segments. Through network effects, the large ecosystem provides a vast support system with expertise and materials with availability through multiple vendors and channels that ensures stable, predictable, and reasonable acquisition and lifetime costs.

A number of changes in the technology flows take place for the supply chain second-wave cloud platforms. The end user is now one of the large preeminent cloud service providers: Amazon, Google, Facebook, and Microsoft in the United States and Baidu, Tencent, and Alibaba in the People's Republic of China. Each of these companies might deploy 100,000 or more servers per year, sometimes much more. The size of these deployments allow them not just to define application-specific SKUs, but an application-specific architecture, or in other words, their own application-specific cloud architecture or ASCP. At the very least, these players subsume most of the validation functions performed by OEMs, and because they are so significant to in-house development, they subsume most of the VAR and SIs as well that used to be present for first-wave enterprise customers.

For the manufacturing of Wave 2 servers, the traditional sequence of *functions*, namely the *design, test, validation, and integration* functions described in Chapter 4, does not change. What changes is who carries these tasks. For first-wave server platforms, OEMs used to carry design, test, and validation. Because of the large market segments involved, the technology providers could afford to dedicate large technical and business teams to a particular OEM. Under a second-wave environment, the CSP is nominally the platform owner. The technology provider still assigns dedicated teams to help the CSP develop a platform. However, it is challenging for CSPs to run the ship as tightly as OEMs do. For one thing, OEMs have decades of experience in honing design, test, and validation processes and have built extensive relationships with the ecosystem, whereas CSPs as latecomers must go through a steep learning curve. Furthermore, and consistent with their desire to use multiple supply sources, a CSP might engage more than one ODM, and although each of the platform's specifications supplied to each of the ODMs might have the same architecture and the same RTL specifications, each ODM will generate a different hardware instantiation. These differences occur even when their engineering teams follow the design rules recommended by the technology provider for board design, possibly using the same design tools. There will be differences in terms of the arrangement of the components in the board and the actual board traces. Likewise, the ODMs might spec different controller chips for management functions or even different suppliers for the resistors, capacitors, and inductors soldered onto the board. The resulting boards will be nominally identical in their logic behavior. In practice, there will be subtle behavioral differences across boards in the ODM offerings. Where electrical margins are tight, there are cases where bugs show up in one design but not in the other. Some analog parameters can actually be very different. For example, there is usually high variance in power consumption numbers at various operating points, between ODM offerings, but often across different batches from the same manufacturers: Whereas one board might exhibit an idle power draw of 80 watts, the next one might draw 120 watts.

The technology flows for reference designs become more complex (see Figure 6-5). Platform development becomes a codevelopment activity involving the CSP, the ODM or OEM assigned to carry out the server manufacturing, and the technology providers. Technology providers now must share their reference designs with the CSP, not just the manufacturer. ODMs play a more prominent role, and instead of their traditional function as service manufacturer for OEMs, they now carry out manufacturing on behalf of the requesting CSP. Some CSPs keep their designs secret, and some actually publish their designs to a public venue or repository. For instance, Facebook and Microsoft publish theirs as contributions to the OCP as shown in the cloud platforms ecosystem in Figure 6-1.

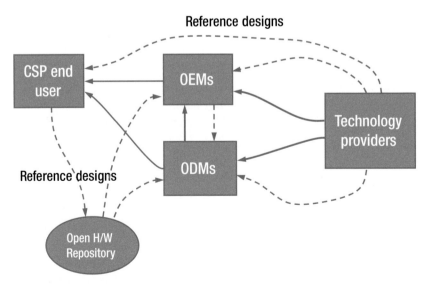

Figure 6-5. *Second-wave [cloud] server supply chain*

The large production volumes involved allow technology providers and ODMs to justify fully dedicated technical and marketing teams to a design project. OEMs still have a play, although they must face significant role changes: There is no longer need for the OEM's traditional customer support functions, nor there is a need to maintain a platform roadmap because the end user owns the roadmap. Different companies have taken different approaches. Hewlett-Packard Enterprise established a close relationship with Taiwanese ODM Foxconn, whereas Dell builds cloud platforms through a dedicated division, Data Center Solutions (DCS) and more recently, Data Center Scalable Solutions (DSS) specialized in manufacturing customized platforms. Dell DSS addresses the needs of CSPs smaller than those that DCS serves[11].

Hardware Development for Third-Wave Platforms

Customization projects for third-wave platforms involve amortizing the investment over a range of 10,000 to 100,000 servers. This means development costs will need to be amortized over a smaller production base compared to the production base of the second-wave players, which was 100,000 units or more. Early observations indicate that platform-building processes for this segment are possible with an incremental evolution over the processes followed by the large CSPs.

There are two factors helping new third-wave entrants.

1. Through precedents created by the pioneering CSPs, the industry has already gone through a learning curve in building ASCPs, at the very least in defining examples of what is or is not possible with an ASCP platform customization approach.

2. An ecosystem for ASCPs already exists that works at least for hyperscale deployments. New entrants need to show the framework is feasible for them. The availability of ASCP specifications for reuse from posted with the OCP[12], lowers the barriers to entry for new platform players. Likewise, there are seasoned providers, ODMs such as Quanta and Wiwynn and OEMs such as Hewlett-Packard Enterprise and Dell with experience serving the pioneer CSPs motivated and willing to expand their market participation with the new entrants.

Although third-wave CSP players might not be as massive in their platform deployments as second-wave providers, there are precedent mechanisms to create a critical mass for ASCP creation through aggregation or pooling, the same pattern that drives economies of scale in the cloud. One is the creation of the appropriate industry groups with an interest in creating platforms for specific market segments. These platforms can serve e-commerce needs, or perhaps small banking. A counterargument is that the potential members of these industry groups compete against each other,

---

[11]T. P. Morgan, "Dell Leverages Hyperscale Expertise for HPC, Clouds and Enterprise," http://www.nextplatform.com/2015/08/24/dell-leverages-hyperscale-expertise-for-hpc-clouds-and-enterprise/, 2015.

[12]The Open Compute Project web site can be found at http://www.opencompute.org/.

making it difficult for these groups to form in the first place. In actuality, this is a case of coopetition, where the desire to emulate the success of the ASCP pioneers trumps centrifugal competitive forces from concerns about working with competitors, or most of the members might operate in diverse geographical regions, and therefore do not compete directly. Furthermore, such a sponsor could be an existing industry group. For instance, co-op consortia including the World Council of Credit Unions and the Cooperatives of the Americas, representing tens of thousands of co-ops worldwide and hundreds of millions of members, are currently specifying digital platforms for their network[13].

The development framework for second-wave platforms is a scaled down variant of processes carried out with OEMs for enterprise servers, where the end user took over the role of OEM, bringing in one or more ODMs to build the resulting designs under contract. Some codevelopment roles were present, where CSPs worked with technology providers to integrate advanced technologies or technologies under development to bring capabilities to market earlier than under the enterprise platform model of the first wave. The early integration allowed building customer-specific variants of these technologies to CSP specifications relative to what was going to be available in the mainstream versions.

Based on the lessons learned from the development of second-wave platforms, we propose a framework, which is an evolution of the framework that governed the codevelopment of second-wave platforms, illustrated in Figure 6-6. The framework encompasses a number of actors, namely a CSP seeking to build an ASCP with application needs and an ODM or OEM with hardware knowledge taking a technical lead to build an ASCP to meet the CSP's needs. The CSP and the ODM or OEM cannot complete the project alone. They bring in relationships with other technology providers as necessary to help with project execution. The presence of an integration lab in Figure 6-6 is a crucial element in the service interactions, where all project participants converge to carry out ASCP integration tasks. The lab accelerates technology development for this project by enabling the participants or *actors* to carry technology development and integration tasks in parallel. This is a crucial time-to-market consideration. It reduces the burden on the actors to deliver a finished technology portfolio before going to market. Technology providers can take a technology under development and make a decision to integrate based on the project requirements, not on readiness based on a roadmap, which ultimately is an artificial deadline imposed by the traditional product planning process. The technology provider can make a decision to move ahead, and integrate based primarily on project requirements and allocate customization resources on that basis as needed under a *directed engineering* development framework.

---

[13]"2nd Conference on Cooperative Competiveness and the Digital Economy," http://dga. kennesaw.edu/cooperativaconf/index.php, 2016.

Project actors bring in their knowledge, experience, and resources to the project in a service exchange to build an ASCP. The motivation for the actors' involvement is the maximization of business value for all participants.

The model is decentralized and relational. It is decentralized in the sense that the engagement pictured in Figure 6-6 is only one instance of multiple engagements occurring in the industry at any given time. There is no platform owner mission control defining when these engagements need to happen. The main motivation for actors to participate in an ASCP engagement is value maximization for each participant. A relational model is different from the traditional goods-dominant logic (GDL) model. Under a product-oriented GDL model, the goal is to sell product, where the most important metrics are *design wins* and widget units sold, and the design wins are transactional. Product sales are one-time events and providers' roadmaps determine continuity. This means that technology consumers must resynchronize their needs at each turn of the providers' technology roadmaps. Resynchronizing means extra work for technology consumers in shoehorning a general roadmap to customer needs, and also extra work for the sales, marketing, and engineering organizations on the provider side in releasing a product line that requires realignment for most every application.

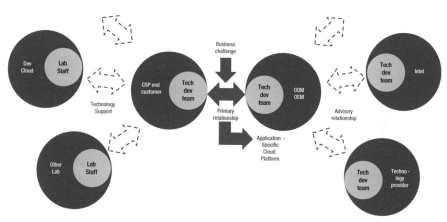

Figure 6-6. *Platform codevelopment framework for third-wave ASCPs*

Given that ASCPs, if successful, evolve and persist across several years or technology turns, a relational model for actors is more appropriate than the one-time transactional model. A technology provider strives not just for a design win, but for an *architecture win*, where ideally the provider's participation persists for the lifetime of the ASCP. At this point, we can say that a technology provider is engaged in a *service* relationship. Under this arrangement, the relationship part overtakes the notion of product. Providers still can measure their business activity using the traditional methods of units sold, perhaps as an accounting method for profit and loss reports. However, the relationship gives technology providers a window to forecast future sales, and perhaps as important, providers get directional input directly from users for future capabilities, and an indication of where new investment should take place. Some companies, especially software companies are "servitizing" their offerings by moving from the current model of granting a perpetual license for a particular software version to a recurring charge model. Adobe has implemented this model with product offerings such as Acrobat and Framemaker;

Microsoft is carrying out a similar strategy with the Office suite and Avid with its Sibelius music notation software. Microsoft offers Office 365 under a subscription model. Furthermore, beginning with Adobe Acrobat XI and Avid Sibelius 8.0, these products are no longer available under a perpetual license. Unfortunately, this change, without the relationship part and accompanying value cocreation strategy, is likely to generate customer resistance.

Some companies have engaged in relationship activities that resemble ASCP value cocreation relationship, such as the technology enabling assist that Intel or any of the large OEMs carry on behalf of technology adopters. Most companies use enabling to support a general technology roadmap rather than customer-specific ASCP platform development.

Hardware Development for Fourth-Wave Platforms

The capability to build and deploy ASCPs afforded the large CSPs nimbleness, by virtue of being able to adapt their own platform to rapidly changing requirements. They were able to attain a sustained competitive advantage as witnessed by their remarkable growth. Amazon AWS, for instance, was able to build a portfolio of cloud services with remarkable breadth, width, and stickiness that essentially define the AWS cloud platform; stickiness in the sense that corporate IT customers find these services extremely useful and valuable. Unfortunately, this state of affairs also creates a quandary: The adopters of these services find themselves unable to draw like services from a second provider. The irony here is that technology has enabled the elimination of single suppliers but has had the unintended effect of creating the same problem at the next layer up of abstraction. Today it is very difficult for a cloud customer to switch providers, because service offerings are generally not interoperable, each with unique service operating models and APIs. Most IaaS providers today focus on datacenter efficiency, in "rack and stack" operations, uptime, and power and thermal efficiency to some extent. There is less emphasis on service interoperability.

Assuming that the ecosystem evolves to a service network by the fourth wave, as depicted in Figure 4-7, there will be strong forces for CSPs to specialize to differentiate service offerings and maximize competitive advantage while reducing the numbers of direct competitors. Interoperability is still possible across infrastructure service offerings through published APIs or the use of standardized APIs. This is a pattern seen in other industries. The automotive ecosystem, for instance, uses bolts normalized for type, thread pitch, and material hardness[14]. Tires also come in standardized rim sizes and aspect ratios. Tire manufacturers can optimize their offerings for long wear, or for high traction or for high-speed operation and be able to command higher revenue, yet interoperability is never in question: Any tire of a given size specification will fit a rim of the same size regardless of manufacturer.

---

[14]Fastenal Company, *Fastenal Technical Reference Guide*, https://www.fastenal.com/content/documents/FastenalTechnicalReferenceGuide.pdf, 2005.

At a first blush, it would appear that if CSPs in Figure 4-7 developed their own customized platform, the ecosystem would devolve into platform chaos. This assumes these players could afford building their platforms in the same way second-wave players did. It does not need to be this way. What is needed is a platform framework that allows innovation from within combined with cross-industry agreement about what interfaces should look like. The state of the art today is less than ideal in this respect, because the contributing technologies do not offer much flexibility when it comes to customization, so this problem needs to be addressed before tackling the interoperability problem.

In a roadmap-driven technology portfolio, technology providers struggle to develop a comprehensive portfolio. This effort is not always efficient in that despite the best efforts during product planning, there will be aspects in technology that do not take hold in the marketplace. What would be useful is a technology architecture that is not as finished, but designed for flexibility of instantiation, to take advantage of a codevelopment process to hone it for particular CSP instances. This requires closer relationships between CSPs and technology providers than those that exist today. The investment in building the relationships will require more effort. However, these relationships will foster future business, bringing additional revenue, and allows the platform owner to defer investment on a capability until there is demonstrated demand. This is consistent with the economic efficiency associated with the cloud. Furthermore, the technical investment in carrying out a technology instantiation with a CSP will be highly focused engineering directed by customer need with higher probability of payoff than roadmap-based effort done on a speculative basis.

Given the degree of specialization expected for CSP services, fourth-wave ASCPs will need to be economically viable in quantities as small as 1,000 units. With these numbers, it will be difficult to justify teams of engineers dedicated to designing an ASCP for just one CSP. Fewer engineers will require increased automated and self-service processes, allowing the automated specification of design variants and the validation of these variants with a lot less labor than what it takes today.

Execution Model for Platform Customization

Figure 6-7 shows an example of an execution model for platform customization for a hypothetical project where Intel becomes a silicon technology provider for an ODM or OEM as the principal partner in an ASCP project. During the initial exploration phase, it helps to become acquainted with the specific pain points the CSP is trying to address with the project. It must high value enough to justify the investment by all the partners. There are ecosystem-scaling considerations for the pain points as well: If the issue has broad manifestation in the industry, it might be worthwhile to bring additional CSPs into the project. This is possible as long as they are compatible or complementary, or work in different geographic regions so they do not see themselves as competitors. Additional scaling might be possible by working this project under the auspices of an industry group.

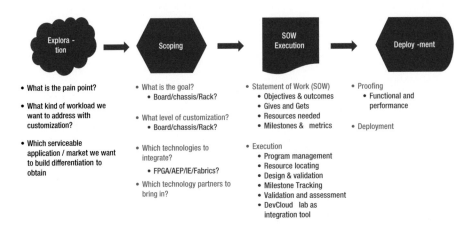

Figure 6-7. Engagement model for platform customization

Project scoping refers to the broad technical design parameters for the project: Are the goals for the project attainable with a custom board design? What additional levels of technology integration should be brought into the project? Chassis level, or rack, row level, or higher? Another consideration is the applicability of emerging technologies to achieve a less expensive or more capable alternative to current technologies. For instance, the use of FPGA might allow the design of a high-performance solution with lower grade and less expensive CPUs; the use of nonvolatile memory DIMM devices plus high-speed networking might enable some CSPs to do away with the direct-attached storage device (DASD) tier for some applications, resulting in very dense, compact form factors. Additional partners could be invited, depending on the stated requirements for the customized platform.

With the technical requirements scoped, the next step is the execution of business and technical processes. There is usually a statement of work (SOW) signed. The degree of formality varies depending on the complexity of the project, the culture, and possible concerns from participants. Once project participants close on the agreements, the technical execution of the project starts. The project goes through the usual design, test, and validation phases of regular projects. There is already an extensive body of development experience for multipartner projects. The only significant addition is the role of a cloud-based integration lab that provides a common view of the platform under development to all project participants.

Deployment encompasses unit testing, with the prototype taken out of the integration lab and deployed in a small field test by the sponsoring CSP. If there is an agreement among the participants, at this point specifications, blueprints, and other intellectual property are posted as a contribution to the industry. There is no obligation to publish every single aspect of the projects. Participants might elect to keep certain components or implementations as black boxes. This is acceptable as long as these black boxes provide clear interfaces to allow functional substitution in future implementations.

The Future for ASCP Design

Processes for building ASCPs for the world's largest CSPs are well established, if not well documented yet. These processes evolved from intercompany processes used by large OEMs to build their platforms. OEMs designed these processes for SHV manufacturing to meet worldwide enterprise server demand, with shipments on the order of 1 million servers per year. OEMs use a segmentation approach to meet general market needs; for instance, low-cost, single-CPU desktop derivatives; dual-CPU large-volume, general-purpose servers that make up most datacenter deployments today; quad CPUs for database back-end applications; and high reliability, availability, and serviceability (RAS) for mission-critical applications.

The intent for segmentation is to cover market needs as broadly as possible. This development model makes it expensive to optimize designs for a specific end user, given that the process to incorporate architectural changes can take years. This left the market vulnerable to demand upsets when new users or new classes of users came up with demand vectors that were orthogonal to features available in the normalized SHV offerings. It was possible to fulfill new applications when price was no object; for instance, aerospace or military applications with budgets that allowed designing customized machines under contract with very small production runs. Lesser applications were less fortunate; they had to get by with SHV offerings that were not a good match for the application, or had go to market with less than ideal capabilities.

Although it might not have been obvious at the time, when the industry could not meet the unique demands from large CSPs starting in 2007, these CSPs decided to become their own OEM. This decision was transformative for the industry. At first, the financial crisis and ensuing demand collapse for the economy at large masked what was to be an epochal change. Even after the world economy recovered, the growth curve for enterprise servers did not recover to its precrisis rate. The IT ecosystem started a rapid transformation to cloud services to the extent that most of the ensuing growth went to the cloud. Actually the growth of the cloud is faster than shown. The enterprise segment contains a cloud component as well for private cloud deployments inside the enterprise.

The pioneering CSPs driving the second-wave ASCPs collaborated with technology providers, starting from existing SHV processes to design, integrate, and deploy the platform capabilities aligned to their requirements, and were able to break even with run rates of 100,000 servers delivered per year. As mentioned earlier, these collaborations are long-term collaborations that persist to this date, having spanned a number of technology generations.

Building on top of the pioneering work by large CSPs, the next segment of CSPs in ecosystem scaling, is still in the second wave, with yearly demands between 100,000 and as low as 10,000. We can expect that some pioneering players, seeking competitive advantage through platform customization, will succeed in building their own ASCPs, meeting platform cost goals by riding on the maturity curve, taking advantage of published reference designs, and reaching out to ODMs with prior cloud platform manufacturing experience.

Third-wave CSP actors are even smaller, with yearly deployment rates on the order of 1,000 to 10,000. Cost efficiencies must make it viable to build ASCPs with production runs one more order of magnitude smaller. There will be two new elements enabling this new class of ASCP players. The first is the use of integration labs, essentially bare metal labs using cloud technology to develop cloud platforms. The integration labs will allow concurrent development of development tasks that used to be carried out in serial fashion. One such example is baseboard validation.

During validation, and under the CSP/ODM/technology provider relationships defined in Figure 6-8, when the CSP detects an anomaly in a board sample for a certain technology component, the first port of call for the CSP is the technology provider, whose technology the ODM integrates into the baseboard. The normal procedure is for the CSP to file an error report to the technology provider. An engineer with the technology provider attempts to replicate the error condition using reference boards, or board samples from the ODM, and comes up with a solution that fixes the error condition. The engineer then interacts with the OEM or ODM carrying out the manufacturing and verifies the problem has been solved. The engineer then reports back to the CSP with an account of the work carried out. For particularly vexing situations, multiple round trips and weeks of regularly scheduled meetings might be required.

Figure 6-8. *Baseboard validation dependency chain*

The hardest problems to solve are hardware race conditions from the subtle difference across board implementations mentioned earlier, or analog transients that corrupt digital states. Race conditions make it difficult to replicate the same behavior on a different set of boards. The existence of a lab in the cloud with bare metal access that allows attaching any instrumentation available in the bench that makes the instrumentation available to all the platform integration parties shortens the whole process by allowing the integration partners to work from a single set of samples, affording them exactly the same view. Problem report replication issues that might take months to complete can now be resolved in days. This part needs to be accomplished ahead of the work to resolve the actual problem.

The transition of CSPs to specialized, service network providers will be gradual. CSPs in some geographical regions might experience competitive pressures, forcing some of the players to specialize for an increased competitive edge, although they will be happy to continue to provide traditional rack-and-stack based services. Others will look at the risks involved in developing ASCPs and decide to source their needs through regular OEM channels, albeit at a possibly higher cost in the long term, or by having to use platforms that match the intended applications less than perfectly.

As with the largest CSPs, for technology providers, this suggests a strategy focusing on CSPs and ODMs willing to take risks and to lead the industry with the goal of creating early successes. These successes can provide the motivation for late entrants to jump in to take advantage of the technology payoff. A complementary approach, mentioned earlier, is that of engaging the support of industry groups for certain technologies as well as groups involved in the promotion of specific verticals such as co-ops or service sectors such as financial services.

The transition for fourth-wave platforms that include the support of IoT will require increased automation. Much in the same manner that the methodology for third-wave platforms introduced the use of cloud technology for the development of cloud platforms, we can expect an increased use of self-service, automated approaches. This will allow expansion of VARs and SIs, who had a diminished role in the transition of platforms from the first wave (enterprise) to the second wave (large cloud). It is within the reach of current technology for ODMs to build baseboards with modules to allow a number of predefined design variants, allowing integrators or CSPs to choose specifications they would like to have; for instance, the number of networking ports, or memory slots, or manageability options. Improved design rules would allow ODMs to manufacture the variants in small batches to satisfy the needs of smaller CSPs.

PART IV

CHAPTER 7

Bare Metal Clouds

Business is not just doing deals; business is having great products, doing great engineering, and providing tremendous service to customers. Finally, business is a cobweb of human relationships.

—Ross Perot

The unit of delivery for the usual IaaS is a virtual machine. This mode of delivery is appropriate when the goal is to carve out a nonfungible resource, namely a pool of servers possibly of different vintages and vendors with diverse forms of storage and heterogeneous network resources, into a normalized service offering: abstracted compute nodes with N processors, M gigabytes of memory, and C network interface controllers (NICs). To customers, the virtualized servers appear homogeneous even though the physical machines on which these nodes are deployed can be different and with varying configurations.

Although the service offering might look homogeneous, the actual quality of service (QoS) that the end user experiences is unpredictable. If the service provider allocates a virtual machine instance to a little used physical machine, the customer will experience great performance. Furthermore, two machines running on the same physical host can appear to deliver excellent networking performance. This is possible if the two machines communicate through the hypervisor's virtual network with no physical NICs in between. Network communication takes place entirely across memory buffers in the virtualized network inside a physical machine. At the other side of the spectrum, one application with heavy I/O to a storage device in the network can monopolize the physical host's NIC and starve other tenants. If the other tenant was unlucky enough to have the two virtual machines land in two different physical servers, this tenant will experience poor network latency and bandwidth. What we see here is that multitenancy exposes customers to the *noisy neighbor problem,* where a workload spike in one virtual machine affects the performance in other virtual machines sharing the physical machine[1].

---

[1]S. Fath-Azam, "The Noisy Neighbor Problem," *Liquid Web,* http://www.liquidweb.com/blog/index.php/why-aws-is-bad-for-small-organizations-and-users/, October 4, 2012.

© Enrique Castro-Leon and Robert Harmon 2016
E. Castro-Leon and R. Harmon, *Cloud as a Service*, DOI 10.1007/978-1-4842-0103-9_7

One of the reasons behind the noisy neighbor problem is precisely the lack of control over the underlying hardware. Therefore, for cases where IaaS QoS control is critical, one approach to address it is to expose a hardware layer in the form of a bare metal as a service (BMaaS). Customers or service providers for whom QoS control is critical, but who still want to deploy virtualized IaaS, now can do so on top of a BMaaS infrastructure they control.

From a QoS perspective, it is irrelevant that performance can be good under some circumstances. The performance varying over a wide range forces customers to plan for the worst, forfeiting the potential benefits when performance happens to be good, or to be constantly on the defensive. Both strategies have a cost. For some applications, the unpredictability of performance can be as bad as any purported performance impact from virtualization. Liquid Web Chief Architect Fath-Azam argued that this variability affects smaller cloud customers disproportionately because larger customers possess the technical might to compensate for these vagaries. As a case in point, Netflix uses virtual machines from Amazon to deliver streaming services[2]. Netflix monitors virtual machines for performance in near real time using homegrown tools such as Atlas and Vector[3]. Virtual machines allocated to busy hosts and showing poor performance, or that are hung or have crashed, can be discarded. There are two challenges.

1. *The environment is dynamic*: A machine showing adequate performance one minute become overloaded the next because the number of machines allocated to a physical host changes continually and the workload for other tenants' machines varies by the second. A group of customers might have a pool of virtual machines in a server at near idle levels until called into service. The provider trusts that peaks and valleys in demand for a large pool of virtual machines, as many as a few hundred per physical host, will cancel out. Although this might be true most of the time, there will be moments where the physical server is overcommitted and the performance as experienced by customers suffers. Therefore monitoring must be carried out on an ongoing basis.

2. *A service provider operates under an economic incentive*: This incentive is to keep physical hosts as busy as possible, in conflict with the performance objectives for the customer. Therefore, if the service provider keeps physical hosts as busy as possible, it also makes it unlikely that the customer will get a virtual machine allocated to a less utilized server. Improved physical host management practices by the operator will bias outcomes toward the low end of the spectrum in the same way it is difficult to find empty seats in today's capacity-optimized airlines.

---

[2]Netflix, "5 Lessons We've Learned Using AWS," http://techblog.netflix.com/2010/12/5-lessons-weve-learned-using-aws.html, 2010.
[3]Netflix, "Linux Performance Analysis in 60,000 Milliseconds," http://techblog.netflix.com/2015/11/linux-performance-analysis-in-60s.html, 2015.

It would appear that to deliver more predictable QoS, providers could perform workload rebalancing across physical hosts by migrating virtual machines across physical hosts. However, workload balancing is not a common practice today because of the operational complexity and restrictions involved. Virtual machine migration is possible only within a predefined server pool, with pool members registered with the hypervisor instances running in the physical hosts. The hypervisor could impose additional restrictions, such as requiring that all physical hosts be in the same subnet. Processes for migrating a virtual machine across a wide area network (WAN) or across hypervisors from different vendors are still experimental.

Although Amazon Web Services (AWS) provides uptime guarantees in its service-level agreement (SLA)[4] for the Amazon Elastic Compute Cloud (EC2) and the Amazon Elastic Block Store (EBS), the SLA offers no performance guarantees, and the only liability is a refund of service fees if a machine becomes unavailable. The underlying fact is that configuration dynamics makes it very difficult to provide these guarantees under the virtualized IaaS model. Sadoogi et al. conducted a performance study on Amazon EC2 and EBS[5] for scientific applications. The main finding of this report is that applications perform well when they rely on only local resources, namely CPUs and direct-attached storage devices (DASDs). Performance is close to the performance attainable with physical machine resources, especially with servers provisioned with solid-state drives (SSDs) instead of the older rotating media devices. However, network latency was longer and bandwidth was lower in the virtualized environment relative to a physical environment. Sadoogi reported degraded QoS for resources accessed via network. Competing virtual machines from different cloud customers create contention for limited NIC and end-to-end network bandwidth. When NIC capacity reaches its limit, computation cannot proceed any faster for the affected applications even when the CPUs are less than fully utilized. This is a classical performance bottleneck situation. Unfortunately, or perhaps because of it, network bottlenecks also mean I/O bottlenecks when a distributed cloud database such as Cassandra or MongoDB is in use because data and metadata transfers occur through the network. With little or no visibility into the underlying hardware environment, and much less of an ability to modify, manage, or control this environment, IaaS customers encountering this bottleneck have little recourse to address QoS woes.

The Case for Bare Metal

A bare metal cloud supports a usage modality where a customer requesting service gets a handle to an actual physical server instead of a virtual machine under IaaS. The customer gets exclusive use of the physical host instead of sharing the hardware with possibly dozens of other unknown customers. Because the customer gets exclusive use to the full machine, type of service usually carries a price premium. How is the bare metal premium justified? There are a number of advantages to deploying bare metal, both from the perspective of the service provider, the provider service consumer, and the ultimate service consumer. Cloud service providers (CSPs) offering a bare metal service are called hardware as a service (HaaS) or BMaaS providers.

---

[4]"Amazon EC2 Service Level Agreement," https://aws.amazon.com/ec2/sla/, June 1, 2013.
[5]I. Sadooghi et al., "Understanding the Performance and Potential of Cloud Computing for Scientific Applications," *IEEE Transactions on Cloud Computing, PP* (99), February 19, 2015.

- *A cure for the noisy neighbor and predictable QoS*: Exclusive access to physical assets means performance side effects from multitenancy become less of an issue. There are no other tenants on the same machine competing for limited network bandwidth. Tenants can range from a single end user wanting control over the hardware to a subprovider, for instance an IT organization deploying a private cloud to business unit customers within a company, or an IaaS CSP using HaaS to implement a differentiated IaaS offering. If a tenant is a provider using bare metal acting as a CSP, this tenant has full control of the machine to set appropriate policies, ranging from pure physical pass-through to carving the machine to define new policies.

  The bare metal concept applies not just to individual server nodes. It enables defining a hosted enclave with almost any component in the datacenter, with any arbitrary topology plus storage resources. Unlike IaaS, if the bandwidth out of a node is insufficient, the customer can request additional NICs installed, or replacements with more ports. The tenant can also negotiate network bandwidth out of the enclave with the host.

- *Relief from nosy neighbor and other security maladies*: Exclusive access to equipment under single-tenancy makes data leaks across tenants less likely. There is a continuum possible for equipment sharing implementations. It can range from single HaaS server nodes with shared network and storage to physically isolated hosted enclaves. There is no best solution in an absolute sense. Every point in this continuum represents a trade-off between a security level and cost and inconvenience. A HaaS service framework allows the customer, not the provider, to define the mix of trade-offs most appropriate to a specific application.

  Another benefit from a bare metal service framework is the ability to deploy hardware-enforced security mechanisms such as UEFI Secure Boot and Intel Trusted Execution Technology (TXT). Hardware mechanisms are in principle much harder to circumvent than software mechanisms. Examples are using the Intel Innovation Engine firmware running inside the CPU and chipset complex to orchestrate hardware security features. Another example is the UEFI secure boot capability and the measured boot mechanisms implemented through Intel TXT. The integration of these mechanisms usually follows customer-specific security policies and therefore they are hard to deploy in multitenant environments. Almost without exception, the lowest common denominator wins and therefore the service provider filters out these capabilities in their virtualized IaaS offerings, and the features are not available even when a customer could benefit from them. The single-tenant HaaS environment removes these barriers.

- *Ditch one-size-fits-all: Hardware the way you like it:* Application-specific customer needs can open opportunities for bare metal providers to deploy application-specific cloud servers (ASCS) as described in Chapter 5. The virtualized environment in IaaS offerings hides these capabilities and therefore the customer cannot take advantage of them even if the capabilities are present in the underlying hardware. The customer must accept the capabilities the provider exposes instead of using the full range of technologies in the physical platform. Unfortunately, this one-size-fits-all approach under IaaS leaves customer needs underserved.

The implementation of an integrated security capability involving TXT would be appropriate to an application-specific cloud platform (ASCP) development project for a highly customized cloud platform. Implementations will likely be domain-specific; for instance, an ASCP to support small banking, as instances of high-value ASCPs deployed in a differentiated service provider environment as envisioned in Figure 4-7. Small banks such as savings and loans and credit unions do not have the heft and critical mass of large banks to afford deploying their datacenters in house. Instead of vertical integration, one way to achieve the critical mass to make these applications possible through industry associations. Stakeholders in an industry association can get together to define a common platform that addresses the needs of its members. Working in this manner addresses the nonrecurring engineering (NRE) cost barrier that smaller players must overcome to get to the competitive benefits of customization that large CSPs realized during the second wave. Given the access to low-level hardware-implemented capabilities, customized bare metal platforms are more expressive than those using virtualized IaaS, and therefore a much better fit to the needs for specialization in the evolved cloud ecosystem.

- *Support for consistent business process management across hybrid resources*: Users get the option to deploy hardware optimized to specific business and application needs. For instance, on the business side, needs might include the use of hardware-based mechanisms to implement controls as required by law under the Sarbanes-Oxley Act, Section 404[6]. These controls would be incorporated into a Statement on Standards for Attestation Engagements (SSAE) No. 16 as specified by the American Institute of Certified Public Accountants[7]. Another example is the implementation of uniform platform power policies across a collection of hybrid resources using Intel Node Manager hardware-based power monitoring. This allows a HaaS customer to monitor physical power consumption in geographically distributed hybrid resource set. This CSP can then define its own policies to allocate this power consumption to customers downstream. The availability of this data opens up a number of business opportunities:

  - Allows breaking up energy costs for separate billing. This is useful for true billing, factoring in time of day or seasonal energy cost variances. Some customers might prefer bearing the cost of risk pricing in exchange for a lower service fee.

  - The implementation of green computing schemes with true allocation of energy costs for competitive advantage.

  - The implementation of uniform power policies, such as power consumption curtailment across hybrid cloud resources.

  - The ability to power down servers physically when not in use to save energy.

- *Support for consistent asset management across hybrid resources*: A bare metal cloud makes it easier for corporate cloud customers to implement hybrid clouds. Hardware represents the lowest common denominator IT operators can use to build up their technical and business processes. Because the complete gamut of features are available to the operator, a corporate IT organization can integrate servers deployed in company datacenters with servers leased from a bare metal provider using uniform policies. With all the hardware features exposed, all options remain open for resource augmentation of in-house resources with HaaS resources. Providers can add hybrid resources seamlessly to deliver a true scalable service to customers, instead of abstracting out platform capabilities to provide the illusion of homogeneity.

---

[6]U.S. Securites and Exchange Commission, *Sarbanes-Oxley Section 404, A Guide for Small Business* (Washington, DC: U.S. Securities and Exchange Commission, 2007).
[7]AICP Aervice Organization Control Reports, "FAQs: New Service Organization Standards and Implementation Guidance," http://www.aicpa.org/interestareas/frc/assuranceadvisoryservices/downloadabledocuments/faqs_service_orgs.pdf.

This management flexibility enables new types of cloud participants in the evolved environment of Figure 4-7: An IaaS provider can enter the business without deploying a single datacenter. The provider can select, draw, aggregate resources from multiple HaaS providers as needed. At the same time, it can build unique, differentiated IaaS services, based on the capabilities of the underlying hardware, and regardless of the location or ownership of resources.

An IaaS provider might have expertise in software-defined infrastructure (SDI) and does not want to be bothered with physical provisioning processes, racking and stacking, and maintaining buildings and the actual physical infrastructure. Instead, this organization can opt to lease physical servers from a HaaS provider, or perhaps multiple HaaS providers.

Using multiple providers reduces business risks from depending on a single provider or even worse, a provider with a single datacenter. Furthermore, using physical hardware allows IT organizations to use uniform processes to manage equipment, regardless of whether the equipment is local, in a corporate datacenter, or remote. In fact, distinctions between equipment in a company datacenter and company equipment in a hosting facility and HaaS equipment from a bare metal provider become blurred. The presumably local equipment might be running in a company datacenter on another continent, whereas the remote equipment could be running in a HaaS datacenter in the same city.

- *High QoS bare metal applications*: HaaS might be appropriate for new classes of customers who up to the present have pent up business needs but might have been reluctant to avail themselves of cloud services and the associated benefits. The largest banks and financial institutions run their datacenters and run highly sophisticated IT operations. Medium-size banks and credit unions might not have the scale to run in-house datacenters and implement business processes out of prepackaged SaaS offerings, or run in-house equipment without adequate expertise, which ironically might expose these organizations to higher levels of risks than the putative risks in the cloud.

  For these financial institutions, the main considerations will be security and reliability, availability and serviceability (RAS), not in deploying lowest cost, bare-bones hardware; therefore being able to deploy hundreds of low-featured, low-cost virtual machines will be of little value when the primary goal is a high-QoS service product. Depending on requirements, the unit of delivery for this service product can be a high-end server similar to high RAS servers that the large financial institutions deploy in house or even a physical slice of such a server.

These servers are highly sophisticated, starting with 4 processors and carrying as many as 32 processors or more and hundreds of hardware threads in their largest configurations. The architecture for these servers is modular and allows for physical partitioning. System administrators can bind CPUs or even cores within a CPU, memory, I/O, and expansion cards to any of the partitions. A number of reconfiguration operations can be done on the fly or in hot mode without shutting down the OS running in the partitions, or powering down the whole machine, such as adding or removing CPUs or memory to a partition. Memory can be configured in a mirrored fashion, storage configured with RAID and multiple network connectivity. If a hard memory error occurs, the module containing this memory can be offlined and replaced with a healthy module.

The features of high-end, sophisticated servers are lost under the present-day IaaS usage modality and therefore under this modality it does not make sense to deploy high-end machines to support a large-volume IaaS offering. Because of this dynamic, the needs from smaller financial institutions remain unserved. They would like to deploy high RAS machines to run financial applications and yet there is currently no offering from cloud providers for this class of service. Nonetheless, due to cost considerations, some applications that require RAS have been migrating to the cloud. However, for the capability mismatch between cloud platform offerings and application needs, this trickle down to the cloud has not fully played out yet, and therefore pent-up demand exists for applications that are too expensive to run in high-end machines in corporate datacenters, but for which there is no appropriate offering for a service to run the applications in the cloud.

In a diversified HaaS ecosystem, a corporate cloud consumer or IaaS CSP can pick the HaaS flavor most suitable for the application.

One possible advantage of IaaS over HaaS is a small quantum for cloud resource augmentation. For IaaS the resource quantum is a virtual machine, which can take a small fraction of a physical machine, whereas for HaaS, by definition, the resource quantum is an entire physical server. Therefore, in theory IaaS allows resource scaling in small increments. In practice, this consideration would apply only to a small business deploying one or at most a few servers. For a company deploying more than a few servers, the decision to deploy one more or one less server quickly becomes a rounding error.

Bare metal clouds open opportunities for emerging players in the evolved third- and fourth-wave cloud ecosystems, operating under different business dynamics. These dynamics might be antithetical to the dynamics driving the largest current cloud providers. These large providers deploy bare-bones, minimalist platforms in centralized, very large datacenters by the hundreds of thousands, striving for cost efficiency through a restricted offering of standardized service products. This modality is the eponymous of the cloud today, with the associated concerns about diminished privacy from nosy neighbors and unpredictable QoS from noisy neighbors. These issues need not be intrinsic to the cloud; large providers can play in both the IaaS and HaaS spaces, and in fact, expose services at multiple levels. Conversely, the demand for specialized services, especially those requiring certain hardware features, will likely create opportunities for niche bare metal providers. In addition to the business and application requirements noted earlier, opportunities will come from the need to fulfill regulatory requirements specific to a country or region such as the enforcement of data locality. It is easier to comply with locality requirements when the data is bound to specific physical machinery.

ASCP Development in the Cloud

Methodologies for the development of ASCPs are currently in a transitionary period. Processes for the development of ASCPs during the second wave were evolutionary developments of the processes used for the development of enterprise servers in the preceding decade. The players were different, with large CSPs taking on the role of enterprise original equipment manufacturers (OEMs), and a narrower feature set for a single customer instead of general-purpose enterprise platforms. The narrower focus reduced complexity, reduced NRE cost, and allowed faster time to market. However, the methodology used evolutionary processes very similar to the OEM platform development processes.

The traditional development methods in use for enterprise platforms very likely will not scale to be of practical use to the smaller CSPs driving the third and fourth waves of cloud platforms. The NRE cost per project per CSP will likely end up being too high, negating any value proposition for the customized platform. Instead of using traditional methods to develop a platform for the cloud, we posit that additional economies are possible using cloud-based processes to develop cloud platforms. In Chapter 6, we discovered that in cloud platform development, the project is a multicompany affair, with significant engineering time spent in executing technical tasks across the participating companies. In particular, under the traditional methodology, validation tasks are presently carried out in a serialized fashion. In this section, we examine how a HaaS lab in the cloud can provide the means to collapse these serial bottlenecks, reducing labor and communication overhead and speeding up development.

The design, development, and manufacturing of an ASCP is a technically and logistically complex mission involving multiple internal and external partners. The platform contains tried and true technology, but also emerging technology components. Whether new or old technology components, they cannot be applied straight from the bottle; even when they are standards-based, components evolve from generation to generation with additional functionality, or existing functionality used in different ways, and it takes a nontrivial effort and investment to ensure they work together. As mentioned earlier, although a CSP is the nominal owner of its ASCP, every ASCP development project is actually a multicompany collaboration. This collaboration encompasses the CSP, the original design manufacturer (ODM) or OEM building the baseboards for the platform, plus a constellation of technology partners providing all kinds of services, including the software platform for the operating environment, middleware and applications, networking and I/O technology, and silicon technology. Other services might include program management and integration services. Figure 6-6 captures the dynamics for this emerging landscape.

Most of the development for first-wave enterprise platforms took place within a single company, with colocated development teams, and with the majority of interactions taking place within the same company. For ASCP development, there are significant cross-company interactions and communication round trips where the interactions are as likely to be intercompany as they are intracompany. The larger distances involved and cultural differences lead to obligatory vetting and filtering of the exchanges. Communication gets slower and more expensive. If an engineer working at validating a board within an OEM company experiences a malfunction, he or she can call the baseboard designer, who might be in the next building. An engineer at a CSP validating an ODM design who experiences a similar malfunction would have to wait until the next scheduled partner coordination meeting. Airtime for the coordination meeting might be limited, and a slot in the agenda for the next instance might not always be available. Beyond that, it might take a few meetings for the CSP engineer to explain the malfunction, and a few more weeks until the ODM is able to replicate the problem and suggest a solution.

During field testing, when a prototype breaks, except for very minor malfunctions, the prototype might need to be shipped back to the factory. The local team might not have the knowledge or the resources and experience to do on-site repair for the new technology. Each incident represents weeks of delay for the technology partner, who might be working under tight product development and product launch milestones.

The current need to ship back defective baseboards is reminiscent of the *sneakernet* a few years ago, where the default mode for data transfer was transporting data in physical media. Although data was understood as not being bound from a specific medium, in practice it was very difficult to transport it, except as physical media. It was an expensive affair to move large amounts of data, either in time, for instance trying to squeeze a 150 MB backup through a 64 kilobit per second modem, or in leasing costs if transmitted through a T-carrier or SONET link.

In a similar vein, we can look at a prototype baseboard as an instance of an abstract architecture represented by the emerging technology. The new baseboard, more likely than not, is not fully functional; it is an imperfect instantiation of the architecture. Removing as many defects as possible from the baseboard is the primary goal of a validation exercise. Having this board hosted at a lab in the cloud and accessible to all partners allows these partners to get a concurrent view of the hardware as well as the ability to manipulate it to any level needed to carry out the validation. The bottom line is that the hardware view provided by a HaaS service in the cloud is an excellent match to assist in cloud platform development.

A Conceptual Architecture for a Lab Bare Metal Service

One application for HaaS is the concept of the virtual lab workbench with an infrastructure in the cloud that strives to replicate an engineer's lab experience with bare metal resources in the cloud. The Platform Application Engineering team in the Data Center Group at Intel started a pilot for a lab-oriented bare metal service. The goal for this installation is to integrate cloud technology into advanced engineering processes, facilitating the work of geographically distributed development teams from different companies engaged in platform development, namely ASCP development. All the methods, techniques, and instrumentation incorporated into the lab workflows are commercially available. Beyond that, the lab does not prescribe or make obligatory use of any particular component. Therefore, the lab can be deployed, replicated, and adapted anywhere in the world both at Intel facilities and at technology partners. Lab implementers can substitute capabilities to fit particular circumstances. The only overriding goal is the implementation of a capability to deliver access to hardware to all relevant project participants to enable successful project completion. The innovation is not in the use of any proprietary technology component, but in the integration of commercially available capabilities toward ASCP development under a cloud vision.

A customer lab environment consists of a private local network, configured to the customer requirements, conceptually illustrated in Figure 7-1. The environment can host one or more target systems or systems under test (SUTs) plus a storage server. Customers access an environment through one or more virtualized portals.

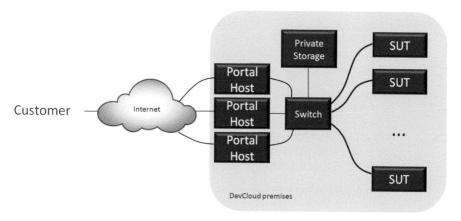

Figure 7-1. *Customer lab environment*

An environment might contain more than one portal to support multiple concurrent projects, perhaps one project Linux-centric requiring a portal running Linux and another Windows-centric. The environment might run a third portal dedicated to running tools. Figure 7-1 shows all networked devices converging into one switch, which is a bit of an oversimplification. The local network could contain more than one subnet, as explained later in this chapter. Once built up, the environment project owner carries administrative rights, including the authority to set usage policies, manage user accounts, and invite additional project participants.

Instrumentation devices supporting remote access appear as additional network nodes: there is one KVM redirection device per SUT. An IP-based power distribution unit (PDU) implements physical power cycling for each SUT and shows up as an additional IP node. The microcontroller in the PDU can switch individual outlets on or off. One IP KVM device can implement not only keyboard, video, and mouse redirection, but also Universal Serial Bus (USB) and serial port redirection as well. Remote users accessing the environment can transfer files to a portal host and to the storage server through drag-and-drop with file transfer tools such as *ftp* or *tftp*. Access to an environment need not be interactive; it can be programmatic through an application programming interface (API) in hybrid cloud style, in which case one of the portal hosts might have an HTTP server to support RESTful protocols.

Each portal host carries a unique IP address. Although the hosts run virtualized, these hosts provide access to physical SUTs in the local network, and therefore access is still HaaS.

SUTs usually sit next to each other within a rack, although there is no particular restriction regarding location within a rack. SUTs that do not fit in one rack can span multiple racks. They do not even need to be continuous. It is perfectly feasible to define a set of SUTs in an environment scattered across multiple racks.

Cost, availability, and customer need determine the level of instrumentation built into an environment, determined by interviewing the prospective guest to get accurate specifications. Overbuilding leads to wasted resources, whereas underbuilding means needs that go unmet. The level of instrumentation ranges starts where IaaS leaves off through a series of rungs of increasing sophistication and degree of hardware control.

- *A software development environment in a dedicated machine*: This machine has a running OS and a development environment running in in the access host. The guest access targeted SUTs doing another SSH or RDP jump from the access host to the target SUTs.

- *The ability to do physical power cycling of a machine*: This capability allows the machine to recover from hard crashes or hangs. It requires the installation of an IP-based PDU. The PDU microcontroller operates as an IP node in the network and implements an HTTP server that allows power cycling the individual outlets where the machine is connected.

- *Machine port redirection*: This capability enables rerouting keyboard and video output to the host window. Additional capabilities could include also rerouting serial port I/O in the SUT to the host window, and even redirecting SUT USB ports to the user's workstation USB ports. These operations run as *out-of-band* operations with hardware devices, meaning without the intervention of the OS, in contrast to *in-band* operations carried through a running OS. The out-of-band I/O redirection also enables setting BIOS parameters and running UEFI commands without need for the OS to be up and running.

- *Low-level hardware manipulation*: When needed, this is possible through a Galileo maker board, or dedicated hardware tools such as in-test probes (ITPs), or the Intel Remote System Controller 2 and test equipment attached to JTAG (Joint Test Action) XDP (eXtended Debug Port) ports. These tools allow setting jumpers in a baseboard, manipulating GPIOs, or reinstalling firmware as needed, including firmware for the Management Engine microcontroller resident in the Processor Control Hub (PCH), as well as BIOS and PCU (Power/Processor/Package/Platform Control Unit) firmware.

A HaaS lab facility mediates a pool of assets provided by one or more sponsoring organizations and a community of users. The design philosophy refrains from imposing any usage model or access restrictions other than those specified by the equipment owner. For instance, when the equipment sponsor specifies access by a certain class of users, the lab facility defines a policy to implement the directive.

Users access the lab facility through commonly available applications such as a web browser, a remote shell program, or Microsoft Windows Remote Desktop connection. No installation of proprietary programs in client machines is required. Authentication is through user accounts and password or certificates. Users using a certificate method need not use passwords at all and accessing the lab facility is as easy as clicking an icon. The facility does not impose any limitation on usage other than those determined by the capabilities of the managed assets.

Baseboard validation might require the allocation of a number of prototype boards across a number of stakeholder organizations. Managing this allocation as a pool of resources allows extending the reach of these assets to a larger stakeholder community. The user community could include engineers in sponsor organizations as well OEMs and ODMs who will take these boards as reference designs to build their own designs, and OSVs and ISVs whose software and applications will eventually run on these boards. In this way, users have total freedom in structuring access to assets. Users can pick the modality most convenient to their business needs, from the usual remote access to a highly integrated hybrid cloud. An integrated hybrid cloud might include USB and SATA redirection, having HaaS machines in the same subnet as the user's network and booting from drives at the user's facility for increased privacy.

The facility increases the efficiency and reach of a limited number of assets through a number of mechanisms:

- *Fast turnover of assets across lab customers*: Reassigning an asset from one customer to another no longer requires shipping of the asset. The lab facility has processes to wipe out newly released assets in short order and place them into the pool. Physical transport would require days to arrange if done within a country, and weeks or even months if done across countries, taking into consideration shipping delays, equipment damage, clearing customs, and training local staff in the use and maintenance of the equipment. Although an OEM might have the skills to perform maintenance and repairs, an ISV only interested in developing applications might look at hardware maintenance as a nuisance. This class of users might not have the time or disposition to carry out these tasks, and even minor mishaps could result in lengthy calls to the factory, draining time and resources from both sides.

  In practice, the logistics of turning over equipment from one project to the next are even more daunting. The criteria for project deconstruction or even determining when a project is finished is oftentimes ambiguous, making it difficult to retrieve equipment on a schedule. For international shipping, the paperwork for re-export of equipment may make it impractical to do so.

- *Pooling of assets brings in inherent process fault tolerance, redundancy, and resiliency*: Under the current methodology, a user might get one board to carry out development. If the board malfunctions, the user will have to ship the board for repairs. Meanwhile development stops and the development project needs to sustain a schedule hit waiting for a replacement board. With pooled resources from the lab, this user can request another machine from the pool and continue working. There is no need to ship the broken baseboard to the factory because the board with the skills to repair it quickly. More likely than not, lab staff will be able to repair, refurbish, and reconfigure a board on site. If a board is removed from the pool, individual users in the group will experience a slight deterioration in QoS: It might take a little longer in the wait queue to get access to equipment or usage slots could become shorter. However, all users in the group can collectively continue making progress, and no one in the ownership group is stranded by a board becoming a single point of failure.

- *Fast update of prototype boards*: Prototype boards are brittle and require frequent updates. Maintaining these boards requires specific knowledge and this knowledge will be useful for a short time. There is no return on investment for members in the ownership group in investing time acquiring skills for maintaining and repairing boards. These boards are used for development purposes for a short time, and therefore the knowledge gained specific to these boards is not reusable. Therefore it makes sense to pay this tax only once for a large community instead of all members of the community having to bear it individually. Pooling frees users from having to carry out repairs, install fixes, and perform firmware and hardware updates.

Asset Management

Assets in the pool retain their identity with respect to the asset owners. Certain assets can be anonymous, especially ancillary equipment. Nonetheless, critical assets can be tagged for life cycle management and tracking at the request of the owner. At their option, equipment owners can designate an asset for their own use or define a class of users allowed to use the asset and the terms of sharing. Owners retain rights for physical access and retrieving the asset from the pool anytime.

A number of access modes to lab assets are possible.

- *Private use*: This is the most common access mode under the HaaS model. The customer gains exclusive access to the equipment in the environment until the environment is explicitly released. No one but the customer or users approved by the customer can have access to the equipment. The only exception is lab staff under the conditions specified by the SLA.

- *Serial exclusive access*: An asset is allocated to a user for a predetermined time. Allocation is usually through a sign-up list. The resources are wiped clean between uses. Revocation of user rights can be achieved through the use of certificates that expire at the end of the allotted time.

- *Community use*: A community of users can share an SUT through the usual mechanism of having multiple accounts in a front-end machine. Multiple front-end machines can also be bound to one SUT. In this case it is the responsibility of the community of users to resolve possible access conflicts to the SUT. This model applies mostly to showcase reference implementations with mostly read-only access, and very little state is left behind after each use.

Security

Security is always a trade-off among security level, convenience, and cost. Therefore, the mix of features in an environment are selected to customer specifications as part of the environment design interview. The goal is to come up with a mix that fulfills customer requirements without being too burdensome, and within the available budget.

- At its most *basic level,* the lab facility offers a number of default security capabilities: The equipment is deployed in a restricted area requiring badge access. Communication between the lab and customer on-premises equipment is encrypted using IPsec standard protocols. Current access to lab accounts is through password security. Certificate-based authentication is available for customers who can take advantage of this process. Within the desired level of security, these processes are designed to be as unobtrusive as possible. Although the allocation of SUTs is exclusive, the virtual machines from unrelated customers can share the same front-end host.

- The next level adds *front-end host isolation,* with only one customer, or customers authorized by the primary customer using the physical front-end host. This environment uses a software-defined network environment (SDN). A customer working in a single SUT shares the rack with other customers, and isolation between customers is enforced by the network partitioning capabilities in the routers and switches in between.

- The *network isolation* option requires allocating a rack to a customer, including a WAN connection and the intervening network equipment.

- *Customer enclaves* represent the highest level of security supported. The notion is similar to that of an embassy, where a host country cedes sovereign rights to the representation of the guest country within an embassy compound. Likewise, a customer enclave in the lab is a comanaged and protected volume inside a locked rack under an SLA. The SLA defines rules for physical access under which lab staff can enter the protected space. For instance the locks may be remotely controlled by the customer and all access events are governed by an access control list, also managed by the customer. Logging could be required for all access events.

Bare Metal Lab Applications

The lab in the cloud service has been useful in assisting operating system vendors to quickly integrate capabilities for the newer processor generations and associated technologies. For instance, the server processor under the code name Skylake-EP in the Purley generation features a higher density topology for connecting the cores inside the CPU instead of the double ring used in the prior generation Grantley, with the processors code-named Haswell and Broadwell. It also features a capability named *integrated I/O* (IIO) that allows networking support directly out of the CPU, as well as the *OmniPath* interconnect to support high-performance computing applications.

Remarkably, a legacy operating system will actually boot on a Skylake-based server, but barely, and literally in legacy or compatibility mode. Intel provides reference drivers for the new capabilities. However, the OS vendor must work with Intel to flush out implementation bugs and carry out performance optimization. In Intel parlance, this work is known as *ecosystem enabling*. Under its business model for technology development, Intel has an interest in ensuring the diffusion of this technology in the marketplace and for customers to realize the value of the new technology as quickly as possible. Unfortunately, an operating system running in legacy mode is not very useful to application developers downstream to take advantage of the new technology. Operating system performance, optimized for prior generations of processors, could be severely handicapped and the new capabilities might not even be available or usable.

There are challenges for Intel, and for ODMs, OEMs and independent hardware vendors (IHVs) building baseboards and products that feature the new silicon, as these are the serial bottlenecks in ecosystem enabling. One challenge is opening the doors to software vendors to start optimizing their applications to the new architecture. This optimization is not possible without a working OS. Therefore, one application for the bare metal service has been making early prototype (alpha) machines featuring the new processor available to operating system vendors.

A limited number of these machines, known as *software development platforms* (SDPs), have traditionally been delivered to developers. However, this is an expensive practice, not only due to the cost of the units, but also due to the cost of the support network behind them. These machines require frequent hardware firmware updates, break easily, and are prone to glitches. As early engineering samples of not-yet-released technology, they become tempting targets for unauthorized intellectual property leaks. One program uses the bare metal lab service to place SDPs in the cloud, as an alternative to physically shipping them to customer sites. Having the machines in one place simplifies the logistics of hardware fixes and upgrades. Firmware upgrades also carry risk. Loading an incompatible set can easily disable a machine.

Debugging and Board Tracing Service

Logic analyzer work in a lab setting done today uses instrumentation attached to a computer front end. Once the instrumentation is in place, engineers can remotely access this front end from their desks to carry out experiments and debugging. This setup enables remote hardware debugging where distance is no longer relevant. An engineer can conduct debugging from an office next to the lab or from another continent. An engineer carrying out ASCP hardware development tasks at a CSP can perform hardware low-level debugging using a platform housed at a HaaS lab provider. There is no particular requirement as to which entity does the hosting. This is mostly a business decision driven by project requirements. The lab host could be the CSP developer, the ODM manufacturing the particular platform, or a third-party, pure-play HaaS provider specializing in providing lab services.

The hybrid algorithm for implementing an emergency default power cap (EDPC) is in principle very simple: a sequenced application of a power throttling action to achieve a fast descent in power demand followed by a power capping action to trim power consumption to a preset level. In practice, the validation of the implementation is complex. Figure 5-2 is actually a simplified depiction of the actual setup. For instance, the PSUALRT# signal nominally goes through a NOT gate, an AND gate and a NOR gate before it reaches the GPIO31 pin in the PCH. In practice, these gates are not discrete. More likely than not, these gates will be embedded in a baseboard complex programmable logic device (CPLD), and correct functioning will depend on the CPLD implementation. Furthermore, the baseboard management controller (BMC) drives the EDPC. Engineers must ensure that gate delays in the CPLD and processing delays in the BMC as well as possible implementation artifacts do not result in undesirable behaviors such as oscillations or undefined states in the digital domain. We cover the EDPC algorithm in more detail in Chapter 8.

The EDPC power management algorithm works in both the digital and analog domains. The digital signals coming from the power supply and the BMC as well as the IPMI programmed commands coming from the BMC adjust platform power consumption by regulating CPU frequency. The instantaneous power consumed by the platform on the DC (direct current) side of the power supplies is the product of the DC bus voltage (VCC) and the current going into the platform.

Actual physics dictate how fast this change can happen. One consideration is stored energy. Shunt capacitance, capacitance to ground, limits how fast VCC can change. Likewise, series inductance limits how fast current can change. There is shunt capacitance and series inductance distributed throughout the system. Without proper tuning, the stored energy can move back and forth between the capacitance and the inductance components. These are effectively power oscillations, often observed in early prototypes. They tend to appear during state transitions, for instance when the BMC releases power throttling after enabling the EDPC power cap. As part of the algorithm tuning, engineers must ensure proper damping of power oscillations with every EDPC activation under all conditions.

Algorithm tuning is an interactive activity, and is very difficult and time-consuming. In a traditional setup, the CSP who owns the platform, the ODM building it, and the technology provider all work independently. The other stakeholders must verify anomalies observed by one entity before they can even start analyzing the issue.

It gets more complicated than that. Because each of the entities carries its own in-house processes, the technology provider could insist that the problem must be replicated on a reference platform before any work toward resolution can be started. If the reference platform does not support the ASCP capability the CSP is developing, a stalemate ensues that leaves all parties unhappy. A common debug platform hosted at a HaaS lab instance circumvents most of these issues. First, the HaaS instance represents a commitment to build an ASCP by all parties: the CSP, technology providers, and the ODMs. In particular, and by virtue of having agreed to join the ASCP development project, the technology provider agrees that the interactions for the project will be carried out on the ASCP and not in a predefined reference platform that might not be a good fit for the project. Second, once the anomaly is isolated and the conditions for triggering it established, there is no need for the other partners to replicate the issue. They can observe the problem directly because they have access to the same machine and have the same visibility. They can use the same machine to try out fixes. The problem resolution process, which might have taken months for hard-to-reproduce problems, can now be completed in a matter of weeks or even days.

Skilled technical work is still required to set up the common debug platform and the target experiments. Lab staff can analyze CAD diagrams of the SUT and solder appropriate tap points. Figure 7-2 shows a prepared board with soldered tap points set to verify the EDPC signal sequencing. In some cases, the monitored logic signals are available from an XDP debug port, but more often than not, detailed debugging of a board will require custom tap points. Selecting appropriate tap points can be a laborious process. The target logic signal might be in a trace buried in the inner layers in a baseboard, requiring monitoring of some other signal that reflects the behavior of the prime target signal.

Figure 7-2. *Customer baseboard with soldered tap points*

Selecting the appropriate signals almost invariably requires the customer to provide CAD diagrams for the SUT boards. Figure 7-3 shows an excerpt of a CAD diagram relevant to a specific board experiment used to study relative timings across selected tap points. In this particular case study, engineers were studying the relationship between signals in taps T1, T7, T8, and T9. In particular, the logic values of T8 and T9 were expected to follow the logic value of T1. T8 and T9 were transitioning as expected when T1 transitioned from high to low.

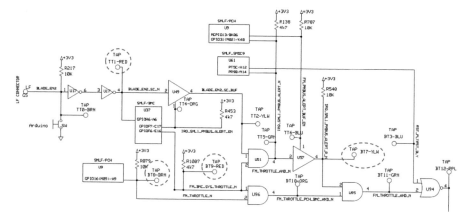

Figure 7-3. *Excerpt from the SUT baseboard CAD diagram showing a few tap points circled in red*

However, when T1 transitioned from low to high it was taking a few more hundreds of milliseconds for T9 to recover. This type of misbehavior is extremely difficult to debug under normal circumstances because there is only visibility at the endpoints. Engineers are left to guess what happens in between. The instrumentation shown allows probing anywhere in between, eliminating the guesswork. This is still a laborious process; identifying the tap points and actually soldering them takes time and involves the risk of board damage. Engineers use an iterative process of carefully adding a few taps at a time, running the experiment until they characterize the behavior of intermediate signals to the point of the root causing the anomalous behavior.

For analyses in the digital domain, lab staff can build appropriate software drivers, sequencers, triggers, and state machines for event capture in the digital and analog domain, and feed the signals into a logic analyzer or oscilloscope (see Figure 7-4). As noted earlier, this is usually a highly interactive process between lab staff and customers. Once the instrumentation is in place, it can be set up for remote access for running series of trials, or if the customer needs to run confidential experiments.

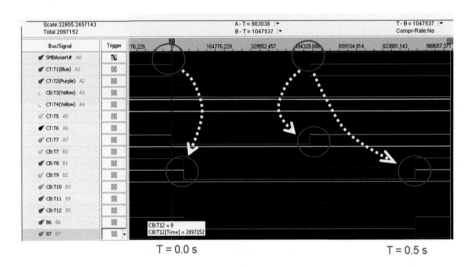

Figure 7-4. *Logic analyzer trace of an experiment*

Before this happens, carrying out the preparations, provisioning, and configuration to support an experiment can take significant time. Even when all the components for a run are in place, certain experiments require bringing a system to a certain state. There is significant time and effort involved in nursing a system to this precise sweet spot. Because of the brittleness of prototypes, this might mean restarting an application for each shot. However, often reloading the operating system is in order or even worse, reloading firmware for each run. Hangs might occur for no particular reason, requiring starting over. Board prototypes might not offer the luxury of in-place or over-the-wire firmware updates; firmware, such as the operating system for a microcontroller embedded in a baseboard or in a chip might reside in an SPI flash chip. Updating the firmware requires physically removing the chip from the machine and reprogramming on the bench. If the machine is in a rack, the operation requires unracking the machine to remove the chip to reflash it with an external flash programmer.

The HaaS lab supports mounting the SPI chip in a switchable socket remotely controlled with a Galileo maker board. This allows redirecting the SPI chip pins to a flash programmer for reflashing remotely and back to the SUT for carrying out experiments. There are no specific flash programmer requirements as long as it allows remote control through a front-end machine application, with the application running in the same user front-end machine or in a separate virtual machine dedicated to tools.

To minimize any proprietary information leaks, users who do not want to leave any state behind can redirect USB to a local workstation or load from a file in the local workstation. The user erases the SPI chip after finishing work, so the bits of an image are either in the user's physical possession or in the SUT only while the user is actively working. Serial redirection should also be trivial.

Alternatively, users can store test images remotely in an encrypted library with password or cert protection, including OS images for fast provisioning and reprovisioning. SUT network ports are usually connected to the same subnet as the front-end machine, with no WAN connectivity to reduce the likelihood of IP leaks.

Once established, these processes save engineers much of the expense and dead time procuring equipment, retooling, and simply cycling the same experiment repeatedly when making parameterized runs.

Establishing supporting lab processes can reduce the drudgery and dead time from repetitive lab tasks. Unfortunately, for engineers working individually there is a steep up-front cost in developing time-saving routines. A lab cloud service allows amortizing the cost of developing advanced processes over a large user community. The advanced environment allows virtualized replicas of an OS and application configuration, or from a library image, obviating the need to reinstall software. If an experiment is known to corrupt a specific software configuration, the machine can be restarted from a virtualized replica, either with a restart from hibernation, or a reboot of a system with a known configuration. Likewise, the lab service offers tooling to reprogram an SPI flash in place without the need for physical access to the machine, from an image library, or from a USB drive in the remote user's possession.

Advanced lab processes can significantly increase the productivity of lab engineers through automation. An automated process makes it easier to experiment with the abstraction than deal with the physical instance of the same. Automation opens the possibility of increasing labor productivity even more, with hardware and software tools not possible before. Under this dynamic, equipment pooling under a bare metal lab service not only increases the reach of scarce, limited, and brittle equipment, but also increases labor productivity. The only downside is that it takes time to devise appropriate automated processes. Lab staff developed the initial set of automated processes. In a more evolved system, we can expect additional automation to be developed by users in collaboration with lab staff. Eventually, and for maximum scalability in a true cloud fashion, there will be metaprocesses that will enable the user community to develop automation without the need for lab staff to intervene.

Platform Power Cycling

As noted earlier, a lab instrumentation features the capability to execute a physical power reset on an SUT. Most software development does not require this capability, where even an OS restart is a rare occurrence. However, preproduction hardware is less friendly and more unstable. This hardware might be prone to hard hangs requiring power cycling to get it unstuck. In addition, some firmware experiments require not just a system shutdown, but also removing power from the machine. We show one implementation that uses commonly available instrumentation. Figure 7-5 shows a portion of the initial screen of the virtualized portal of an environment with SUT "Blue" running Red Hat Enterprise Linux.

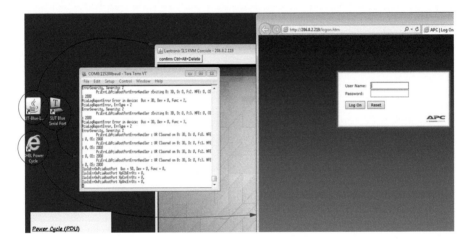

Figure 7-5. *Virtualized bare metal lab service portal screen*

There are three icons on the left and the respective expanded windows on the right. The Java icon runs the front end of a Lantronix KVM redirection device showing the SUT screen running Linux. The terminal display captures the serial port output of the SUT. This implementation uses an inexpensive generic RS-232 to USB converter, with the RS-232 side connected to the SUT serial port and the USB side connected to a USB port in the portal server mapped to a USB port in the virtualized host access host. The SUTs for this environment use outlets from an APC IP PDU. The controller hosts an HTTP server. The browser window shows the output of the IP PDU server.

The operating system captures output of the serial port when running. This makes serial port monitoring useful to detect when the SUT has been powered on and it is going through the power-on self-test (POST) sequence. Unfortunately, the Lantronix window does not autorefresh; it requires a mouse click to refresh. Observing the serial port relieves the user from having to click constantly to find out if the OS is up and running. With a serial port monitor, the user can expect the OS to signal its presence a few moments after the serial display stops.

Enter the login credentials for the IP PDU as shown in Figure 7-6.

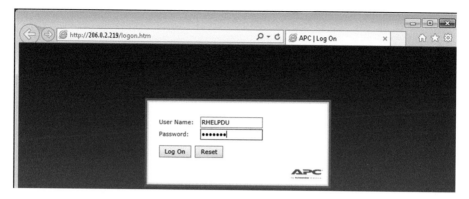

Figure 7-6. *Logging into the IP PDU*

The IP PDU home screen opens, as shown in Figure 7-7.

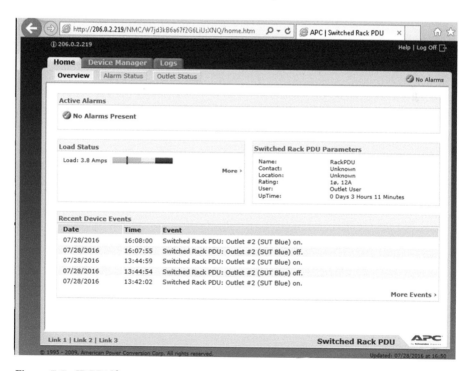

Figure 7-7. *IP PDU home screen*

Click the Device Manager tab, then click Control in the left menu. A screen with the outlet inventory opens, as shown in Figure 7-8.

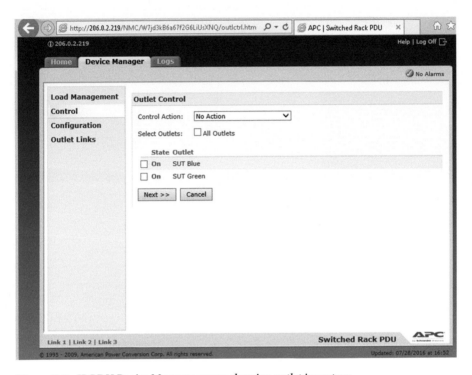

Figure 7-8. *IP PDU Device Manager screen showing outlet inventory*

To power cycle the Blue SUT, click the SUT Blue check box, and from the Control Action pull-down menu, select Reboot Delayed, as shown in Figure 7-9.

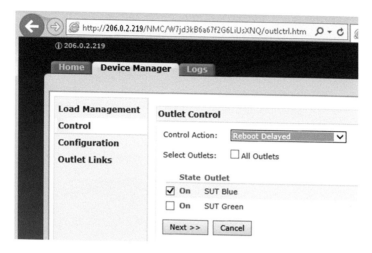

Figure 7-9. *Selecting target SUT and power cycling action*

Click Next once. The confirmation screen shown in Figure 7-10 appears.

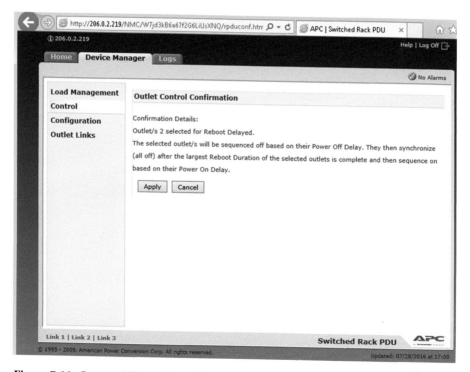

Figure 7-10. *Power cycling confirmation screen*

Now click Apply. After this action, the SUT will be power cycled and the IPKVM window will black out. A few seconds later, the serial window will start displaying content. It will continue to do so until the operating system wakes up and starts capturing the content of the serial port. Make sure to terminate the PDU session at this point by closing the respective (APC) window. The IPKVM might need to be restarted as well.

After a few minutes, after restarting the IPKVM session, you will see the login screen reappear, as shown in Figure 7-11. The appearance of this screen completes the power cycling sequence.

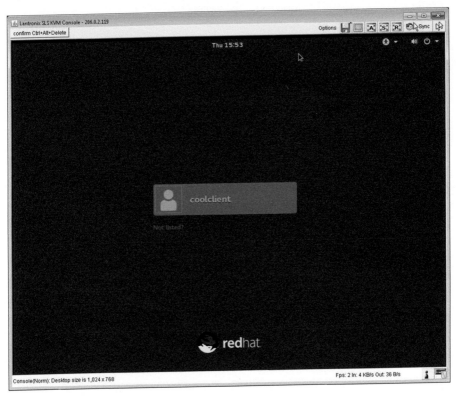

Figure 7-11. *Operating system login screen after a physical power cycling*

Technology Sandbox Service: Bare Metal lab as a Marketplace

At the business level, a bare metal remote lab facility under a co-development model with participation of multiple technology partners can define a *technology marketplace.* Assume a service network ecosystem as depicted in Figure 4-7. Each CSP member in this ecosystem provides specialized services, drawing from services from other providers, as shown in Figure 7-12. To go to market, this service provider also brings in a unique "secret sauce" that justifies its market presence and usefulness to players downstream. This secret sauce can take many forms:

- *Functional integration*: The service provider integrates services from supporting providers and delivers a unique capability, perhaps with a strong geographic component. An example is an income tax return service specific to a country's tax laws.

- *Service scaling integration*: The service provider aggregates capabilities from various providers into a convenient and scalable version available to consumers downstream. Quintessential examples are the marketplaces in Amazon Marketplace and eBay.

- *Unique intellectual property*: The service provider has unique IP, which combined with services from supporting providers and technology from partners, allows the provider to deliver a unique service offering.

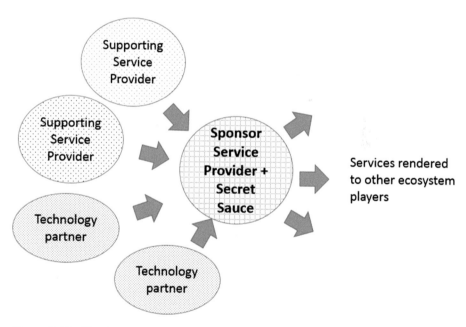

Figure 7-12. *Cloud service provider ecosystem dynamics*

The lab marketplace framework is recursive: The service provider need not be a single service provider; it can be another service network or even another marketplace. An example is a cooperative banking or a credit union or small banking network offering certain banking services such as a consumer remittance service. The service provider becomes a service maker sponsor, assembling a network of communications providers, applications providers, and technical and business support. A credit union wishing to deliver this service can plug into this network to integrate the remittance service into its financial services portfolio. Integration includes brand identity. The service or service network provider gets to choose the type of brand identity. Here are some possible options:

- *Invisible and seamless*: A consumer making a money transfer does not even realize the presence of an outsourced network actually performing the service.

- *Subtle*: The consumer is informed "This transaction completed through the FFF Financial Network," or that the consumer's credit union is a "Member of the FFF Financial Network."

- *Branded transactions*: The identity of the facilitating provider becomes secondary. Major credit card providers use this approach.

Another important role in the service marketplace dynamic beyond the roles of supporting service provider, technology partner, service sponsor, and service consumer, is that of the metaservice provider, namely the entity sponsoring the marketplace in the first place. An example of a metaservice provider is BlankSlate[8], a digital market agency whose mission is to establish local connections among brands, businesses, publishers, and audiences.

Vendor motivations for taking a metaservice provider role are diverse. For instance, Microsoft, with its Azure-in-a-box stack, seeks to extend the industry reach of the Microsoft Azure platform to add value to enterprise datacenters. A subset of Azure functionality that otherwise would run in Microsoft cloud datacenters can now run at other service provider datacenters or at customer datacenters, with a uniform application and operational model[9]. This model is useful for cases where data location is constrained geographically. Revenue models are also diverse: The metaservice provider or the sponsor service provider can realize revenue from advertising, charging for consulting services, charging for software licensing, or through transaction fees.

In a HaaS lab marketplace, each lab environment defines a stall or sandbox in the cloud. Each sandbox is a BMaaS instance allowing a tenant complete control over the hardware. The tenant of a sandbox is either a technology partner or a CSP with goals to integrate emerging or advanced technologies. Technology providers announce their presence and availability in the lab marketplace. The sponsor service provider has the option of openly announcing its participation, inviting one or more technology providers to apply and join their project, or operating discreetly, inviting only technology participants as needed. Technology partners can install demonstration versions of their stacks. A service provider can bind its service to the technology provider's stack instance, or negotiate with the technology provider to install a fresh stack in the sponsor provider environment. Intel is deploying a pilot instance of the bare metal lab in Hillsboro to enable rapid diffusion of advanced technology under the Intel Cloud Insider program. There is no charge for participation. However, participants must enroll and become active members in the program.

---

[8]See http://www.blankslate.com/.
[9]I. Thomson, "Microsoft Unbuttons Shirt, Teases Glimpse of Azure-in-a-Box Stack," *The Register*, January 26, 2016.

Once the sponsor service provider builds its stack, there are a number of postintegration actions:

- *Deploy the newly minted stack*: Deploy it to the sponsor service provider's datacenters.

- *Publish the stack architecture for ecosystem and scaling*: The sponsor service provider has discretion of leaving parts of the architecture as black boxes, respecting the provider's desire to keep the secret sauce components secret. Another entity trying to offer a similar service would need to re-create, reimplement the black boxes, or license this capability from the sponsor provider.

Figure 7-13 summarizes the relationships among service providers, technology partners, and the rest of the ecosystem. Whether coordinating factory resources through cloud APIs, or using a lab partition as a beta sandbox, or the CSP initially linking the sandbox implementation to its datacenters as a prior step to migrating the stack to the datacenters, there is an implementation process continuum, given that all the environment instances are in the cloud. Project participants have the option to pick any point in this continuum for the best business and technical outcomes.

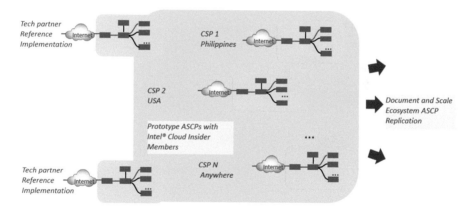

Figure 7-13. *Lab marketplace life cycle*

A HaaS lab marketplace eases the path to adoption of emerging technology. The HaaS lab marketplace alleviates capital expense (CapEx) issues. For small companies the few servers might represent an insurmountable cost barrier in the way to carrying technology assessment. Larger companies might require the assessment teams to go through a procurement process that takes several months. We can see that the same dynamic that played out server procurement in traditional datacenters also applies to technology assessment. The same issues propelled cloud computing in the first place, and therefore we can expect a similar acceleration for technology assessment from the application of cloud methods. For instance, the marketplace connects service providers and technology partners directly in a single, small community. Service providers can speed up time to solution deployment, which also benefits technology partners through accelerated sales cycles. On top of that, sandboxes provide access to both hardware and software, enabling fast and efficient platform customization, which is exactly the goal for third-wave cloud platforms.

HaaS Lab Federated Architecture

A hierarchical architecture allows delivering the capabilities mentioned thus far in a system of arbitrary size. At the highest level, the lab is a federation of labs, shown in Figure 7-14. These labs can be geographically dispersed. Each lab represents a building or datacenter location, and within each lab, one or more logical divisions can exist. We call these divisions *pods*, possibly defined by departmental or divisional boundaries. A pod in turn consists of one or more *rows* of *equipment racks*. Racks house the SUTs plus the ancillary service hosts. Service hosts are physical servers running a virtualized environment containing front-end host virtual machines that end users see.

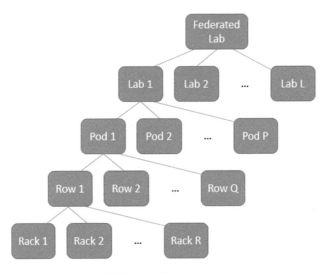

Figure 7-14. *HaaS lab hierarchical structure*

Virtualized front-end hosts allow serving a large community of end users while minimizing hardware requirements for ancillary support equipment. In most cases, host workloads tend to be interactive, with low processing demands; hence it makes sense to consolidate as many virtualized front-end hosts as possible into the fewest service hosts. Physical front-end hosts are also possible when called for due to security, performance, or other special requirements.

At the next level of detail, we see a *pod command center*, shown in Figure 7-15, usually housed in a rack, serving the rows within. Each row in turn carries a *row command center*, also usually in a dedicated rack. Each row command center in turn connects to one or more physical *service hosts*.

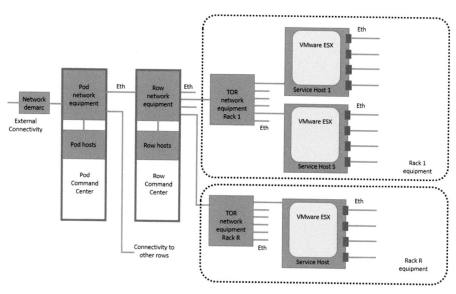

Figure 7-15. *Haas lab relationships between pod, row, and rack structures*

Figure 7-16 depicts a service host in detail. A service host runs a hypervisor, in this case VMware ESX defining a virtualized network and one or more user *front-end hosts*. An end user accessing the facility logs into a designated front-end host. The hypervisor connects the virtualized network to physical NICs. These NICs can be of any of four types:

- *Server*: This is the application NIC assigned to the OS running in the SUT.

- *BMC*: This is the NIC assigned to the management network, connected to the BMC.

- *Control network*: Auxiliary lab equipment controllers are connected to this network, for instance a Galileo board controller to manipulate GPIOs.

- *Spare*: This port is for future expansion and is not in use in the current architecture instance.

In addition, controllers such as a Galileo board or the Intel RSC2 also require a front-end host. It is probably easiest to retain these front-end hosts in their original physical instantiation. However, virtualizing this front-end host will forgo the need for the extra hardware, and setting up the virtualized version is no more time consuming than provisioning the physical host. The USB connection or connections can be mapped to physical controller host instances where required. Currently, both the Galileo board and the RSC2 require this type of connection.

If we move to the right of Figure 7-16, we can observe an actual SUT layout. Customer requirements define the actual layouts. Obviously, layouts that are more complex require more effort and time to set up, and hence the actual layout deployed is usually the simplest that gets the job done. Figure 7-17 depicts two example layouts. For SUT 1 the customer requires manipulating a certain GPIO in the baseboard.

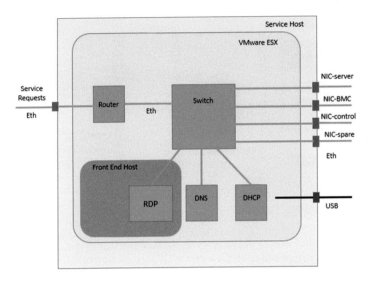

Figure 7-16. *Service host detail*

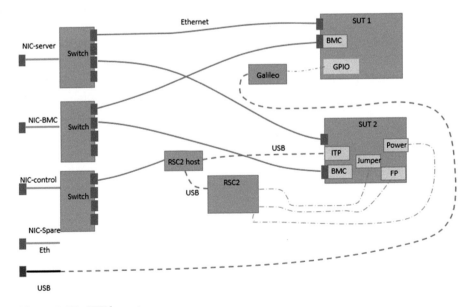

Figure 7-17. *SUT layouts*

GPIO stands for *general-purpose I/O*. A GPIO is a pin in a chip that acts as a digital control line and can be used for multiple purposes depending on the chip application. GPIO pins can be used for different purposes at different times. The different modalities introduce complexities and the possibility of bugs. On the other hand, pins in a chip are usually at a premium, and GPIOs help reduce the pinout numbers. Also, adding a pin to a chip in production is not practical, and GPIOs could be the only way to implement a certain function.

Monitoring and setting GPIOs is usually not necessary for production boards, but might be essential for debugging and verifying the correct functionality of a baseboard subsystem. A GPIO may be implemented as a floating gate with a pullup resistor. If the pin is left hanging, then the GPIO takes on a default state of a logical 1. If the pin is grounded, then the GPIO takes on the value of logical 0. This grounding can be done manually, but this method is usually not practical even when the machine is physically present. The features in a circuit board are small, and manual grounding can result in unintended damage due to static discharge or touching an unintended part of the circuit board. If the machine is racked, physical manipulation is out of the question, even if the machine is present. The recommended method is to manipulate GPIOs through a microcontroller. Figure 7-17 shows SUT 1 with a Galileo microcontroller board connected to a GPIO within. The Galileo needs a USB connection to a front-end host. In this case the front-end host is virtualized and runs in the service host. The Galileo virtual front-end host is connected to a physical USB port in the service host as shown.

SUT 2 in Figure 7-17 shows a more elaborate setup using an RSC2. The RSC2 also requires a front-end host. In this case the lab customer has requested that the physical front-end host be retained, as shown. The RSC2 enables physical power cycling of the SUT plus access to an in-test probe, jumpers, and the front panel in the SUT.

The lab architecture just presented is not prescriptive. Labs in a federation could be peer labs within a company, deployed in different geographical regions, or they could belong to different companies or providers. As in any federation, and following the spirit of the cloud, the federation is loosely coupled.

A lab might use alternative means to deploy a capability, for instance using Arduino controller boards instead of Galileo. It can even offer a subset of capabilities, such as access through a single web portal and therefore a single IP address, with a flat network configuration, where all servers appear as local network peers. This means that the whole lab looks like a single environment of the canonical architecture. This setup might be objectionable to some customers: Even though the web interface might attempt to regulate the visibility of the SUT nodes in the pool, in reality, all the servers reside in a single subnet, and therefore the walls between customers are very thin from a security perspective and the web environment can be easily subverted. Labs must advertise or describe any known operational limitations as disclaimers in the description of capabilities and in the SLA.

Appendix: Sample Lab Service Level Agreement

This document defines the data management processes in practice at the HaaS customer access lab (the lab). The lab customer is herein referred as "Lab Guest." The policies are in place with the following objectives:

- Define coordinated processes to safeguard data and applications to be hosted in the lab, thereby minimizing risks of data breaches and leaks.

- Clarify roles and responsibilities in the collaboration toward the long-term objectives for the lab as per Lab Guest memorandum of understanding. The main goals of the project are as follows:

  - Carry out a performance assessment of a number of Lab Guest critical applications to determine application and hardware requirements.

  - Perform application architecture mapping to current generation server platforms. This work includes optimization recipes from the performance assessment with optimally configured platforms to deliver result in the shortest time scale possible.

  - Develop a strategic application architecture mapping to next generation platforms. This includes the use of application-specific baseboards to allow a close match between application requirements and advanced silicon technologies in a cost- and energy-efficient combination.

The above notwithstanding, the likelihood of adverse outcomes can be minimized but not eliminated altogether, and therefore Lab Guest and Intel agree to not hold each liable should any of these adverse outcomes ever happen.

Hosting the engagement at the lab allows lab staff to carry out the tasks of profiling and optimization more effectively. A significant part of the work will be carried on advanced prototypes that might require frequent diagnostics and troubleshooting. Having the platforms at the lab will shorten the time and expense for issue resolution.

General Considerations

Here are some considerations governing the relationship between Lab Guest and the lab.

- There are no explicit limitations in the lab architecture or equipment configuration, except for

  - Mutual considerations of cost.

  - Any action in conflict with preexisting Intel IT or corporate data policies.

- The actual lab configuration is determined by mutual agreement. The issuance of corporate policies is beyond the authority of project participants and therefore if a corporate policy conflicts with a project policy, it cannot be grandfathered into this project.

- The intent for this infrastructure is to be responsive to Lab Guest's business requirements. The infrastructure will be dynamic, to be built over time, as fast as technology development and resources will allow. For a certain level of infrastructure build-up, Lab Guest determines whether the risks are acceptable for specific data and code drop milestones.

- A regular joint Project Development Team (PDT) meeting will be established to coordinate ongoing security and technical issues and for reporting, initially weekly and then every two weeks as needed.

Lab Access

- Lab staff will provide access to the lab to authorized Intel and Lab Guest engineers.

- There is a double physical perimeter around the Lab Guest equipment: access to the lab room and access to the Lab Guest equipment inside locked cabinets.

- Access to the lab room is granted only to Intel employees in an Access Control List (ACL). This access is subject to expiration and needs to be renewed regularly for employees with demonstrated need. Intel employees not in the ACL or non-Intel visitors can enter the lab only if escorted by a person in the ACL.

Lab Access Logs

- In the event of an incident such as break-in or loss of equipment, the security team will have access to logs in the lab perimeter and can review the data without need for approval from HR Legal in order to investigate the incident.

- Log access requests by third parties or even by Intel staff will require escalation and HR Legal approval. The HR Legal team may decline the request. Approval is granted on a case by case basis. The project team needs to work with the HR Legal Team to understand the turn-around time.

- Support provided during business hours, 8:00–5:00, M–F, U.S. Pacific Time Zone. The expected turnaround time is from one to three hours.

Physical Access Security and Access Control Lists

- Racks for this project will be provided with simple locks front and back. Keys to locks will be held by the supporting local staff. Racks will be placed inside a caged area for exclusive Lab Guest use. There will be no other equipment inside this cage than equipment designated to the project.

- Access to the caged area will be via magnetic badge, RFID, or biometric mechanism. The cage locking mechanism will be connected to a service node enforcing the ACL and implementing the logging function. Lab Guest manages the ACL. The security service node is connected to the WAN using the same connectivity as other service nodes. Lab Guest can log into the security node at any time to retrieve access logs, edit the ACL, and configure the security node to notify reportable events through text or email. The logs will only contain project-related events.

- Passive mechanisms such as hard drive encryption are possible as an additional layer in case of a physical breach, subject to technical, performance, or implementation cost impediments.

Hardware Maintenance and Upgrades

When changes to the server need to be done such as upgrading memory type/size, swapping processors, or reboot systems or make changes to BIOS/FW configurations, Lab Guest will provide a clear list of tasks that needs to be done to Intel Engineer. Upon mutual agreement and approval, engineer will procure the key to the rack, open the rack, and perform required changes. Upon successful changes, rack will be locked and key will be handed to lab staff. A log of changes that are performed are captured in a spreadsheet and an email will be sent to the key Intel and Lab Guest stakeholders confirming the changes performed.

Storage Locker

Lab staff provide a storage locker space to store Intel Security Team approved items inside Intel Facility. The type equipment to be stored and space required needs to discussed with lab staff.

Lab Data Storage

Any documentation, software, or hardware left behind for safekeeping will be logged with the lab staff. Lab staff will manage the items in the locked storage area.

Media Transfers

- Any device with storage capability, including hard drives, SSDs, memory cards, USB keys, and servers are to be registered and approved with Intel Security prior to being carried into an Intel facility and submitted for inspection by Intel Security upon leaving the Intel premises.

- Any data Lab Guest deems sensitive needs to be encrypted on-disk using a non-dictionary passphrase if it will reside outside of the locked rack, be transported off-premises, or outside the jurisdiction of lab staff.

- All test results or related data requires written or email approval for public disclosure.

- Upon removal of media from lab: if request is to return media to Lab Guest it may be hand carried out of the lab and must be protected with approved encryption. Otherwise, for device removal, it must be wiped with shred or secure erased and CD/DVD media must be destroyed. All media removal from the rack must be logged.

Network Security Policy

The policies described in this document assume a logical separation of concerns. Intel provides the advanced platforms and access control in the form of a lab platform. Lab Guest becomes a tenant in the lab and owns the data and applications under test at all times. Lab Guest manages all data transfers and application installation and provides explicit authorization to lab staff to carry out administrative and application optimization tasks at Lab Guest's discretion. The lab is effectively a bare metal cloud. All the physical equipment except for the WAN facing router is assigned exclusively for this project with no multi-tenancy. None of the cloud subnets will be connected to the Intel corporate network.

The following infrastructure will be in place to enforce data integrity:

- An external DMZ, ("xDMZ") managed by lab controls connections, forwarding, manages inbound and outbound security, and detection of DOS attacks, port scan attempts, detection of script kiddies, etc. and establishes and maintains connection channels from the outside cloud to the lab.

- Lab Guest's DMZ ("eDMZ") for controlling access, forwarding, etc. as above, only between the external connection and internal connection(s). eDMZ can support DHCP, DNS, Port Forwarding/Reversing, DOS, Certificate manager, Gateway, Bridging, etc. as docs the xDMZ.

- Up to four iDMZ for controlling access, forwarding, etc. as above, only between the VM Host

225

- *iDMZ01*: Control plane DMZ—Connections at the overall control/data plane at the first layer into the SUT. Again, the DMZ will consist of DHCP, DNS, Port Forwarding/Reversing, DOS, Certificate manager, Gateway, Bridging, etc.

- *iDMZ02*: Control plane DMZ—Connections at the overall control plane of the data layer within the SUT physical layer(s). Front end for a smart switch, load generator and SUT control layer manipulation, certificates, DNS, gateway, etc.

- *iDMZ03*: Data plane DMZ—Connections at the overall data plane of the data layer within the SUT physical layer(s). Front end for a smart switch, load generator and SUT data layer manipulation, certificates, DNS, gateway, etc.

- *iDMZ04 (Optional)*: I/O control of test instruments, logic analyzers, JTAG interfaces, Serial port interfaces, etc.

- IPSEC will be deployed optionally to protect the connection(s) and data layers, subject to considerations of complexity of use increases as the level of IPSEC/VKE layers is notched up. Protocol and payload encryption are optional subject complexity tradeoffs. Likewise on whether certificates should be static or dynamic. Dynamic certificates can be set to expire at a predetermined time. They can lead to increased security, at the expense of more complex certificate management.

  Host and client are required to have a matched set to establish a connection. The Cert manager verifies the connection(s) and then signs off.

  Dynamic certificates are constantly changing as well as the connection. This can be applied to the connections, protocol, and payload layers

Security measures exact a performance, convenience, and usability penalty. However, when possible, the encryption engines of the processor(s) and the TCP offloading, packet defragmenter, VM packet tunneling, etc., will be deployed using Intel's hardware accelerated engines.

Physical Security Policy

The initial setup envisions a lab administered DMZ connected to the WAN router to vet WAN connections. The services for running this DMZ are implemented as virtual machines in an assigned physical server. The lab administered DMZ connects to an inner Lab Guest administered DMZ acting as front end to the platform SUTs, workload generators, and application subnet(s).

- *No security setup is foolproof.* The initial setup is multilayered and includes placing the equipment in a badge access room. There is a tradeoff between minimizing risks and inconvenience. For instance, hard drive encryption means Lab Guest needs to intervene and provide the hard drive passcode for every reboot.

- *Lab Guest owns the access control list* to the application subnets. Access list members encompass lab staff, Intel platform and application engineers, and Intel system administrators.

- As a tenant, *Lab Guest provides access rights to lab staff* to carry out their roles, including workload characterization, profiling, optimization, collect data, perform analysis, change the server BOM, and update BIOS settings upon acceptance from Lab Guest team.

- *Data anti-backflow mechanisms* can be installed in either DMZ per mutual agreement.

- *Visitor badges.* When customers enter the Intel premises, the customer will visit the security area, provide required credentials, and procure the visitor badge upon successful verification. A lab staff host will escort the Lab Guest visitor into the Intel premises and datacenter lab all the time.

- *Access codes, login, or decryption passwords* will be treated as sensitive information, and will not be written down or stored electronically in an unencrypted format, and will not be shared with anyone unless explicitly allowed by both lab staff and Lab Guest access approvers.

- *BIOS* will have passwords set. Lab Guest decides who has access to the passwords.

- *External removable media ports* (such as CD-ROM, DVD, SD, USB or eSATA, but not limited to this list) should have boot capability disabled in BIOS.

- A minimum of two *Kensington cables* should be provided that can be securely anchored to the rack, for the purpose of locking any removable media.

- *Inventory control.* Equipment will be audited monthly to ensure nothing is missing from expected inventory.

- *Photographs & cameras.* Digital cameras and video cameras are not allowed in the datacenter area without written approval from Intel Security.

- *Lab Guest visit checkout.* The customer will be escorted to the main visitor area where customer will hand over the badge to the Intel Security Team.

- *Physical access to lab facility.* The datacenter is equipped with the badge reader. The access is allowed for approved personnel only. When customer wants to enter the lab, a lab staff member will escort the customer into the lab.

Termination and Deconstruction

At time of engagement decommissioning, all data will be physically recovered and transported by Lab Guest, or destroyed in keeping with industry best practices such as ATA Secure Erase, Gutmann method, degaussing or physical destruction of media compliant with DoD 5220.22-M. This applies to any and all sensitive data or intellectual property, configuration, intermediate data generated, or results not explicitly allowed for retention or delivery to either party.

Any customer-installed devices, such as video recording equipment for managing security or magnetic media for data transfers, will be securely stored in a manner consistent with Cloud Lab policies, until such time as equipment can be responsibly recovered by Lab Guest.

CHAPTER 8

■ ■ ■

Service Strategy and Examples

Southwest Airlines is successful because the company understands it is a customer service company. It also happens to be an airline.

—Harvey Mackay

Let us explore ways to put the concepts in the previous chapters to work. The motto "Think globally, act locally" applies here. A crucial piece of insight from the concepts we have discussed so far is that, given that the cloud is intrinsically service-oriented, understanding and internalizing the notion of service is a necessary condition to success in cloud space. We discovered in Chapter 4 that long-term planning approaches, successful in the first wave in the enterprise cycle, are less effective in the fast-changing cloud markets. It became necessary to shorten the process by engaging with end users, not just to gather requirements for future products, but also to actually jointly plan, design, and even manufacture the platforms. Organizations need to embrace cloud internally to succeed in cloud markets. This approach brings additional benefits: Embracing a service culture and taking advantage of cloud technology to speed up internal processes will actually endow the organization with the agility and timeliness it was seeking to succeed in the cloud market.

We covered processes for service transformation in Chapter 3, describing a number of steps that organizations can take to adopt and embrace a service culture. Common wisdom and experience from service-oriented architecture (SOA) transformation projects suggests that executive support is essential for this transformation to take place. However, imposing a top-to-bottom service-oriented diktat is not practical, realistic, or even desirable. A more realistic goal is to identify opportunities to use service-oriented thinking to bring up immediate and positive local changes, albeit small, as part of a larger service transformation strategy. Early successes bring confidence in the organization and a self-reinforcing virtuous circle that fosters further experimentation and creativity from participants. The journey, with its associated learning, goals for continuous improvement, and measurement of outcomes, is more important than practicing a specific methodology. From this perspective, a service-dominant logic (SDL) strategy emphasizing symmetric value-for-value exchange provides more immediate feedback mechanisms than a goods-dominant logic (GDL) approach. The GDL approach is more

© Enrique Castro-Leon and Robert Harmon 2016
E. Castro-Leon and R. Harmon, *Cloud as a Service*, DOI 10.1007/978-1-4842-0103-9_8

product and product feature-centric, and more normative in terms of these features, where there is a temptation to offer a feature portfolio in a take it or leave it fashion. As mentioned earlier in the book, feedback loops still exist as part of product planning, but these are longer than those in an SDL environment are. Some features might be obsolete by the time the product hits the market.

In the spirit of acting locally, but within a global perspective, we start with a service macroarchitecture that lays out a landscape for technology enabling the service economy, helping identify some immediate actions. The macroarchitecture extends the NIST cloud model up toward the notion of a service-oriented economy, and downward toward the hardware that makes up the NIST cloud. We follow the macroarchitecture with examples in specific fields where change can happen:

- The integration of power management from platform power to integration at the industry level under an automated demand response (ADR) framework where a datacenter behaves like a servicelet to power utilities.

- The Alzheimer's Organization federated database.

- The bring your own device (BYOD) phenomenon in IT organizations.

The approach in these examples is evolutionary. It allows immediate action toward increasing an organization's nimbleness or reach within the industry under a strategic vision but avoids the disruption associated with an organizational remake. These case studies represent vertical slices across the layers of the macroarchitecture. Activities that work horizontally within one layer are also helpful to bring immediate benefits of the cloud and a service approach to an organization. One example is the notion of a cloud-based lab service discussed in Chapter 7.

A Service Macroarchitecture

In computer engineering, the term *microarchitecture* refers to the machine organization below the instruction set architecture (ISA), including the description at the register transfer level (RTL) logic and the underlying electrical circuitry implementing each of the instructions in a processor. As a processor goes through successive generations, the instruction set stays essentially the same, able to run the same software, even though the microarchitecture, the underlying implementation, might go through radical changes to improve performance, and reduce the size and power requirements. In this situation, the processor represents a useful abstraction to preserve programming compatibility across multiple generations.

Going in the opposite direction, the term *macroarchitecture* describes the environment above the processor level, including programming languages and environments, compilers, assemblers, and hypervisors. We use the term *service macroarchitecture* to span a service-oriented ecosystem universe, all the way to the notion of a service-oriented economy. Figure 8-1 shows these relationships in the form of a service cloud stack. The column at the right provides a few examples without an intent to be comprehensive.

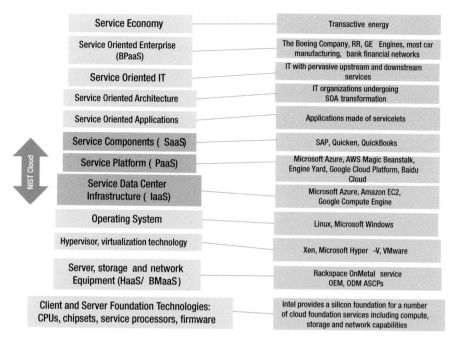

Figure 8-1. *Cloud macroarchitecture*

We use Figure 8-1 as our visual roadmap for the discussion in the rest of the section. Note the SaaS, PaaS, and IaaS, entities at the core of the NIST definition for cloud computing, occupying just a small portion of our universe in the middle of the stack[1]. The macroarchitecture broadens the scope of the NIST vision higher up toward business and economic concerns, and toward the bottom to its technology foundation.

The macroarchitecture stack roughly maps to the service network depicted in Figure 4-7 as we connect service providers in each of the rungs in Figure 8-1 to service relationships. A service provider at any level carries relationships with other providers downstream, upstream, and possibly between peers. This pattern is easier to see if we rotate Figure 4-7 a quarter turn counterclockwise. Figure 8-2 shows the result. The technology providers are now at the bottom of the graph, and the cloud end customers appear at the top. The graph emphasizes servicelet relationships among the participants in a service network using a conventional definition of a service producer–consumer relationship, not in the strictly symmetric value cocreation as defined by Vargo and Lusch[2].

---

[1]P. Mell and T. Grance, *The NIST Definition of Cloud Computing*, Special Publication 800-145 (Washington, DC: National Institute of Standards and Technology, U.S. Department of Commerce, September 2011).
[2]R. F. Lusch and S. L. Vargo, *Service-Dominant Logic: Premises, Perspectives, Possibilities* (London, UK: Cambridge University Press, 2014).

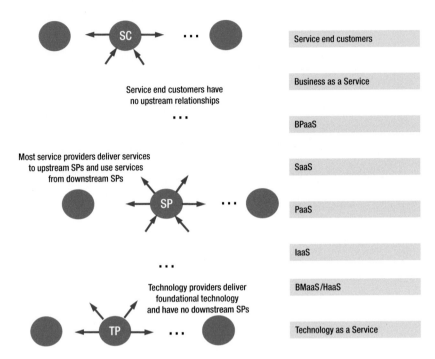

Figure 8-2. Service network in the cloud ecosystem

Preserving this asymmetric view is necessary to analyze the service provider-consumer relationships and the role of cloud service providers (CSPs). Under this view, we can still apply the definition of a service as the "application of competences (knowledge, skills, and resources) by one entity for the benefit of another entity in a non-coercive (mutually agreed and mutually beneficial) manner"[3]. The service consumer applies some form of payment or compensation for the services rendered. Vargo and Lusch looked at this payment as a credit for future services.

Documenting the context for a service relationship analysis is essential for the analysis to be meaningful. For instance, an employee working for a CSP who uses the one of the productivity applications under Office 365 SaaS by Microsoft is an end user for the purposes of the analysis, unless the CSP embeds Office 365 application programming interfaces (APIs) or service capabilities into their offerings. Likewise, an automobile manufacturing company makes extensive use of services in its supply chain. However, if it designs, manufactures, and sells its vehicles under a GDL framework, this company is also a leaf node in its service network. On the other hand, this company is a service provider if it provides leasing and financing services to its customers. This service is

---

[3]R. Schmidt, A. Kieninger, et al., "Meta-Services—Towards Symmetric Service-Oriented Business Ecosystems," *AIFB Proceedings of the Second International Workshop on Enabling Service Business Ecosystems* (ESBE'09), 2009.

complementary to the company's main line of business of manufacturing vehicles. This was the case of the former General Motors Acceptance Corporation (GMAC), divested from General Motors to become Ally Financial, Inc.

In the cloud service network depicted in Figure 8-2, services exist at multiple levels, roughly following the service macroarchitecture layers. The correlation is not exactly one-to-one because a specific application domain might not have a presence in every layer. Beyond that, an entity in the macroarchitecture such as a company could be service-oriented in some aspects but not in others. Here are some examples.

- In the initial cloud of circa 2007, the lowest level service available and the service that started the cloud was IaaS; therefore there were no downstream service providers. Bare-metal service offerings appeared later, around 2009[4].

- IaaS and HaaS providers initially did not have downstream server platform providers because the platform suppliers were all traditional product-oriented GDL platform providers. The first instances of a framework for technology platform as a service took place with some large CSPs participating in the second-wave cloud platform.

  Even then, the occurrence of this pattern was not a traditional service relationship in that the service providers entered a service agreement with a technology platform provider, given that there was no precedent for such an infrastructure. However, the service relationship patterns of value cocreation and value-for-value exchange were there.

- Large automobile manufacturers have a highly evolved downstream network of suppliers, very close to a service network. If we look upstream, there are parts of their business that are effectively service-oriented, such as leasing services and contracts with rental companies, but other parts are still very much GDL, such as automobile sales through dealer networks.

It is important to acknowledge that political and certainly business and economic considerations prevail over technical concerns in the uppermost layers, starting with service-oriented IT. Service orientation becomes a lens through which to understand organizational and technological relationships and dynamics to predict and optimize outcomes, rather than purely expressing architectural intent. It is safe to say that today no organization, whether governmental or any private enterprise, is intentionally service-oriented top to bottom.

In the upper layers, service components or servicelets provide the foundation for service-oriented applications, which in turn provide the basis for an SOA in a service-oriented IT organization. For most organizations, these concepts represent aspirational

---

[4]A. Bridgewater, "What Is Bare-Metal Cloud?," *Computer Weekly,* http://www.computer-weekly.com/blog/CW-Developer-Network/What-is-bare-metal-cloud, September 6, 2013; M. S. V. Janakiram, "Why Bare Metal Cloud Is in Vogue," *Computer Weekly,* http://www.computer-weekly.com/news/2240227924/Why-is-bare-metal-cloud-in-vogue, September 2, 2014.

goals and a framework for strategy making toward a more efficient use of technology resources. Some of these constituencies argue for caution in favor of proven, traditional GDL frameworks, against refactoring processes and resources behind an SDL framework. Actual practice is messy, with IT organizations in continuous transformation and with raging debates between various constituencies, not just about service-oriented versus product-oriented strategies, but also in deciding an optimal path for embracing SDL.

Complex organizations, such as the IT organization in a large corporation, will exhibit islands of service in an otherwise GDL sea. Likewise, aircraft and automotive manufacturing companies have a supply chain and design federated network understandable in terms of a federated service network. However, these companies market their products from a very traditional GDL perspective, focused on assumptions about the intrinsic value of the goods offered instead of the value-in-use. This approach can lead to contradictory marketing strategies where aircraft manufacturers tout bigger windows and the spaciousness of advanced aircraft[5], with these features being defeated, when airlines requesting more seats per row[6]. Meanwhile, seat pitch gets smaller with each succeeding technology generation, at least in the economy cabin, from as large as 34 inches in the 1980s to a bone-crushing 28 inches on some budget airlines today. Likewise, automotive manufacturers use a supply chain network to feed their factories and a dealer network to deliver the finished product. An end-to-end service-oriented analysis of these networks could yield optimizations that are not obvious from a traditional GDL perspective.

The evolution toward a service-oriented economy in advanced economies has been running its course for at least a century, if not more, providing a backdrop for service-oriented enterprises. Service-oriented business processes, supported by service-oriented technology applications, will coexist with GDL processes in most organizations for the near future, with a constantly moving, uneasy boundary. These dynamics occur within companies as well as across regional industries.

Change usually takes place after a crisis, where contradictions from a GDL perspective become unsustainable, and a fear of losing everything takes over. An example comes from the notion of value-in-use concept for SDL versus intrinsic value in goods under GDL. When market dynamics make a product less valuable, and the vendor attempts to keep the price constant under the intrinsic value premise, demand for that product will fall. The vendor can use supply-side marketing strategies to create awareness about product features to stoke demand. Unfortunately, this strategy will not work if the lower demand is because the product has become less useful to users. A service-aware marketing strategy would focus more on the demand side, looking at the customer value-in-use dynamics, taking into account that users determine product valuation, not the seller.

The cost efficiency and accelerated feedback loops between actors driving service-oriented frameworks ensure that market signals of trouble ahead come up much earlier, and perhaps even more important, SDL practitioners can recognize these signals and act on them on a timely basis. This is one aspect of business agility under SDL. Service practitioners are keenly aware of this dynamic, for fear of being left behind by nimbler players.

---

[5]See http://www.boeing.com/commercial/777x/.
[6]W. McGee, "Think Airline Seats Have Gotten Smaller? They Have," *USA Today,* http://www.usatoday.com/story/travel/columnist/mcgee/2014/09/24/airplane-reclining-seat-pitch-width/16105491/, September 24, 2014.

The layers underneath the NIST cloud comprise the technology foundation for the cloud: OS, hypervisors and hardware. The lowest layer comprises silicon-based technologies providing the physical building blocks for application-specific cloud platforms (ASCPs): processors, network and I/O controllers, firmware, baseboards, and thermal designs. The next layer up comprises processing, network, and storage equipment. In layers further up, we see the hypervisor or OS running on the bare metal, and above that, the OS.

As in the layers above the NIST cloud, technology foundation layers today are predominantly product-oriented but changing at a fast pace. At the lowest layers, GDL technology purveyors, the majority today, face challenges when attempting to participate as service providers in a service ecosystem. Product features have traditionally defined technology markets, whether measured in terms of nanometers for semiconductor feature sizes, millions of instructions or floating-point operations per second (MIPS or FLOPS), or network speeds. For technology providers, participating in a market in terms of pay-for-performance basis sounds like a laudable goal to provide relief from boom-and-bust, lumpy revenue patterns toward a more continuous and steady service revenue that delights shareholders. There are a number of considerations for executing on this strategy:

- There are no shortcuts; in particular no amount of marketing repositioning can reverse a trend where a product is considered less valuable by customers.

  - In the long term, changes in revenue can only reflect changes in value delivered to customers.

  - Transfer of risk toward the technology provider represents an opportunity for value added, for instance where a provider commits to a certain level of application performance as opposed to a certain product feature.

  - Achieving great service and a customer relationship is not free. It requires added investment in human resources. This is incompatible with companies driven by product margin. GDL companies will need to weigh the risk of lowering margins to attain a more stable revenue stream and go after higher market participation.

- A technical framework makes it easier to chart a service transformation strategy for technology providers. Chapters 4 through 7 exemplify one such framework with the notion of ASCPs as CSP-oriented customized platforms and a platform roadmap. The ASCP model covered in Chapters 4 through 7 represents a radical rethinking for building hardware platforms to tend to the needs of CSPs today and to the needs of the Internet of things (IoT) market in the near future. This rethinking comprises processes for both platform creation and development, namely processes for ASCP development as well as platform deployment in the form of HaaS or BMaaS in support of existing services such as IaaS as well as emerging services such as the concept of a lab service supporting concurrent multiparty platform development.

235

Service concepts have also become more prominent in the software layers, especially with open source. Peter Levine, former CEO of XenSource, posited that for open source, technology represents a level playing field given that all players have access to the basic technology[7]. He advocated for the concept of *open source as a service* where participants use the commonly accessible open source technology base, and combine it with unique homegrown capabilities and a service offering. The homegrown capability can be a physical appliance or a differentiated service offering that includes not only the open source technology base, but also knowledge in a specific domain with few competitors.

Change with service in mind is also taking place with vendors of proprietary software. Some changes are relatively minor, with vendors migrating from a perpetual license for a defined instance and version of a software product to a subscription model as discussed in Chapter 6. With this change, the vendor is seeking to maximize revenue and to convert an otherwise lumpy revenue pattern from selling licenses to a recurrent revenue model. In this case, there is little change with the product offering, which remains firmly in GDL territory. Terry Myerson, Executive Vice President, Windows and Devices Group, declared in his blog about Microsoft Windows 10 that this version of Windows might be the last version a customer ever buys, at least for a given device. He went on to say, "Once a Windows device is upgraded to Windows 10, we will continue to keep it current for the supported lifetime of the device"[8]. The implicit goal is to convert Windows as a platform for service delivery. Under this model, access to product features associated with a particular Windows release, Windows XP, Windows Vista, or Windows 7 or 8.1, are no longer relevant as a marketing strategy. For this vendor, a clean break with the past is neither practical nor desirable because of the short-term revenue implications. Customers still need to pay for a license for each new device they deploy, and therefore Microsoft remains primarily under its current (GDL) revenue model. This action subtly acknowledges that the notion of intrinsic value is not holding up for the Windows OS, and therefore Microsoft reduced the book value of this portion against future revenues[9]. Given that this revenue could not be realized, perhaps due to signals from the slowing of the PC market, Microsoft, making virtue out of necessity, is taking advantage of the value brought up by regular updates to build a relationship with Windows customers. The execution of this strategy has not been without hiccups, with customers annoyed by nagware and heavy-handed tactics to compel them to upgrade older versions of Windows to Windows 10 and the occasional botched upgrade.

[7]P. Levine, "Why There Will Never Be Another Red Hat: The Economics of Open Source," *Tech Crunch*, https://techcrunch.com/2014/02/13/please-dont-tell-me-you-want-to-be-the-next-red-hat/, February 13, 2014.
[8]T. Myerson, "The Next Generation of Windows: Windows 10," https://blogs.windows.com/windowsexperience/2015/01/21/the-next-generation-of-windows-windows-10/#aDEISgA57FcjT7ED.97, January 21, 2015.
[9]G. Keizer, "Windows 10's Upgrade Model Temporarily Wipes $1.6B from Microsoft's Books," *ComputerWorld*, http://www.computerworld.com/article/3060177/microsoft-windows/windows-10s-upgrade-model-temporarily-wipes-16b-from-microsofts-books.html, April 22, 2016.

Another classic conundrum is the question "Does IT matter?" Carr raised it in his well-known *Harvard Business Review* article[10]. In that article, Carr indicated that IT deployments had the features of built-out infrastructural technology with commonly available commoditized components. In fact, the trend toward commoditization has gone well beyond Carr could have imagined in 2003: It is not just economically viable to outsource application development, but most in-house application development has become impractical. Likewise, for some organizations it has also become impractical to deploy applications when a commoditized instance is available in the cloud, such as most human resource applications, e-mail, storage services, and office productivity. Therefore, in the best of outcomes, the deployment of these technologies allowed an organization to reach parity with similar organizations, negating any competitive advantage. IT strategy devolves to a defensive approach that emphasizes cost reduction, late technology adoption, and risk minimization. GDL companies follow this approach, consistent with the prevailing culture. A clear indicator of this dynamic is companies where the CIO reports to the CFO, with these companies looking at IT as a cost to be contained.

In spite of these dire predictions, IT organizations still exist and thrive today. The most successful found that an SDL approach provided the way out of this conundrum, where IT becomes an engine for business transformation, and more explicitly, an engine for business service transformation. Under this new dynamic, the goal for IT is not to fulfill a checklist of capabilities that every business has just to reach parity. Instead of traditional capabilities "bleeding" to the cloud, these organizations use the cloud to amplify their capabilities and reach, and exhibit a nimbleness they could not achieve with in-house resources. Instead of burdening business units with rigid processes, these enlightened organizations focus on business value by helping the same business units create advanced processes aligned with the company's mission[11].

The macroarchitecture in Figure 8-1 is a useful tool to highlight relationships in the observable service universe and to connect cloud technology to the economic ecosystem it supports. This ecosystem spans multiple companies and organizations. The entities within are not monolithic at all; they are loosely coupled and act in a federated manner, bound more by business rules than APIs, especially at the topmost layers. Figure 8-1 and Figure 4-7 are related; the relationship becomes obvious after rotating Figure 4-7 as explained earlier. This puts original equipment manufacturers (OEMs) and original design manufacturers (ODMs) close to the bottom and cloud service end consumers at the top. A service network forms when a service provider at any level establishes relationships with other providers upstream, downstream, or between peers. A service provider usually delivers services to other providers upstream and uses services from providers downstream. A large company such as Microsoft can have a presence at multiple rungs in the macroarchitecture, as an OS provider, and as a PaaS provider with Windows Azure, or application provider with Office 365 and Outlook.com.

---

[10]N. G. Carr, "IT Doesn't Matter," *Harvard Business Review,* 5–32, May 2003.
[11]E. Castro-Leon, R. Harmon, and M. Yousif, "IT-Enabled Service Innovation: Why IT Is the Future of Competitive Advantage," *Cutter IT Journal, 26* (7), 15–21, July 2013.

Service Relationship Patterns

There are three types of relationships in the cloud service macroarchitecture, illustrated in Figure 8-2.

- *Upstream relationships*: A CSP engages in upstream relationships with its customers, whether they are end user organizations, corporations, or individual consumers, or to other CSPs higher up in the macroarchitecture stack or service network.

- *Downstream relationships*: A CSP could rely on services from other CSPs. The latter comprise its *downstream relationships*. Although not part of the service network, a CSP also has downstream relationships with product or asset supply chains; for instance, equipment suppliers.

- *Peer relationships*: This primarily applies to technology partners, be it CSPs or technology or business providers engaged in delivering a service or portfolio of services. The partners, when working jointly, attain a competitive technical or business competitive advantage that otherwise they would not have.

Peer relationships need not be formal or explicit. For instance, all Microsoft Cloud Platform System portfolio adopters for the Microsoft Azure cloud-in-a-box are peers although they might not know each other, and each has a downstream relationship with Microsoft Azure as a technology provider and Microsoft as a CSP. Likewise, all the customers of a CSP are peers and have a downstream relationship with that particular CSP. Partnerships in peer relationships are important. CSPs are not the primary creators of cloud services[12]; businesses and individuals are and constitute the actual source for cloud services. Services come from ISVs and application developers, content creators generating anything from ringtones to movies, blogs, and news reports to product reviews, to product specifications and technical papers and presentations, as well as technology providers that make possible the processing, storage, and conveyance of the applications and content. The combined contributions of these players have continued powering and transforming the industry relentlessly since cloud technology took off in 2007.

Participants in each of the layers form a global service network through upstream, downstream, and peer service relationships. These relationships are constantly evolving, reflecting the highly dynamic nature of the cloud. Here are a few examples of service relationship patterns without an attempt at being exhaustive.

- *Service hosting*: Any node in a service network that is not a terminal (leaf) node in the service network delegates supporting services to one or more CSPs downstream. A service hosting entity is also a service provider.

---

[12]J. McIntyre, *IBM SmartCloud: Becoming a Cloud Service Provider* (IBM Redguides for Business Leaders, REDP-4912-00, December 12, 2012).

- *Service consumer or service user*: A service consumer is simply a customer of a CSP. This service consumer in turn can be another CSP drawing services from CSPs downstream.

- A distinguished service user is a service end user, an individual or organization benefiting from the service, but it is not a CSP. An individual using a cloud-based e-mail service is an end user. A corporation providing a cloud-based e-mail service to its employees is also a cloud service end user. The ultimate goal of a service is to fulfill the economic needs of an individual or organization in an efficient value-for-value exchange. Service end users are top leaf nodes in a service economy with no one above them. On some occasions, a corporation that appears to be an end user organization might not be an end user; it can be that the user is the IT organization outsourcing certain internal or private cloud capabilities to an outside CSP.

- *Service aggregation*: A service aggregator bundles and resells services from providers downstream. An example is an IaaS provider using third-party HaaS services in certain locations to deliver IaaS services in certain locations; that is, with specific location metadata characteristics. This applies, for instance, with health care users, where identifiable patient data must stay within a country or region. Where deploying a datacenter in that region cannot be justified because of technical, regulatory, or time-to-market issues, it makes sense for a CSP to outsource the physical infrastructure to a third-party HaaS provider. Aggregation could be motivated for purely business reasons: A storage provider with name recognition might decide to bundle and rebrand generic storage services from storage providers downstream.

- *Service partners*: Technology providers collaborating with a CSP to extend or increase the CSP's service capabilities extend the service network. What is interesting in this dynamic is that the technology contributors might be very traditional product-oriented, goods-dominant logic (GDL) companies. The potential revenue from these collaborations can nudge these organizations toward a more service-dominant logic (SDL) approach to business, hopefully generating new business opportunities.

Note that the distinction between a service *provider* and a service *consumer* is purely conventional. In reality, both parties in a service transaction engage because they both benefit. In other words, the transaction takes place within a context of value *cocreation* where both parties benefit. The service provider usually gets monetary compensation for services rendered. From an SDL, this compensation is a credit for future services; for instance, a service aggregator paying for services downstream.

Cloud Power Management

Power management, as a technology capability, constitutes a good proof point to illustrate some of the concepts of the cloud macroarchitecture just covered, as well as to highlight approaches for ASCP platform customization, and some capabilities initially developed under a GDL framework eventually become part of the service universe.

Let us start by defining a few essential concepts for the purposes of the discussion, such as energy, power, and thermals. Defining *energy* from an abstract perspective is surprisingly difficult. For now, let us look at energy as a capability to make a change on a physical system; in other words, without energy, nothing happens. If the system is mechanical, energy is the capability to carry out work, such as making a hydraulic or a steam turbine spin. Energy can take many forms: thermal as the amount of energy it takes to heat a room, or electromagnetic, such as the solar energy it takes a set of solar panels to charge a battery. Energy can change from one form to another, such as converting electric energy to light, heat, or motion.

As hard as it is to define, we can measure energy very precisely. A conventional unit of energy is a *joule*. In mechanical terms, a joule is the energy it takes to overcome a force of one newton over a distance of one meter. Alternatively, in electrical terms, a joule is the energy dissipated in one second by a current of one ampere running through a resistor of one ohm.

The next concept is the notion of *power*. Power is a measure of energy intensity, in joules expended per second. One joule per second defines a *watt*. This unit is rather small, applicable to measurements within a baseboard or single server. Beyond that, a more practical unit is a *kilowatt* (KW) for the purposes of measuring power in racks and *megawatts* (MW) for measuring power at a datacenter level. A common dual-CPU server idling consumes about 100 watts. This server, if driven hard and with a large memory configuration, can draw 500 watts. It is highly unlikely that servers in a rack reach this level at the same time. A good rule of thumb for a power allowance in a rack will be about 16 KW for a rack provisioned with 40 × 1U servers and about 8 KW for a rack provisioned with 20 × 2U servers, with a 1.75-inch pitch per rack unit in a standard EIA rack. Higher server counts per rack are possible with blade form factors, where power draw can reach 24 KW or more.

Older datacenters that have not been thermally optimized can rarely support higher densities than 8 KW per rack. Thermal optimizations that deploy racks front to front and back to back alternatively, known as cold aisle/hot aisle layouts, can sustain up to 16 KW racks. Deploying rack densities beyond 16 KW usually requires complete airflow isolation where hot air exiting the back of a row of a rack flows into a special compartment, or extracted through chimneys on top of each rack, flowing into an exit plenum where it never mixes with the incoming cold air.

Deploying racks beyond the thermal capacity of a datacenter will result in hot spots. Servers caught in a hot spot might undergo a process of *thermal throttling*, where protection logic inside each CPU slows down processor frequency to reduce heat generation. Servers under thermal throttling go through a speed reduction of about two thirds of the normal operating frequency. Unfortunately, the reduction in application performance with processor frequency is not linear. This kind of slowdown increases the contention for resources in the running application, where performance yield goes down faster than frequency. Hot spots are difficult to stamp out because they move around, depending on the operating states of the servers involved. Short of a datacenter thermal redesign, the only recourse for datacenter operators is to pare down the number of servers per rack, resulting in scores of half-full racks. This is acceptable for recently deployed datacenters where power demand has not yet caught up with the datacenter capacity and there is room to spare. However, this solution becomes very expensive later in the datacenter life cycle where available power cannot be used because of thermal limitations in the layout. This means inefficient use of capital spending for power infrastructure, which runs at around US$12.5 million per delivered megawatt according to the Uptime Institute[13].

In many cases, the term *power management* is used as a generic term for a discourse that also encompasses *energy* management and *thermal* management. Being aware of this distinction helps clear up the resulting ambiguity.

Power Management Macroarchitecture

At this point, it will be useful to take a technology capability, namely power management, and map it to some of the elements of the cloud macroarchitecture just described. Let us examine some of the reasons motivating cloud operators to deploy a power management capability. As explained earlier, we use power management as a generic term to denote power, energy, and thermal management.

- *Power is a limited resource.* If there is not enough of it, this could trigger a service interruption where the operator cannot deliver on a service-level agreement (SLA) promise.

- A corollary is that the power management as a practice enhances *business continuity*, and its application will harden a system against outages under certain, predetermined scenarios.

- More generally, the operator wants to avoid *adverse scenarios* due to improper application of power. Adverse scenarios include inefficient use of resources and equipment damage.

The operator of a service stack achieves power management through a series of overlapping layers of technology. Each layer contains sensors and actuators managed by one or more controllers. The CPU is at the root of power management as one of the more energetic components in a technology stack. The CPU can account for one half to two thirds of the power consumed in a server, with memory power taking a good chunk of the remaining power budget.

Figure 8-3 depicts a macroarchitecture for power management in a service ecosystem, in the same spirit for the cloud macroarchitecture in Figure 8-1. Figure 8-3

---

[13]W. P. Turner and K. G. Brill, "Cost Model: Dollars per KW Plus Dollars per Square Foot of Computer Floor," *Uptime Institute,* http://www.five9sdigital.com.php5-7.dfw1-1.websitetestlink.com/wp-content/uploads/2009/09/Uptime-Institute-Cost-Model-Calculations.pdf, 2009.

comprises multiple logical levels, from the CPUs in the servers all the way up to the cloud, in a similar style to the levels in Figure 8-1. The relationship is not exactly one-to-one; there might be a need to include more levels, for instance, if a power analysis involves microarchitectural subsystems inside a CPU.

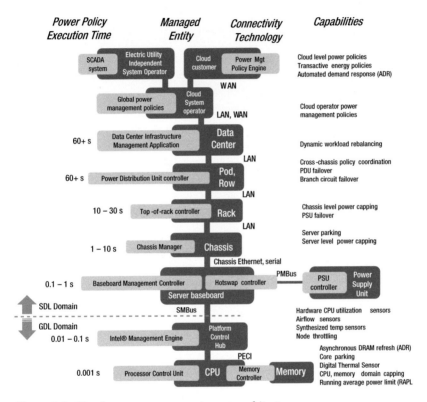

Figure 8-3. *Cloud power management macroarchitecture*

Listed on the right of Figure 8-3 are examples of capabilities that exist at specific logical levels in the macroarchitecture. Each capability uses downstream capabilities to implement functionality and carry its mission. The downstream capabilities are encapsulated in such a way that it is easy to understand the workings of a capability at one level in terms of capabilities of the level immediately below. On the left of Figure 8-3 is the boundary of the lowest level at which service-oriented offerings are available today. This boundary has historically been migrating downward since the inception of the cloud in 2007, and today it is located at the ASCP level for the largest CSPs. It is higher for smaller service providers that still purchase OEM products either directly or through distribution channels.

Here is a brief rundown of the capabilities highlighted in Figure 8-3. Note that this list is not exhaustive. New capabilities reach the market as the market goes through the learning curve.

- *CPU domain capping*: A more technical name for this capability is *running average power limit* (RAPL). The *power control unit* (PCU), a microcontroller embedded in the CPU, can regulate the power consumption in the CPU itself through power and thermal sensors and actuators instrumented in the CPU itself. Note that the PCU cannot see outside the CPU, and therefore is not equipped to regulate server power. An external entity, the ME, must tell the PCU in each of the CPUs to regulate power consumption up or down to adjust CPU power consumption so server power is within a preset goal. *Memory RAPL* is a related capability to regulate memory power consumption. The memory controller does that by regulating memory bandwidth, including powering down a subset of memory links.

- *Digital thermal sensor*: The digital thermal sensor (DTS) is a counter inside the CPU, negative during normal operation. DTS keeps track of the temperature below the thermal throttling that would induce the PCU to declare an emergency and put the CPU in low-frequency mode (LFM), the same mechanism triggered by PROCHOT#. PROCHOT# is actually a bidirectional signal. If the CPU gets too hot and enters thermal throttling, the PCU asserts PROCHOT# to alert other entities in the baseboard that a CPU has entered thermal throttling.

- *Core parking*: The PCU can shut down one or more cores to reduce power consumption.

- *Asynchronous DRAM refresh (ADR)*: When a power loss takes place, ADR triggers a nonmaskable interrupt (NMI) to flush CPU caches and put memory in self-refresh mode. This mechanism helps the implementation of routines to preserve memory data after a power failure.

- *Node throttling*: This is the action of placing a CPU in LFM. The goal of LFM is to reduce power draw from a CPU as much as possible without crashing applications. Node throttling reduces CPU operating frequency by as much as two thirds, with a commensurate reduction in power demand.

- *Synthesized temperature sensors*: The average exhaust temperature of air coming out of a server is difficult to measure. It is actually more accurate to synthesize this value. If we know the inlet temperature, the air mass flowing through the server, and the power consumption, it is possible to compute the temperature increase using a fluid dynamics model. This is the notion of a synthesized temperature value. These values are useful for computing the temperature profile of a datacenter using a computational fluid dynamics (CFD) model.

243

- *Airflow sensors*: It is possible to estimate the airflow rate through a server by correlating it with fan speed using an appropriate computational model. For Intel-based servers, the ME carries out these calculations. The telemetry is available through Intelligent Platform Management Interface (IPMI) messages to the ME.

- *Hardware CPU utilization sensors*: Most operating systems have an estimator for CPU utilization. Intel-based servers have very accurate hardware sensors that provide an estimate of CPU utilization by measuring the percentage of time the CPU spends idling (technically, in the ACPI package C6 state). The software sensors are slow, taking several seconds to execute. The hardware equivalent is out of band very fast through an IPMI call through the network. This would allow an application to estimate the utilization of not just one machine, but that for a whole cluster.

- *Server-level power capping*: This is a capability implemented by Node Manager for Intel technology CPUs. It allows allocating a power target for a specific server. This is done through an IPMI call to the target server, from the network.

- *Server parking*: Server parking is the action of shutting down a server for the purposes of reducing power demand. This is appropriate in virtualized environments or environments where servers in use provide computational resources, with data residing elsewhere.

- *Power supply unit (PSU) failover*: The action of having redundant PSUs take over and continue powering a set of machines even after one or more PSUs trip.

- *Chassis-level power capping*: Chassis-level power capping allows allocating a collective power target to all the nodes inside a chassis in a blade system. The chassis manager can orchestrate this action, assigning individual limits to each of the nodes and capping them using Node Manager.

- *Branch circuit failover*: For equipment fed by redundant branch circuits, continued operation after the outage of one of the feeder circuits.

- *Power distribution unit (PDU) failover*: For servers in a rack fed from redundant PDUs, continued operation after the failure of one of the PDUs.

- *Cross-chassis policy coordination*: Refers to chassis-wide power management policies, especially for equipment allocated to a customer in a HaaS setting.

- *Dynamic workload rebalancing*: Shifting workload from a group of servers to another in response to a thermal or power event. It does not need involve an advanced capability such as virtual machine migration. It can be as simple as shutting down a group of servers and restarting the workload somewhere else.

- *Cloud operator power management*: Refers to global power policies that a cloud operator implements in a datacenter.

- *ADR*. ADR stands for Automated Demand Response and allows a power utility to activate a prenegotiated power curtailment agreement with a datacenter. This is useful for region-wide power optimization during periods of high electricity when the utility is running out of generation resources or has limited capability to wheel in power from outside the region, due to insufficient transmission capacity.

- *Transactive energy policies*: Transactive energy is essentially a power management cloud that operates at the service economy level (Figure 8-1). Transactive energy is a framework that enables carrying out energy policies at a regional level, across boundaries spanning different companies, government, and eventually international boundaries, enabling market participation of distributed energy resources and using pricing signals.

- *Cloud-level policies*: This refers to regional country-wide coordination of energy policies, for instance policies toward reduction of carbon footprint or across multiple energy resources, spanning CSPs, the cloud ecosystem, and government agencies. An example is Advancing Cutting-Edge Technologies and Strategies to Reduce Energy Use and Costs in the Industrial, Agriculture and Water Sectors, an initiative issued by the State of California[14].

Server Power Control

To illustrate how a capability at one level relies on lower level layers, let us look at *server power control*. Server power control is a common feature in standard high-volume servers (SHVs). It is an out-of-band mechanism using the IPMI protocol where a management entity can command a server to define an upper bound for power consumption at a certain level, say 270 watts. Power consumption in a server is proportional to workload demand. If a server is running capped at 270 watts, the capping mechanism will not allow the server to draw more than 270 watts. If the server is currently running over 270

---

[14]California Energy Commission, http://www.energy.ca.gov/contracts/index.html.

watts, the capping mechanism will bring power consumption down to 270 watts. Capping imposes operational limits:

- If the power consumption is over 270 watts when the cap becomes active, it reduces performance yield because the control mechanism reduces the operating frequency in processor cores.

- If the server is currently operating below 270 watts, a cap at 270 watts reduces performance headroom and makes the server less responsive in case there is an uptick in workload demand as it imposes frequency restrictions.

How does power capping work? Conceptually, capping functions through a simple control feedback loop, as shown in Figure 8-4. A microcontroller embedded in the *processor control hub* of the chipset, the Intel Management Engine or ME, shown in Figure 8-3, runs an application implemented in the ME firmware, Intel Node Manager. The server is fitted with an instrumented PSU under the PMBus standard[15]. An I2C[16] bus connection runs between the power supply and the ME, allowing the ME to sample server power consumption in real time. If there is a cap in effect, the ME firmware commands the CPU to adjust its power draw up or down until the sensors in the PSU indicate that the server power draw is within target.

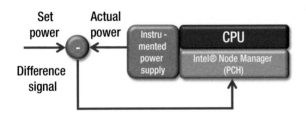

Figure 8-4. Server power capping control feedback loop

Node Manager is essentially an embedded agent, present in every server and implemented in firmware that obviates the need to run software agents in the server. This is actually an important consideration regarding the responsiveness of the control loop. A software agent cannot take power readings faster than one sample every few seconds. According to the sampling theorem, it will take several samples for the control loop to converge after a power cap changes. This is under ideal conditions. In practice, shifts in CPU power can take less than a second, so a software entity might not be able to sample power fast enough for the control loop to converge. The ME can sample power once every 10 to 100 milliseconds, ensuring precise power readings. The power-capping feature is accessible through an industry-standard Intelligent Platform Management Interface, or IPMI. The managing entity issues the command to the Ethernet management port in the target server. The baseboard management controller (BMC), another microcontroller

---

[15]See http://pmbus.org/Specifications/CurrentSpecifications.
[16]I2C is a serial bus invented by Philips Semiconductor. The physical layer consists of a pair of wire traces that runs through a baseboard connecting the managed entities.

that regulates baseboard management functions, catches this command and relays it to the ME for execution. A second advantage of a firmware agent is that it is out of band. It is operational independent of the OS, meaning that it works even when the OS is hung, or not active. Operational costs are also lower, as there are no third-party fees for the agents, nor there is associated maintenance labor for keeping possibly hundreds of thousands of servers updated.

How does the ME regulate CPU power consumption in turn? There is a communication channel between the ME and the CPU called Platform Environmental Control Interface (PECI). Through PECI, the ME invokes a capability in the CPU, RAPL. RAPL allows the ME to set a target power draw for the CPUs in the server, just enough to comply with the server target power.

We were able to describe a server power capping capability with just three logical levels in the power management macroarchitecture. The CPU appears as a black box for the purposes of ME CPU power management, where the ME commands the CPU to a certain power level, and the CPU responds, for practical purposes, instantly. In this way, it is possible to understand a specific power capability without having to dive into multiple levels of the power management macroarchitecture ad infinitum. In actuality, the implementation of RAPL involves another control loop. The PCU, a microcontroller embedded in each of the CPUs in a server, regulates power consumption for that CPU. The PCU implements a complex algorithm involving sensors and actuators monitoring power consumption for each of the cores in the CPU as well as voltage regulators, frequency control and temperature sensors. However, because all of these entities reside inside the CPU chip, signal propagation is fast, and the control loop for PCU commands actually converges in less than one millisecond, at least one order of magnitude faster than the control loop implemented in the ME. This solves two problems:

- The ME does not need to worry about transients in the RAPL loop. As mentioned earlier, RAPL responds instantly for practical purposes.

- Second, similar to sampling issues with a software agent mentioned earlier, the ME would not be able to sample entities inside the CPU fast enough to achieve effective control. The PCU, acting as a surrogate of the ME, takes care of changes inside the CPU that occur too fast for the ME to handle.

There is a third benefit from an architectural perspective: clean abstractions. The PCU deals with entities inside the CPU, which would not be that meaningful at the ME level. This approach reduces design complexity, cuts engineering costs, and minimizes the occurrence of bugs. In fact, it allows engineering teams to work in parallel and more or less independently.

Power Management ASCP Solution Approach

As discussed in the previous section, a power management capability targets specific scenarios and can comprise one or more of the levels in the macroarchitecture. We covered the example of server power capping in the previous section. As in any complex problem, a divide-and-conquer approach makes solution design more tractable. This divide-and-conquer approach allows breaking up any complex scenario into solution subsystems that involve just a few logical levels in the macroarchitecture, ideally no more than two or three.

We also applied simplifying assumptions to analyze the different subsystems individually without worrying too much about interference across subsystems. We took advantage of the fact that the different levels operate at their own time scales. Figure 8-3 captures the approximate time scales associated at each level. We call these response times, and they roughly correspond to the rise time in response to a step function stimulus, namely the time for the output response to rise to the half-power level, roughly 0.707 of the target value.

In this section, we discuss architectural design considerations for a power management capability embedded in the Open Cloud Server (OCS) platform for the Open Compute Project (OCP) as an instance of ASCP server customization. As with previous ASCP designs, this solution addresses a specific problem in a cloud platform. The OCS platform architecture is extremely efficient and parsimonious in the use of hardware. It is a blade in chassis design with 24 or 48 blades for chassis deployed for compute functions. Traditional rack designs assume two PSUs per node with 1 + 1 redundancy. This design dictates a PSU large enough to allow a maximally configured server to continue running in case the other PSU fails, plus some margin. Under this design, PSUs operate at a fraction of their rated power, where they are the least efficient. Applying the same pooling approach seen in cloud computing, the OCS design uses a pool of six PSUs to power all the nodes in a chassis. This will allow 5 + 1 redundancy for most configurations except the heaviest, meaning that if one PSU fails, the chassis can continue operating with the remaining five PSUs. A heavy configuration means all blades populated, with a large portion of memory slots also populated.

There are additional efficiencies possible even with this design: Were PSUs dimensioned for peak power draw from the servers, we would see the same underutilization scenario as with the 1 + 1 case. On the other hand, having all servers simultaneously draw peak power is a very unlikely event.

For ASCPs with pooled PSUs, one way of reducing hardware cost is to provision the PSUs not for peak power, but for maximum efficiency during normal operations, and then handle power peaks for what they are, namely exceptional and infrequent events. Under these conditions, for example, if power demand from the chassis exceeds PSU capacity a few minutes per day, a recourse would be to use active control, namely power capping, to reign in power draw for those minutes without much impact on performance yield, instead of the conventional approach that relies on the margin from PSU overprovisioning. Unfortunately, this approach involves extra cost, both in acquisition and operational cost: It requires heavier and more expensive electronic components, and higher energy costs due to lower efficiency. Active control means that the recovery mechanisms are out of sight, and do not represent a burden during normal operations, but spring into action as soon as an emergency occurs.

Recovering from a PSU fault involves reducing power demand immediately to keep the nodes in a chassis operating within the operating envelope of the remaining power supplies. When one PSU trips, there is a sudden increase in power demand in the remaining PSUs. Initially this power comes from the energy stored in the PSU's capacitors. This is not sustainable. If the remaining PSUs can't sustain the power demand from the blades, a power demand reduction needs to execute within one tenth of a second or the voltage in the direct current (DC) bus will fall below the operating threshold, causing the remaining PSUs to trip. The chassis manager orchestrates this action. Unfortunately, from the macroarchitecture, we know that it will take the chassis manager on the order of 1 to 10 seconds to execute a chassis-level power capping action, and by the time the action is complete, the whole chassis would have crashed. The solution approach is transitioning the system through a series of safe modes within the time constraints imposed by the PSUs while minimizing their side effects. There are three stages:

1. *Throttling*: This is the server equivalent of an aircraft performing an emergency dive to avoid hitting an obstacle. PMBus-compliant PSUs have a logical signal named SMBAlert#. The hash mark (#) indicates logical complement. This means that SMBAlert is normally 1, and is active low when it transitions from 1 to 0. The failing PSU issues a distress signal by asserting its SMBAlert#. This action initiates the recovery sequence for the whole chassis. All the nodes in a chassis as well as the chassis manager monitor this signal. In the nodes, SMBAlert# is routed to the PROCHOT# signal. PROCHOT# is the same signal that the CPU uses when it overheats and needs to trigger thermal throttling. The difference is that in this case the trigger is a PSU failure. The assertion of PROCHOT# commands the PCU to place all the cores in the CPU in LFM, reducing the normal operating frequency by two thirds down to about 800 MHz. This mode of operation is called LFM. The action also reduces power demand by about two thirds in less than 4 milliseconds. It can act this fast because it is implemented in hardware. The goal here is to reduce power demand immediately to a level below that needed to keep the chassis running and to recover from all but the most severe contingencies. For an OCS chassis, the range of contingencies includes the loss of one to four PSUs.

2. *Emergency default power cap (EDPC)*: Most applications will continue to run with the CPUs in LFM, but so slowly that little work can be done. The second phase is a local action within each node where the BMC establishes a predetermined power cap. This power cap is severe enough to allow the chassis to ride out most of the PSU fault scenarios. There is no time to coordinate actions across nodes and therefore each node executes this action autonomously. Coordination will take place in the next phase. However, the default power cap will restore enough performance to allow applications to continue running. Because the BMC initiates this action and the action stays local within the board, the BMC can establish the EDPC in less than a second. EDPC power levels require configuration ahead of time. It is possible to assign unique default power cap values to each node, depending on the workloads they carry. Still, the EDPC needs to be set so the total chassis demand will be below the most severe fault scenario considered.

3. *Chassis-optimized power cap*: Establishing a chassis-optimized power cap requires the intervention of the chassis manager. The chassis manager can tally up the number of working PSUs, the available remaining power, and the workload priorities for each node, and then establish a postfault operating envelope. It might take several seconds for the chassis manager to establish a postfault operating envelope. In the most severe cases, if a capping action is insufficient to restore acceptable performance in higher priority applications, the chassis can shut down nodes running less critical applications.

With this introduction, let us now look at some solution considerations to enhance operational continuity in a cloud datacenter as an example for a cloud macroarchitecture application.

Power Management for Business Continuity

In a cloud environment, the cost of energy to power a server as fraction of total cost of ownership (TCO) is significant. A server drawing 350 watts at 100 percent duty cycle, assuming an electricity cost of $0.11 per KWh, will cost 350 watts × 24 hours per day × 365 days per year × $0.11 per KWh, or about US$337 per year, or a lifetime cost of US$1,000 assuming a three-year refresh cycle. If the server purchase price is US$4,000, the cost of powering it will be about 20 percent of the hardware TCO, not including other ancillary costs such as cooling and labor.

From a business perspective, perhaps a more relevant cost consideration than energy is opportunity cost. This is the cost of lost business in terms of revenue and damage to reputation should a server become unavailable after a power incident, taking its workload down with it. A blade system with 24 nodes can easily run 100 to 400 virtual machines. That is up to 10,000 virtual machines for the chassis, representing service delivered to perhaps hundreds of accounts. The damage to the business from a chassis crash can be much larger than the value of energy saved from efficiency gains.

Power and thermal incidents rank high in terms of root causes for server outages and therefore power and thermal management rank high when it comes to business continuity planning. For practical purposes, the price of energy is inelastic during an emergency. Offering to pay more for energy during a crisis will not increase the number of kilowatt-hours available. The opposite might actually be true, with less supply available due to equipment malfunction during an emergency. Under these circumstances, if there is a shortfall, and if mitigating measures are not in place, there will be no options left to avoid adverse business outcomes.

The default practice to manage these deficits during a crisis is through resource overprovisioning: configuring systems with extra power supplies or provisioning PDUs from independent circuit feeds. This way, servers can sustain an unplanned reduction in supply and continue running.

The main drawback of overprovisioning is cost: Having a PSU as a spare just in case, a part costing tens or even hundreds of dollars, is inconsistent with current business practices, when procurement is monitoring materials costs down to the level of cents.

Furthermore, a solution at one level can become a problem at a different level. As noted earlier, datacenter power is a finite resource, to the point of limiting the amount of deployable equipment, and not by rack capacity, especially with older datacenters. Overallocated power becomes stranded power, reserved just in case of need for some indeterminate future. A midlife, low- to midpower density but otherwise perfectly operational datacenter ends up populated with power-limited half-empty racks with poor power and space utilization and poor return on investment.

Business Continuity Usages

Business continuity in the context of datacenter design and operations refers to the set of measures and processes to enable continued operations in through emergencies. Disaster planning involves defining and profiling a range of incidents and defining measures to improve resiliency against such occurrences. Business continuity analysis cannot be an unbounded exercise: Ensuring 100 percent uptime over an indefinite time would require infinite resources. A design process for business continuity usually involves a process of triage, identifying risk factors along with the associated measures to mitigate their effect. The analysis becomes the basis for an eventual business continuity plan.

Preserving business continuity in the presence of power and thermal contingencies boils down to managing the potential imbalance between power supply and demand. Given that supply is inelastic, this leaves demand management as the next option. Sensors and controls in server platforms are useful to shape workload demand in a timely manner to fit a workload profile. Demand shaping is not without side effects. It affects application performance or quality of service to various degrees. Imposing power limiting will slow down workloads or even cause software timeouts or crashes.

The range of power-management-related contingencies considered for an installation depends on business goals and an assessment of risk factors for the installation. Table 8-1 captures a few examples. Each contingency is associated with a set of usages and actions to mitigate its effects. Another important parameter is the time scale within which the actions need to take place before system crashes and loss of workloads.

Table 8-1. *Power Management Contingencies*

Contingency	Usage	Actions	Time Scale
Total loss of utility power	Maximize refueling window	Power capping subject to workload priority	1 day to 1 week
Local hot spots	Reduce heat generation	Power capping subject to workload priority with temperature monitoring, reconfigure venting	1 hour to 1 day
Loss of PDU in dual-feed system	Coordinate breaker policies	Regulated chassis throttling	1–10 seconds
Loss of PSU	Reduce PSU overprovisioning	Fast regulated chassis throttling	10–100 milliseconds

If utility power is lost, the system switches over to battery backup power for a few minutes, just long enough for the cogeneration system to kick in. Battery banks need to last long enough for the diesel engines or gas turbines to get started and reach full strength. With cogeneration in place, the next critical juncture is to make fuel last until the next resupply. Do not assume the normal resupply time for the purposes of disaster planning. A number of datacenters that lost power but otherwise survived the earthquake had to shut down after running out of fuel. Planners did not anticipate the disruption of highways that prevented deliveries by tanker trucks. Beyond that, there was damage to refineries and pipelines[17].

Table 8-1 lists a few example power-related contingencies considered in a business continuity exercise. An essential characteristic for each contingency is the reaction time to manage an event. A datacenter running on cogeneration might last up to a week, whereas if the event involves a server losing a power supply, the fault requires handling in less than 100 milliseconds.

Local hot spots could develop due to workload intensity or specific local circulation patterns. Rebalancing workloads such as moving workloads in the hot spots to cooler areas in the center can take care of some hot spots. Persistent hot spots might indicate flaws in the datacenter thermal design and hence could require refining the thermal design, perhaps through a power, thermal, and possibly CFD analysis. The relentless drive to optimize operational efficiency has also led to the trimming of operating margins. One particular usage is high ambient temperature (HTA) operation of datacenters to save on cooling costs. Under a traditional practice operating with a thermostat set at 21°C, a 10°C spike is inconsequential. In actual practice it is impossible to maintain an even temperature throughout a facility. Hot spots always develop. If the set temperature is now 27°C, variations of 5°C are possible. Unfortunately, if the spike occurs in a hot area already at 32°C, a spike to 42°C could lead to equipment failure.

The narrowing of operating margins is not the same as cutting corners unless done in a haphazard way. Instead, these considerations represent a careful weighing of cost versus benefit. Where there is little control over contingencies, the traditional approach is to design in ample operating margins. This leads to systems designed for the worst possible event through resources held in reserve. Specific trade-offs change over time. Improved technology enables data-driven approaches that allow users to quantify, manage, and rebalance risks. A user can decide to hold the level of risk constant and cash in on the improved contingency management capabilities, or use the new capability to reduce risk. Large CSPs deploying tens or even hundreds of thousands of nodes are usually in the first camp with concerns about holding down platform bill of materials (BOM) cost, whereas enterprise customers running mission-critical applications are more inclined to go for the higher reliability route.

[17]M. Zaré and S. Ghaychi Afrouz, "Crisis Management of Tohoku; Japan Earthquake and Tsunami, 11 March 2011," *Iran Journal of Public Health, 41* (6), 12-20, 2012.

Power Limiting vs. Capping vs. Throttling

We use the terms power *limiting, capping,* and *throttling* with very precise meanings for the purposes of contingency analysis. Let's take a short side trip to define them before continuing the discussion (see Table 8-2). These terms refer to power management control actions needed to handle the emergency. The outcome sought under the emergency is continuing operations by reconfiguring and optimizing the system to best work under the impaired conditions imposed by the event. Users might experience some loss of performance, but at least the workloads continue to run without interrupting or losing transactions.

Table 8-2. *Power Management Terminology*

Term	Server Context	Automotive Analogy	Remarks	Drawbacks
Power limiting	Keep power draw within predefined bound	Stay within the 55 MPH speed limit Engine governor	Goal is not to exceed limit in first place	Limit is usually static, e.g., set at boot time Imposes preset performance limit
Power capping	Bring chassis power draw to a lower target bound	Moved to a 35 MPH zone Let go of gas pedal or brake gently	Some leeway on how fast to reach the cap targets Minimize impact on application performance	Performance impact when actively capping Relatively slow acting
Power throttling	Roll back chassis power draw as quickly as possible	Deer in headlight situation: Stomp on the brakes and slow down as quickly as possible without damage to vehicle or deer	Emergency: Reaction time is prime consideration; performance impact takes backseat	Severe impact on performance Power regulation not possible

Power Limiting

The goal of power limiting is to prevent the power demand from a server from exceeding a predefined power consumption boundary. The concept is similar to the notion of a speed limit when driving a vehicle.

One example of speed limiting is a driver observing a posted speed: A driver in a 55 MPH zone watches the speedometer against the speed limit and makes sure the vehicle does not exceed it. A second example is the speed governor built into most present-day cars. When a vehicle is driven at full throttle on a roadway with no speed limits and the vehicle reaches its maximum design speed, say 155 MPH, a computer-controlled engine governor will kick in and cut off fuel to keep the vehicle from exceeding that maximum design speed.

Likewise, in a power-managed data center, a management application can impose a power allocation on a chassis smaller than what the chassis would draw under a full application workload. Power-limiting mechanisms are the least intrusive; they do not exert control unless the system is about to hit the power limit.

Beyond that, to reduce BOM costs, the group PSUs feeding the chassis might be overcommitted: The nodes in the chassis can potentially draw more power than what power supplies can muster. A power-limiting policy ensures the power demand from the nodes stays within policy-imposed boundaries.

Figure 8-5 illustrates power limiting at work: Power demand follows a daily curve. The critical moments are the periods under peak demand where the servers, if left by themselves, would have exceeded the prespecified power draw limit.

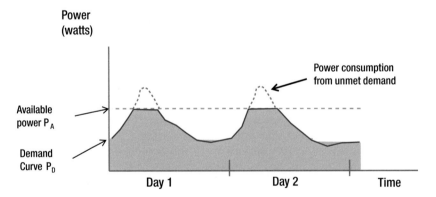

Figure 8-5. *Power limiting scenario*

The power limit can be dynamic or static. A static limit can be set at boot time, usually through a BIOS sheet parameter. In this case changing the limit requires a reboot. Some platforms use a proxy metric, such as a P-state limiter, in lieu of power and a poor predictor for power consumption. Platforms provisioned with Intel Node Manager are capable of dynamic power limiting, using server power directly as the control variable. The power control mechanism is out of band; that is, it works with or without the OS. This allows setting power limits right at power-up, making it easier to enforce datacenter-wide power limits.

Power Capping

Dynamically changing a power limit leads to the power capping or power regulation scenario shown in Figure 8-6. The red line represents the power budget imposed on a chassis or rack. *Power margin* is the difference between the power budget and the actual power demand. The scenario in Figure 8-6 is for a dual-PSU server where one of the PSUs trips, taking with it half of the available power. Furthermore, this is a server with no overprovisioning, requiring both PSUs present when operating under high load. Cloud platforms can operate in this manner for highly provisioned systems. As noted, when the PSU trips, available power drops by half and the power margin becomes negative. If power demand does not drop fast enough, it will hit the shaded area. This could overload the remaining PSU, causing it to trip, too. The server crashes at this point.

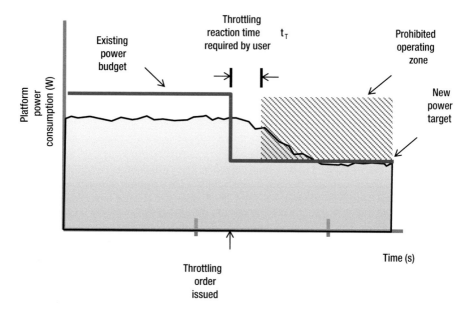

Figure 8-6. *Power capping scenario*

For Intel-based servers, the technology of choice for achieving power regulation is through Node Manager capping. A Grantley server can reach its target power in between a 0.1 second and 1 second. For the prior generation, Romley, this time is about 3 or 4 seconds. The automotive analogy for this situation is a vehicle moving from a 55 MPH freeway to a 35 MPH commercial or residential zone. It is sufficient to lightly apply brakes or even let the vehicle coast to the new speed, even if the vehicle exceeds the new 35 MPH limit for a few seconds. Law enforcement will usually tolerate this small transgression. However, driving at 55 MPH in a 35 MPH zone is not sustainable and a law enforcement action will eventually ensue.

Figure 8-6 shows power descending after the contingency from a power capping action following the contingency. For this particular application, power capping alone does not address the platform requirements. It takes too long to reach the new power target. Note that the throttling time is a nominal quantity. It does not mean the machine will crash every time the contingency takes place. What this means is that the behavior is out of spec and the machine is at risk. The operator will want to remove this risk as much as possible.

Power Throttling

The OCS platform requires a descent within 100 milliseconds. Node Manager power capping is too slow for this application, as shown in Figure 8-6. The SMBAlert# throttling mechanism described earlier provides the desired fast descent to avoid the prohibited zone. This mechanism is fast acting but does not allow adjustment. It is an all-or-nothing mechanism, and behaves like the reflex reaction from touching a hot iron.

The automotive analogy for throttling is a driver hitting the brakes for maximum deceleration to avoid a collision with another vehicle, animal, or pedestrian. The goal is now to reduce speed in the shortest possible time. The main figure of merit is throttling time, a time window to reach the target power level.

Distributed Throttling

Figure 8-7 illustrates the effect of throttling one node. The OCS platform requires that all the nodes in the chassis and operating under the pool of six power supplies, must be throttled at once. The SMBAlert# signals from all PSUs are wired OR, a fancy way of saying they are bundled together, and routed through the chassis backplane to the nodes and the chassis manager. This solution, although simple, suffers from some drawbacks. For instance, the chassis manager gets an alert about a PSU tripping, but has no means of discovering which PSUs failed or how many. In addition, the communication between the chassis manager and the managed nodes is through serial lines, which is slow and makes broadcast communication to the nodes difficult. We proposed an improved design in Chapter 5, illustrated in Figure 5-5.

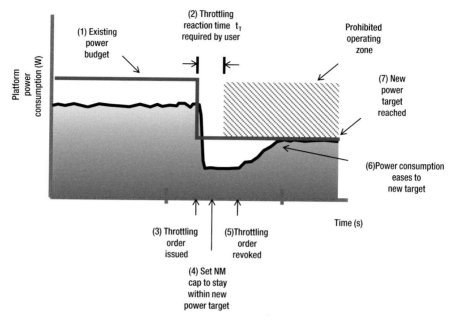

Figure 8-7. *Power throttling scenario*

The Regulated Chassis Throttling Problem

Regulated chassis throttling ensures recovery at the chassis level from the loss of one or more PSUs in a pooled PSU system such as the one deployed with OCS. Let us put together the conceptual three-stage approach discussed earlier, namely throttling, the EDPC and chassis-optimized power cap (CPC) with the technology features just discussed. Table 8-3 summarizes the approach. The approach is federated and hierarchical where a local controller uses local sensors and makes local decisions, and exports these capabilities as policies to the next level up. This is a key architectural consideration. For instance, the chassis manager would be an inappropriate entity to carry out throttling: Throttling needs to be done fast to keep the whole chassis from crashing. If the chassis manager were in charge of this action, it would need to do a broadcast to the managed nodes that would take the better part of a minute. This is unnecessary because the mechanism is already implemented in hardware through the propagation of the SMBAlert# signal.

Table 8-3 introduces one new element: closed loop system throttling (CLST). This is a routine encapsulating the PROCHOT# capability. Although it is possible to drive PROCHOT# directly from SMBAlert#, it is simpler to delegate this function to the ME. Operating PROCHOT# involves subtleties unrelated to the throttling that would be unnecessarily complex if handled by the triggering PSU. For instance, PROCHOT# is overloaded. If asserted too quickly after the start of the CPU power-up sequence, it will actually trigger a fault-resilient boot sequence (FRB) where the server boots with one CPU or even one core within a CPU. The ME takes care of unrelated housekeeping functions. It also adds related capabilities that increase the effectiveness of throttling, by temporarily removing power from the server fans on assertion of CLST. By design, the baseboard has built-in flexibility to route SMBAlert# in a number of ways when it arrives at the baseboard: to the BMC, the ME in the PCH, and connected to PROCHOT#. A *complex programmable logic device* (CPLD) takes care of the routing. Engineers test a number of combinations during validation before deciding which one will work best in the production boards.

Table 8-3. *Three-Stage Distributed Power Cap*

Stage	Time Scale/ Implementation	Description	Sought Effects	Side Effects
1. Throttling	10–100 ms hardware, ME firmware	PSU controller triggers global CLST	Fast power rollback prevents DC bus voltage collapse	No power regulation; severe performance impact; LFM is it
2. Local node Policy: Default Power Cap (EDPC)	0.1–1 s BMC firmware	BMC releases CLST hold, sets prestored local power cap	Safe mode operation, quick exit from LFM	Policy is not globally optimized
3. Global node Policy: Chassis Optimized power Cap (CPC)	1 s–1 min S/W in chassis manager	Chassis manager releases local policy, sets globally optimized postevent policies	Globally optimized per-node postfault policies	Takes time to compute and propagate; system might have crashed without 1 and 2

Adding a prestored local policy now defines a three-stage algorithm.

1. Figure 8-8 depicts the first two stages through EDPC. The ME, BMC, and the chassis manager all get the SMBALERT# signal at the same time from a PSU in distress (Step 2 in Figure 8-8) but react at different speeds. The ME in each node reacts the fastest. As soon as it sees SMBAlert# activated, the ME invokes its CLST routine (Step 3), placing a "crowbar" in the system to hold it and to prevent it from crashing. The ME completes CLST in about 4 milliseconds to take care of any power deficit immediately and well ahead of the distress threshold of 100 milliseconds.

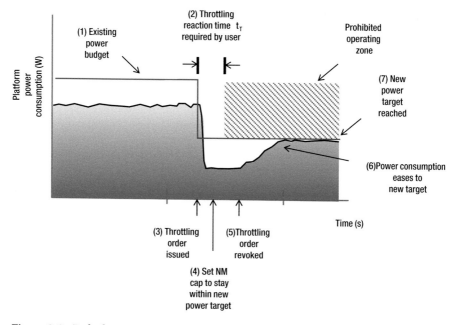

Figure 8-8. *Default power cap algorithm*

2. The BMC also receives SMBAlert#. When SMBAlert# arrives to the BMC, it triggers an interrupt. The interrupt handler wakes up, issues a local node policy, and releases the CLST hold (Steps 4 and 5 in Figure 8-8). Releasing the CLST hold allows power consumption to rise gently, up to the limit set by the EDPC (Steps 6 and 7 in Figure 8-8). This sequence takes about 1 second. The system is now in a safe, albeit suboptimal configuration. The EDPC power level is preset, perhaps based on workload profile. There is no opportunity to change it during a node recovery sequence

3. Finally, the chassis manager, also wired with SMBAlert#, fires up another interrupt. When the interrupt handler wakes up, it performs a state estimation across all PSUs and nodes and computes a globally optimized configuration. Because of the complex orchestration, the event handler might take between 30 seconds and 1 minute to execute the global optimization. The handler has plenty of time to complete its job because the two prior stages have taken care of the immediate emergency. In the current OCS version, there is no logic for the chassis handler to determine which power supplies failed. The chassis manager cannot even determine the number of failed PSUs. The recovery scenarios are somewhat limited. If the BMC assumes one failed PSU, but the actual scenario is two down, very likely additional PSUs will trip after the recovery sequence, bringing down additional PSUs and making the system inoperable. Figure 5-5 depicts an improved design.

The benefit of the initial CLST throttling application is gaining thinking time for the chassis manager to devise, put in place, and enforce a postfault policy coordinated across nodes. Unfortunately, this can take several seconds. The chassis manager needs to interrogate the PSUs through PMBus to ascertain the nature of the fault, look at the workload profile, and assign power quotas for each node.

As mentioned before, CLST reduces the DC power demand by a half to two thirds by placing all CPUs in LFM. This action erases the power deficit, allowing the system to continue operating indefinitely even after the loss of a power supply.

A perfect power response would trace the red line in Figure 8-8 exactly. The response of the composite algorithm avoids the prohibited zone, but is less than perfect as imposed by the current state of the art.

The postfault regulation profile does not require capping all nodes at the same level. The specific approach is application dependent. For instance, it is possible to prioritize the nodes in a chassis by the workloads they run into high and low priority. If continued operation under limited power requires rationing, the chassis manager grants a larger allowance to the high-priority workload.

The chassis manager manages power allocation to the nodes in a chassis. A higher level controller, for instance, a top-of-rack controller, can be tasked to carry out power policies across chassis. If a chassis runs impaired after recovering from a PSU failure, the top of rack manager can migrate some of the workloads and command the chassis manager to shut down the vacated nodes.

Managing Hot Spots

The time scale for the development of hot spots in a datacenter is much slower than the time scales associated with the breaker coordination problem. The buildup could take several hours and hot spots might appear during peak demand. However, the problem is much more complex, three-dimensional, and time varying. CFD simulations indicate that although some hot spots are persistent, some shift over time. The persistent hot spots are probably due to deficiencies in the thermal design of the datacenter, and are better addressed through a power and thermal assessment analysis and planning exercise.

Unfortunately, research on managing hot spots is relatively sparse. Again, CFD simulations suggest that they are difficult to stamp out. Attempts to manage them by regulating underfloor vents do not work too well. The actions change airflow patterns, but the hot spots do not go away; they just immediately move a few feet away, in any direction, in a 3D version of Whac-a-Mole.

Controlling heat emissions through power capping works better. However, hot spot shifting still occurs to a certain extent. Given that the problem has not been solved in general, the recommendation is to build a real-time temperature map using information from server inlet sensors and synthesized exhaust temperatures available through IPMI calls to each node, and a cautious application of Node Manager capping only when servers are about to reach the upper limit of the target temperature.

Automated Demand Response

We have illustrated the implementation of power management as customizable capability for an ASCP capability. If we go up in the hierarchy of Figure 8-3 near the top, to the concept of ADR, we can see an illustration of a service network relationship. Please note that although organizations such as Lawrence Berkeley National Laboratory (LBNL) have been carrying out intense research since the early 2000s[18], these capabilities are still nascent, especially ADR for datacenters. The Electric Power Research Institute (EPRI) completed one of the first proofs of concept in 2016[19].

An electrical grid has little stored energy of practical use. There is some energy in the rotating mass of power generators, in the electromagnetic fields in electrical machinery and transmission lines, and perhaps a few pumped storage stations, but the amount of stored energy is minuscule compared to the daily demand. Datacenters deploy energy storage devices, such as batteries, flywheels, and ultracapacitors, for very specific applications. For instance, standby battery banks take over after a power outage. Their mission is to keep the datacenter running through power blips, where energy is lost for a few AC cycles, or for no more than a few minutes after an outage to allow diesel or gas generators to fire up and come online. As in a hybrid vehicle, the battery does not have stored energy to function as the main propulsion method, but to help the main source bridge operational gaps. In a vehicle, for instance, it allows turning off the internal combustion engine during vehicle stops. The bottom line is that for any electrical grid, generation and consumption must always be in balance.

---

[18]Berkeley Lab Demand Response Research Center, https://drrc.lbl.gov/openadr; G. Wikler, P. Martin, B. Shen, G. Ghatikar, C. C. Ni, and J. H. Dudley, *Addressing Energy Demand Through Demand Response: International Experience and Practice* (Lawrence Berkeley National Laboratory, Report LBNL-5580E, 2012).
[19]M. Sweeney et al., "Server Demand Response via Automated Hardware Management," In *Proceedings of 2016 ACEEE Summer Study on Energy Efficiency in Buildings*, 3-1–3-12, http://aceee.org/files/proceedings/2016/data/papers/3_877.pdf, 2016.

Resolving power imbalances requires the application of mechanisms with undesirable side effects. One mechanism is lowering the supply voltage. This condition is effectively a brownout. Given that power is a product of voltage and current, lowering the voltage generally reduces the power demand. Another mechanism, albeit more drastic, is load shedding, essentially disconnecting certain workloads. As in the preceding example, contingency plans for load shedding are not always in place or enforced. Shedding is also highly disruptive to the affected customers, an emergency procedure, more akin to a controlled crash rather than a power management method.

Demand response is gentler method for addressing power imbalances. It refers to a process where a power utility sends a power curtailment request to a customer. The transaction takes place under the terms of a previously arranged contract where the customer gets some form of compensation or reward for the sacrifice. These transactions also define a service relationship in a power management service network. For this discussion, we focus on the relationship between an electric utility and datacenters. Although this is not current practice today, there will be strong financial and environmental incentives for ADR relationships between utilities and datacenters, as it becomes practical from a technology maturity perspective. Because of complex economic, political, and governance issues, it might not be practical for utilities to work directly with datacenters; therefore a new intermediary might arise in the form of a cloud system operator. This system operator carries out the recruitment, workload classification, negotiation of agreements, and fulfillment of power management policies and requirements by datacenter participants. Under this arrangement, datacenters function as service providers and utilities function as service consumers.

The subject of early demand response experiments included building management systems through the adjustment of thermostat settings, deferring water heating, and precooling buildings. These workloads are inherently slow acting and therefore the traditional process of a utility operator calling the customer by phone is sufficient. A system administrator on the customer side executes the request after receiving it. If the workload is a building, the administrator adjusts thermostat settings, shuts down expendable workloads, and dims lighting systems using the building management system. An incremental improvement came with e-mail and faxed notifications. These processes allowed handling requests as part of a day-ahead forecast.

Time is of the essence when it comes to the types of events handled by ADR. A day-ahead ADR can address static energy imbalances. For instance, it allows utilities to issue ADR requests to address an anticipated shortage in generation the next day, or for seasonal energy planning.

They would be useful to address expected imbalances over a 24-hour cycle but insufficient to address contingencies such as the one that led to the July 2012 India blackout that affected 620 million people and the 2003 U.S. Northeast blackout affecting 55 million people. Datacenter workloads represent a new class of fast-acting workloads that are useful beyond balancing electricity supply and demand over a daily cycle, but allow power regulation fast enough to address transient imbalances that otherwise could result in unplanned outages.

Automated Demand Response for Datacenters

Datacenters present two kinds of workloads: the power demand from the building infrastructure and the demand from the information and communication technologies (ICT). The concept of *power usage effectiveness* (PUE) captures the relationship between the two types. This metric, developed by The Green Grid, is defined as the ratio of total facility power over the power dedicated to ICT equipment. A typical corporate datacenter today has a PUE of around 2.0, which means the datacenter is consuming as much power cooling and lighting it as it spends on ICT equipment.

PUE has historically been trending down, primarily because facilities that are more efficient require less energy expended in cooling. The most efficient datacenters have a PUE between 1.10 and 1.20, which means they run their cooling system in economizer mode most of the year, with mechanical cooling turned off. Some might rely on convection cooling instead of fans. From a demand response perspective, this means that the infrastructure side of datacenters is becoming less and less significant as a target for a demand response strategy. This puts the ICT side of datacenters at the forefront. High-volume servers, because of the large number deployed, take the lion's share of ICT power in a datacenter.

Server workloads behave quite differently from cooling workloads. Servers of recent manufacture consume little power when idling. This is the *notion of power proportional computing*. Ideally, power consumption in a server should be linear with workload intensity, all the way to zero. In practice, there is a floor when a server is idling of about 80 watts for the more recent machinery. If a workload varies in intensity during the day, the server power demand will reflect this variation. Furthermore, as we saw earlier in the chapter, it is possible to move a server along this curve, regardless of workload using power capping technology.

Although manual execution of demand response directives is time consuming and onerous, they are sufficient for slow-acting mechanical workloads such as air conditioning that might take hours to react. However, sensors and controllers in servers allow changing their power demand in a matter of seconds or even fractions of a second. A slow-to-execute demand response mechanism would not be practical or able to take advantage of these capabilities. This means manual demand response methods are no longer practical for datacenter workloads and therefore automation becomes obligatory. Automation means using computers to coordinate distributed resources. This is another manifestation of the pattern in technology evolution noted in[20] where business processes that initially involve an interaction between a human and a machine eventually become fully automated. This puts IT at the forefront in making demand response possible.

---

[20]E. Castro-Leon, "Consumerization in the IT Service Ecosystem," *IEEE IT Professional,* September/October 2014.

Datacenter Participation in Demand Response

For utilities, the generation scheduling needs to take place within the limitations of the device: Nuclear generation is difficult to throttle and therefore takes on a role of baseline generation, holding a constant level through the day. On the other hand, it is relatively easy to throttle diesel generators up or down, but this flexibility comes at a high cost per kilowatt-hour for the fuel consumed. Renewable sources such as wind and solar photovoltaic are subject to the vagaries of weather and offer little scheduling flexibility. This means that when wind is blowing and wind turbines are peaking, another type of generation must be curtailed to keep the grid power balanced.

During normal operations, working toward peak demand requires increasingly more expensive and easy to regulate generation sources. Utilities enforcing time-of-day pricing charge more during these periods. Utilities hold some capacity in reserve for the worst days. If the last watt is used, the price of electricity effectively becomes infinite: No more power can be had at any price.

In practical terms, an electricity supply system shows symptoms of distress well before the last watt has been allocated. Generators and transmission lines are dynamic systems. When driven hard, they become prone to oscillations, and therefore their reliability and ability to absorb disturbances becomes more limited.

New construction to meet increased demand is not always a feasible alternative. The siting, licensing, and construction time for a new transmission line or large generating plant can stretch for several years, if not decades. The largest plants have a lower operating cost per kilowatt. However, they would represent a poor use of capital if used a few minutes per day for peaking.

The ability of datacenters to regulate demand in matter of seconds makes them useful for demand response applications beyond cost arbitrage, involving business continuity, where the survival of the system is at stake.

The economics of demand response are compelling. Early trials suggest that the cost of workload curtailment ranges from $125 to $300 per KW of reduction. This needs to be compared against the capital cost for new generation that ranges between $500 and $5,000 per installed KW [8, 9], and the $11,500 capital cost per KW deployed power in datacenters [13]. In the case of the application of demand response to preserve system stability, the value of the power curtailed is unbounded when the alternative is a regional blackout.

A datacenter presents a concentrated demand point to a utility, typically on the order of 1 to 100 megawatts. It would take anywhere from 50 to 5,000 residential units spread over several square miles to reach similar demand levels. From this perspective, the returns from implementing an ADR strategy targeting datacenter workloads can be large and be realized much faster than trying to achieve the same over a large number of diverse residential customers.

Furthermore, unlike current practices in residential power monitoring and control, much of the compute, network, and storage equipment and supporting infrastructure is state of the art and already instrumented for power monitoring and control. Interoperable frameworks to extract and convey management data are also in place. However, there are no known previous efforts to use these capabilities on a large scale.

Demand management is useful for peak shaving. It helps utilities defer capital investment and allows reliable operation even when equipment upgrades are not feasible or cannot be deployed in short order. For instance, the process for siting, construction, and deployment of a new transmission line can take decades. Datacenter operators realize an economic benefit through incentive rates from enlisting in a demand response program.

As an additional benefit, because of their concentrated demand and cogeneration capabilities, the participation of datacenter customers can have a positive effect on system reliability and dynamic stability. Generation from wind and solar energy tends to have a deleterious effect on system dynamic stability. Generation operators have an economic incentive to inject as much power into the grid when the wind blows or the sun is shining regardless of the state of the grid. This generation usually happens at remote sites and wheeling this extra power can overload a transmission line. It is possible to tailor ADR operational policies to address not only supply and demand imbalances and pricing mechanisms, but also to optimize system stability margins using built-in monitoring and control mechanisms. This can be in the form of curtailing loads to reduce the likelihood of losing synchronization on a transmission line, or even reshaping workloads for continued operation under impaired conditions after an incident or even a catastrophic event. The goal is to make the system more resilient against an ensuing cascading failure that would lead to a regional blackout.

The benefits of demand response are threefold, primarily during peak power demand:

- Environmental in the form of avoidance of generation and associated emissions and transmission losses, which tend to be largest during peak demand.

- Energy pricing arbitrage, applying demand response whenever it is less expensive than purchasing an equal amount of energy at spot prices. Even for vertically integrated operators, with company-owned generation facilities, generation costs during peak demand are also highest.

- Enhanced grid reliability through quick workload demand curtailment.

The benefit of the last alternative is potentially unbounded when the alternative is a system collapse. Its implementation requires fast coordination of distributed energy resources spanning multiple companies. The implementation of this alternative requires an advanced distributed IT capability not possible before cloud computing.

Architecture of Demand Response

A commonly understood communication framework is essential to manage the complexity of demand response deployments. The LBNL developed one such framework, OpenADR. LBNL developed version 1.0 and ceded the standard to the Organization for the Advancement of Structured Information Standards (OASIS). At the time of writing, work toward OpenADR 2.0 is in process under the auspices of OASIS.

As shown in Figure 8-9, an ADR customer can connect to a utility through a number of methods

- Directly, as shown in configuration a.

- Through a proxy as in configuration b.

- Through an aggregation service, as in configuration c.

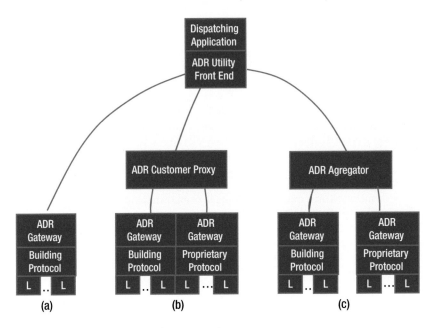

Figure 8-9. *Current ADR deployment architecture*

A customer might find it convenient to participate in a demand response exercise through a proxy service offering a simplified signup process and demand response interactions, while preserving the identity of the customer to the utility. A third modality is through an ADR aggregator, where the aggregator negotiates specific terms with each of the customers and presents a single logical interface to the utility.

Figure 8-10 shows the detail of a datacenter workload showing infrastructure devices supporting BACnet and Modbus. Figure 8-11 shows a detail for servers under the ICT.

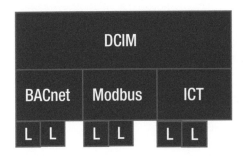

Figure 8-10. *Detail of a datacenter workload*

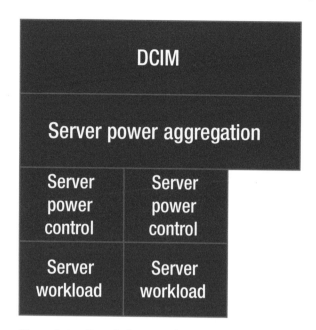

Figure 8-11. *Detail of a server (ICT) workload in a datacenter*

Server power control is implemented in the server's firmware such as Intel Node Manager, as described earlier in this chapter. Power demand control is enforced using the IPMI protocol on top of Ethernet networks. An aggregation layer allows combining power demand targets and consumption readouts. Intel Data Center Manager: Energy Director is an example of this application. The *data center infrastructure management* (DCIM) application in turn provides OpenADR services and drives the aggregation layer through a RESTful API.

OpenADR deployments are built on top of preexisting management frameworks. For instance, if the target workload is a commercial building the ADR gateway software interfaces with the building management system for the target site.

OpenADR 2.0 defines the concept of virtual top node (VTN), the same as resource energy controller (REC) in[21] in the role of manager or aggregator. A VTN manages one or more virtual end nodes (VENs). The concept is recursive whereby a VEN can take on the role of VTN to lower level entities, shown in Figure 8-12.

[21]G. Horst, *Concepts to Enable Advancement of Distributed Energy Resources* (Palo Alto, CA: Electric Power Research Institute, February 2010).

267

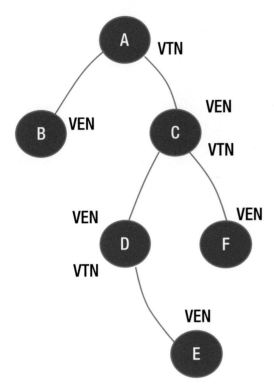

Figure 8-12. *Virtual top nodes and virtual end nodes under OpenADR 2.0*

We already see hints of this dynamic in Figure 8-9. Under this concept, demand response deployments are effectively instances of service networks as described in[20] and[22]. This becomes more evident if we redraw Figure 8-9 as a service network, as shown in Figure 8-13. The ADR proxy case has been omitted for simplicity. In a cloud environment, the utility–customer relationships need not be strictly hierarchical, and therefore more than one utility might be involved. This is particularly true in datacenters with redundant utility feeds.

[22]E. Castro-Leon, J. He, and M. Chang, "Scaling Down SOA to Small Businesses," In *Proceedings of the IEEE International Conference on Service-Oriented Computing and Applications,* 99–106, 2007.

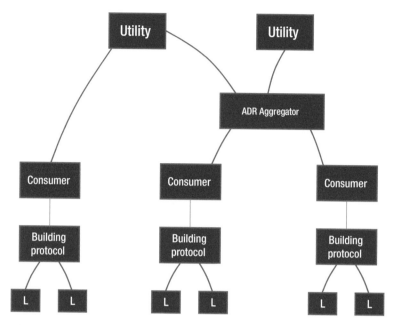

Figure 8-13. *A demand response service network*

It would appear that a VTN is an energy consumer and a VEN an energy consumer. Although this is true for a direct connected customer, this is not necessarily true under the recursive model. The availability of cogeneration resources blurs this relationship even more, where a datacenter backup generator can inject power into the grid on request from a utility, under an OpenADR relationship. Likewise, a backup battery installed in a server rack can potentially make that rack an energy producer under some circumstances.

The Future of Demand Response

As happened with the cloud, quality of service considerations will likely become central to ADR transactions. Workloads exhibit different qualities, and therefore will be valued differently from a demand response perspective. For instance, the fast curtailment capability of server workloads could be useful for improving grid stability margins, whereas the slow regulation of mechanical cooling will be more useful for day-ahead forecasts. Table 8-4 provides a few examples of workload "flavors." We can anticipate efforts for workload standardization as this takes root in the industry.

Table 8-4. *Workload Behaviors in Datacenters*

Workload Type	ADR Implementation, Private to Datacenter Operator	Behavior Exposed in ADR Contract
A	Business critical, can't be touched	Not exposed in an ADR agreement
B	Apply server power cap; can be capped indefinitely; some tolerable performance impact	Limited reduction in X kilowatts in 5–10 seconds, can be held for long times; moderate compensation
C	Apply server power throttling to selected workloads; server power demand goes down by 50% in 100 milliseconds or less; application throughput drops by 75 percent or more; DC operator negotiates the cost of this hit with business customers	Large KW reduction very fast; the utility will need to give the user lots of points
D	Turn off chiller compressors for a few minutes; DC coasts on available refrigerant supply	Moderate KW reduction; may take minutes to take effect and can be used only for limited time; relatively cheap
E	Shut down expendable workloads such as replicated web server front ends; datacenter operator negotiates impact of this action with business customers	Moderate KW reduction; may take minutes to take effect; can be used indefinitely; moderate number of points
F	Shut down plenum fans; duration limited by acceptable temperature rise	Low KW reduction; takes seconds to take hold; can be held for limited time; relatively cheap
G	Raise datacenter ambient temperature set point	Moderate KW reduction; attainable power reduction hard to measure and can take hours to stabilize; relatively cheap
H	Turn on cogeneration	Requesting utility pays energy cost plus premium
I	Switch to alternate utility provider	Requesting utility pays arbitrage costs plus premium

We can also support highly dynamic behaviors with machine-to-machine negotiation between transaction parties and automatic discovery and configuration. The normal practice today is for humans to conduct service negotiations and to sign a written contract. As service offerings under ADR become standardized, we can expect service negotiations to become standardized as well, subject to automated negotiation processes from machine to machine.

Security is another aspect that requires further investigation. The potential for breaches in power grids is amply documented. A pervasive adoption of demand response will likely increase the vulnerability surface of a grid, and at the very least, increase the risk of distributed denial of service attacks. Current demand response communications use encrypted HTTPS exchanges, not unlike those used for financial and health care transactions. It remains to be seen if these mechanisms are sufficient to carry demand response transactions.

A technical challenge, perhaps of a lesser degree, is a commonly accepted method to determine the baseline for demand curtailment. Server workloads are highly dynamic and change by the second. Under currently available technology, set power targets are defined in an absolute number of watts to be consumed by a machine. Once the limits are in place, it is not easy to determine the consumption level if the cap is removed.

As demand response adoption becomes more pervasive, we can expect a rich ecosystem developing, with curtailment watts traded as easily as generated watts. Beyond the enabling of demand response transactions, the accounting and reconciliation of the transactions will need advanced IT capabilities.

Mass Customization of IT

If we go back to Figure 6-2, the most recent events in the large-scale evolution of service networks in the cloud have paradoxically enabled the delivery of increasingly finer grained IT. When a large enterprise broke up a monolithic application into easier to understand, loosely coupled servicelets under an SOA, the resulting servicelets were still internally sourced servicelets. Some servicelets were plain and generic, such as a Network Time Protocol (NTP) service to synchronize a group of distributed machines.

A web service call made it easy to vector these calls to outside at a lower cost than building and maintaining an equivalent capability in house. Likewise, it became possible to vector capabilities implemented through shrink-wrapped software, through calls to an external provider hosting instances of the same software. The host could be the software vendor or a third-party hosting provider. This process led to the ubiquitous deployment of standardized applications in the cloud. An example is Microsoft Exchange, with the service hosted on Microsoft datacenters[23], or as SaaS through third-party datacenters[24]. This dynamic started the ball rolling toward the formation of a service network ecosystem.

Once in the wild, these servicelets became available to other customer companies. The larger customer base brought in economies of scale, with the cost of having a certain capability going down to a fraction of its in-house equivalent. Smaller corporations that struggled to deploy two or three servers in a back room were now able to deploy

---

[23]D. Wlodarz, "Why Office 365 Beats Hosted Exchange for Small Business Mail," http://betanews.com/2013/03/15/why-office-365-beats-hosted-exchange-for-small-business-email/, 2013.
[24]Microsoft Exchange Server Hosting, Rackspace, https://www.rackspace.com/en-us/email-hosting/hosted-exchange.

sophisticated human resources applications, or most any application they needed to conduct their business. They actually had multiple choices, for instance, running a mail server stack on top of an HaaS or IaaS offering, or renting a preconfigured and maintained server offering from a third party such as Rackspace, or using an SaaS offering from Microsoft.

One significant cost factor in the economies of scale achieved is labor: An small or medium-sized business (SMB) with five servers still requires at least one staff person, whereas a cloud operator with one staff member can tend to anywhere between 100 and 500 servers. Although their practices might be controversial in terms of economic impact and job creation, cloud companies are notoriously parsimonious in their use of labor in their quest to achieve economies of scale.

This transition took the industry to the next milestone shown in Figure 6-2, from large IT to a new period with IT-empowered SMBs. The concept of *enterprise service bus* (ESB) as a conduit to facilitate the interactions across servicelets played a significant role in the implementation of corporate composite applications. API portals, essentially a marketplace where servicelet developers can post or publish their wares, took the role of ESBs.

There are two more transitions in this service-driven application evolution. The next transition is technically evolutionary, but had a profound social and economic impact in the years between 2010 and 2016. The same servicelet technology that SMBs were able to afford due to the cloud's emerging economies of scale became increasingly granular to the point that individual consumers could use them and perhaps more important, afford them. The resulting revolution is, of course, the revolution of the smart device, essentially a connected pocket computer that allows consumers to access composite applications that used to be the exclusive purview of corporations. We call this trend the *consumerization of IT*. For this period, examples of new marketplaces for application are the Google Play Store, the Apple App Store, or the Samsung Galaxy Apps digital distribution platforms.

Figure 6-2 covers one last transition, consistent with the ASCS evolution model. This transition is also consistent with the pattern of the automation of processes and technologies initially created to facilitate human–machine interactions. Under this pattern, with advancing automation, the scope of these processes widens, adding machine-to-machine interactions to the mix. This is the transition from personal IT to IoT in consumer space. The transition also brings the second Internet, the cloud-based Internet, to a full circle: The first Internet was the human-to-machine web Internet, automated through web services and REST protocols. The second Internet is the service-based cloud Internet, where increasing automation of service governance leads to IoT. However imperfectly, humans still drive this ecosystem for their benefit. There are a number of drivers behind this dynamic:

- *Automated service negotiation*: Surprisingly, most service setup today is manual, involving actual face-to-face negotiation of terms between prospective service providers and consumers to settle issues related to the SLA and fees. Even the simpler alternative of signing up to a service through a web interface involves pure human intervention and judgment. Evolving standards and technology will enable a fully automated service life cycle management, from discovery to assessment to enrollment to service teardown.

- *Humans as point of integration*: Using humans as a point of integration is usually not a good idea for a well-functioning service ecosystem. Humans can get bored, tired, or might feel that the integration tasks should be carried out by someone else. Examples of humans as a point of integration are a health care system that requires a patient to sign up for a primary care provider, and sign up again for the pharmacy service surrendering the same data. An IoT system with poor integration is a residential climate control that forces the consumer to change seasonal set temperatures and enter changes in daylight saving time.

- *Lower transaction costs*: Service life cycle management is still a significant hurdle today. IoT brings a promise to lower this cost.

- *Monetization of metaservices and service metadata*: This item has been a primary motivation for Internet companies to enter business, and will become a bigger consideration as the cloud Internet transitions to IoT, with new entrants to the market.

We cover two examples in the remainder of this section, the phenomenon of consumerization of IT and the Rachio sprinkler system.

Consumerization of IT

The transition from composite applications during the SOA era in the early 2000s to IT for SMBs using cloud-based servicelets to personal IT has been reflecting back to corporate IT under the consumerization of IT trend. This is the practice of workers using laptops, smart devices, and hardware and software tools they own to carry a double duty at work. Because of this, this practice is also known as *bring your own device* (BYOD)[25]. BYOD and the related concept of *bring your own application* (BYOA), have been transformative to IT in the sense that they have redefined IT's role in the enterprise from a centralized technology purveyor, assessor, and gatekeeper to a facilitator in a more federated environment, although not without challenges. Consumerization brings an inversion of roles where users, not IT, drive technology adoption and change.

This change is fundamental, and is not going away anytime soon, driven by the need for business efficiency and nimbleness and by cultural change as the change of guard from the boomer to the millennial generation takes place. Ironically, perhaps the segment least concerned of all is the end users and the employee community using their devices as they always had and who expects these devices simply to work and deliver value in a corporate setting the same way they had in their personal life and past work assignments.

The service dynamic in the cloud can go a long way toward explaining the impetus behind BYOD. Perhaps it can also provide some insight into possible strategic approaches on how to manage and take advantage of the trend to maximize the beneficial impact

---

[25]D. Evans, "What Is BYOD and Why Is It important?," *Techradar.com*, http://www.techradar.com/news/computing/what-is-byod-and-why-is-it-important-1175088, October 7, 2015.

to the actors involved. This benefit comes in terms of improved productivity for workers and reduced capital and operational costs to corporations as well as the aperture of new opportunities. In other words, exploring the driving forces behind consumerization is an essential exercise to make sense of the current dynamics of transformation and disruption and to ensure IT continues delivering value to the enterprise.

We can think of three primary drivers behind BYOD: The first is the transition to the service economy we have been covering in this book. This driver, in turn, brings two more: a redrawing of the enterprise boundaries, and the new social contract. Let us go over each item in the following sections.

Consumerization and the New Social Contract

The enterprise workforce has become more diverse, especially after the crisis precipitated by the financial sector in 2008. The role of transient staff has increased. These include contractors in workforce augmentation agencies and service providers as well as independent professionals and part-time employees. Full-time employees, the traditional audience for IT services, is getting proportionately smaller. This eminently transient workforce bring their own tools. Relatively short tenures means it is not practical for these professionals to adopt existing processes. Temporary teams might bring tools they are comfortable with, such as tools for project tracking and management or customer relationship management (CRM) and use them totally outside the purview of the IT organization. Because establishing a local infrastructure would not be practical, these tools are usually SaaS based and accessed through mobile devices.

Even when corporate applications and data are involved, employees entering the workforce place less value on corporate-issued tools and would rather continue using their personal devices. Temporary employees find it more productive to use their own devices. This creates enormous pressure on IT organizations to address these requests and to support personal devices.

The New Enterprise Boundaries

Large corporations today such as aircraft and automobile manufacturers have effectively become gigantic systems integrators managing complex supply chains. Smaller companies follow the same dynamic to a lesser degree or participate in a number of supply networks. This means that corporate applications and data are routinely accessed by a very diverse community. When application components or whole applications such as e-mail messaging get outsourced to the cloud, the notion of inside versus outside the enterprise gets blurred, with corporate processes using resources outside the traditional enterprise perimeter.

In this environment, the user community with its diversity is not concerned about distinguishing between inside and outside resources, and expects to use devices, data, and tools in the same way they always have. Effectively, IT no longer has control over devices to connect with corporate data and applications. A heavy-handed approach in managing BYOD will likely alienate users who will end up sidestepping IT altogether. There are no simple solutions to this quandary, but it helps to understand the dynamics behind this change, covered in the next section.

Transition to the Service Economy

With globalization, the world economy has become service oriented. For all advanced economies, the economic value from services such as financial, travel, legal, and health care services exceeds that of manufacturing, agriculture, and extractive industries. One of the practical effects of the transition to the service economy has been the adoption of cloud computing.

A look at Google Trends[26] points to at least a circumstantial correlation between service transformation in IT and BYOD. The tool lists the relative frequency, or in other words, the popularity of web searches for the terms *SOA, cloud computing,* and *BYOD.* Each term is normalized to its peak frequency with a numerical value of 100 assigned to the peak. The graphs in Figure 8-14 show data plotted from 2004 to the present. The term SOA came first, with its hockey stick inflection point outside the data. Our estimation is that the inflection took place around 2002 or 2003 at the onset of web services technology and peaked in 2007. Its popularity as a term diminished slightly after 2007. The seasonal peaks at the end of the years 2011 through 2014 constitute an interest topic for speculation. Perhaps it is due to CIOs putting pressure on their service transformation task forces for not "doing enough" to incorporate cloud technology at the end of each fiscal year in anticipation of presenting to a report to the CEO. The hockey stick inflection for the cloud takes place at the end of 2007. The popularity of the term tapers off during 2012. Because we know that the cloud is not going away anytime soon, we surmise that cloud computing has become a mainstream term in the IT community. Finally, the inflection point for BYOD does not take place until 2011, more than three years after the onset of cloud computing. Our conjecture here is that it took this much time for the IT in the service economy for servicelets to go into the wilderness, undergo a transformation into pure, cloud-based composite applications, and come back into the corporate world, brought in by entrepreneurial workers wielding BYOD.

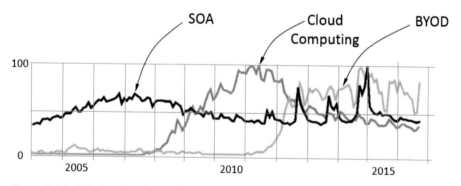

Figure 8-14. *Relative Google search frequencies for SOA, cloud computing, and BYOD since 2004*

---

[26]See https://www.google.com/trends/.

Moving forward, the notion of internal assets versus those outside the enterprise has changed radically compared with the status quo of centralized IT at the onset of the service revolution in technology starting in the early 2000s. The focus at that time was on tight management of corporate assets. Let us look at the enterprise boundaries before the service transition in what we call the IT classic era and at how these boundaries evolve with the service transition and adoption of cloud computing. We can do this thought experiment by drawing the enterprise boundaries on top of Figure 6-3, which yields Figure 8-15. During the classic IT era, enterprise boundaries were easy to discern. If an asset was inside the corporate walls, it was inside the enterprise boundaries. Even each corporate laptop was "inside" even if traveling: It was a corporate-owned asset running corporate-sanctioned applications and maintained by corporate IT. Every laptop had a corporate bubble protecting it. Today, things are not so clear. For one thing, application servicelets, which started in house at the outset of SOA, started going into the wild. Therefore, corporate applications now run on assets owned or operated by third parties.

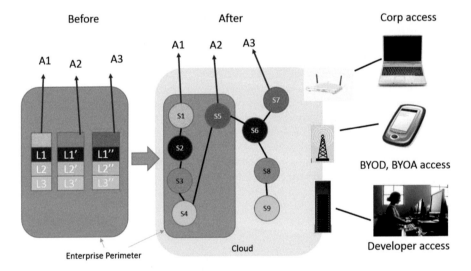

Figure 8-15. *The evolving enterprise boundaries*

Servicelets can be native, intended from the beginning to support cloud-based composite applications. In practice, legacy applications can be "servitized" and retrofitted as servicelets by slapping an API on top of the application. Conversely, software designed as a servicelet can be made to behave as a self-standing application through a thin GUI making calls to the servicelet's API.

As the bottom line, the reengineered application must support multimodal access, also shown in Figure 8-15:

- Traditional access by corporate employees.

- BYOD and BYOA access by the general public.

- App developers interacting through the company's published interface in an API portal.

Once servicelets "escaped" into the wild, as third-party offerings available to any developer, new business opportunities surfaced and developers started building applications that before would have been created inside the enterprise. Because the ecosystem involved is essentially the whole computer industry, including corporate and individual consumers, the rate of evolution has accelerated notably. Most new applications die quickly, but the ones that survive can develop a customer base of hundreds of thousands in just a few months. This is the context from which consumerization developed, with a profound economic effect: very expensive datacenters costing hundreds of millions or even billions of dollars into delivered applications accessible for a few dollars per month, or even free to the consumer. The audience for these applications grew from one for a complete solution stack built in house in a corporation, to a few hundred large corporations, then for a few tens of thousands of SMBs to millions or tens of millions of individual users. Under the consumerization paradigm, individual users became familiar with these applications and brought them back to the enterprise, completing a full circle.

A strong contributing factor to the adoption of BYOD is the preferences of the millennial generation just entering the workforce, which grew up in this environment. From this perspective, it makes perfect sense to continue this modality at work, for both access devices, either a mobile device or PC client, to connect to the cloud-based applications behind them. This is what brings us to the notion of BYOD and BYOA today.

What about tomorrow? BYOD is primarily, and once more human–machine interaction. There are inklings of a new circle starting with machine-to-machine interactions in the form of IoT. We are talking about devices such as printers, webcams, and drones acting as network nodes. Outsourced printers are becoming ubiquitous, with printers deployed on premises, managed by a service provider as a service, with the customer paying for the page count.

Changes brought by the consumerization of IT will likely redefine the role of IT. What we see is actually the proverbial tip of the iceberg. The impetus behind BYOD are long-running trends of economics and technology evolution: A transition to a service economy in advanced economies is fundamentally changing relationships between organizations and workers, and in the process transforming how IT is delivered to constituents. Consumerization is also a reflection of the blurring of enterprise boundaries, in part due to the changing relationships.

An IoT Service Network Example

In another example of mass customization of IT, the sprinkler controller system described in this section exemplifies a small startup can put together an advanced IT capability taking advantage of existing servicelet components without spending millions of dollars in basic research and development that the project would have cost even ten years ago. The output of this development is a connected controller appliance, essentially an IoT device that sells for about US $250 and an associated servicelet. Individual consumers can deploy the appliance and bind the appliance to the servicelet. Consumers can also bind any edge device they already own, be it a smartphone, PC or tablet and bind these edge devices to the servicelet to add a human interface to the application at no extra cost. These service relationships form a mini-ecosystem around the individual consumer, shown in Figure 8-16. The compute and network infrastructure for this application represent an investment of several billion dollars, and yet individual consumers can enjoy a slice of this infrastructure under a service framework for the cost of a short flight, much in the same way can afford to use a seat in an aircraft worth hundreds of millions of dollars. Likewise, the process of installing an instance of the sprinkler service orchestrates a complex set of distributed resources behind the scenes, yet most of this complexity is hidden to the individual consumer, to the point that an installation by a specialist is not necessary for consumers of average technical skills. Most any person capable of installing an operating system or an application in a PC can carry out the sprinkler installation successfully.

The Colorado startup Rachio offers a residential sprinkler controller service. This is an early example of a fourth-wave, device-oriented IoT network backed by a number of cloud services. Figure 8-16 shows the local service network for this system.

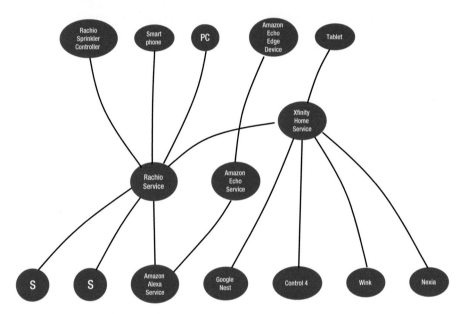

Figure 8-16. *Local IoT ecosystem for the Rachio Iro sprinkler controller*

Time-to-market and capital investment considerations do not make it practical for Rachio to operate in-house datacenters, and therefore the Rachio service depends on a number of support services, some unnamed, shown by the circles with an S at the bottom left of Figure 8-16, and some publicized such as the Amazon Alexa voice platform[27]. There are aggregation service platforms that in turn take the Rachio service as one of their feeders. Shown in Figure 8-16 are Amazon's Echo service and the Comcast Xfinity Home Service, which provides a glass pane for a number of services such as Rachio, Google Nest, Control 4, Nexia, and Wink, among others. A user can operate the system through a number of edge devices. Figure 8-16 shows three: a smart phone and a PC

---

[27]"How Do I Use Alexa with My Rachio?," *Rachio.com,* http://support.rachio.com/article/483-how-do-i-use-alexa, 2016.

communicating directly with the Rachio service, and a tablet mediated by the Xfinity Home Service.

The Rachio service manages a swarm of sprinkler controllers, an example of which is shown in Figure 8-17. Each Rachio controller connects to the Internet through a Wi-Fi access point. The Rachio service runs in a datacenter in the cloud and provides a web server. Consumers access their controllers through edge devices, which can be a laptop or desktop PC, or an app running on a tablet or a smartphone as shown. Figure 8-17 also shows a screenshot of the controller app, running on an Android smart phone functioning as an IoT edge device. Figure 8-18 shows the web browser interface running on a laptop. The sprinklers can be accessed, albeit indirectly, through the aggregator services. This distributed scheme provides a certain level of fault tolerance. For instance, the residential sprinkler controller can cache some of the service information, including user authentication to allow edge devices connected to a local area network (LAN) to talk directly to the controller to turn sprinkler heads on or off without having to mediate the operation through the Rachio service. This capability is helpful if the link to the Internet is down.

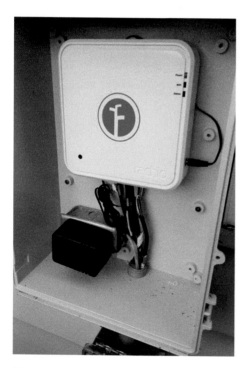
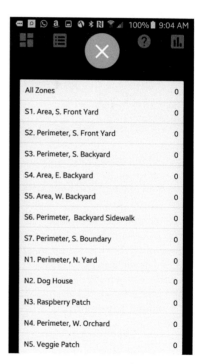

Figure 8-17. *Rachio Iro sprinkler controller and smart phone controller interface*

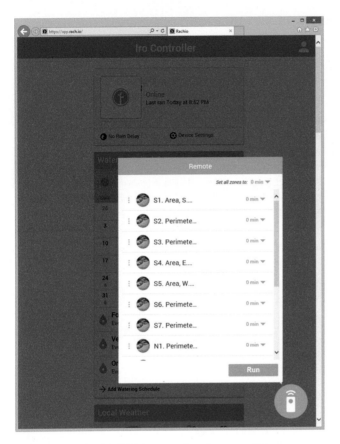

Figure 8-18. *Rachio Web browser interface on a PC*

As mentioned earlier in the chapter, automation is an important aspect of an IoT service. By default, the Rachio system makes adjustments to the irrigation schedule autonomously. For instance, it might skip a scheduled watering if rainfall exceeds a threshold. It will also make seasonal adjustments to watering times. The system sends automatic e-mail notifications for each action (see Figure 8-19). The system does not require user intervention except for deviations from the present schedule; for instance, to start a manual irrigation cycle.

We've made a Seasonal Shift to Veggie patch on Iro controller.

In September, this schedule ran for 46 minutes. In October, this schedule will run for 26 minutes.

N3. Raspberry Patch has been adjusted from 12 minutes to 6 minutes N4. Perimeter, W. Orchard has been adjusted from 17 minutes to 9 minutes N5. Veggie Patch has been adjusted from 17 minutes to 9 minutes

Figure 8-19. *Excerpt of a Rachio Iro end user e-mail notification*

The Global Alzheimer's Association Interactive Network and Cloud Platforms in Precision Medicine

President Obama announced the Precision Medicine Initiative in his 2015 State of the Union Address with a US $215 million investment in the President's 2016 Budget[28]. PMI is an approach for disease prevention and treatment that factors in the patient's genetic makeup, environment, habits and lifestyle to determine a customized strategy to manage disease. The current challenge for this approach is data intensity. The emerging Electronic Health Record data cloud, as complex as it is constitutes only a small component of the data in an eventual PMI system. Eric Dishman, the PMI director at the National Institutes of Health notes "The precision medicine data processing challenges are the biggest of the big data problems – bigger than meteorology, bigger than astronomy, bigger than physics. Those were traditionally the fields that required the most number crunching..." Degenerative diseases such as Alzheimer's, diabetes, cancer and Parkinson's, currently difficult to manage at best, are good targets for PMI.

An early practice for PMI includes linking up or federating research databases across institutions in multiple geographic regions. Examples are the Collaborative Cancer Cloud[29] and the Global Alzheimer's Association Interactive Network (GAAIN). We will focus on GAAIN in the following discussion. GAAIN is a collaborative project involving the Alzheimer's Association in partnership with the Laboratory of Neuro Imaging (LONI) at the University of Southern California (USC) and the National Center for Alzheimer's

---

[28]*Fact Sheet: President Obama's Precision Medicine Initiative*, The White House, Office of the Press Secretary, https://www.whitehouse.gov/thepress-office/2015/01/30/fact-sheet-president-obama-s-precision-medicine-initiative
[29]E. Hayes, *OHSU, Intel Sign up 2 Major Cancer Centers for Ambitious Cloud Project*, Portland Business Journal, March 31, 2016.

Disease Research and Care at the University of Geneva. Funding for the computational infrastructure of the project comes from the US National Institutes of Health Big Data to Knowledge grant.

The goal for these federated databases is the sharing of patient clinical data as well as research data sourced from possibly multiple institutions and present it in useful forms to users in the broader research community. The extraction and processing of this data must respect patient confidentiality as well as to comply with rules and policies imposed by the data owner. Researchers and eventually clinicians want to use this data to identify indicators correlated with quality of life and life span for Alzheimer's patients. This data can suggest social and behavioral factors that affect the progression of the disease while reduce healthcare costs. Researches also hope that the analysis of the federated data will provide insight into the root cause of the disease, helping improve treatments and even identify preventive measures to delay the onset of Alzheimer's symptoms.

Because of their distributed nature, it is not surprising that these data "clouds" or "networks" form a service network as described in Figures 4-7 or 8-2. Some repositories are small, representing perhaps a single lab or research project, with relatively simple authentication and access control, while others are large, institutional data stores. As in the First Web, most of these repositories provide a Web interface for access by humans and may lack APIs for machine-to-machine access. The data may also be subject to local policies, location restrictions as well as legal conditions such as redistribution.

Figure 8-20 captures the high-level architecture of GAAIN. GAAIN defines a service network not unlike the sprinkler system service network shown in Figure 8-16. A critical component is the GAAIN central server, mediating interactions across data sources. A GAAIN data partner is the owner of a particular data source.

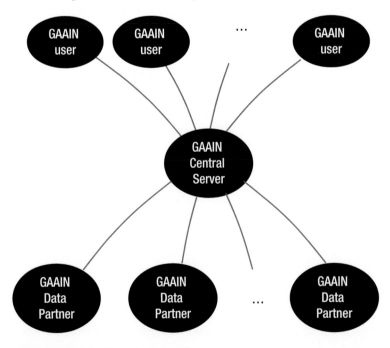

Figure 8-20. *GAAIN service network*

Figure 8-21 depicts the high-level architecture of a data partner client (DPC). The DPC is a Java container deployed on a DPC host or on a separate computer provided by the GAAIN project. When the central server sends queries to a DPC, all retrieved data coms from a derived database in the container. The data owner decides the subset of the original source database allowed to reside in the derived database.

Participation in GAAIN is voluntary. The structure of the DPC is designed to lighten the setup and administrative burden on the DPC data owner. Regardless, the GAAIN project follows a set of global policies that with every DPC deployment:

- **Control.** GAAIN data owners retain control of their data at all times, including revocation rights and can disconnect the DPC from the GAAIN network anytime. To minimize the possibility of leaks, no cached data is ever copied to permanent storage in the central server.

- **Light footprint**. The central server accessing the derived database reduces the burden on the DPC's local production system. The data export operation is done at a time convenient to the data owner to minimize disruption to normal operations.

- **No copy policy**. As hinted above, all data in permanent storage stays under the control of the repository owner, including the derived database. Some data may be cached in the memory of the central server during query processing. If the data owner disconnects a DPC, the central server removes all the cached data from its memory.

- **Security**. The interactions between the central server and a DPC use HTTPS and Transport Layer Security (TLS). The enrollment process between GAAIN and a new data partner that includes the initial key exchange.

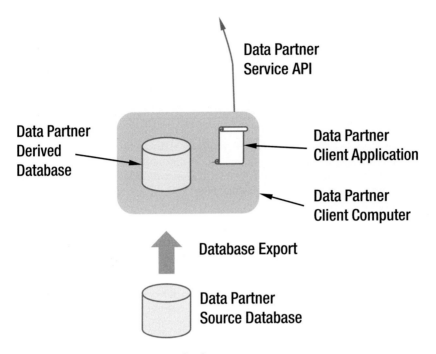

Figure 8-21. *GAAIN architecture for data partners*

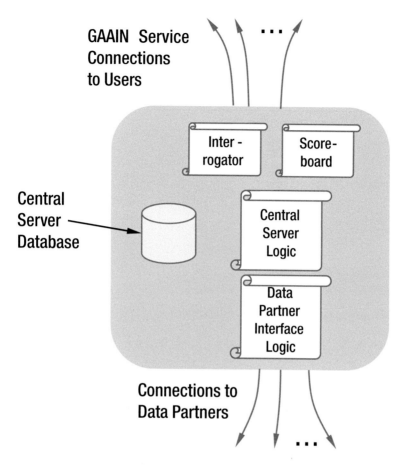

Figure 8-22. *GAAIN architecture for the central server*

GAAIN users interact through the central server. The central server presents two main interfaces to users, the scoreboard and the interrogator. The scoreboard is publicly accessible and presents a list of data partners as rows in the scoreboard with a list of data attributes such as age, gender, handedness and race, as columns and the number of subjects for each data partner and attribute. The inspection of the scoreboard gives the researcher an idea of the extent of data available before using the interrogator.

The interrogator enables the researcher to define specific cohorts based on chosen attributes. The researcher usually start by defining a baseline cohort to be compared with a second cohort. As the researcher adjusts the definition of the second cohort by selecting additional attributes, the interrogator updates the results interactively.

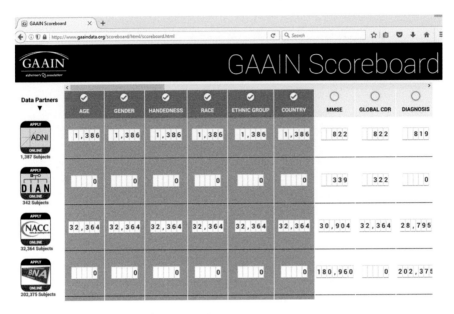

Figure 8-23. *Partial screenshot of the GAAIN Scoreboard*

Figure 8-24 depicts a screenshot of an attribute description from the interrogator.

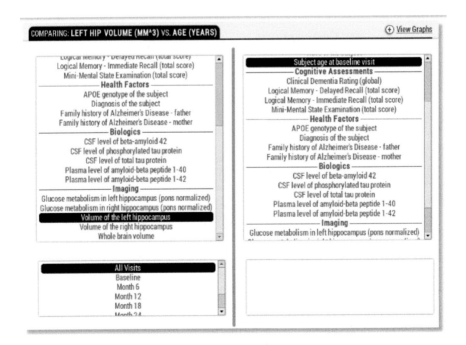

Figure 8-24. *GAAIN interrogator attribute description*

Figure 8-25 shows a scattergram from a query to the interrogator, and Figure 8-26 shows the query result in bar chart form.

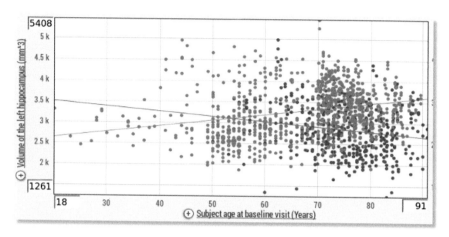

Figure 8-25. *GAAIN interrogator scattergram*

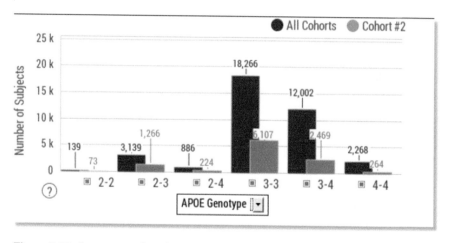

Figure 8-26. *Interrogator bar chart*

The GAAIN network is already a bona fide cloud in its initial inception and deployment. Data partners live as PaaS layer in the cloud macroarchitecture. Data partners are implemented as physical computers deployed at the data partner premises, or as a Java container hosted in a data partner host or a computer provided by GAAIN deployed in the data partner premises. Pushing the GAAIN compute resources at the DPC to the cloud may simplify the on boarding or enrollment logistics as well as the day-to-day operations. These computers can run as virtualized IaaS or as a physical machine from a hardware-as-a-service (HaaS) provider.

Data partners may choose to run on HaaS to minimize the risk of data leaks across virtual machines. Given that the central server is a keystone component, it probably should run as HaaS if deployed in the cloud for the security reasons mentioned and for scalability. It may be easier to carry out upgrades through the HaaS provider than to purchase a new server to be deployed on premise. GAAIN administrators own and manage DPC computers whether in the cloud or on premise. Under this assumption the GAAIN administrators can easily implement, upgrade and deploy changes in the DPCs without ever having to ship machines. For data partners who can't let data out of premise, the data repositories can be attached to the DPCs in the cloud using encrypted channels.

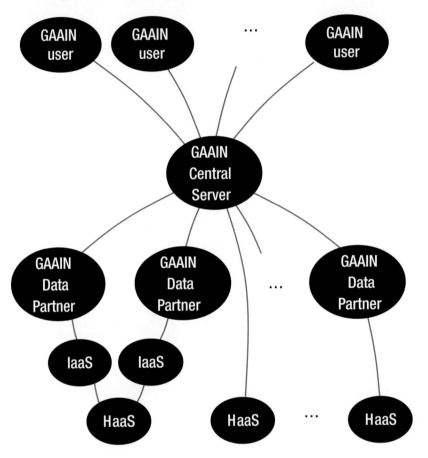

Figure 8-27. Evolved GAAIN Service Network

PART V

CHAPTER 9

■ ■ ■

Cloud as a Service Evolution

There is at least one point in the history of any company when you have to change dramatically to rise to the next level of performance. Miss that moment – and you start to decline.

—Andy Grove

The previous chapters covered some fundamental aspects of the service dynamics as applied to IT and how service dynamics define the cloud and cloud processes. We also discussed how the enterprise platforms that characterized the first wave of standard high-volume (SHV) servers evolved into second-wave cloud platforms under a service dynamic with strong customization and built-to-order components. The second wave drivers and adopters were the largest cloud service providers (CSPs) worldwide with the concept of *application-specific cloud servers* (ASCPs). A competitive advantage for these players and initial barrier to entry to smaller players was the nonrecurring engineering (NRE) cost to design and manufacture the desired customizations. However, as platform providers and consumers went through the learning curve and achieved increasing technology maturity, the benefits of customization became democratized and available to smaller CSPs.

The democratization of ASCPs defines the third wave, on the upswing at the time of writing. The dynamics driving the third wave are the same ones that characterized the first wave: Technology sharing with a larger user base brings economies of scale. The benefits of scaling are generally greater than potential losses from new competitive entrants. In many cases, there is no downside at all because the potential competitors operate in a different geographic region or in other market segments. Processes that facilitate platform customization for third-wave players include standardization through platform industry groups such as the Open Compute Project (OCP) and the increasing use of cloud technology to develop cloud platforms. We can also expect working groups in various cloud service domains, such as e-commerce and small banking, to band together and define cloud platforms optimized for a particular service domain.

The evolution of the fourth wave for cloud platforms is just starting. This fourth wave will provide the platform foundation for the Internet of things (IoT), the servers in the cloud that will energize the *servicelets* that make IoT work. For this transition, we can look at the transition of the first web-to-web services as a pattern: The first Web was a technology to enable a universal client computer to facilitate human–computer

© Enrique Castro-Leon and Robert Harmon 2016

E. Castro-Leon and R. Harmon, *Cloud as a Service*, DOI 10.1007/978-1-4842-0103-9_9

interactions. The transition to web services occurred when web technology became useful to facilitate universal machine-to-machine interactions.

Likewise, a defining characteristic for the fourth wave will be increasing levels of automation through machine-to-machine interactions. Because of the need to supportmachine-to-machine interactions, IoT architects will find that HaaS access will make IoT end-to-end device integration easier to design, execute, and operate. This automation will facilitate not just the interaction across the service providers of today for service orchestration and management through a service life cycle, but also the orchestration, management, and service integration of the machines that make up the IoT. Actually, a *thing* in the IoT can be small, like a mote, but can also be large, such as an automobile or even a ship or aircraft. However, these devices constitute the visible portion of the IoT universe. There is a much greater mass of IoT "dark matter" not readily visible supporting IoT functionality.

Some IoT applications are intangible: Their edge devices do not have atoms allocated to them and reside as applications in other devices, such as the Siri and Cortana concierge services, with Siri running in Apple iPhones and iPads, and Cortana running on client devices running the Windows 10 operating system. The Amazon Echo service works through dedicated devices, but very likely the instantiation of edge devices is more a business decision rather than a strict technical necessity[1]. In particular, Echo uses the Alexa application programming interface (API) that runs in the cloud[2].

We believe the demand for the servicelet infrastructure to support emerging IoT capabilities is very much a dark horse at the present, if anything because flashy IoT edge devices get the lion's share of the industry's attention. The success of these devices does not depend on the direct revenue they generate, but in their capability to channel other cloud services, not just from their sponsoring companies, but from third parties as well. Each successful IoT service will create a platform with associated ASCPs as well as an ecosystem supporting it. Some of the ASCP demand will come from existing cloud players. Apple, Amazon, and Microsoft are good examples, but a good portion of this demand could come from emerging organizations that do not exist today. This demand is a dark horse if only because it is not on the industry's radar. Figure 9-1 extrapolates Figure 4-12, depicting a steeper demand curve to account for the participation of IoT ASCPs. This demand is on both sides of the second- and third-wave growth curves because of the participation of incumbents, to which we add the contribution of emerging or new participants.

---

[1]"Amazon Echo," *Wikipedia,* https://en.wikipedia.org/wiki/Amazon_Echo, 2016.
[2]"Create a Smarter Home with Alexa: Introducing the Smart Home Skill API," *Amazon Developer,* https://developer.amazon.com/public/solutions/alexa/alexa-skills-kit/content/smart-home, 2016.

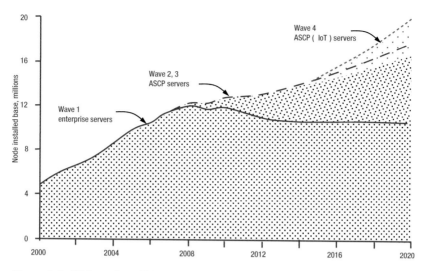

Figure 9-1. *Elaboration of Figure 4-12 showing extrapolation for IoT server demand*

In this chapter, we cover topics related to evolutionary changes in the service ecosystems we see today that we can expect in the future. The first topic is the role of *metaservices* and service metadata in an evolved service governance framework. The second is a quintessential service ecosystem: the smart city, with a government whose primary mission is to provide services to its residents.

Metaservices, Service Metadata, and Service Governance

Advances in IT have the potential to bring disruptive changes in business processes. Disruptions come from new degrees of transparency to process components from these changes, or can alter the cost relationships in these components. FedEx is a classic example. This company started an overnight package service on April 17, 1973. Although the capability to carry out overnight package deliveries was innovative by itself, given the existing infrastructure at the time, FedEx went beyond that. The company's greatest contribution was the notion of a tracking number, initially used internally for quality control[3]. Externalizing this capability also allowed FedEx to export logistical efficiencies to their customers. This capability proved to be as valuable to customers as fast shipping by adding predictability to customers' business processes. Exporting process efficiency is one enduring pattern for successful cloud services. The driving principle is actually

---

[3]R. Baldwin, "Shipshape: Tracking 40 Years of FedEx Tech," *Wired Magazine,* https://www.wired.com/2013/04/40-years-of-fedex/, April 17, 2013.

not new; Ronald Coase documented it back in 1937 in his theory of the firm, arguing that reduced transaction costs drive increased business efficiency[4,5].

Intermediation, Disintermediation, and Reintermediation

Another enduring pattern for services is the pendulum between intermediation and disintermediation. In some cases, the introduction of a service triggers a disintermediation; that is, the elimination of process intermediaries. Classic examples are the elimination of travel agents during the dot-com era and a trend toward self-service, for instance, in automobile fueling stations, cashiers replaced by automatic teller machines, and airport ticketing kiosks. At the time FedEx started, moving cargo by air was a slow and inefficient process that negated the main advantage of air transport. Cargo was at the mercy of the intervention of forwarders to pick up and deliver the cargo at the source and destination and to orchestrate the cargo routing[6]. Getting to the destination before the consolidation of the air industry often involved two or more hops across different carriers and it was up to the forwarders to orchestrate the interline transfers. FedEx took charge of the package pickup and delivery as well as the air transport. It also established a system of hubs, starting with its hub in the Memphis International Airport to minimize the number of transfers.

The management of the complex logistics required an IT capability to match that included the ability to track packages in transit in real time. In the early 1980s, Internet capabilities were rudimentary and cellular carriers were not yet in business, and therefore FedEx developed a private Internet of sorts along with a wireless network to allow real-time communication throughout the company, including drivers[7]. Today it would be possible to build a similar capability of FedEx's cost out of commonly available servicelets from a bevy of CSPs, but FedEx had to build its platform from scratch at great expense. The investment paid off and FedEx was able to exact a first mover advantage in its line of business. FedEx enabled a process of disintermediation from the existing carriers delivering an expensive and unsatisfactory service followed by reintermediation using centralized company resources.

Disintermediation and transparency do not follow a continuous progression. In the first half of the twentieth century, for workers, performing an accounting query might have been as simple as walking to the next room and speaking to the appropriate clerk.

---

[4]R. H. Coase, "The Nature of the Firm," *Economica, 4* (16), 386–405, November 1937.
[5]R. H. Coase, "The Problem of Social Cost," In *Economic Analysis of the Law: Selected Readings,* D. A. Wittman, Ed. (Oxford, UK: Blackwell, 2007).
[6]Curiously, a similar problem existed with early e-mail routing with the *uucp* server application, which required the sender to specify a complete routing path for the intervening machines using the '!' ("bang") notation, such as *ogc!intel-gw!inteloa!egcastro*. Today this routing is automatic: The user only needs to know the recipient host name and user name, using the user@hostname notation. The Domain Name System (DNS) takes care of locating the host, and the Simple Mail Transfer Protocol (SMTP) routes the message. This notation is still in use today, as an audit trail mechanism if the user cares to find out about the routing of a message after its arrival.
[7]C. Evans, "10 Facts That May Not Know About FedEx," *IntegraCore,* `https://blog.` `integracore.com/packaging/10-facts-that-may-not-know-about-fedex/`, 2013.

The introduction of mainframes and centralized IT in the 1950s changed the landscape, an example of reintermediation, the introduction of new intermediaries, essentially the IT organization managing the mainframe behind the glass walls. Consolidation and centralization of functions brought improved operational efficiency with a lower cost per query. For information consumers this change was not necessarily beneficial, as queries might have had to wait until the next batch run and new application requests had to wait for years. The pendulum swung in the opposite direction in the 1980s with the industry adoption of the personal computer and packaged software. Fulfilling the need for an application became as simple as going to the store and purchasing shrink-wrapped software to fit the purpose.

The industry adoption of cloud computing at the beginning of the millennium brought another wave of reintermediation. It became less expensive to outsource certain IT functions such as payroll, e-mail, customer relationship management (CRM), and expense reporting to SaaS providers and for some companies, these functions went out the door to cloud providers. As in the mainframe era, there were economies of scale through the reuse of a common infrastructure across multiple corporate customers and from the domain expertise of the service providers.

Service Metaproperties: Service Metadata and Metaservices

As in prior occurrences of business process transformation, the wide adoption of the service paradigm not without side effects, primarily in the loss of transparency as an IT process gets outsourced and crosses a service boundary. We see this phenomenon every day: a corporate employee or an individual consumer booking travel or enrolling for health care benefits. Sometimes the handoff is obvious: The employee logs in from a corporate web site, where the web site links to an American Express maintained web site. Sometimes the identity of the service provider is less obvious: The engine to find a lowest fare route might be using an analytic engine from another provider, and going through APIs from the various airlines involved for discovering specific route and fare information. In other instances, the web site discloses the technology of the service provider instantiated for a particular application, such as site-specific instances of the Google search engine. Most newsfeeds today work in this manner, functioning as curated aggregation sites from content providers that in turn aggregate their content, effectively defining another service network, as depicted in Figure 8-2.

There are a number of considerations under this dynamic.

- Assume that by default any service offering is the front end of a service network behind it. Even when the service provider acts as a purveyor of physical entities, such as a HaaS provider, and the user gets a handle to a physical server, that server might have been outsourced to a third-party HaaS provider.

- The service consumer would find it useful to have a priori indication of quality of service (QoS), to be able to assess the pedigree of any third-party component services in an offering, as well as security and privacy practices in effect across all services and subservices involved.

- Loose coupling is desirable for most cloud services, meaning that the service implements a functional capability, but does not impose specific process requirements; for instance, synchronization requirements or a specific management framework.

- The service provider of a composite application is responsible for the service guarantees under the service's service-level agreement (SLA), for carrying out service governance and orchestration of servicelets.

- A service consumer needs access to information about the service offering. Some information is relatively static, such as the billing rate. Some information is dynamic, for instance the charge for the service since the last billing. This capability usually requires invoking a method from a provider API. Additional information might be related to scheduled outages or service performance and quality.

- A service consumer who is also a service provider might need the information from aggregated services downstream to shape the information passed to service consumers upstream as well as to shape security and availability policies. For instance, the provider might decide to use an alternate service if one of the feeder services downstream anticipates downtime.

- There is no invisible hand guiding service orchestration toward ever more efficient composite service offerings. The desire to decrease transaction costs often leads to attempts at cost shifting between servicelet providers. Misguided attempts from some players to shift cost can result in poor offerings and unsustainable dynamics.

  For instance, major airlines' efforts to cap costs from subcontracted regional feeder airlines have led to less experienced pilots being paid salaries below poverty levels, which in turn has reduced the number of people choosing this career well below sustainable levels. The extensive use of the self-service model for trip reservations and check-in has resulted in extremely poor customer satisfaction.

  Health care systems usually require customers to register for each of the services: primary care provider, optometry, dentistry, pharmacy services, and so on. This could reflect inadequate use of service metadata to implement some basic capabilities, such as a single sign-on, and forcing the end user to take on a role as a point of integration.

Even though servicelets in the cloud are presumably location independent, to assemble a composite application, the solution architects and engineers involved must document the application architecture, publish the application parameters in the application's registry, and identify the set servicelets needed to build and stand up the application. The engineers also need to extract information from the servicelet to ascertain that the servicelet specifications meet the minimum security, performance, and uptime requirements for the application singly and when working together and identify alternative servicelets to minimize application downtime.

Mechanisms for service metadata exchange are essential in service architecture, design, and operations. An entity managing a composite needs information about each of the constituent services. In other words, needed is a capability to carry out *servicelet introspection* to retrieve sufficient information about a servicelet. Application managers maintain this information in a database or registry. This information allows the service architect to select the most appropriate servicelets for a future composite application from internal or external offerings. Information in this repository allows service architects to determine the suitability of the various servicelet alternatives, to validate composite functionality during application testing, and to carry out security and performance policies. Information in this repository is also essential during operations to enable performance and security management, and to identify standby service instances when needed to manage service reliability.

Additional documentation might include instructions on how to allocate additional service instances for reasons of failover or to increase application performance. This documentation is essential not just during the application lifetime, but also before for planning purposes, and after application decommissioning for appropriate disposition and postmortem. Note that failover is an administrative policy that prescribes actions to be taken in case of a servicelet failure. The aspirational goal is to have automatic failover procedures to minimize downtime after a servicelet malfunction. System administrators can use manual procedures as long as the procedures stay within the service level promises to customers.

David Linthicum introduced the notion of *metaservice*[8] as data about a service or servicelet for the purpose of service life cycle management. This is similar to the notion of *metadata*. In informatics, metadata is commonly associated with information about stored data to organize the data and make it easier to search and retrieve. Metadata access and replication policies are important factors in the information retrieval performance; and improperly designed, they can become a bottleneck. Metadata is an important consideration in a company's data strategy. Metadata is essential in defining the structure of warehouse repositories aggregating information from multiple sources.

The notion of metadata is central to many disciplines, including the Dewey Decimal System for cataloging books in library and information science, and the EXIF data recorded with every frame by many digital cameras[9]. The notion of metadata is also essential to the business model of the leading social media companies like Facebook, Google, and Twitter. For these companies, revenue from metadata is so valuable that it allows them to deliver content to their user community essentially free or at nominal cost. Metadata is also at the core of privacy controversies in the industry. Cloud metadata constitutes an emerging field. Most of the literature about metadata in the cloud actually

---

[8]D. S. Linthicum, *Cloud Computing and SOA Convergence in Your Enterprise, A Step-by-Step Guide* (Reading, MA: Addison-Wesley, 2010).

[9]*Understanding Metadata* (Baltimore, MD: National Information Standards Organization, 2004).

refers to metadata management for information stored in the cloud, about performance issues, replication policies, and the optimal configurations for specific applications[10].

Therefore, the notion of metaservices, as defined by Linthicum, is incomplete for characterizing cloud-based services. Linthicum conceptualized the notion of a static description of a service under metaservices, but did not capture the actionable parts of life cycle management, such as service creation or adding users. For the purposes of this discussion, we retain the terms *metadata* and *metaservice* but under the conceptual view proposed by Rainer Schmidt[11]. According to Schmidt, a service is a three-dimensional entity. The main dimension encompasses a service's *functional properties*. Functional properties such as its API and provided access methods define the main capabilities that a service implements. However, the service capabilities alone might leave its users wanting. This service could have a powerful API and offer high performance. However, users might decide to pass on this offering in favor of another one if the provider cannot offer performance guarantees, or if the service is easy to hack. Another common item about a service is its billing rate. These essential, albeit static parameters about a service constitute the service's *metadata*, which corresponds to the second dimension under Schmidt's nomenclature under a service's nonfunctional properties. This notion of metadata is similar to the existing notion of metadata for databases and roughly corresponds to Linthicum's notion of metaservices.

Furthermore, services must support procedural actions to carry service management: life cycle actions such as service discovery, standing up a service instance, and decommissioning a service instance. A service consumer might be interested in the current service charges since the last billing cycle by invoking the appropriate API method. This API is not part of the functional capability of the service. Instead, it belongs to another service supporting the main service. In other words, this service is a *metaservice*. Note that we are using Linthicum's term under a different meaning. Metaservices comprise the third dimension under Schmidt's nomenclature.

The volume encompassed along its three dimensions defines the *value of a service* to a customer, as shown in Figure 9-2. A service might have a rich and powerful API. However if its performance and security specifications are poor or not disclosed (metadata items), or it has poor or nonexistent mechanisms for QoS redress or capacity scaling (metaservice items), the service can be a poor value or a poor fit for a certain application.

---

[10]A. Verma, S. Venkataraman, et al., *Efficient Metadata Management for Cloud Computing Applications* (Champaign, IL: University of Illinois, 2010), https://www.ideals.illinois.edu/handle/2142/14820; G. Shankaranarayanan and A. Even, "The Metadata Enigma," *Communications of the ACM, 49* (2), February 2006.

[11]R. Schmidt, A. Kieninger, et al., "Meta-Services–Towards Symmetric Service-Oriented Business Ecosystems," *AIFB Proceedings of the Second International Workshop on Enabling Service Business Ecosystems (ESBE'09)*, 2009.

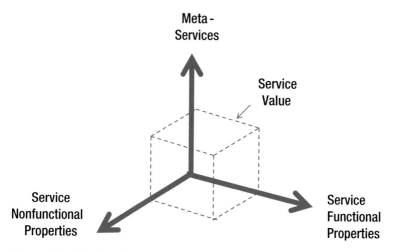

Figure 9-2. *The three dimensions of service value*

The meta-aspects are both relative and recursive: *relative* in the sense that the meta- designation depends on a particular context. A service provider might decide to outsource all or portions of the metafunctions; for instance, relying on a third-party certificate authority for issuing certificates to implement a service's ID management capability. Such a certificate authority provider would be a service provider in its own right, beholden in turn to its particular metadata and metaservices. Hence, someone's metadata might be someone else's main product. Meta-aspects are *recursive* in the sense that a metaservice, in addition to possibly being a service in its own right, can also carry its own metadata and metaservice attributes. The manageability aspects of a service map directly to a cloud service's metadata and metaservice where manageability monitoring is captured under metadata and the manageability control aspects are enforced under a metaservice.

Lack of transparency and the lack of maturity under the metaconcepts of a cloud service limit its value to customers and hence its rate of adoption or applicability. It makes it difficult for solution architects to estimate the security and service level implications of the composite application. From a solution integration perspective, the actions involved in integrating a service component can be as relevant as the detail of the main capabilities rendered.

Services are subject to service level agreements, or SLAs. As noted earlier, the World Wide Web was initially an open framework for humans to access applications over the Internet. The human-machine interactions eventually evolved into web services with machine-to-machine interactions over the Internet. We expect a similar evolution for SLA setup, with labor-intensive negotiations for service setup today giving way to automated processes not too far into the future.

Service binding for a composite application as well as the assessment of a service's SLA is often a manual process today. We can expect increasing levels of automation in the near future, with SLAs becoming machine-readable and service assessment and selection automated following preestablished policies.

Some applications today are monolithic because current analytic tools very provide little insight about global behaviors based on the characteristics of the individual components. The availability of metadata will allow making predictable QoS assessments for a whole application, based on the analysis of the metadata of the service components. The transparency brought up by metadata will make it easier to build IT applications with best-of-breed service components (servicelets) in a way that will be easier to refactor as business conditions change; for instance, implementing scalable performance and incorporating security procedures as needed. It will be possible to fine-tune the delivered QoS through the manipulation of the individual servicelets. The assumption is that the means will exist to estimate the delivered QoS in a provable way; that is, through the application of mathematical formulas using servicelet metadata.

As an example, a solution architect for a provider might determine that to reach the advertised QoS, the back-end storage availability needs an increase from 98 percent to 99 percent. An in-house solution might require reengineering the storage subsystem in the company-owned datacenter.

A more agile, service-oriented solution might involve leasing additional storage capacity, perhaps from another storage provider, and deploying a mirror copy of the data, or perhaps switching to another provider altogether with a different and more stringent QoS profile. The offline analysis of the metadata and the metaservice specifications for candidate services can yield a useful assessment of the future performance of the candidate services.

In principle, this process is not much different from building a portfolio of investments in finance with a target set of behaviors by integrating a set of instruments with desired characteristics and aided by the services of ratings companies. A financial advisor is an example of a service provider who makes a living dealing with metadata management, information about fund portfolios. The different funds in an advisor's portfolio represent downstream servicelets. Today, most of these funds are managed manually, by poring over fund prospects (metadata). Tools exist to automate at least some of the repetitive tasks of portfolio evaluation, effectively defining a service network relationship.

Automated metadata management is a function of technology maturity. We can expect less human intervention in the future, and automated machine-to-machine negotiations to become more prevalent, following the pattern of human-to-human to human-to-machine to machine-to-machine interactions associated with technology evolution. The expectation is that negotiations that used to require human-to-human interactions between service providers and consumers with lengthy and protracted negotiations taking months to close will morph into humans interacting with portals, with time constants shrinking to days, and eventually machine-to-machine, with transactions associated with building composite applications closed in a matter of minutes.

This new environment will foster the creation of new classes of service providers, more horizontally focused in a rich and agile service-oriented application environment. Metadata is a highly valuable commodity that has allowed the largest CSPs in the world to thrive. Personal information, or information generated by individuals, is also metadata. Google monetized metadata in its search engine through ad placement. Amazon can increase the traffic in its e-commerce sites by leveraging product reviews (metadata) generated by customers. Facebook intersperses ads when displaying friends' information (user metadata) and newsfeeds.

As the cloud market matures, we can expect increasing interoperability. An early example is the Eucalyptus environment, which can manage either Eucalyptus or Amazon EC2 IaaS instances using the Amazon Web Services (AWS) API[12]. Eucalyptus, after its acquisition by Hewlett-Packard, is being reengineered to support multiple environments including OpenStack and VMware ESX. In a mature market, a service's metaproperties (metadata plus metaservices) will become a differentiating factor for users considering selection among a bevy of functionally similar offerings.

The benefits to date from monetizing this metadata in consumer space have been highly asymmetric. Users might benefit from a number of "free" services and applications. However, the recurring revenue the CSP derives from the use of this metadata is larger, allowing the CSP to pay for infrastructure and services and still make a tidy profit. The aggregate value of the metadata store is probably several times the yearly revenue. Very likely, consumers voluntarily surrender metadata during service sign-up and companies extract it through data mining of proprietary or public records in addition to collecting metadata from sales and customer service operations. The consumer rarely gets direct compensation for the value of this information. Our prediction is that this degree of asymmetry will diminish slightly as corporations with high financial stakes become consumers for service metaproperties and assert their needs. These corporate customers will be involved to ensure the metaproperty offerings align with their business goals.

The business model for service metaproperty providers will likely be different. Instead of "free" services, corporate customers will treat service metaproperty providers like any other service provider, subject to an SLA. The aggregate value of service metadata and metaservice revenue in an evolved service economy will likely be much larger than the value of personal metadata. There are fewer companies than there are individual users, but the value of a single company's metadata could run into the hundreds of billions, if not trillions, of dollars. It would appear that the service metadata of a customer company's composite application using only publicly available servicelets might be public information, but it is not. The particular parameters of a service instance and service orchestration information can provide insight into the company's most guarded secrets. In view of that, corporate customers will demand that this information be kept confidential as a condition to engage in business. If only because of their financial might, corporate service consumers carry more weight than individual consumers to make sure service providers act according to their interests.

Metaservices are services on their own right and therefore do not carry any special distinction as a service. That said, metaservices and metadata management also constitute a highly specialized type of service, and following a trend toward specialization seen in other industries as they mature, we can expect a number of CSPs to rise to the occasion and make a business of providing these services. These companies can sell trusted and curated metaservices and service metadata trust in the same way that a company like Verisign provides trust certificates.

---

[12]"Eucalyptus (software)," *Wikipedia,* https://en.wikipedia.org/wiki/Eucalyptus_(software), 2016.

A valuable capability that service metaproperties will enable is common manageability processes for composite applications. If we go back to Figure 6-3, although a service might be bound to more than one requester, each application instance is essentially a tree of contributing services, with each service made up of lower level services, following the layers in Figure 8-2. For CSPs, the leaves of the application tree usually end up in a physical server from some HaaS provider, internal or external. The service profile for a given application, abstracted in Figure 9-3, can be very dynamic. The application could bind to subordinate services in real time depending on operational demands from customers: More service instances can be added for additional performance, or a service might fail over to a functionally identical service offering in case of a malfunction in an existing service. Here are some essential considerations to enable service assessment during discovery and enable runtime service management:

- *Service introspection*: Service introspection encompasses more than the properties of the top-level services. In Figure 9-3, the composite application using service S1 might want to ascertain not just the specific properties of S1, but also the properties of the services underneath, in a recursive fashion. There are nuances in discovery capabilities. For instance, S4 might decide to keep the service topology it uses secret for business reasons. S4 can still provide consolidated information that will allow the user of S1 to carry out certain policies: S1 might offer energy metadata for each one of the calls, or rolling energy estimates. In this case, it might be sufficient for S4 to present consolidated energy numbers for the hardware platforms involved in each service call. This brings the next topic.

- *A capability at one level becomes a policy at the next level up*: The customer for S1 might impose specific restrictions, such as specifying instances of S3 that do not contain a competitor's offerings, or in the case of geographic restrictions, specifying that the service resources be located in a certain location. For power management, processor power usage can be controlled using the processor running average power limit (RAPL) mechanism. S1 is too high in the abstraction chain to specify RAPL settings for the CPUs running S7, S8, and S9. However, it can issue policies to S4 specifying that the application be run only during the wee hours of the morning to minimize energy usage.

- *Distributed management*: It is possible to carry certain policies cooperatively across all services involved. For example, to compute energy consumption, S1 is not required to interrogate every service in the tree. It suffices to interrogate S2, S3, and S4. S4 totals S5 and S6, and S6 accumulates S7, S8, and S9. Likewise, for service billing, S1 charges its customers the cost of using S2, S3, and S4 plus its profit margin.

In general, a service provider is responsible for managing the QoS for all subordinate services, and for meeting its own SLA. It also decides the granularity of the management policies: Some service providers might decide to present a single, all-encompassing bill, whereas others might decide to use a la carte pricing. The choices are situational. Breaking energy out as a separate item might be useful for high-performance computing where energy use is a prime consideration. This enables the consumer to procure energy separately if need be.

Composite application

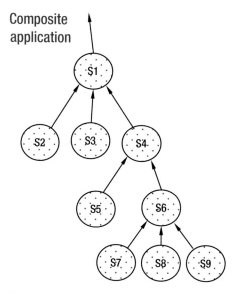

Figure 9-3. *Composite application architecture*

More often than not, the service metaproperties for most service offerings today are incomplete, and in many cases do not properly document the actual capabilities of the service offering. This is the origin of the common complaint that cloud disintermediation brings poorer QoS. This need not be the case. Because of economies of scale and concentrated expertise on the part of providers, we can expect third-party servicelets to be a better performing alternative than the in-house alternative. As reluctant as service consumers might be to acknowledge this fact, if this were not true, the cloud would not have taken off. As the industry matures, metaproperties will become more and more of a differentiator for a service offering. We can expect service providers to pay more attention to metaproperties as they become a make-or-break differentiator in the cloud and ultimately will determine the providers' bottom line.

Smart Cities and the Internet of Things

In 2008, for the first time in history, over half of the world's population lived in urban areas. By 2050, the United Nations projects that two thirds of the world's 9.7 billion people will live in cities[13]. Population growth pressures on municipal infrastructure in addition to resource constraints have led to new conceptualizations and policy prescriptions that place the city at the core for developing innovative solutions to make the world a better place. The smart city concept represents a compelling platform for IT-enabled service innovation and adoption. It offers a view of the city where service providers use IT to engage with citizens to improve the quality of life while innovating and optimizing city operations. Some researchers expect the number of smart cities to increase from 21 in 2013 to more than 88 in 2025, with 31 in Europe, 25 in the Americas, and 32 in the Asia-Pacific region[14]. By 2020, forecasts for the global market for smart urban services will exceed US$400 billion per year[15]. Frost & Sullivan forecasts a US$1.5 trillion global market opportunity in smart city energy, transportation, health care, building, infrastructure, and governance[16].

The smart cities concept provides a laboratory for innovation on how information technologies can improve the quality of life while optimizing the city operations. With the decaying of postindustrial urban centers and the rapid population growth in emerging economies, there is intense pressure to redesign existing cities and to design new cities from the ground up to become green and efficient by providing transportation systems, energy grids, and public services that will enable the livelihood of city dwellers. The emerging IoT technologies, abetted by the cloud, are fundamental for the development of smart cities. Correspondingly, we believe smart cities represent the most important market for IoT applications. An IoT integrated cloud-oriented architecture under a service framework, consisting of intelligent networks, software, sensors, human interfaces, and data analytics, is essential for value creation. IoT smart-connected products and the services they provision will become essential for the future development of smart cities[17].

What Makes a City Smart?

The smart city concept is not new. For more than 100 years, urban planners and engineers have pursued the goal to make city design and management more scientific[18]. Some researchers view the smart city concept as an outgrowth of the late 1990s smart

[13]M. Totty, "Five Cities That Are Leading the Way in Urban Innovation," *The Wall Street Journal*, April 21, 2016.
[14]L. Arrowsmith, "Smart Cities: Business Models, Technologies, and Existing Projects," Information Technology Service research report (IHS Technology, May 30, 2014).
[15]S. Singh, "Smart Cities: A $1.5 Trillion Market Opportunity," *Forbes*, http://www.forbes.com/sites/sarwantsingh/2014/06/19/smart-cities-a-1-5-trillion-market-opportunity/, June 19, 2014.
[16]Frost & Sullivan, *Strategic Opportunity Analysis of the Global Smart City Market* (New York, NY: Frost & Sullivan, August 2013).
[17]G. Falconer and S. Mitchell, *Smart City Framework: A Systematic Process for Enabling Smart + Connected Communities* (Executive Report, Cisco Internet Solutions Group, 2012). http://www.cisco. com/web/about/ac79/docs/ps/motm/Smart-City-Framework.pdf
[18]P. Hall, *Cities of Tomorrow: An Intellectual History of Urban Planning and Design in the Twentieth Century*, 3rd ed. (Malden, MA: Wiley-Blackwell, 2002).

growth movement that advocated policies for urban growth management[19]. Smart growth is urban planning that concentrates growth in urban centers to reduce sprawl by increasing urban density, public transit, walking, and bicycle use. Smart cities might address such issues, but the primary orientation is to connect physical, social, business, and government infrastructure with ICT innovations to leverage the collective intelligence of the city. Representative smart city definitions include the following:

- The *use of smart computing technologies* to make the critical infrastructure components and services of a city—which include city administration, education, health care, public safety, real estate, transportation, and utilities—more intelligent, interconnected, and efficient[20,21].

- A city combining *ICT and Web 2.0 infrastructure with other organizational design and planning efforts* to dematerialize and speed up bureaucratic processes and help to identify new, innovative solutions to city management complexity, to improve sustainability and livability[22].

- The *application of complex information systems* to integrate the operation of urban infrastructure and services such as buildings, transportation, electrical and water distribution, and public safety[23].

- A city may be called *smart* when investments in human and social capital and traditional (transport) and modern (ICT) communication infrastructure fuel sustainable economic growth and a high quality of life, with a wise management of natural resources through participatory government[24].

- Smart cities are *complex ecosystems composed of heterogeneous interconnected networks of enabled things* providing sensing and actuating facilities such as traffic sensors, security cameras, traffic lights, citizens' smart phones, and facilities for management and organization[25].

---

[19]D. Bollier, *How Smart Growth Can Stop Sprawl* (Washington, DC: Essential Books, 1998).

[20]J. Hartley, "Innovation in Governance and Public Services: Past and Present," *Public Money & Management, 25* (1), 27–34, 2005.

[21]D. Washburn, U. Sindhu, S. Balaouras, R. Dines, N. Hayes, and L. Nelson, "Helping CIOs Understand Smart City Initiatives," *Growth, 17,* 2009.

[22]D. Toppeta, *The Smart City Vision: How Innovation and ICT Can Build Smart Livable Sustainable Cities* (Milan, Italy: Think: The Innovation Knowledge Foundation, 2010).

[23]C. Harrison and I. Donnelly, "A Theory of Smart Cities," *Proceedings of the 55th Annual Meeting of the ISSS-2011, 55* (1), 2011.

[24]H. Schaffers, N. Komninos, M. Pallot, B. Trousse, M. Nilsson, and A. Oliveira, "Smart Cities and the Future Internet: Towards Cooperation Frameworks for Open Innovation," *Future Internet Assembly*, 431–446, 2011.

[25]G. Merlino, D. Bruneo, F. Longo, A. Puliafito, and S. Distefano, "Software Defined Cities: A Novel Paradigm for Smart Cities through IoT Clouds," In *Ubiquitous Intelligence and Computing and 2015 IEEE 12th International Conference on Autonomic and Trusted Computing and 2015 IEEE 15th International Conference on Scalable Computing and Communications and Its Associated Workshops (UIC-ATC-ScalCom)*, 909–916, 2015.

The definitions share a common theme of combining ICT with investments in human and social capital and modern urban infrastructure and services to create sustainable economic growth and a high quality of life for citizens. The Merlino et al. definition specifically defines smart cities as complex ecosystems of IoT infrastructure that facilitate the management of the smart city applications and capabilities. This definition exemplifies the dominant approach to smart city development today. Smart cities use ICT to sense, analyze, and integrate the key information of core systems in running cities. A smart city can make intelligent responses to different kinds of needs, including daily livelihood, environmental protection, public safety, city services, and industrial and commercial activities. Similarly, smart can describe cities that have deployed, or are currently piloting, the integration of ICT solutions across three or more different functional areas of a city.

The functional areas include mobile, transport, energy, water, sustainability, physical infrastructure, governance, safety, and security. The goal of smart cities is to be more effective and efficient at handling resources and providing services to citizens. For older cities, smart city development includes the rethinking and rebuilding of urban infrastructure, utilities, and services and adding technology-based, especially smart system-based applications. Therefore a city may be deemed smart when investments in human and social capital, physical infrastructure, and city services are integrated with ICT services to drive innovative approaches to sustainable economic growth, responsible stewardship of natural resources, and participatory governance to create a high quality of life[26].

Numerous benefits develop from the applications of ICT in smart cities. These benefits include the following:

- Improving the utilization of existing infrastructure capacity to reduce the need for new construction, yet increase capacity.

- Reducing resource consumption, especially water and energy, and reducing CO_2 emissions.

- Developing new services for citizens such as real-time transportation guidance and e-government services.

- Monitoring energy, water, and transportation demand to improve capabilities to manage peak service demand.

Recent technological advances have accelerated the development of the smart city. The pervasiveness of digital sensors and digital control systems for the management of urban infrastructure have enabled applications such as traffic sensors, building management systems, and digital utility meters. High-speed fixed and wireless networks connect sensors and smart systems that allow real-time information analysis to improve operational performance. Smart phones, the semantic web, cloud computing, and IoT promote real-world interfaces and applications[27], and embedding the latest advances in

---

[26]V. Albino, U. Berardi, and R. M. Dangelico, "Smart Cities: Definitions, Dimensions, Performance, and Initiatives," *Journal of Urban Technology, 21,* 2014.
[27]A. Gyrard and M. Serrano, "A Unified Semantic Engine for Internet of Things and Smart Cities: From Sensor Data to End-Users Applications," *2015 IEEE International Conference on Data Science and Data Intensive Systems,* 718–725, 2015.

mobile and pervasive computing, wireless networks, middleware, and agent technologies into the physical spaces of the city[28].

Smart City Development

Innovation and global competition are driving the development priorities of cities. The European Commission identified three priorities for a social cohesion policy to drive the development of smart city solutions[29]:

1. *Competitive Policy* to attain competitiveness in research, innovation, and the upgrading of skills to support the development of the knowledge economy.

2. *Labor Market Policy* to sustain employment, facilitate social cohesion, and reduce poverty.

3. *Sustainable Development Policy* for smart land use, reducing water use, reducing greenhouse gases emissions, and improving energy efficiency.

The prioritization provides strategic guidance to city officials to develop strategies and initiatives to support the development and implementation of smart city business models. Similar approaches are underway in Asia and the Americas, typically in the form of public-private partnership (PPP) initiatives.

Smart city business models are unique for each city depending on needs, resources, citizen expectations, and development goals. However, most smart cities depend on a technology platform that consists of[30]:

1. *High-capacity broadband infrastructure* that combines cable, optical fiber, and wireless networks.

2. *Physical infrastructure* augmented with embedded systems, smart devices, sensors, and actuators for real-time information processing.

3. *Applications* to enable real-time communications and collaboration to enable engagement between citizens, institutions, and businesses.

A primary benefit of smart cities is the initiation of large-scale participatory innovation processes that can enable more effective and efficient government and a

[28]J. Rico, J. Sancho, A. Díaz, J. González, P. Sánchez, B. Alvarez, L. Cardona, and C. Ramis, "Low Power Wireless Sensor Networks: Secure Applications and Remote Distribution of FW Updates with Key Management on WSN." In *Trusted Computing for Embedded Systems*, 71–111 (New York, NY: Springer, 2015).
[29]H. Schaffers, N. Komninos, M. Pallot, B. Trousse, M. Nilsson, and A. Oliveira, "Smart Cities and the Future Internet: Towards Cooperation Frameworks for Open Innovation," *Future Internet Assembly*, 431–446, 2011.
[30]J. Lee, M. Hancock, and M.-C. Hu, "Towards an Effective Framework for Building Smart Cities: Lessons from Seoul and San Francisco," *Technological Forecasting & Social Change, 89*, 80–99, 2014.

higher quality of life for the public. Smart cities engage relevant stakeholders to develop innovation ecosystems. Schaffers et al, indicated that ecosystem frameworks typically emphasize three initiatives[29]:

1. *Business innovation economy* includes clusters for new business incubators, technology parks, universities, manufacturing, services, health care, tourism, and enabling infrastructure to include seaports, rail hubs, airports, and financial districts.

2. *City infrastructure and utilities* initiatives to provide services to citizens such as smart communication networks, smart grid networks, alternative energy, smart water management, environmental monitoring, real-time alerts, safety, smart transport, personal mobility, and parking.

3. *City governance* initiatives such as e-government services, engagement with citizens, and monitoring and measurement for evidence-based governance.

Smart City Frameworks

In arriving at a detailed framework model of a smart city, it is useful to categorize its components. IT infrastructure and applications are essential for smart cities. Smart city initiatives apply smart computing technologies to critical infrastructure components and services. The goal is to reduce the time between insight and action, enabling citizens at every level to collaborate and act with confidence. We address three of the most common frameworks used by smart city developers: the Technology, People, and Institutions Framework, the Smart City Initiatives Framework, and the IBM Smarter Cities Framework.

Technology, People, and Institutions Framework

This framework focuses on the core components of a smart city[31] and comprises technology, factors, and institutional factors.

- *Technology factors* include IT infrastructure and applications, prerequisites for enabling user engagement, and willingness to collaborate and cooperate among citizens and public and private organizations to energize a smart city.

- *Human factors* comprise human infrastructure, human capital, and education for urban development. Smart, committed, and engaged people are critical for the success of smart cities.

---

[31]T. Nam and T. Pardo, "Conceptualizing Smart City with Dimensions of Technology, People, and Institutions," *Proceedings of the 12th Annual International Conference on Digital Government Research: Digital Government in Challenging Times*, ACM, 282–291, 2011.

- *Institutional factors* encompass smart governance and policymaking for the design and implementation of smart city initiatives. Smart governance is a cornerstone of the smart city where smart city ecosystem actors engage in service development and use including accommodating human factors relevant to the adoption of new technologies.

The Smart City Initiatives Framework

This framework includes management and organization, technology, governance, policy context, people and communities, economy, infrastructure, and the natural environment[32].

- *Management and organization*: Smart city initiatives leverage intensive use of ICT and require strong management and organizational capabilities.

- *Technology*: Smart computing and IoT technologies integrated with city infrastructure and services are at the core of the smart city concept. They are the key drivers of smart city initiatives.

- *Governance*: Smart city projects involve multiple stakeholders requiring innovative and effective governance in terms of laws, administrative rules, judicial rulings, and practices that prescribe and constrain government activity.

- *Policy context*: Smart cities involve the interaction of technology with political and institutional components. Policy creates conditions that enable urban development.

- *People and communities*: Smart city projects affect citizens. The goal is to foster more informed, educated, and participatory citizens. To that end, smart city initiatives enable citizens, and their communities, to become engaged users and participate in the governance and management of the city.

- *Economy*: A core purpose of a smart city is to foster innovation and to increase economic competitiveness. Initiatives include smart economy, smart people, smart governance, smart mobility, smart environment, and smart living. Smart ICT systems are central to that capability.

- *Infrastructure*: ICT infrastructure and its integration with physical infrastructure is essential to the development of the smart city. Sensors, smart systems, wireless mobile, and Wi-Fi networks enable the development of service-oriented ICT systems.

---

[32]H. Chourabi, C. Nam, S. Walker, J. Gil-Garcia, S. Mellouli, T. Pardo, and H. Scholl, "Understanding Smart Cities: An Integrative Framework," In *Proceedings of the 2012 Hawaii International Conference on System Science (HICSS-45)*, 2012.

- *Environment*: Smart cities are about environmental sustainability. ICT applications enable the effective management of natural resources such as water, waste water, energy, land use, and green spaces.

IBM Smarter Cities Framework

The IBM *Smarter Cities framework*[33] consists of three dimensions: planning and management, infrastructure, and people, with subcategories as presented here.

- *Planning and management*: The goal for smarter city planning and management is to enable a city to realize its full developmental potential while maintaining efficient day-to-day operations. Insights from data analytics inform solutions that can help a city remain vibrant and safe for citizens and businesses.

  a. *Public safety.* Increasing public safety is one of the quickest methods to produce quantifiable results and shape public opinion. Public safety agencies can gather and analyze data for traffic, weather, crime, health matters, security breaches, hazardous materials, fires, potential disasters, and so on, and deliver actionable information to their stakeholders in near real time. This data informs governmental activities such as emergency management and law enforcement. Capabilities such as big data analytics, data visualization, and real-time collaboration and coordination enable better planning, operations, and postactivity assessment.

  b. *Government and agency administration.* The goal is to reorient government policies to guide sustainable smart growth that will meet the needs of citizens and business.

  c. *City planning and operations.* Smarter cities use smart systems and data analytics to design, implement, and manage operations. The goal is to maintain efficient day-to-day operations.

  d. *Smarter buildings.* Commercial and residential buildings use a third of global energy. In North America, buildings consume approximately 72 percent of electricity, account for 12 percent of water use, and generate 60 percent of nonindustrial waste. By 2025, buildings will consume more energy than the transportation and industrial sectors combined. Smart buildings with smart sensors

---

[33]IBM, *IBM Smarter Cities: Creating Opportunities through Leadership and Innovation* (Armonk, NY: IBM Corporation, 2014). http://www.ibm.com/smarterplanet/us/en/smarter_cities/overview/index.html

and control systems can measure, sense, and assess the condition of critical building systems such as HVAC, energy use and demand response, elevators, lighting, fire, elevators, air quality, water provision and use, security and access control, as well as monitor the operations of the computer networks and applications.

- *Infrastructure*: Infrastructure services are fundamental for making a city livable in terms of both necessities and comforts for citizens and businesses.

    a. *Energy.* The development of smart grids using digital sensors, advanced ICT networks, and big data analytics can help utilities more effectively manage supply and demand and enable more efficient energy use through intelligent distribution management systems.

    b. *Water.* Smarter water management adopts a holistic view of water and waste water systems that integrates and visualizes data on consumption, quality, flow, and pressure. Sensors embedded throughout the water sources and infrastructure provide for big data analytics-driven solutions for the real-time tracking and reporting of conditions and system-wide water management.

    c. *Transportation.* For most cities, it is not possible to build new roadways, rail systems, or ports. However, capacity can be increased by embedding sensors and location technology into the transportation infrastructure and using cloud-based real-time analytics to reduce congestion and transport times. The goal is the development of an intelligent transportation system across all modes of transport.

- *People.* Smarter cities support the needs of each citizen within the service ecosystem through social programs, health care, and education.

    a. *Social programs.* Solutions in this space make it easier for citizens to access social programs for better life outcomes and ensure that service organizations can deliver effective citizen-centered services with better results. Programs include social assistance, family services, employment services, and disability management.

    b. *Health care.* In 2010, 30 percent of all computer data worldwide was medical images not connected to a smart system. The goal for smarter health care is to enable better diagnoses, help professionals treat illness, find ways to cure disease, and enable individuals to make smarter choices about their health and care.

    c.   *Education.* Smarter education analytics applications can provide integrated K–20 solutions, preschool to graduate degree, to support teaching as well as learning outside the classroom. The challenge is monitoring student performance and developing innovative teaching methods to improve learning outcomes.

Although the IBM Smarter Cities Framework is the most comprehensive in terms of scope and detail, all of the frameworks are conceptually similar. As the field moves forward, we will likely see a deepening of the conceptual dimensions. When the smart city concept first emerged, the IoT was not yet technologically feasible. Now that smart sensors, devices, and networks are realities, the city has the possibility of achieving its smart potential. The work of integrating the theoretical and conceptual framework for the smart city is still in flux. There are common elements in the proposed frameworks. The word *smart* is commonly associated with *technology, digital, intelligent, ICT,* and *big data analytics.* The definitions just presented indicate that smart cities involve an integration of human capital, physical infrastructure, and ICT. The smart cities frameworks are in the mainstream of this conceptualization.

Smart Cities and the Internet of Things

Smart cities make use IT to beneficially transform operations, work, and the life of citizens. The IoT represents an integrated smart system architecture of sensors, software, networks, and corresponding interfaces that hold the promise to do just that. IoT systems provide real-time awareness and integrate people, processes, and knowledge to enable collective intelligence for smart decision making.

Smart City Systems

To be effective, smart systems need to be instrumented, interconnected, and intelligent. Instrumentation enables the collection of timely high-quality data through embedded sensors that communicate over wireless or wired networks. For example, devices such as smart meters for gas, electricity, and water continually monitor the supply and demand for these utilities. Interconnection creates the communications among data, systems, and people. Recently major cloud, network, and device providers such as AWS, Google, IBM, Cisco, AT&T, Dell, Intel, GE, Microsoft, Oracle, Siemens, Qualcomm, Huawei, Salesforce, and Samsung have announced plans to support IoT[34]. Forecasts indicate that more than 50 billion smart things and 5 billion people will connect to the Internet by 2020[35]. That works out to 300,000 new *things* connected to the Internet every hour. The interconnections among people, objects, and systems across the framework of the city will enable new ways to gather, share, and act on information.

---

[34]B. Butler, "Most Powerful Internet of Things Companies," *NetworkWorld,* http://www.networkworld.com/article/2287045/wi-fi/wireless-153629-10-most-powerful-internet-of-things-companies.html#slide1, April 4, 2016.
[35]N. Earle, "50 Billion Things, Coming to a Cloud Near You," *Cisco: The Platform,* http://blogs.cisco.com/news/50-billion-things-coming-to-a-cloud-near-you, June 10, 2015.

Intelligence in the form of new computing models, algorithms, and advanced analytics will enable better decisions and outcomes for cities and their citizens. Smart connected objects will generate tremendous amounts of useful data to enable the development, deployment, and use of smart products and services. For example, statistical models can predict traffic flows, energy and water supply and demand, educational performance, safety problems and solutions, and the efficacy of medical treatments to enable better outcomes and lower costs.

IoT Network Requirements

The emerging smart city concept has many definitions and approaches, as we have reviewed. However, all smart cities have at their core a highly capable ICT system with a network of sensors, wired and wireless broadband connectivity, and advanced data analytics that enable the intelligent, efficient, and environmentally friendly services for citizens. The following requirements are essential for the integration of smart systems with IoT-based smart products and services in a smart city context.

- *Sensors*: Sensors are essential components for IoT-based smart products. The amount of data these sensors create is large. IoT devices will communicate over the regular communication channels such as cellular or Wi-Fi. The collective bandwidth available for these devices to send the data is a major limiting factor. One approach to deal with this is to equip end-node sensors with processing capability to analyze, interpret, and select data for interpretation at the end node. Data exceptions and statistical information pass on to the cloud[36].

- *Security*: A smart city network with a large number of end nodes is subject to cyberattack, which can critically affect smart city infrastructure such as dams, electricity grid, bridges, airports, and water supplies. Security is required at four levels: secure storage for sensor data, secure in-memory databases, secure communication, and secure execution environment. Secure sensor data will enable secure analytics, interpretation, and secure actuation of the critical parts of the infrastructure. An authentication mechanism for secure access by authorized users is required for the right kind of access.

---

[36]D. Gunduz, K. Stamatiou, N. Michelusi, and M. Zorzi, "Designing Intelligent Energy Harvesting Communication Systems," *IEEE Communications Magazine, 52* (1), 210–216, 2014.

- *Fault tolerance/fail safe*: Key infrastructure elements require fault tolerance and fail-safe capability in the event of a power failure or disaster. Battery backup is essential to ensure the sensing function would continue for some length of time. Second, critical infrastructure needs to include redundancies to ensure the IoT system can continue to operate in adverse conditions. Intrusion and theft deterrence is essential to facilitate asset recovery or decommissioning to ensure that data is secure and malware is not introduced to the wider system[37].

- *Energy harvesting*: Many smart city devices are in locations where power connections are not available. Running thousands of devices on batteries is not a viable option. In such environments, smart sensors and actuators must be embedded with energy harvesting mechanisms that allow the devices to operate for 10, 15, or even 20 years without human intervention Energy can be harvested from photovoltaic solar cells and, in some instances, ambient sources[36].

- *Connectivity*: The IoT network provides for slow as well as fast sensors. For closed-circuit television security and traffic systems such as those in major cities, it is important that most of the video analytics processing occur in the camera itself. Data can then be available for real-time streaming and network viewing. For example, when there is no traffic problem, there is nothing to communicate to the cloud. In the event of an accident, the smart solution can allow streaming and remote viewing of video data by city emergency services.

- *Manageability*: Because a large number of smart devices and sensors can be widely placed geographically at large distances, the IoT network must incorporate means to allow remote management of these devices. This could include remote delivery of OS patches, profiles, new analytics algorithms, and key management of parameters. For example, a presidential visit to a city might require remote management of traffic lights, so the entourage may pass smoothly through the city[38].

---

[37]Y. Peng, Q. Song, Y. Yu, and F. Wang, "Fault-Tolerant Routing Mechanism Based on Network Coding in Wireless Mesh Networks," *Journal of Network and Computer Applications, 37,* 259–272, 2014.

[38]M. Makkes, R. Cushing, A. Oprescu, R. Koning, P. Grosso, R. Meijer, and C. de Laat, "Smart Cyber Infrastructure for Big Data Processing," *2014 IEEE Optical Fiber Communications Conference and Exhibition,* 1–3, 2014.

- *Mesh-networked devices*: IoT devices need to be able to communicate with each other without going to the back end, share the data among end nodes, and communicate with other devices in the vicinity for group processing. For example, a specific end node might sense a chemical spill in one area, and then interrogate nearby nodes to see if the other nodes are sensing the same phenomenon. The decision making through combined intelligence of multiple nodes can help in making better decisions.

- *Open APIs for citizens to enable service creation*: Smart cities can generate large numbers of data sets from networks of devices and sensors. Much of this data is stored and not analyzed. The smart city network should allow access to common sharable data and becomes a platform for the development of innovative applications. For example, utility companies can use the data to gain accurate information on electricity, water, and gas usage to improve resource planning. Public transportation providers can use data on arrival, departures, level of utilization, and loading to model more efficient routing. Citizens can plan trips and transportation mode choice based on desired activities and locations[39].

- *Back-end or cloud storage*: This is where data and statistics are stored, analyzed, and postprocessed to enable insights over time for decision making. For example, a range of weather data (temperature, pressure, humidity, etc.) coming from a large number of edge devices collected over time can help predict microclimates in specific areas of the city.

- *Sensor network communication*: IoT devices use several methods of communication. Some might require 3G or 4G wireless networks. Smart meters and home devices might need Z-Wave or ZigBee, and some might require Wi-Fi, BLE, or 6LoWPAN depending on the type of sensors and IoT devices used in the framework[40].

IoT Systems Architecture

In countries with a strong private sector, most technology expertise also resides in the private sector. By default, governments delegate most of the infrastructure services and even the delivery of services to private entities. These services are available as mostly unregulated services, such as services from media companies, or as regulated monopolies

[39]M. Foulonneau, S. Turki, G. Vidou, and S. Martin, "Open Data in Service Design," *Electronic Journal of e-Government, 12* (2), 2014.
[40]J. Espina, T. Falck, A. Panousopoulou, L. Schmitt, O. Mülhens, and G. Yang, "Network Topologies, Communication Protocols, and Standards," *2014 IEEE Body Sensor Networks Conference*, 189–236, 2014.

or oligopolies, such as power utilities, cable and broadband services. Occasionally services are integrated through public private partnerships, such as traffic enforcement cameras.

On the left side of Figure 9-4, we see some of the levels from the cloud macroarchitecture model. We also see a number of servicelet examples and their approximate location in the macroarchitecture universe. IoT sensors and actuators are close to the bottom, at the hardware level. Mobile devices most consumers carry today are essentially roaming computers studded with sensors. As such, mobile devices appear at multiple levels in the macroarchitecture.

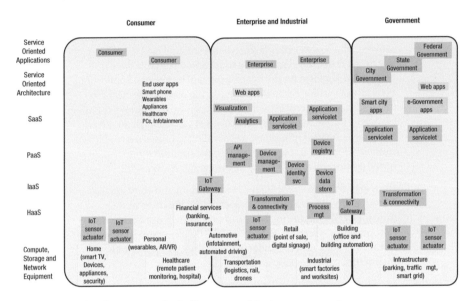

Figure 9-4. *Cloud ecosystem, including smart cities in government space*

Applications that consumers use, for instance, the sprinkler controller described in Chapter 8, appear at the top under service-oriented applications. However mobile devices are also studded with sensors, such as atmospheric pressure, temperature, GPS locators and accelerometers, and therefore these sensors appear at the hardware level near the bottom. These devices can also be recruited to provide intermediary services, such as relay stations for implementing a mesh network, in which case they may also be represented in the mid-region. Bain & Co. identified a number of ecosystem segments for IoT sensors[41]. Any other sensor types not in the list are captured as IoT sensors and actuators in all of the IoT segments.

---

[41]A. Bosche, D. Crawford et al., Defining the Battlegrounds of the Internet of Things, white paper, April 27, 2016, http://www.bain.com/publications/articles/defining-the-battle-grounds-of-the-internet-of-things.aspx

An IoT system integrates information from vast arrays of sensors. This information needs structuring for existing networks, screened to ensure integrity and security, processed and stored so it becomes usable to the eventual consumers. IoT sensors are discrete motes providing information about pressure, temperature, activity, sound or video feeds, or specific events such as a door opening. These sensors can be self-standing such as street video feeds, automated weather stations, or retrofits on legacy equipment. Newer equipment will likely have embedded sensors. Local processors, hubs sitting at the edge of the sensor network, do the initial processing (see Figure 9-4). A traffic camera monitoring a road crossing uploads only events where there has been a red light violation[42]. Some of the pre-processing can be done within the device itself assuming sufficient computational resources. Otherwise a process management or a transformation and connectivity servicelet carries these computations. The Cloud Standards Customer Council defines some of these servicelets[43]. For simplicity, Figure 9-4 does not capture the links representing service relationships between servicelets, such as those shown in Figures 8-13 or 8-16.

Data from the sensors and sensor hubs is untrusted by default. Gateway computers take this information and screen it to make sure it has not been corrupted or tampered with. Qualified data is forwarded to a datacenter for consumption. Today this process takes place within a single company or governmental entity. However, for scalability purposes, these tasks can be delegated to service providers under contract. For maximum scalability and interoperability across multiple stakeholders and organizations, the implementation protocols need to be industry standard open protocols to the extent possible.

Datacenters carry out extensive processing on the aggregated and sanitized sensor data using the visualization, analytics or application servicelets shown in Figure 9-4. Data analysis, storage in databases, or aggregation and preparation for real-time consumption are typical processes. Public API services (see Table 9-1) allow exporting applications to the cloud through web services-based APIs[44]. These APIs are available, in turn, for applications in other organizations. The resulting functionality becomes consumable by a variety of client PCs, tablets, and mobile smart devices. Under this architecture, sensor data incorporates into a service network. The owner of the data and the owner of the infrastructure could be different entities. This architecture places no particular restrictions on ownership, which is assigned based on technical or business considerations.

---

[42]Y. Yoon and J. Chun, "Tracking Model for Abnormal Behavior from Multiple Network CCTV Using the Kalman Filter," In *Computer Science and Its Applications*, 933–939 (Berlin, Germany: Springer, 2015).

[43]Cloud Customer Architecture for IoT, Cloud Standards Customer Council (2016), www.cloud-council.org/deliverables/CSCC-Cloud-Customer-Architecture-for-IoT.pdf

[44]A. Bridgwater, "Intel Mashery: How to Manage an API," *Forbes*, http://www.forbes.com/sites/adrianbridgwater/2015/02/12/intel-mashery-how-to-manage-an-api/#4de7bc0d75fa, February 12, 2015.

Table 9-1. *IoT Systems and Implementation Protocols*

IoT System	Implementation Protocol
Corporate, government, consumers	Web services, REST application access control
Application APIs	Manageability: OMA DM, TR-069, web configuration, IPMI, Redfish
Cloud datacenters	Runtime environment: Java, Lua, OSGI, Mashery
Gateways	Security: Open SSL library, certificate management, secure boot, encrypted storage
Sensor hubs and sensors	Connectivity: ZigBee, Z-Wave, cellular 2G/3G/4G, Bluetooth, serial, USB, VPN, Wi-Fi, MQTT

Smart City Strategy Development

The smart city service ecosystem includes many actors, which include citizens, politicians, city planners, IT network providers, software companies, smart device and service providers, research firms, and academicians, all investing time and other resources to fulfill their vision of a smart city. The convergence of the cloud, inexpensive bandwidth, wireless networks, smart phones with social and information apps, and the consumerization of IT at work and home as covered in Chapter 8, coupled with the rise of the IoT network concept, is disrupting the old bureaucratic, slow-moving, high-cost, and ineffective city business model[45]. As the IoT and the smart cities trend converge, businesses and cities are already moving forward.

Smart city implementations for smart connected things exist for security systems, automated tollbooths, airline check-in machines, automated teller machines, self-service retail checkout, and smart vending machines. As the technology deploys, the challenge for city and business executives is developing a disruptive ICT-enabled business model. Adding intelligence to old objects and infrastructure or designing new smart systems, smart products, and smart services, although necessary, is not sufficient for disruptive impact or competitive advantage. Technology, to be truly disruptive, must disrupt customer value.

Lubin and Esty studied how managers dealt with disruptive market megatrends issues[46]. The authors researched the total quality management (TQM) and IT megatrends of the 1980s to determine how managers dealt with megatrend scale disruption. Although most managers perceived that their decisions could profoundly affect the future competitiveness or even survival of their organizations, they did not develop a strategic vision or plan to embrace the emerging market disruption to their advantage. After assessing successful companies, they identified four distinct stages for

[45]E. Castro-Leon, "The Consumerization in the IT Ecosystem," *IEEE IT Professional, 16*, 20–27, 2014.
[46]D. Lubin and D. Esty, "The Sustainability Imperative," *Harvard Business Review, 88* (5), 42–50, May 2010.

navigating a megatrend from initial efficiency-based strategies to becoming disruptors themselves. The stages are as follows:

1. Reduce costs.

2. Reengineer products and processes.

3. Transform the core business.

4. Create new business models.

We used these stages to illustrate the smart city strategy development model in Table 9-2. Although development of smart cities is has been in progress for some time, the emerging reliance on IoT and big data analytics is beginning to demonstrate impressive results. Most smart cities initiatives, such as those in Singapore and Barcelona, involve the reengineering of existing cities by retrofitting new infrastructure[47]. Other initiatives, such as those in Songdo, South Korea, and the Yujiapu Financial District in China, are greenfield smart cities, designed to that vision from inception[48]. In all instances, planners would be wise to navigate the strategy development stages to inform the transformation of existing cities and for new smart cities to begin with best practices from project inception.

Table 9-2. *Smart City Strategy Development Model*

Stage	Megatrend Strategy	Smart City Innovation Strategy
1	Reduce costs, waste, and risks	Reduce operating and environmental costs from existing operations and infrastructure such as energy, water, safety, and transport. Reduce carbon footprint from computing, especially datacenters. Develop standards and regulations to manage operations and risks.
2	Reengineer and redesign products, services, and business processes	Engage all actors in the city service ecosystem to identify potential solutions. Pilot projects to test new business model assumptions. Rethink and redesign infrastructure and processes, and migrate from passive products and services to intelligent solutions. Incorporate ICT smart capability into all infrastructure, business processes, and applications.
3	Transform the core business and integrate new ideas	Launch the smart city business model. Build trusted relationships with all service ecosystem actors including citizens, suppliers, partners, and employees. Develop infrastructure, processes, applications, and organizational culture that embraces and drives smart city success.
4	Develop new business models for disruptive innovation and differentiation	Develop the smart city as a platform for creating innovative solutions. Address new market opportunities with new solutions. Become recognized as a leader of the smart city megatrend.

[47]A. Caragliu, C. Del Bo, and P. Nijkam, "Smart Cities in Europe," *Journal of Urban Technology, 18* (2), 65–82, 2011.
[48]J. Kim, "Making Cities Global: The New City Development of Songdo, Yuijapu and Lingang," *Planning Perspectives, 29* (3), 329–356, 2014.

Smart City Implementations

This section discusses two smart city implementations, Singapore and Barcelona, which have employed IoT-based initiatives successfully. Singapore topped the Global Smart City rankings for 2016 with Barcelona, London, San Francisco, and Oslo rounding out the top five[49]. In 2015, Barcelona won the top award. The Barcelona Smart City program and the Singapore Smart Nation program provide different perspectives for the implementation of smart city programs. Cities need to rank high on six smart indicators to gain global smart city status: Smart Economy, Smart Environment, Smart Government, Smart Mobility, Smart Living, and Smart People. Citizens live in a vibrant culture where an open government promotes sustainable living practices, green spaces, and makes wise decisions and investments in the future.

Barcelona Smart City Program

Smart City Barcelona implements a broad variety of citizen-oriented technical programs. Barcelona seeks to provide services by using ICT throughout the development and implementation of its smart city model[50]. Smart City Barcelona features an efficient bus transit system, bicycle sharing program, smart parking, waste management, smart LED lighting, renewable energy, mobile services, participatory government, and its innovation district[51]. The Barcelona smart city model identifies 22 smart city initiatives including ICT networks, information flows, environment, mobility, energy, water, solid waste, nature, buildings, public space, open government, innovation, and smart services. Barcelona is saving more than US$58 million with smart water technology, and parking revenues have increased more than $50 million through its smart parking program[52]. The city has more than 500 km of fiber-optic network[53]. It is developing a series of projects to support a smart city initiative to create integrated Internet and telecommunications for the city.

Using Cisco's Internet of Everything IoT solutions, the smart city project has developed in three technological layers. The first layer consists of sensors deployed throughout the city. These sensors are supporting smart water, smart lighting, and smart energy management. The open source Sentilo sensor and actuator platform provides access to data generated by a citywide sensor network. The data is available to both legacy and new applications to support numerous services. The second layer is the city's operating system (City OS), which will aggregate and analyze all data from the various city

---

[49]Juniper Research, "Singapore Named 'Global Smart City-2016,'" Juniper Research, Ltd., https://www.juniperresearch.com/press/press-releases/singapore-named-global-smart-city-2016, 2016.
[50]See https://www.shbarcelona.com/blog/en/ for resources and news available for smart city Barcelona.
[51]"Ten Reasons Why Barcelona Is a Smart City," *VilaWeb.cat*, http://www.vilaweb.cat/noticia/4175829/20140226/ten-reasons-why-barcelona-is-smart-city.html#, February 26, 2014.
[52]I. Capdevila and M. Zarlenga, "Smart City or Smart Citizens? The Barcelona Case," *Journal of Strategy and Management, 8* (3), 266–282, 2015.
[53]V. Walt, "Barcelona: The Most Wired City in the World," *Fortune*, http://fortune.com/2015/07/29/barcelona-wired-city/, July 29, 2015.

applications using big data modeling and predictive analytics, when completed. The third layer provides the customer interface for sharing data and analytics from the City OS with both city government and private external data users. The three-layer "urban platform" is a developing model for IT-enabled service innovation[54].

With respect to the strategy development model, Barcelona has successfully transitioned through the first and second stages. At present, it is solidly in the third stage and making progress toward the fourth. Regarding Stage 3, the old ways of doing business remain in place as a backstop. As innovative ideas develop and prove capable, they will replace legacy systems as cross-project synergies prove successful. The continuing development of the three-layer urban platform for ITC-enabled service innovation will bring Barcelona solidly into Stage 4 territory, ready for the development of potentially disruptive new business models. With its comprehensiveness, the Barcelona Smart City program is a leading example for smart city projects worldwide[55]. It embodies many of the smart city dimensions in the IBM Smarter Cities framework.

Singapore Smart Nation Program

The long-term goal of Singapore is to become the first smart nation. If global acclaim is the measure, then Singapore has arrived. Singapore achieved the top Global Smart City ranking for 2016 in the Juniper Research ranking[56]. In addition, Singapore came in second, behind Switzerland, in the 2015–2016 Global Competitiveness Report[57] and second, following Hong Kong, in the 2016 Index of Economic Freedom[58]. It has been at, or near, the top of these rankings for a decade. Singapore is certainly doing things right. Singapore's vision of a smart nation involves its world-ranked universities, medical centers, R&D resources, significant investment capital, and technology incubators. Singapore has the world's fastest broadband and wireless networks and a dynamic digital economy. Its strategy addresses six priorities: urban density, aging population, health care, mobility, energy, and water. The challenges are as follows:

- Singapore is the world's third most densely populated nation at 8,000 people per square kilometer, with more immigrants expected.

- Like other nations, Singapore's population is growing older, with 20 percent of the population forecast to be over 65 years old by 2030, up from less than 10 percent in 2016.

[54]Cisco Systems, *IoE-Driven Smart City Barcelona Initiative Cuts Water Bills, Boosts Parking Revenues, Creates Jobs & More*, Whitepaper, Cisco Systems, http://www.cisco.com/assets/global/ZA/tomorrow-starts-here/pdf/barcelona jurisdiction_profile_za.pdf, 2014.
[55]L. Laursen, "Barcelona's Smart City Ecosystem: A Big Investment in Data-Driven City Management Starts to Pay Off," *MIT Technology Review*, November 18, 2014.
[56]Juniper Research, "Singapore Named Global Smart City."
[57]K. Schwab, *The Global Competitiveness Report 2015-2016* (Cologny, Switzerland: World Economic Forum, 2015), http://www3.weforum.org/docs/gcr/2015-2016/Global_Competitiveness_Report_2015-2016.pdf
[58]T. Miller and A. Kim, *2016 Index of Economic Freedom* (Washington, DC: Institute for Economic Freedom and Opportunity, 2016). http://www.heritage.org/index/ranking

- Aging populations put pressure on individual health care facilities, hospitals, and extended care facilities.

- For a population of 5.4 million, there are 1 million cars on the road. Roads cover approximately 12 percent of the land area. The number of vehicles and roads cannot increase to accommodate growth.

- Power consumption in Singapore increased by 33 percent between 2005 and 2015. An additional increase of 30 percent is forecast for 2050.

- With a high population density and a lack of natural resources, Singapore requires efficient use of critical resources, especially water. The city-state imports 90 percent of its water from Malaysia[59]. Strict water management, desalination of seawater, rainwater collection, and reuse of waste water are strategies to address this issue.

Singapore is developing a technology-driven entrepreneurial ecosystem to address these issues. Entrepreneurial ecosystems consist of domains including markets, industries, technologies, resources, policies, and culture. Within the ecosystem, there are collections of actors playing roles such as providing knowledge, skills, resources, infrastructure, technology, and finance[60]. Entrepreneurial ecosystems are made up of networked organizations or communities that can facilitate innovation. They are platforms with strong network effects. Singapore has given the entrepreneurial ecosystem strong government support. From 2005 to 2014, the number of Singapore startups increased from 24,000 to 55,000. In 2013, Singapore technology businesses raised US$1.7 billion in venture funding, eclipsing competitors Japan, South Korea, and Hong Kong. More than 40 percent of all startups in Southeast Asia originated in in Singapore[61].

At the core of the Smart Nation program is the most extensive effort to collect data on all facets of daily living ever attempted by a city[62]. Government-deployed sensors and cameras, augmented by citizen-owned smart phones, monitor activities of people, infrastructure, buildings, and resources such as energy and water throughout the city. This includes the cleanliness of public spaces, crowd densities, traffic concentrations, and movements of individual vehicles. The program will eventually affect the lives of every person in the city. Because 80 percent of Singapore residents live in public housing, the government has more leeway to experiment with different smart city applications.

---

[59]M. Totty, "Five Cities That Are Leading the Way."
[60]The Economist, "All Together Now: What Entrepreneurial Ecosystems Need to Flourish, Special Report: Tech Startups," *Economist.com*, http://www.economist.com/news/special-report/21593582-what-entrepreneurial-ecosystems-need-flourish-all-together-now, January 18, 2014.
[61]M. de Villiers, "Why Does a Smart Nation Matter? Singapore, A Tech Innovation Hub, Is Tackling Tomorrow's Big Challenges Today," *Forbes.com*, www.smartnation-forbes.com, 2016.
[62]M. Watts and N. Purnell, "Singapore Is Taking the 'Smart City' to a Whole New Level," *The Wall Street Journal*, April 24, 2016.

The data from the IoT system feed into the Virtual Singapore online platform with the goal of providing the government with a view of how various systems and behaviors are performing in real time. Big data analytics will enable effective emergency response, crowd and traffic control, efficient water and energy use, and waste management. Other applications are communicable disease control, health and lifestyle monitoring, care for the aging, and appliance use in the home. Specific examples include the following[63]:

- *Sensor mapping*: The Singapore government has installed sensors and cameras in buildings, on roadsides, and in other areas to monitor traffic, pedestrian movement, weather patterns, and emergency and safety-related events. Real-time data displays on a 3D digital map that shows how the city is functioning. The clickable and zoomable map displays every building, facility, road, and public space on the island nation. It enables the government to determine where to build new buildings; specify features such as building dimensions, materials, windows, and solar orientation to ensure efficient energy use; and locate transit and other mobility services. For emergencies, smart phone GPS data can locate users and enable the communication of safety instructions.

- *Smart homes*: Monitoring elderly citizens and enabling them to live independently is a priority. Therefore, dwellings are being equipped with sensors, monitoring devices, and smart appliances. Toilet sensors monitor the number and type of flushes to provide general health information to monitor and share with family, caregivers, and health providers via smart phone apps. Other sensors indicate if appliances remain on inadvertently, heating and cooling use, and water and energy use.

- *Smart traffic*: Singapore's toll roads use satellite-linked sensors and devices, in addition to smart phones, to track every registered vehicle in the city in real time. Vehicle tolls are automatically charged by the distance traveled. Traffic advisories and congestion pricing encourage drivers to take alternate routes or drive at off-peak times. Parking fees charge automatically by time and location.

The Singapore government states that the smart city technology programs will improve government services by improving connections with citizens and encouraging public and private-sector innovation. The initial applications are encouraging, but the ecosystem is still is its development stage. Privacy issues are still a work in progress. Law enforcement can use any data collected without citizen or court approval. Issues of data privacy, security, and user safety are not resolved, although the Singapore government indicates that data anonymization is the standard practice, where possible.

---

[63]N. Purnell and J. Watts, "Singapore's Smart Nation: The Singapore Government Is Testing an Ambitious Range of Smart City Technologies to Aid City Planners," *The Wall Street Journal*, http://graphics.wsj.com/singapore-smart-city/, April 24, 2016.

Conclusions

The smart city movement is becoming the next big thing for the development of innovative new cities and the transformation of older ones. The momentum for this transformation seems to be in the right direction. Most of the major technology companies view smart cities as the major market opportunity for IoT. These companies have highly evolved smart city strategies. In addition, there are now dozens of cities worldwide that are pursuing the smart city concept.

Given all the data breaches at all levels of government as well as business, cybersecurity is hardly a strong point for IoT or smart city systems. As more sensor-enabled smart objects network onto the Internet, the potential for greater and more damaging data thefts and system takeovers accelerates. Already, there is circumstantial evidence of drive-by-wire Internet-connected vehicles being hacked. Attackers have hijacked security cameras, digital video recorders, smart thermostats, and alarm systems.

Privacy is another major issue that smart cities need to address. Many citizens worry about the privacy of smart meters. Lower energy use might mean the resident is not home. Electronic medical records are a huge privacy risk, as the Healthcare.gov experience in the United States has demonstrated. A lot more effort toward trust building based on privacy protections and data security needs to happen before smart cities gain citizen acceptance.

The smart city concept is gaining acceptance, at least with government and technology providers. The long-term potential of smart cities is compelling for citizens, the environment, and the economy. However, innovative applications of smart ICT cannot automatically create a smart city. Collaboration with smart citizens is essential. In addition, it is difficult to determine how smart a city really is. Merely adding a smart dimension to a dumb object is not enough. As we have seen in this chapter, considerable variability exists in defining what a smart city is, what dimensions are most relevant, and what applications have the most benefit for citizens and other ecosystem members.

■ ■ ■

Cloud-as-a-Service Epilogue

If someone asks me what cloud computing is, I try not to get bogged down with definitions. I tell them that, simply put, cloud computing is a better way to run your business.

— Mark Benioff, CEO of Salesforce.com

The information and communications technology (ICT) industry has gone through multiple concurrent upheavals since the turn of the century in its role to support the business. We covered the democratization of IT in Chapter 6 where IT jumped the corporate walls, and became affordable and increasingly granular. Early instances of this trend were small and medium sized businesses and individual consumers in the form of BYOD and smart devices. The trend continues throughout all industries today. Taken further, it has become practical for deployment with embedded devices in the form of the Internet of Things (IoT) as discussed in Chapter 8. A second transformation relates to the sourcing of technology. Shortly after the technology crash of the early 2000s, the downward revision of IT budgets encouraged IT strategist to focus on the outsourcing of application development and integration. A few years later, the focus switched to concerns about application and solution in sourcing. Today the focus is about services sourcing, both in sourcing and out sourcing. The switch to services has upended entire supply chains. This transformation to IT services underlies the growth in demand for data center servers that continued after the financial crisis of 2008. However, this growth in IT services is taking place in the cloud space, opening the door for large cloud service providers such as Amazon, Google, Microsoft, Facebook, Baidu and Alibaba as well as hundreds of emerging providers worldwide.

Growth in servers deployed in traditional enterprise settings, either with hardware dedicated to fixed applications, consolidated or not, has stagnated. The new demand is going to deployments by public cloud service providers, by private clouds in the enterprise, or hybrid public-private cloud solutions. The rapid advancement of cloud computing technology has lowered costs and increased the scale, reach, and scope of cloud solutions is behind these upheavals. After ten years, cloud adoption

E. Castro-Leon and R. Harmon, *Cloud as a Service*, DOI 10.1007/978-1-4842-0103-9

across industries is still growing exponentially[1]. This growth continues in spite of initial misgivings regarding QoS, SLA guarantees, security, noisy and nosy neighbors, integration issues and many other issues[2]. We believe that early cloud technology proponents and adopters, whether motivated by opportunity or a desire to keep up with or outmaneuver competitors, have engaged a technological tailwind that benefits success. As we can see by the results of many new cloud business models, it is hard to argue with success. This tailwind has been hiding in plain sight all along, in the -as-a-Service concept related to everything cloud.

The goal we set for this book is to use the principles of service science to provide insights for the business dynamics behind service innovation in cloud computing[3]. A basic view within service science is all businesses are service businesses. Therefore, there is an ongoing shift in perspective from the traditional goods-dominant logic (GDL), which is product oriented, to a service-dominant logic (SDL) that views service as a collaborative effort between service system actors for the co-creation of value. The juxtaposition of these alternative frameworks, one fading and the other assuming a dominant position, provide an opening for understanding the dynamics of the emerging cloud service ecosystem. The GDL approach, which views services as units of output, is simpler because it derives from traditional IT practice. It attempts to map a set of process requirements, for instance the life cycle of a server in a data center into a set of product requirements. Business planning and product development then becomes an exercise of "improving" the product's feature set, abstracting out the actual intended usage. This approach may have been feasible in slowly changing environments and market situations that allow a company to go through the entire development cycle without significant changes in requirements. Perhaps this was true in the past, and perhaps vendors could nudge customers to stay the course. This is no longer true today. The cloud service ecosystem has leveled the playing field. Customers who are not completely satisfied can always go to another supplier.

The cloud is inherently service-oriented, and therefore a service-oriented supplier carries an inherent competitive advantage over a more traditional product-oriented supplier. Unfortunately, the GDL mindset deeply embeds in the corporate culture and ethos of an organization. It influences market definition, product development, business processes, human resources, marketing, customer relationships, and enterprise strategy. A transformation from GDL to SDL for an organization is one of the hardest transitions possible, requiring a strategic remake of the entire enterprise and its external ecosystem. We addressed these issues with our discussion of service innovation, service thinking, and service transformation in Chapters 2 and 3. For organizations intent on succeeding in the cloud space, the first step toward this transformation is internalizing the dynamic

---

[1] Hynes, S., Cloud Platforms vs. On-Prem – A Guide for the Rest of Us, LogEntries.com, September 24, 2014. Available at: `https://blog.logentries.com/2014/09/cloud-platforms-vs-on-prem-a-guide-for-the-rest-of-us/`.

[2] Paul, F., 7 Cloud Computing Objections — Debunked! AllBusiness.com, September 2015. Available at: `https://www.allbusiness.com/7-cloud-computing-objections-debunked-16666004-1.html`.

[3] See Chapters 1, 2, and 3 for the discussion of service innovation, service science, the conceptual foundations of the service-dominant logic (SDL), and the service transformation process.

of the service orientation inherent in the cloud. This will enable organizations to embrace change as an essential component to relating to customers. In principle, a service offering in the cloud can track and anticipate customer desires much more nimbly than a product offering. The cloud service system accommodates changing requirements, as they are inherent in the user experience and the relationships within the service ecosystem.

The concept of platform is common across the GDL and SDL universes. In the GDL universe, a platform is a shorthand for a set of primarily physical features for a set of applications; whereas in the SDL universe a platform, often multi-sided, explicitly supports service exchange relationships within the cloud service ecosystem. The feature set for a GDL platform changes slowly, with changes preferably bundled in product generations, such as model years in the automotive industry. A GDL platform may have a single owning company that manages a supply chain behind this platform. In contrast, a SDL service platform is in constant development, precisely one of the motivations for the DevOps methodology. An example today is OpenStack. A service platform may not have a formal owner; it might be a consortium or a loosely organized developer group. It is multidimensional because a large platform may have presence at multiple levels in the macro architecture. The associated service network is explicit, and industry participants may enter at any of the levels and nodes in the service network where they have strengths. Players establish relationships with service providers downstream as well as their customers upstream in a highly dynamic environment. We addressed service-oriented platforms in the form of application specific cloud platforms (ASCPs) in Chapters 4 through 7.

This book seeks to link the essential service orientation of cloud computing with the principles of service innovation and its service science and service dominant logic foundation to provide deeper insight on the technical and business dynamics behind cloud computing. Given the dominant emphasis on services in the developed world and the growth of services in emerging economies, there is a tremendous opportunity for service innovation in the cloud. In the spirit of service, we hope cloud practitioners and business strategists find these insights useful to improve business and technical outcomes in their organizations, and that in turn will share their experience with their service partners in the industry at large.

Index

Get the eBook for only $4.99!

Why limit yourself?

Now you can take the weightless companion with you wherever you go and access your content on your PC, phone, tablet, or reader.

Since you've purchased this print book, we are happy to offer you the eBook for just $4.99.

Convenient and fully searchable, the PDF version enables you to easily find and copy code—or perform examples by quickly toggling between instructions and applications.

To learn more, go to http://www.apress.com/us/shop/companion or contact support@apress.com.

Printed in the United States
By Bookmasters